THE GREAT RELIGIONS OF
THE MODERN WORLD

The Great Religions of the Modern World

CONFUCIANISM · TAOISM · HINDUISM

BUDDHISM · SHINTOISM

ISLAM · JUDAISM · EASTERN ORTHODOXY

ROMAN CATHOLICISM · PROTESTANTISM

Edited by Edward J. Jurji

PRINCETON UNIVERSITY PRESS

PRINCETON NEW JERSEY

290
J979g

Entry in 1943-48 CBI
NO LC. #
A 46-33

Printed in the United States of America

PREFACE

It is the purpose of this book to indicate the genius, development, and spiritual core of the major contemporary religions. This also is a study of religion in its relation to the world crisis. The central theme of the symposium—originally proposed in a preliminary formula—was really achieved by the persistent endeavor of the contributing group; and, in due course, it was adapted by each author to the peculiar nature of his subject. It is hoped that the result of our concerted effort may provide a background of understanding to all who, as lay reader, historian, philosopher, comparative religionist, apologist, missionary, or parish minister, wish to approach the great religions in the light of their affirmations and impact upon human society and culture.

In keeping with the above purpose the authors have sought to express themselves as simply as possible. For example, diacritical and orthographical symbols have been omitted in the spelling of foreign words even when they would normally be required according to certain systems of transliteration. In short, the reader visualized for this book is a general reader, not a technician.

The editor desires to acknowledge the counsel and encouragement of Datus C. Smith, Jr., Director of Princeton University Press. George F. Thomas, Professor of Religious Thought at Princeton University, read the manuscript and offered many valuable suggestions. In this joint volume, the willing cooperation and mutual esteem of the several writers concerned lays each under heavy indebtedness to all the others. In connection with the chapter on Roman Catholicism, appreciation is due to the Right Reverend William A. Griffin, D.D., Bishop of Trenton, who graciously granted an Imprimatur. Insofar as the mechanics of the volume are concerned, Miss Gladys Fornell, and the Press staff, have been constantly helpful. To all these, as well as to my wife, Nahia Khuri Jurji, I am deeply grateful.

Edward J. Jurji

Princeton, N. J.

v

CONTENTS

		PAGE
PREFACE		V
CONFUCIANISM	LEWIS HODOUS	I
TAOISM	LEWIS HODOUS	24
HINDUISM	JOHN CLARK ARCHER	44
BUDDHISM	AUGUST KARL REISCHAUER	90
SHINTOISM	DANIEL CLARENCE HOLTOM	141
ISLAM	EDWARD J. JURJI	178
JUDAISM	ABRAHAM A. NEUMAN	224
EASTERN ORTHODOXY	JOSEPH L. HROMÁDKA	284
ROMAN CATHOLICISM	GERALD G. WALSH	307
PROTESTANTISM	JOHN A. MACKAY	337
WHO'S WHO OF AUTHORS		371
INDEX		373

Confucianism

LEWIS HODOUS

THE Confucian group has had a continuous history for about twenty-five centuries. For almost twenty centuries it has been the ruling group. During these years the Chinese built up and held together the largest social-political structure in history. While many forces cooperated in this process Confucianism was the formative one. Today at Chu-fu the descendants of Confucius are carrying on the cult to their great ancestor and the great teacher of China. According to Y. C. Yang all Chinese are basically Confucianists with a leaning toward Buddhism and Taoism.

Confucianism is a modern term coined by the Catholic missionaries. The Chinese employ the term *Ju-chia,* literati, meaning the followers of the teaching of Confucius which was inherited from the sages of antiquity, embodied in the classics, interpreted by the commentators and philosophers, and now is in process of adjustment to the modern world.

Confucius (551–479 B.C.) lived in an age when the feudal system and its institutions were dying and a new China was emerging. He was of humble origin. Up to the age of thirty-five he was unknown. He studied the ancient governments and ceremonies and established a school in which he trained a few disciples. In the latter half of his life he visited different states seeking an opportunity to put his teaching into practice, but the rulers of these states were too much occupied in holding their insecure positions to pay much attention to him.

The China of his day consisted of a number of states under the Chou emperor. In the early years of the dynasty, when the royal prestige was high, the emperor was able to settle quarrels between claimants for political power in the various states. But after 800 B.C. the authority of the ruler was disregarded by the vassals. Strife and confusion followed. The strong conquered and absorbed the weak. The cement which held the feudal social order was cracking and disintegrating.

In this situation three problems emerged. One was the problem of the source of sovereign authority. The answer of Confucius to this problem was that sovereign authority roots in the mandate of Heaven. The second problem was that of the legality or constitutionality of political power in the several states. Increasingly this was claimed by several aspirants. The solution of Confucius was the restoration of the waning authority of the Chou emperor as ruler and as priest. The third difficulty was the growing confusion in the social order. To meet this Confucius advocated loyalty to Heaven, to the Chou emperor, filial piety, but especially the education of rulers of character and ability.

The most important contribution of Confucius was the training of disciples, who, with their successors, collected the pre-Confucian works, edited, and interpreted them. They also compiled the sayings of Confucius and Mencius and produced the Great Learning and the Doctrine of the Mean as well as numerous other works. During the Han dynasty (206 B.C.–A.D. 220) the Five Classics were assembled.[1] In A.D. 252 they were engraved on stone tablets in the capital, thus providing a standard authoritative text. Later to the Five Classics were added the Four Books.[2] The two collections constitute the bible of Confucianism.

COSMOLOGY

Confucius left open several problems. One was that of cosmology. In the latter part of the fourth century B.C. the *yin-*

[1] The Five Classics include: The Book of Changes, Yih Ching; The Book of Poetry, Shih Ching; The Book of History, Shu Ching; The Book of Rites, Li Chi; and Spring and Autumn, Chun Chiu. They may be found in *The Chinese Classics,* by James Legge. Oxford, 1893–1895.

[2] See *Analects of Confucius,* by W. E. Soothill. World's Classics, 1937; *Analects of Confucius,* by Arthur Waley London, 1938; *Mencius,* by L. A. Lyall. London, 1932; *The Great Learning and The Mean-in-action,* by E. R. Hughes. Dent, 1942.

yang theory was formulated, and the Confucianists adopted it. According to Chu Hsi, who flourished in the thirteenth Christian century and is reckoned as the greatest Neo-Confucianist scholar, the universe and every particle in it are composed of two principles which are coeternal, infinite, distinct, but inseparable. (*Li,*) the psychic principle, (is the principle of movement comparable to the *élan vitale* of Bergson.) *Chi* is the material principle (which gives the *Li* a point of contact.) The two principles operate through two modes: *yin* (the negative mode,) characterized as dark, cold, passive, and female; the *yang,* (the positive mode,) characterized as light, warm, active, and male. These two modes operate through the five agents, water, fire, wood, metal, soil. These agents are composed of varying proportions of the two modes. Water, for example, has a great deal of *yin,* and very little *yang.* Fire, on the other hand, has much *yang* and little *yin.*

Matter is conceived as a great globe which begins to move when informed by the psychic principle. During the movement the two modes are gradually separated, but as the speed increases they mix again and give rise to the five agents which form all beings. The first pair of each species is produced by spontaneous generation. Then from the two all the rest come by transformation.

The universe is creative, has beauty, utility, and potentiality. These emerge respectively in the seasons, creativity in the spring, beauty in the summer, utility in the autumn, and potentiality in the winter. These qualities in the universe emerge in man as the constant virtues of love, justice, reverence, and wisdom. Man accordingly is good because he possesses this endowment of Heaven.

The presence of the psychic principle makes all men equal. In this philosophical theory, which came from Mencius and was broadened and deepened by Buddhism, Chu Hsi ran counter to the social situation in China which denied it. Chu Hsi met the objections by explaining that all men are fundamentally equal because they have a portion of the *Li.* Their differences arise from the different grades of the material principle. Thus this

3

profound theory and the inequalities of Chinese life were harmonized. All men are brothers. One of the philosophers of that time put it thus: "The people are my brothers, and inferior beings are my companions."

The philosophy of Chu Hsi favored a patriarchal government. The emperor was regarded as a saint and as the father and mother of the people who could do no wrong. The actual government was in the hands of a dominant minority of the Confucian group.

ETHICS OF CONFUCIANISM

Confucius left open another problem, namely, that of the source of evil. Mencius held that human nature is good, being the deposit of the Tao which is good. Evil according to his doctrine is due to environment, or to education, or to lack of forethought, or to wrong judgment of life's values.

This pragmatic view of evil did not satisfy the scholars of Neo-Confucianism. Buddhist philosophy deepened their insight into the mystery of evil. According to Buddhism evil in human life was due to cosmic ignorance which conditioned phenomenal existence. To meet this challenge the scholars felt compelled to place the source of evil in the material principle *Chi*. But this principle is essential in the universe because through it the universe takes form. This principle is originally good and pure. The evil creeps in not because the universe is blinded by illusion but because enmity and strife enter with the process of differentiation which accompanies the functioning of the material principle. The evil is not in the original state of the universe. To the Neo-Confucianists this theory made the ethical values secure and at the same time opposed the escape-salvation of Buddhism. Furthermore, it emphasized the duty to return to the psychic principle *Li* and not be enslaved by the material principle *Chi*. This theory reaffirmed the doctrine of Mencius that human nature is good. In due time this teaching was embodied in the Three Character Classic (San Tzu Ching) ascribed to Wang Ying-lin (1223–1296) which was memorized by all students up to the year 1912.

4

Another problem which Confucius left open was, "how can a man become good?" Neo-Confucianism taught that the mind could be transformed by the study of the principles underlying human history and by right education which included study of the classics and following the example of the sages. To this was added, from Buddhism, the practice of meditation.

Ethical life is conceived in the Five Relations. These are the ruler-subject, father-son, husband-wife, elder-younger brothers, and friend-friend relation. The sovereign should be benevolent, the subjects, or officials, loyal. The husband should be just, the wife obedient; the father kind, the son filial; the elder brother considerate, the younger obedient. Friends should be faithful. Each individual is thus subject to three pressures. The first is from above, the elders and ancestors. The second is from the sides, the equals; and the third is from below. This system has developed highly integrated social groups held together by privileges and duties.

The family is the basic unit in Chinese society, all three of these relations having to do with it. The pattern of the family rests upon the succession to the cult of ancestor worship or to the paternal stock (*tsung*) and to the patrimony. Thus the principles of the religious, economic, and political life are rooted in the family and in ancestor worship. Filial piety is the keystone of the Chinese ethical order and embraces all the virtues of human nature. Confucius organized life about Goodness. His successors made filial piety the center. Filial piety includes not only service to the dead and obedience to the living, but ordains that any act which dishonors the parents is unfilial. In modern as well as in ancient China loyalty to the ruler or state was the completion of filial piety.

The relation of teacher to pupil is scarcely less important. It belongs to the friend-friend category. The teacher is also conceived as the intellectual and moral parent. This relation has been somewhat disturbed in recent years; there are signs, however, that it is regaining its importance.

The ruler-subject relation is being clarified. In pre-republican China the state rested on a divine mandate. The emperor was the son of Heaven. There are indications that point toward a continuation of this theory in modern form. Sun Yat-sen is the father of modern China. He is a sage who has based his "Three Principles" upon cosmic reality. The emperor has been replaced by the state and its representatives. The "subject" of imperial China has become the citizen of a democratic state.

The Confucianists hold that moral conduct is not merely the endowment of the Universal Order, Tao, but is also dependent upon man. The purpose of justice is to give each man his place. Man is father, son, elder brother, friend, or citizen. Each status has certain privileges and certain responsibilities. This means that each individual lives in a system of loyalties which he owes to others and which others owe to him.

The rites control these loyalties and prevent the individual from neglecting them. The rites fix the individual in his relationships and direct him in the performance of his duties in these relationships. The rites are not merely rules of etiquette, they are a way of life in human relations and in relations beyond the human. In other words they are also religious, a fact which has sometimes been overlooked. In the period of the Contending States (403–221 B.C.) the theory was developed that in religion the reality of the spirits was not necessary. But the ceremonies were necessary for the peace of the individual and the security of society. Accordingly rites were developed as forms of social control while the reality of the gods was obscured. This has persisted to the present time.

Music was also a means of harmonizing the individual in himself and with society. The Confucianists governed by rites and music. Rules and punishments were employed to promote rites and music. The rites and music were modeled upon Heaven. The universe was originally harmonious. The rites and music were established to improve the universe, make it more beautiful.

In the past few years, music and the closely related poetry have been employed widely to stir up patriotism. According to the Book of Rites "Poetry is what gives the first stimulus to character; ceremonial is what gives it stability; music is what brings it to full development."

There are two norms which Confucius proposed and which have been the ideal since his day (Heaven has placed these norms in man,) Stated simply (one) is that man should do to others what he desires them to do to him. This is the principle *chung*, loyalty. "What we ask of the son we should give to the father. What we ask of the official should be given to the ruler. What we ask of the younger brother should be given to the elder brother. What we ask of the friend should be given to him."

From another aspect we should not do to others what we do not wish ourselves and should do to others what we wish ourselves.

"What you hate in him who is above, do not do to the one below. What you hate in the one below, do not do to the one above. What you hate in your elders, do not do to your juniors. What you hate in your juniors, do not do to your elders. What you hate on the right hand, do not do on the left hand. What you hate on the left, do not pass on to the right. This is called *shu*." All men have desires. All men know what they desire. This should be the standard in their behavior to others.

The happiness of life is to be achieved not in the result but in the act done in good conscience regardless of consequences. The Confucian theory is that good should be sought in the act, in the process, and not in the result. "The gentleman is not to grumble at Heaven nor blame men." Mencius said: "The gentleman follows the model and thereby awaits the order of Heaven." Doctrine of the Mean states: "The gentleman abides in change and awaits the mandate of Heaven."

The Confucian group has always stressed the doctrine of rectification of names, that is, rectifying of terms—giving to things names that truly describe them, in order to distinguish between right and wrong. A name was regarded not merely as a symbol but as conveying the essence of the object or idea. This was expressed by Confucius when asked about government in these words, *"Chun chun, chen chen, fu fu, tzu tzu."*

7

(Let ruler be ruler, official be official, father be father, and son be son, this is government.)

THE CULT OF CONFUCIANISM

Worship of Shangti. Confucianism was established as the state religion by the emperor Wu-ti (140–87 B.C.) and held this position till 1912. The emperor was the high priest. The literati were the teachers. The faithful were the scholars and the gentry of the towns and villages. The cult consisted of the worship of Heaven and Earth, the ceremony to Confucius, and ancestor worship.

The center of the state religion was Shangti or Heaven. Shangti, meaning the ruler above, was the high god during the Shang period. The term *Ti* was also used to designate the ancestors of the ruling house. Heaven was worshiped by the Chou rulers before they conquered the Shang. It came to be used as the general term for the ancestors of the ruling family who were supposed to be located in the sky. After the conquest of the Shang by the Chou the two terms were combined to form Hao Tien Shangti, the Shangti of Exalted Heaven, or Huang Tien Shangti, the Shangti of Imperial Heaven. Personal traits were ascribed to this being but a clear conception of vital personality was never achieved. Later the term Tao, Universal Order, obscured the personal traits of Shangti. At present the term Shangti is employed for the term God by the Protestant churches along with the term Chen Shen, True God. The Catholics have adopted the term Tien Chu, Lord of Heaven.

The annual offering to Shangti was made by the emperor accompanied by the highest officials at the winter solstice on the round three-terraced marble altar south of the capital. On the north side of the top terrace facing south was the tablet of Shangti. On the left and right were the tablets of the ancestors of the reigning dynasty. On the second terrace were arranged the tablets of the sun, moon, the seven stars of the dipper, the five planets, the twenty-eight constellations, the signs of the zodiac, the clouds, rain, wind, and thunder. In the first month of the year the emperor made an offering at the Temple of Prayer for a Good Year, known to Westerners as the Temple of Heaven.

Opposite the great enclosure of the altar of Heaven was a large park. In this was a square altar of two terraces to the Divine Husbandman, Shen Nung. Here also was the field on which the emperor plowed the first furrow and thus inaugurated agriculture. Near by was the temple of Jupiter, the Star of the Great Year, so called because Jupiter makes one revolution in about twelve years and is regarded as the ruler of time.

North of the capital was the square altar of two terraces to Sovereign Earth. Around the altar were deep trenches with water representing the earth surrounded by four seas. On the top terrace were the tablets of Sovereign Earth and the imperial ancestors. The time of worship was the summer solstice. There were also tablets of the five sacred mountains, the four seas, and the four streams.

Across from the altar to Sovereign Earth was the temple of the goddess who presided over the weaving of silk. She was worshiped by the empress and was added to the pantheon after the Christian era. In the sixteenth century the temple was built in the palace grounds for the convenience of the empress.

Besides these there were appropriate ceremonies to the patrons of medicine, war, cannon, palace doors, porcelain kilns, granaries, fire, walls and moats, and literature. Kuanti, a hero of the Three Kingdoms (A.D. 220–265) was deified at the end of the sixteenth century. Also there was the god of the polar star and the Great Eastern Mountain, Tai Shan. Among the lesser gods of the imperial pantheon there was considerable turnover during the centuries.

This worship of Heaven and Earth, imperial ancestors and heroes grew up during the course of centuries. In the fourth century B.C. it was strongly influenced by astronomical knowledge from the Mediterranean world. The new astronomy became the celestial pattern for the rising empire. The polar star about which the heavens revolve became the symbol of the emperor surrounded by his loyal vassals and counselors. Shangti was personalized. This was the contribution of Moti, or Mo Tzu (*ca.* 479–381 B.C.), a philosopher, who lived between the time of Confucius and Mencius. This personal god was regarded as having a righteous purpose in governing the world. The world of man and the realm of nature were viewed as an organism. The ethical was embedded in the natural and was regarded as a force which evoked response in nature. Injustice and oppression in government were disturbing elements and were followed by signs, such as eclipses of the sun and moon, and by the appearance of comets. In some cases nature responded to such acts by warnings such as earthquakes, landslides, and extraordinary phenomena. The literati employed these signs and warnings to curb the oppressive measures of the bureaucrats who surrounded the emperor. This humanistic motive operated as late as 1910 when Halley's comet made its appearance in our corner of the universe and caused consternation among the Manchu oligarchy. The emperor abdicated in 1912.

The offering to Heaven was regarded as the keystone in the arch of empire. It rested upon the theory of the state which is analogous to the pattern of the family. The emperor as the son of Heaven was the head of the cult and of the patrimony. Heaven was his father to whom he owed the service of a filial son. The relation to Heaven included the control of men and gods. The emperor had the mandate of Heaven to rule the world. This mandate was not perpetual but was dependent upon the character of the emperor. The relation of the officials and the literati to the emperor was not based upon the political point of view but upon the religious. The problem of the present government of China is how to conserve this aspect of the tradition.

Cult of Confucius. The cult of Confucius originated with his disciples. In due time the Master became the symbol of the people's political unity and cultural life. This symbol was vitalized in the Confucian group who viewed China's culture as a whole, appropriated it, interpreted it, and embodied it in the political and cultural heritage. The Confucian group thus became the incarnation of the growing Confucian tradition. It combined politics, ethics, and education, and suffused them with a spirit of reverence and devotion. Confucianism then became a religion. It lived on while dynasties rose and fell and conquerors marched and retreated. Even when the other-worldliness of Buddhism lured the minds of a people already weakened by suffering, distracted by confusion, and decimated by war, the cult of Confucius, though it passed through many a dimout, never suffered a total eclipse.

The high spots of the historical process reveal the general trend. The first emperor of the Han dynasty visited the tomb of Confucius. In A.D. 442 a temple was erected at Chu-fu, the place of his tomb. In 505 one was erected at the capital. This was canonization. From now on honors multiplied. Tai Tsung of the Tang dynasty (A.D. 618–906) put the cult on a new basis. In 630 he decreed that all districts in the empire build temples to Confucius with statues of the Master dressed in royal robes. This universalized the cult. In 647 he made the Confucian Temple the Hall of Fame for scholars and officials. In the capital he established imperial colleges in which the Confucian classics were taught. Graduation from these colleges, examinations, and special examinations by the emperor became the doors into official life. This made Confucius not merely the patron of the Confucian group, but the patron of the government and the symbol of national unity. In 665 Confucius was given the title of Supreme Teacher. In 735 he was granted the title of King, in 1013 that of Supreme Saint, and in 1330 his descendants were ennobled. After 1530 the images in many Confucian temples were replaced by tablets so as to avoid the semblance of idolatry.

In 1905 the examinations for civil office based upon the classics were discontinued. This took away the political basis of the cult. After 1912 the study of the classics was dropped in the government schools, though it continued in some private schools. The abdication of the Manchu dynasty and the establishment of the Republic obscured the meaning of Confucianism but at the same time introduced a period of a new evaluation of the Master.

Ancestor worship. Ancestor worship has been called the religion of the Chinese. During the Shang period (1766–1122 B.C.) it was a fertility cult. During feudal times it was the custom to have a personator of the dead at the offering, a child descendant representing the dead. As the feudal system disintegrated the character of the family changed. Personal relations of father and son replaced the formal relations of lord and vassal. The family of the common people followed the pattern of the aristocratic family. Filial piety became the center of the new family. The child was taught "not to move one step without thinking of one's parents, not to utter one word without thinking of one's parents."

The tablet took the place of the personator. It became animated by a special ceremony after the name of the deceased was written upon it, and the dot was placed over the character *chu* meaning the abiding place of the soul of the dead. Along with the tablet portraits of the dead were also made. They were consulted before making important decisions; for it was believed that the intentions of the dead could be discovered by the facial expressions on these portraits.

The funeral rites occupied an important place. By them not only were the dead made happy but the status of the family was reinforced. Funerals were elaborate. Moti, or Mo Tzu, who came after Confucius, states that "When a member of the people dies they use up the family property. When a feudal lord dies they empty the treasury of the country." Coffins were made of solid timbers to preserve the body. The site of the grave was selected by a geomancer. It was located at the confluence of celestial forces and offerings were made at the critical times in the periods of nature. Thus ancestral worship was intimately connected with the agricultural cult.

In addition to these customs there grew up stories to stimulate the cult. A filial son chastised by his mother lamented: "She is old and unable to chastise me properly." A mother who liked fish was brought some in midwinter by a son who melted the ice by his breath. Marital authority was promoted by filial piety. Thus a young wife being courted by another man cut off her nose saying: "Dishonored by mutilation who will look at me?"

Later the theater also took its part in stimulating filial piety. All these means bolstered up parental and marital authority at a time when the family was adjusting itself to the freer situation of postfeudal times.

Ancestor worship is now passing through another crisis. The growth of modern industry in the cities is breaking down the peasant family. The individual is becoming conscious of his freedom and demands the right to choose his occupation, his partner in life, and the place where he shall live. The small families have increased in number. Divorce is more common. In the last few years the Chinese have realized that the family cannot guarantee complete security, and are placing their faith in the nation.

But ancestor worship is still the religion of the Chinese. Modern ancestor worship centers about the tablet, the funeral, and the grave. The tablets are kept in the main hall of the house, or in a special cabinet to four or five generations. After that they are placed in the ancestral temple. The worship in the house is simple. The priest on the occasion is the head of the household— the father, grandfather, or the eldest son. In the worship of the clan the senior member takes the leading part.

The offerings placed before the tablet consist of food, incense, flowers, and candles. The food is served hot with chopsticks placed beside the dishes. When all is ready the head of the house lights three sticks of incense, comes before the tablets and holds them as high as his forehead. Then he places the incense in the incense burner, and either performs the *kou-tou,* three kneelings and nine knockings, or simply bows three times. Sometimes the ancestors are invited to be present, important matters are announced to them and they are asked for a blessing.

The times of offering vary. In pious families candles and incense are burned on the first and the fifteenth day of the month. More formal offerings are made on the anniversary of the birth and death of the departed. At the important festivals special offerings are made. The most important offering is on the last day of the year when the whole family gathers in a reunion including the living and the dead. Offerings are also made at the time of special announcements such as betrothals, weddings, births, and deaths. When the revolution was successful, Sun Yat-sen made the announcement at the imperial tombs at Nanking to the ancestors of the Ming dynasty (A.D. 1368–1644), the last Chinese dynasty.

In the spring the Chinese sweep the graves and make a special offering to the soul in the grave. In the autumn the people make a special offering by burning sheets of paper with pictures of warm clothing and trunks and other necessities for the dead. Besides the regular ancestor worship, offerings are made to the wandering spirits of the dead who have no one to provide for them. In many communities elaborate services are held to ferry such spirits through purgatory where they are suffering punishment.

In its long history ancestor worship has passed through many changes. It is connected with the basic belief that the world of man and of those who have passed on are not two worlds but make one whole. The Chinese lives with his ancestors and his ancestors live with him and in him.

The ancestor cult guarantees the succession of property rights, not merely physical property but what we call good will. The ancestors are supposed to transmit good influences which reside in the bodies of the dead. The tombs are in the fields and by their magic power contribute to the fertility of the fields. This connection gives ancestor worship a solid basis in the economic and social life. Connected with the clan ancestral temple are fields, the income from which is used for offerings and for the support of worthy students of the clan. The clan temple is common property and in times of need a member of the family may find refuge in it. He finds a bed and a rice bowl awaiting him.

The cult also supports the marital rights, the morals of the community. Chinese morality has its center in the family and filial piety is the fountain source that inspires this morality. This is operative today when the old patterns of life are breaking up. The family is still the enduring pattern.

In East China one clan was reported as giving each soldier, going into service, land to raise one hundred and ten pounds of rice. Before the enlisted man leaves he kneels before the ancestral altar and the clan elder gives him the following charge: "You must be loyal to the state, thereby winning glory for your ancestors. You must never be afraid to die. Nor should you desert your ranks. Last of all you must never surrender to the enemy." Devotion to ancestors is still an important force in modern China.

CONFUCIANISM AND OTHER SYSTEMS

Confucianism has great digestive and assimilative capacity. It developed from the primitive religion and adopted the High God, Shangti and Heaven, the cult of Mother Earth, the god of the soil, and the cult of the ancestors. It had a share in the creation of the cultural heroes Shun, Yu, Shen Nung. In the fourth century B.C. the new astronomy began to seep in from the West and during the Han dynasty (206 B.C.–A.D. 220) Confucian scholars organized the state religion around the new view of the Heavens. In the Han period Confucianism also assimilated the belief in a personal God, which came from the opponent of Confucianism, Moti, or Mo Tzu.

During the period of the Contending States (403–221 B.C.) Confucianism was greatly influenced by Taoism. Mencius (372–289 B.C.) advocated the dogma that human nature is good because it is a deposit of the Tao, the Taoist basic reality. During the Sung dynasty (A.D. 960–1279) Confucianism developed a metaphysics under the stimulus of Taoism and Buddhism.

Confucianism has revealed during its long history a great leavening power although it is not a missionary religion in the modern sense. For the Confucian group was profoundly conscious of the world as "one world." They hoped to bring the blessings of Confucianism to the whole world, not by force, but by the civilizing power of its values. This is expressed in the Book of Rites as follows: "When the great Tao was operative, all under Heaven were ruled by justice. Sages and men of ability were chosen as rulers. Sincerity and peace ruled. Therefore men loved not only their parents, nor treated as children only their own sons. Provision was made for the aged till their death, the able-bodied were employed and children were properly brought up. Due provision was made for the widows, orphans, childless men, and the sick. The right of men to work that suited them, and of women to good homes, was recognized. The production of goods was so regulated that nothing was wasted, while useless accumulations for private use were regarded with disapproval. Labor was so regulated that energy was stimulated while activity for merely selfish reasons was discouraged. Thus there was no room for the development of a narrow egoism. Robbery and outrage were unknown. Hence there was no shutting of the outer gates. Such was the age of the Ta Tung-World Brotherhood."

This cultural leaven has been spreading for about twenty-five centuries. The shamanistic elements of the folk religion were sublimated by it, or repressed. Human sacrifice and orgiastic rites were tabooed. The love songs of the Book of Poetry were moralized. The animistic gods were brought under the Confucian code of propriety. As Chinese political power advanced southward and westward Confucianism won new converts.

Taoism as a philosophy opposed the Confucian ethics. As a religion it made them the basis of its teaching. The Buddhists appropriated ancestor worship and the ethics of Confucianism. The foreign conquerors of China became more Confucian than the Chinese. The Jews of Kaifeng have been completely assimilated. The Moslems are slowly but surely becoming Chinese. The most notable accomplishment of Confucianism was its victory over Buddhism. This was achieved not merely by assimilating the contributions of Buddhism to Chinese culture, but also by the fact that Confucianism was rooted in the Chinese rural family, the unit of Chinese cultural and political life.

Confucianism in Japan. The Analects was introduced into Japan in the third century by Achiki; and a Korean scholar, Wani, taught it to the crown prince. The constitution of Shotoku-Taishi (573–621), though claimed to have been based on Buddhism, was derived from Confucianism so far as its moral tenets are concerned. In the seventh century the University of Nara used the Chinese classics as textbooks. The Chu Hsi school (Shushi) founded by an ex-Buddhist priest was influential throughout the Tokugawa period. It was the foundation of the educational system. At the end of the eighteenth century a decree prohibited contrary doctrines.

The Chinese profoundly influenced ancestor worship as practiced in Japan. Amaterasu, a nature god, was transformed into the ancestress of the imperial house. Not only Amaterasu, but many other nature gods, have become humanized through the influence of Chinese ancestor worship. In China filial piety was the supreme virtue. In Japan, however, the emperor, the embodiment of the state, became the object of the highest loyalty.

Dr. Inouyé summarized the influence of Confucianism on modern Japan in this manner: "That the majority of those who participated in the making of the New Japan toward the end of the third period consisted of Confucianists is an undeniable fact ... of all the branches of Confucianism, the Chutsze School and the Wang Yang-ming School produced most pioneers of the new era. ... It may be added that the readiness with which our people grasped and adapted the newly introduced Western civilization was in the main due to the mental training they had received from the study of Confucianism throughout the Tokugawa age." [3]

The Imperial Rescript on Education formulated by Emperor Meiji and promulgated October 30, 1890, shows evidence of Confucian influence: "Ye, Our subjects, be filial to your parents, affectionate to your brothers and sisters, as husbands and wives be harmonious, as friends true; bear yourselves in modesty and moderation, extend your benevolence to all; pursue learning and cultivate arts, and thereby develop intellectual faculties and perfect moral power."

Confucianism in Europe. In 1662 Intorcetta published a work entitled, *Sinarum Scientia,* containing a sketch of the life of Confucius in French and Latin and translations of the Great Learning and the Doctrine of the Mean in Latin. Confucius was not described as an idol worshiper nor as an atheist. In 1687

[3] Okuma, *Fifty Years of New Japan,* vol. II, pp. 62, 63.

was issued a work entitled, *Confucius Sinarum Philosophus.* It contained an introduction and the Analects, Great Learning, and the Doctrine of the Mean, with commentaries. On this work the Jesuits based other works, among them, *La Morale de Confucius.* Here they informed lay readers that this morality came from the source of natural reason, an idea welcome at the beginning of the Renaissance. This work marks the high point of the knowledge of Confucius in Europe.

Pater Noël of Prague in 1711 published the six classics, being the reproduction of the three mentioned above and Mencius, Hsiao Ching, and Santze-ching. Noël puts less stress on the missionary interest and much more upon Chinese wisdom. In his introduction he says: "This translation I hand to you, dear reader, not only that you may learn to know what the Chinese have written, but that you may do that which they have thought right." He adds, "As often as you read the teaching of the Chinese, bethink yourself of the life of Christians. May Jesus become the cornerstone of both." At the turn of the seventeenth and eighteenth centuries there were many works on the culture and history of the Chinese.

Among the intellectual leaders of Europe, Leibnitz (1646–1716) was one of those open-minded men who enter into other cultures and feel themselves into the thought of others. The first production of Leibnitz which gives his view of Confucius is found in *Novissima Sinica* (1697). It is a collection of facts about China gathered from the Jesuits. In the introduction he treated Confucius from the viewpoint of Protestant Germany; stated, furthermore, that the two highest cultures of man were meeting at the ends of the earth, and hoped that Russia might serve as a bridge between the two to its own enrichment. To be sure the West surpassed China in mathematics, astronomy, logic, and metaphysics; but in the ordering of life and in state morals China surpassed the West. In the same book Leibnitz wrote: "Who would have believed, indeed, that this people would have surpassed us who are grown in conventional morals with forms of an established life? Though we may be equal to them in cleverness, in industry, and surpass them in contemplative knowledge, they surpass us in practical philosophy, i.e. in their ethical and political arrangements. So great is obedience to superiors among them, the respect for old age, the almost religious cult of ancestors that a bad word against them is not heard and is regarded as patricide is among us." He went on to the effect that the Chinese should send missionaries to teach Europe the practice of their natural theology. He said: "Therefore I believe if a wise man were made judge, not over the form of beautiful goddesses, but over the superiority of people that he would hand the golden apple to the Chinese, if we did not surpass them by a superhuman good, namely, the divine gift of the Christian religion."

CONFUCIANISM SINCE 1912

Under the Republic the cult of Confucianism has had a varied history. Under President Yuan Shih-kai (1912–1916) it enjoyed a brief revival—he made in 1914 an offering to Heaven at the round altar south of Peking. In the constitution Confucianism was recognized as intimately related to the Chinese state. Chen Huan-chang, a pupil of Kang Yu-wei and a Ph.D. of Columbia University, tried to establish a Confucian Church and build a Confucian University in Peking, but without success. In Shansi Governor Yen established Heart-cleansing societies to cultivate the values of Confucianism.

The long connection of Confucianism with the monarchy made its retention under the Republic seem to be an anachronism. Its emphasis upon the past, upon obedience to the authority of the elders, its support of the patriarchal system made it appear to be an obstacle to the free citizen of a republic. Those who had drunk from the shallow wells of modernism regarded it as another superstition to be discarded with Buddhism and Christianity.

Its nadir was reached in 1928 when the national government ordered the offering to Confucius to cease. In 1931, when Japan took over Manchuria and soon planted its guards within a few miles of Peiping, China needed a symbol of its political and cultural unity. It turned to the ancient roots of its unity and power. The ceremony to Confucius was revived (in 1934) and was conducted at Chu-fu by the high officials of the Kuomintang.

The Confucian temples were repaired. The old musical instruments were restrung. The old ceremonies were made vibrant with the spirit of old China conscious of its mission in the modern world. The study of the classics was revived. Plans were made for the repair of the temple at Chu-fu at government expense. August 27, the alleged birthday of Confucius, was made a national holiday. The title of the oldest male of the Confucian family was changed from "Duke of Extended Sagehood," granted in 1233, to "Sacrificial Official of the Late Teacher." The Three Principles of Sun Yat-sen—racialism, democracy, and livelihood—were grafted upon the Confucian system.

In line with this revival of Confucianism is the New Life Movement established by Generalissimo Chiang Kai-shek at Nanchang, Kiangsi, in 1934. This movement reveals the trend in Chinese thinking and life. Four fundamentals provide the basis of the movement.

1. Regulated attitude, *Li*. The people are to be trained to take a new attitude toward nature as revealed in modern science. They are to be trained in a new attitude to modern society as expressed in rules and etiquette. They are to be oriented in a new attitude toward the nation by accepting a new discipline.

2. Right behavior, *Yi*. These new attitudes are to be expressed in conduct in accordance with natural law, social rule, and national discipline. Life should be orderly, disciplined, obedient. The habits of solidarity and calmness should be cultivated and disorganization, irresponsibility, and perfunctoriness should be opposed. Life should be productive, frugal, persevering, self-reliant and not extravagant, luxurious, idle, slovenly, and covetous. Life should be artistic. Good manners should be cultivated. Tidiness and truthfulness should be emulated as against vulgarity, carelessness, and hypocrisy.

3. Honesty in personal, public, and official life, *Lien*. What agrees with *Li* and *Yi* is right; what does not agree is wrong.

The people are to be trained to do what is recognized as right and to oppose what is recognized as wrong.

4. Honor, conscientiousness, *Chih*. When a man recognizes that his actions are not in accord with *Li, Yi,* and *Lien* he feels ashamed. When he is conscious of the wrongdoing of others, he is disgusted. But this consciousness must be genuine and thorough so that he will strive to improve the good and get rid of the evil.

This movement has kinship with Confucianism. The virtues inculcated are the time-honored Confucian virtues brought up to date—propriety, justice, integrity, and a sense of shame. The New Life Movement is a popular movement. Its roots are in classical tradition, but its motivation arises out of the depths of the Chinese mind and the needs of the time.

Thus by the philosophical interpretation of the "Three Principles," by the restoration of the service to Confucius, by the weekly ceremony to Sun Yat-sen, and by the inauguration of the New Life Movement the Chinese are adjusting their ancient heritage to modern times.

The metaphysics of Confucius may be called idealistic. Confucius believed in a Regulating Order, *Tien Tao*. This power was imaged in the Princely Power. Confucius believed in Celestial Providence which charged him with his mission and protected him. He was in communion with this power.

When Confucianism became the national religion the concrete ideas of Heaven, Shangti, faded and became abstract principles of organization which united different acts of the state ceremonial. For a time during the Han dynasty a personal God was worshiped. By the time of Chu Hsi the divine in the universe was reduced to the psychic principle *Li* and to the material principle *Chi*. Confucianism was the state religion in the sense that the state was the basis of the religious faith. To Confucius the state had been the creation of Heaven. To his successors Heaven was the creation of the state.

As a religion Confucianism developed a civilization and a state which have had a long and continuous history. This state was governed not by force but by moral suasion. The basic pattern of the system is man in relation to the universal order which includes the human order. To Confucianism the eternal order is fixed. The cosmic laws and the great gods desire the well-being of men. The laws and customs of society have the same goal. To attain happiness it is necessary to make the right adjustments to the universal order. If men are afflicted by natural calamities and social disorders it is due to the lawless action of the state and society. The ethics of Confucianism have been most effective in the family and in institutions based on the pattern of the family such as guilds and secret societies. The individual can serve Heaven and his ancestors best by developing his Heaven-given nature. The good man need have no fears.

The trend in China seems to be toward a synthesis in at least three directions. This process is illustrated in the temple of Confucius at Nanking before the war in 1937. In the highest place in the temple was the tablet of the Master. Somewhat below it was a marble bust of Sun Yat-sen, the father of modern China. On the pillars were portraits of Newton, Lavoisier, Pasteur, Lord Kelvin, Galileo, James Watt, Dalton, and Benjamin Franklin. Confucius represents traditional values, Sun Yat-sen modern nationalism, while the portraits on the pillars stand for modern science. Thus out of the religious and social chaos is emerging a synthesis between the East and the West.

SELECTED BIBLIOGRAPHY

THE FIVE CLASSICS:

The Book of Changes, Yih Ching; The Book of Poetry, Shih Ching; The Book of History, Shu Ching; The Book of Rites, Li Chi; Spring and Autumn, Chun Chiu. The Five Classics may be found in The Chinese Classics. By James Legge. Oxford, 1893–1895.

THE FOUR BOOKS:

Analects of Confucius. By W. E. Soothill. World's Classics, 1937.
Analects of Confucius. By Arthur Waley. London, 1938.
Mencius. By L. A. Lyall. London, 1932.
The Great Learning and The Mean-in-action. By E. R. Hughes. Dent, 1942.

Origin and Development of the State Cult of Confucius. By John K. Shryock, New York, 1932.

History of Chinese Philosophy. By Feng Yu-lan, translated by Derk Bodde. Vol. I. London, 1937.

Confucianism and Modern China. By Reginald F. Johnston. London, 1934.

A Short History of the Chinese People. By L. Carrington Goodrich. New York, 1943.

Taoism

LEWIS HODOUS

TAOISM started as a philosophy and developed into a religion in the Han dynasty (206 B.C.–A.D. 220). In Taoism the emotional, spontaneous, imaginative side of Chinese life comes to expression. As a philosophy Taoism sought unity; not the unity of organization but rather the unity of organism. The mystics sought union with the Tao so that they might bring unity and peace to the distracted world in which they lived. As a religion Taoism sought power over nature and over man by adjustment with the Tao through magic.

The basic intuition of the Taoist mystics is the Tao. During the fourth century B.C. a new astronomy came to China. The heavens were regarded as revolving about the solid block of the earth with the polar star as the pivot. This revolution was marked by the interaction of the negative principle *yin* and the positive principle *yang*. These two principles operated through the five agents or forces—water, fire, wood, metal, soil. These operations produced all the phenomena of earth, day and night, the seasons, man and the activities of man in response to the natural forces. This movement of the heavens about the earth was called the Tao by the Yin-yang philosophers. They formulated their theory in the phrase, "One *yin,* one *yang* is the Tao."

The Taoist mystics accepted this view but found it inadequate. They sublimated it by the mystic trance and believed that they attained ultimate reality and were able to identify themselves with it. The Tao Te Ching begins with the statement: "That which is ordinarily called the Tao is not the real Tao any more than a mere name is the real thing. As nameless It is the origin of Heaven and Earth. As having a name It is the mother of all things."

The Tao then is the physical concept of the way of the heavens in relation to the earth, transfigured and deepened by the mystic trance. The Tao is universal but not transcendent. It produces all and yet is not above all. It is not a person or an individual. It is the basic, cosmic energy which informs all. It is in all the phenomena of nature and yet not of them.

The other important term of the Taoists is *Te*. *Te* means to receive. When things receive the vital principle, that is *Te*. The Tao Te Ching puts it this way: "The Tao gives them life. Through moral power It nourishes them, through substance gives them form, by environment It completes them." The Tao is universal energy. *Te* is its activity. Thus *Te* includes both the physical and the moral aspects of nature and the life of man.

TAOIST LITERATURE

Taoism produced an extensive literature. The chief sources of philosophical Taoism are the Tao Te Ching and the Chuang Tzu Book. The Tao Te Ching has been attributed to Lao Tzu, of the sixth century, B.C., but this is questioned. It consists of sayings from various sources—which are embedded in much older material—and deals with the Tao, ethics, and government. It was compiled in the latter part of the fourth century B.C. It is mystic poetry of a high order with an admixture of common sense.

Chuang Tzu (369–286 B.C.) or Chuang Chou is one of the greatest Taoist thinkers. He occupies a high place among the philosophers of the world. The Chuang Tzu Book consists of thirty-three chapters and may be divided into three parts: inner part, chapters 1–7, by Chuang Tzu himself; outer part, chapters 8–22, by the pupils of Chuang Tzu; miscellaneous chapters, 23–33, by writers belonging to later traditions.

Taoism is treated also in a large collection, Tao Tsang, which numbers over 5,500 portions. Several codifications of it were made through the centuries, and during the Ming dynasty (A.D. 1368–1644) it was published twice. A new collection was in process of printing in Shanghai when the war broke out in 1937. These works bear no signature as a rule; they are supposed to come from Heaven. Many of them are by Ko Hung (*ca.* 270–350) and other Taoists. The collection is divided into three parts and twelve classes. Although it is the great source for the study of Taoism, it remains little known in the West.

The mystical experience differentiates Taoism from Confucianism. The root of Taoist philosophy is not in observation, reason, or discussion but in the mystic trance. The Taoists regarded books as the "dregs and remnants of the ancients." Reason should be abandoned because it obscures knowledge which is innate. The real knowledge is not the knowledge of sensuous things but knowledge of the Tao. This knowledge cannot be attained by study or by effort. The way to obtain it is the mystic path.

The mystic path practiced in ancient China resembles the mystic practices of all times. There is a period of isolation, detachment from the world of things. Then comes a period of abstinence corresponding to the *via negativa* of the medieval mystics. This leads to a vision, *via illuminativa,* and finally may be followed by union, *via unitiva,* with the Tao.

The mystical experience resembles conversion. The disciple had to enter a new life before he could qualify for full membership in the Taoist community. This is vividly described in Chuang Tzu: Yen Hui cried: "the Yen Hui who did not attain this state is I, Yen Hui. When I shall have attained this state, I shall be a Yen Hui who did not exist before."

This conversion is attained by a process called by Chuang Tzu, "the renewing of the heart." "Unify your attention. Do not listen [to that perceived by] the ear, but listen [to that perceived by] the heart. Do not listen [to that perceived by] the heart, but listen [to that perceived by] the soul [*chi*]. That which you understand does not come by the ears, but by the heart. The spirit should then be empty and take hold of reality. The union with the Tao is not obtained except by emptiness. It is this emptiness which is the renewing of the heart." (Chuang Tzu, chapter 4.)

The mystic experience does not come without a conflict between the "heavenly" and the "human." The human is the normal personality. This artificial and illusory self must be eliminated and the heavenly will then take full possession. Then follows ecstasy which is described in the following words: "His body was like a piece of dry wood, his heart like ashes." (Chuang Tzu, chapter 23.) Lieh Tzu supposedly of the Chou period (*ca.* 1027–256 B.C.) who belongs to this school describes it as follows: "That which was interior and exterior [in me] became interpenetrated. I had the same perception through the eyes as through the ears, through the ears as through the nose, through the nose as through the stomach. All sensations were melted together. My heart became concentrated. My bones and my flesh were liquefied. I did not have any feeling of that to which my body was attached, on which my feet were placed. At the mercy of the wind I went eastward and westward as a leaf, as a dry stalk, so that I did not know whether the wind carried me, or I carried the wind."

This ecstasy sometimes was completed in the union with the Tao. The Taoist philosophy arose out of this mystical experience. The mystical experience divided nature into two aspects. One was that perceived by the senses. This sensuous world was mere appearance. This is expressed beautifully in the *Musings of a Chinese Mystic* [1]: "Once upon a time, I, Chuang Tzu, dreamt I was a butterfly, fluttering hither and thither, to all intents and interests and purposes a butterfly. I was conscious of following my fancies as a butterfly, and was unconscious of my individuality as a man. Suddenly I awaked, and there I lay, myself again. Now I do not know whether I was then a man dreaming I was a butterfly, or whether I am now a butterfly dreaming I am a man."

Yet this sensuous world has its function. The Chuang Tzu Book expresses it thus: "The raison d'être of a fish-trap is the fish. When the fish is caught, the trap may be ignored. The raison d'être of a rabbit-snare is the rabbit. When the rabbit is caught, the snare may be ignored. The raison d'être of language is an idea to be expressed. When the idea is expressed, the lan-

[1] By Lionel Giles. Wisdom of the East Series. Page 49.

guage may be ignored. But where shall I find a man to ignore language with whom I may converse?"

The problem of the Taoists at this period was the overcoming of the relativities of their time. Many world-views were struggling for mastery. The solution of this conflict could not be made by classifying phenomena according to their similarities. This to the Taoists was an arbitrary way of solving the problem. Their solution consisted in viewing all experience as parts of the Whole. This Whole is not transcendent. The solution is to be found in the unity which interpenetrates all and embraces all.

To the mystics the Tao was the fountain of the ethical qualities which the saint or holy man must embody in himself. When he does so the world will submit to his guidance not because of his physical power, but because of his moral character. This has found expression in the widespread view that only the good man can bring peace and prosperity to China.

The Tao is impartial. It plays no favorites. This means justice. The Tao Te Ching states it this way: "Heaven is everlasting and the earth is eternal. The reason why heaven and earth are perpetual and enduring is because they do not exist for themselves. Therefore they exist forever." This impartiality includes being impartial to the self. The complete man is unselfish, selfless, without egoism.

The Tao is orderly. There are no collisions in the universe. The reason for this is that all things operate in mutual compliance. This is also the great trait of the wise man and of the Chinese people. There is much mutual compliance in the crowded villages. The Chinese like to talk things over. They often settle local conflicts, or prevent them by a feast. There is much self-government among the people. The mystics practiced forbearance, tolerance, mildness, and self-abnegation and to some extent at least promoted these qualities among the people.

The finest insight of the mystics is that the Tao is humble. "The great Tao overflows everything. All things depend upon It for their existence. Yet it does not desire the reputation of Its meritorious work. It completes its meritorious work and assumes not the reputation of doing so. It loves and nourishes all beings and does not make Itself the owner. It is always without desire. It may even be mentioned in small things. All things are dependent upon It and yet It does not make Itself their master." "The highest natural virtue is like water. The virtue of water is to benefit all beings and to occupy the place that all men hate." This is applied to the complete man. "When the meritorious work is accomplished and fame follows, then the person retires. This is the Tao of Heaven."

The outstanding quality of the Tao is spontaneity. The term used is *wu-wei* and is usually translated as "inaction." The term means "not to do anything for," that is, not to meddle, not to interfere, to let nature take its course. "The Tao acts constantly without effort and yet there is nothing which It does not accomplish." Chuang Tzu states it thus: "To rule the empire without effort, that is heavenly. Teaching the empire without effort, that is synonymous with virtue." The Tao Te Ching states it thus: "Heaven and Earth have the greatest excellence, yet they do not say a single word; the four seasons follow their clearest laws, yet they do not discuss; the myriad of beings have their perfect laws and yet they do not speak. The holiest man is spontaneous. This is called imitating Heaven and Earth." The classical statement of this quality is: "Busy yourself with no business." This quality was found to be most difficult to attain. It was misunderstood and easily degenerated into *laissez faire* and inaction.

POLITICAL PRINCIPLES

Taoism consists not so much of doctrines as of activities making for corporate well-being and salvation. Its mystic religious insights were part and parcel of political principles which the mystics sought to realize in the confusion of the time.

Their first effort was to realize a world where there was no interference with freedom and where special privilege did not limit the privileges of others. The walled towns with their officials and soldiers were living on the taxes of the peasants.

The rulers of these city-states claimed that their position was granted them by the favor of Heaven. They were chosen to rule the peasants. This the Taoists denied, saying: "Heaven and Earth have no selfish interests. They treat all things as straw-puppets. The sage has no selfish interests. He treats all men as straw-puppets."

The straw-puppets were used in sacrifice and honored during the sacrifice, but after the offering was over they were thrown upon the wood-pile. The meaning is not that Heaven disregards all, is neutral to all, but that Heaven does not grant special privileges to any whereby they may exercise control over men.

Out of these insights grew the practice of nonresistance and condemnation of militarism as practiced by the rulers of the walled cities.

The mystics attacked also the moral and legal restraints advocated by the Confucian group. One of the keenest ironies is in the following passage: "When the great Tao is done away with, then we have benevolence. When wisdom appears, we have hypocrisy. When the five relations are not at peace, then we have filial piety and love; and when the country is in rebellion, we have the loyal official." Again, "Do away with saints and discard your wisdom and thieves will disappear."

The Taoist mystics developed the ideal of the small state. "[I am thinking] of a small country with a sparse population. They may have many leaders at their disposal, but do not use them. They may regard death as unpleasant and yet do not move away. Although they possess boats and carts, still they do not use them. Although they have armor and weapons they do not set them in array. Let them cause the people to make knots or strings and use them instead of writing. Then they will enjoy their food, their clothing will be beautiful, their dwellings peaceful, their daily life happy. Although neighboring countries may be near enough so that they may see each other and may hear the crowing of the roosters and the barking of the dogs, the people will reach a great age and die and still not have any intercourse with each other."

ECONOMIC PRINCIPLES

These early mystics tried to integrate their mystic religion with life. They censured the materialism of their day. They looked with critical eyes at the luxurious customs of their day. They urged government frugality and light taxes. "That people go hungry is due to the fact that the rulers waste taxes. That people are difficult to govern is due to the meddlesomeness of the rulers." "The more beautiful the palaces, the more barren and neglected the fields. To adorn oneself with beautiful garments, to carry sharp swords, to be glutted with food and drink, with treasures in abundance—this means robbers and begging. These have nothing to do with the Tao."

The mystic stressed the principle of maximum contentment with minimum content. "There is no greater calamity than not to be contented. There is no greater evil than continually increasing desires. Therefore note, he who understands sufficiently to be content is continually content."

TAOISM AS A POPULAR RELIGION

When Chin Shih Huang Ti became emperor in 221 B.C. the country needed peace. He adopted Taoism because its principles of spontaneity and noninterference, which were readily transformed into *laissez faire* and inaction, promised cooperation with the diverse elements of the empire. The first emperor of the Han dynasty also favored Taoism though he realized that he needed a group with a historical perspective. His successor adopted Confucianism as a state religion. This did not prevent the development of Taoism as a popular religion.

During the disturbed times of the second century A.D. two leaders formed sects which are the parents of present day Taoism. One was Chang Ling who produced a book of charms. Those who received his teaching gave him five measures of rice. The other was Chang Chueh who induced the sick individual to confess his sins in a quiet place, make an offering of wine and read the Tao Te Ching and pray. He also exacted five measures of rice for this service. The confessions in three forms were carried to a mountain, buried in the ground, and soaked in a river and thus were communicated to the genii of Heaven, Earth, and Water. Chang Chueh with his brother Chang Lu gained possession of Shensi. His adherents were known as the Yellow Turbans who carried all before them, but were finally subdued.

At the beginning of the third century A.D. a sectarian movement which centered in Szechuan opened a dynasty of so-called Taoist popes with the title of Celestial Teacher borne by the family of Chang. These religious chiefs levied a tax upon the faithful and their descendants finally established themselves at Lung Hu Shan in Kiangsi. They were officially recognized in 748. From this seat they dispensed charms and orders. They had control over the Taoists living in families, geomancers, fortune-tellers, and doctors. The family of Chang were dispossessed by a communistic section of the National Army in 1927.

In the course of time this expanding popular Taoism attracted to itself and gradually assimilated many groups with various doctrines. One of these originating on the shores of Shantung developed the idea of the Immortals. Long life was not in the tradition of Taoism. The ancient Taoists regarded the body as not worth preserving. These Immortals were located in the mountains of Central Asia and were presided over by the Queen of the West, Hsi Wang Mu. In her garden was a peach tree which bore fruit once in a thousand years and whoever partook of it would never die. They also developed the legend of the Isles of the Immortals in the Eastern Sea. The First Emperor—Shih Huang Ti, of the Chin dynasty (221–207 B.C.) whose system of government lasted until the twentieth century—sent an expedition to these islands. Later were developed the legends of the Immortals in the moon.

With the Immortals is connected the elixir of life. Disease and death are due to a lack of bodily energy which may be supplied by certain foods and drugs. The mystics abstained from ordinary food, and practiced breathing. There was the story of one who could breathe through his heels. The purpose was to take in as much of the *yang* force as possible and keep it. These

32

hermits lived on seeds and plants and thus added to the foods and pharmacopoeia of the Chinese.

In the experiments with the elixir of life all sorts of substances were placed in a caldron made according to specifications. The fire beneath it was kindled by the pure fire of the sun, the water was the dew collected from a metal surface exposed to moonlight. After three years in the caldron the elixir was called "small perfection" and could cure a hundred diseases. After six years it was "middling perfection" and a draught of it would prolong life. After nine years one draught would confer immortality.

This elixir, however, did not produce Immortals who ascended into Heaven. Various excuses were invented to explain the failure. The material was not good, the heat was not sufficient, the time was not favorable. This failure led to the practice of inner methods. The heart had to be pure and quiet. A new theory of man was developed. He was a small microcosm (Heaven and Earth) and so everything is already in man. He does not need to go out for anything. Within the body are three centers called the "three elixir fields." Within these fields there is the mysterious medicine which can be manipulated, and spiritualized, and then made to return to the respective field. In the body natural fire of the heart is transformed into pure spiritual fire, natural water of the kidneys into spiritual water.

Another influence in Taoism is that of Moti, or Mo Tzu. During the Han period (206 B.C.–A.D. 220) only the Taoists could stand up against the Confucianists. Many of the groups came to the Taoists for protection. The followers of Mo Tzu, being pacifists, were not too popular in this warlike age. The Mo Tzu influence is revealed by the adoption of gods and spirits, prayer and offering. Later Mo Tzu was placed among the Immortals and to him were attributed powers of controlling spirits and producing the elixir of life.

Another practice connected with Taoism goes by the name of *feng-shui,* wind and water. The theory behind this is that, since man is born on the earth and returns to the ground, the place of his dwelling and his burial must be decided by the cycle of the five forces. The manipulators regarded the earth as a cubic block. This was set in the midst of the sky and was surrounded on four sides by the twenty-eight mansions of the moon. Since the Han dynasty these observations on earth have been correlated with the Heavens.

The theory behind *feng-shui* was that *yin-yang* permeate the earth and produce all things. One breath or vapor permeates the body of the progeny and the bones of the ancestors. This being the case the misfortune of one can influence the other.

This theory is the expression of the profound sense of the Chinese unity and continuity of the family. This unity and continuity are due to the constitution of nature itself. In this there is no reference to demons, or to good spirits. The family is the product of the universal force. It is subject to this force. Out of this grew the ethics of the Chinese. Man is the product of universal forces, is subject to them, is connected with the ancestors by them. The science of *feng-shui* is the abstract projection of filial piety.

Taoism as a religion needed a center about which to organize its ritual and values. This was found in the new astronomy introduced from the West. The five forces (water, fire, wood, metal, soil) were connected with the five planets, the *yin* and *yang* principles and the seasons. Astronomy connected Taoism with the Heavens and their influence upon the agricultural life and the destiny of man. Many of the gods of Taoism have an astral origin. To these were added gods adopted from Buddhism and from the secret sects.

In due time the Taoists, whose religion of nature was close to popular beliefs, appropriated local and domestic gods and placed them in a hierarchy after the pattern of the officials of the empire. They superimposed upon the human situation a divine administration. At the head was Yu Huang Shangti, the Jade Emperor. Under his rule were all the gods and goddesses and spirits in the universe. They established the idea that each individual had three genii in charge of him and these reported on every fifty-seventh day of the cycle of sixty days to the governor above. This kept alive the sense of individual responsibility. The principal moral censor was the kitchen god who reported on the last day of each month and at the end of the year to the Ruler Above.

The local gods and the genii formed an intermediary group. They could shorten or lengthen life according to the merit of the individual; thus the Taoists did away with fatalism. These gods were associated with the soil and so were in contact with the souls of the dead. The great attention paid to tombs makes this connection natural. The officers in charge of life were conceived as functionaries in Hades. Through the influence of Buddhism to the effect that human acts were rewarded after death, Taoism developed at least from the eighth century A.D. a code of sins. Each sin, as well as the good action compensating it, was precisely described and duly rewarded.

The God Tai Shan is chief in the hierarchy of infernal inspectors of men's deeds. In every village the god of the ground is under the authority of Tai Shan. Outside of the eastern gate of the large walled cities there is usually a temple of Tai Shan. The courts of Hades are represented with the punishments for the various sins. The God of the Walls and Moats is also an important god in this hierarchy. In some of these temples there is also a feminine divinity, a daughter of Tai Shan. She is called the Princess of Azure Clouds, and bears the name of Dawn. Her acolytes preside over the first days of birth. She herself gives birth. Tai Shan is honored because he is a great deity of rural China. Agriculture and the veneration of ancestors are connected with him.

TAOISM AND OTHER SYSTEMS

Taoism as a philosophy suffered many distortions. Its basic intuition of a spontaneous reality is difficult to apprehend and more difficult to hold. Spontaneity readily degenerated into *laissez faire* and nonaction. The lack of a concrete norm invited all sorts of fancies and vagaries. When Taoism was favored by Chin Shi Huang Ti many local superstitions sought shelter under its hospitable roof. The disciples of Mo Tzu, being pacifists, went underground during this warlike time and provided Taoism with a belief in spirits and the rewards and punishments. Later this stream merged with Buddhist karma and produced the moral bookkeeping of rewards and punishments in present day Taoism.

The *yin-yang* theory through its differentiation of diverse kinds of cosmic breath gave a basis to Taoist breathing. The new astronomy supplied not only stellar gods, but a center about which the new religion was organized and connected with the Heaven above and the peasant's need below.

The exorcism of the northern shamans, incantations, the legends of the Immortals, of the Queen of the West, the Floating Islands in the East, the Immortals in the moon transformed a mystic philosophy into a popular religion.

But the largest influence on Taoism was Buddhism. When the Buddhists came to China the Taoists became their hosts. The Buddhist monks were called *Tao jen,* the term used for Taoist hermits. The Taoists discovered that the Buddhists had gone much further along the mystic way. Early translations of Buddhist sutras made considerable use of Taoist terms.

The Buddhist trinity, Western Paradise, hell, the order of monks, karma, transmigration, gods and goddesses were taken over from the Indian religion. Taoism became a Chinese edition of Buddhism. Buddhism not only introduced gods and images, it personalized the natural forms of Taoism and thereby transformed the character of ritual. In the folk festivals ritual was regarded as a magical process stimulating nature to act in the desired way. A personal god, however, required a different kind of approach and so prayer was introduced alongside magical formulas and incantations. Buddhism deepened the meaning of religion. The Taoists made offerings to the gods for material benefits; thank-offering expressed gratitude for anticipated favors; the gods were really used and not worshiped. The Buddhists condoned the practice, but insisted that the gods made spiritual blessings which were also available to the believer. They emphasized faith, defining it as the hand which takes hold of Buddha.

This new attitude in religion brought in by Buddhism began to transform the demons. They were partly sublimated by the atmosphere of hope so characteristic of Mahayana Buddhism. This is a long story and it is not easy to evaluate this aspect of Taoism. Some people hold that the Chinese live in constant fear of demons and the many popular stories about them seem to confirm this. But though the Chinese believe in demons and discuss them the question arises whether they are more than mere symbols of undesirable things to be avoided. There is an extensive literature on demons, and the stories are well written, widely read and enjoyed. All this leads one to suspect that these stories are a genre of literature similar to our mystery stories. Dante consigned some of his contemporaries to special places in the Hades of his day. Chinese writers have given similar honored places to officials who failed them in the state examinations.

Another contribution of Buddhism was the hope of personal immortality. The Taoist mystics believed that they were able to attain immortality through their mystic practices and through the elixir of life. But Mahayana Buddhism offered this hope to all. Immortality did not depend upon offerings, or one's station in life, but was connected with the character and conduct of the individual. A moral relation was established between this life and the condition of the soul beyond this life by the theory of karma, the equivalence of deed and reward. This proved to be a great boon in easing the tensions of life. Poverty and wealth, sickness and health, happiness and misfortune were not only explained by this formula, but were made endurable.

To the great mass of the people, however, karma was vague. The Taoists made it understandable and practical by a system of religious arithmetic. To each evil deed was attached an appropriate punishment either in this life or in the next. All this was clearly expounded in a popular work entitled, *Book of Rewards and Punishments by the Great Supreme*.[2] This work states the principles underlying the system as follows:

[2] Tai Shang Kan Ying Pien, published during the Sung dynasty A.D. 960–1279.

"The Great Supreme says: Misfortune and fortune have no door; men themselves incur or win them; recompense follows virtue and vice, as the shadow follows substance.

"Consequently in Heaven and on earth there are genii noting the sins of men and cutting off from their lives periods proportioned to the slight or great offenses. When their periods of life are shortened, little by little the people become needy; they encounter many sorrows; they are the objects of hatred by others; punishments and troubles pursue them; prosperity and happiness shun them; evil stars strike them with plagues. When the curtailed periods of their life are completed, they die. . . .

"For all great sins of men twelve years of life are cut off; for small sins one hundred days. . . .

"If at death there remains guilt unpunished the punishment extends to the descendants of the culprits."

The system also provides punishment in Hades which was taken over from the Buddhists, adapted to Chinese conditions, and became a vital force in the imaginary environment of the Chinese.

Again, Buddhism fructified Taoist ethics. The root of Buddhist ethics is in the love of all beings. This love is based upon the religious insight that every living being has the Buddha nature and is on the way to Buddhahood. Philosophical Taoism and Confucianism promulgated the teaching that all men have an endowment of the Tao, but these systems lacked the personal motivation. The *Book of Rewards and Punishments by the Great Supreme* brings out clearly this new motivation in the following passage:

"The good man is aware that all beings of the earth, the plants, the birds, the animals on land and in water, all that has life, have been created by Heaven and earth. Heaven and earth gave rise to them because they feel pleasure in the beings. If you cannot protect them, at least do no harm to them. The good man, while walking and seeing at his feet a blade of living grass, lifts his foot and passes without treading upon it. Neither does he deliberately kill an insect, however small it may be, all this comes not only from the love for beings, but at bottom from the love of Heaven and earth."

This passage is especially interesting because of the statement that love for beings springs from the love for Heaven and earth. In China love for Heaven was unthinkable until it was introduced by Mahayana Buddhism.

Taoism was not always on the receiving line. It gave to Confucianism the basis of the theory that human nature is good. Later it made a large contribution to the metaphysics of Neo-Confucianism. Its great contribution to Confucianism, Buddhism, and the Eastern world was through its intuition that ultimate reality is spontaneous. This Taoist insight came to fruition in the meditative sect Chan-men, founded by a simple monk. Buddhism brought to China Indian quietism with its regimen of abstinence, contemplation of dead bodies, and other practices to impress the dogma that this world is suffering. This with elaborate Buddhist ritual, organization, theology, libraries of scriptures, confused and alienated the Chinese mystics. They believed that if Buddha had anything to say to the individual he could do it without all this paraphernalia. The Tao was spontaneous and spoke to man without trumpery. One of the early converts to this view advocated the necessity of beating the ghosts out of the Chinese people. By ghosts he meant the Buddhist hierarchy and all its works.

This immediate enlightenment experienced by a simple monk developed into a mystic activism which transformed certain aspects of Buddhism and Confucianism and is today as Chan in China and Zen in Japan a religious force of considerable power.

MODERN TAOISM

Taoism in modern China is divided into two schools, the Northern and the Southern. The Northern school emphasizes meditation, and metaphysical speculation, and practices breathing.

The Southern school was located at Lung Hu Shan (Kweiki Kiangsi province) until 1927. It was headed by the so-called

Taoist pope who had charge of Taoist priests living in families and dispensed charms, amulets, and incantations.

Behind modern Taoism is the basic concept of cosmic energy of which Man is a part. By obedience to this energy he can obtain health, wealth, offspring, and a peaceful life. By opposing it he will meet misfortune, disaster, and death. It operates through many forces called gods and demons. These forces and the methods of employing them are known to certain specialists. Many of the methods are the common possession of the people passed on by hoary tradition.

Another fundamental idea of Taoism is a philosophy of government. The emperor in the Confucian system regarded as the son of Heaven is to the Taoists the manifestation of the Tao. He and his officials are endowed with a special amount of this cosmic power or *Te*. The emperor is a model for all men. A good ruler will have a peaceful, harmonious state. If the state is in disorder this is evidence that the ruler has lost this power of the Tao, that Heaven is displeased with him. It is then the duty of men to assist Heaven in removing the ruler and to co-operate with Heaven in establishing a new order. At this point the theory of Taoist spontaneity comes out. The Taoists co-operate with nature in meeting difficulties and overcoming them.

This philosophy of government, which is endemic in China and not consciously articulated, gives rise to numerous societies—some of them secret—which spring up to meet any critical situation in the nation. These societies have no creed, but they have a ritual. The members are made blood-brothers by the ancient and sacred ritual of exchanging blood. It was celebrated in the novel of the *Three Kingdoms* when three men, of whom Kuanti was one, made a pact to stick to each other through life and death. There are other such brotherhoods celebrated in poetry and story. These societies are not communistic, but they often believe in share-the-wealth plans. They often rob the rich and help the poor.

These societies have a long and interesting record. The Pai Lien Chiao, the White Lotus, goes back to the time of the Mongol dynasty. It has had several incarnations. The Society of Heaven, Earth, Man (San Ho-hui) has eight rebellions to its credit during the last one hundred and fifty years. The great Tai Ping rebellion which ravaged China between 1850 and 1864 and which had a Christian slant drew its support from these secret orders. The secret order is the social pattern of Chinese society in conflict and confusion.

It would be difficult to overestimate the influence of these societies on modern China. After the Republic was inaugurated the universal slogan was *tu-li* "stand alone." Freedom was interpreted without the sense of responsibility which real liberty demands. While this attitude weakened the family and folk responsibility, it did not produce individuals with a sense of responsibility to the new social order. After the revolution the students smashed the idols, soldiers occupied temples and monasteries, while the government not only frowned upon popular festivals but discouraged and even prohibited them. The old gods were dethroned but new gods with authority did not emerge spontaneously. To meet this situation many of these societies set up more inclusive gods. Some of them placed above their old gods the God of all Religions. Christianity, Islam, Buddhism, Confucianism, and Taoism were viewed as ways of salvation under the direction of the God of all Religions. For example, in a model prison in Peking in 1912 there was a lecture hall. Behind the chair of the speaker were five images: Christ, Lao Tzu, Confucius, John Howard (the eighteenth century English philanthropist), and Muhammad.

The chaotic social and religious situation spread abroad a sense of pessimism and frustration. To meet this these societies provided quiet places for meditation and thus promoted certainty and unity of conviction and an assurance that they had found a synthesis of truth. Again, in China religion and conduct belong together. These societies are a powerful ethical force elevating the moral tone of the community as well as that of their members. They emphasize such values as sincerity in human relations and honesty in business. They hold their members to a high moral code and act as a brake at a time when moral values are skidding toward chaos. But they go beyond the cultivation of the personal life and try to meet the suffering brought about by the dislocation of the social order. They minister to the wounded soldiers, to the refugees, and to the needy in the large cities.

Religion in China is connected with politics. It expresses the emotional and esthetic aspects of life while conduct and politics express the active aspects. These societies are very influential in government policies as well as in practical administration. They exert a powerful pressure not merely on local officials but on the national government. China is still governed by men rather than by law and these societies are able to exert influence upon the leaders who are behind the modern government.

On the whole the trends of these societies are toward conservatism and sometimes toward reaction. Their influence on policies and administration is quite evident, but many of these orders have programs for the future political organization of China. As a rule they do not advertise them. This would bring about their dissolution.

Taoism has always been most prosperous in times of trouble and confusion. Again it is running according to form. As a religion it has numerous gods symbolizing natural and social forces. On the level of magic it promises wealth, health, and happiness. On the higher level it offers psychic integration by meditation and discipline. It has stimulated reform in government and has attempted to bring harmony in the social and religious confusion of the time.

The object of Taoism as a mystic philosophy was to obtain power over self, over men and nature, and to bring unity to the distracted and suffering people of that period of Chinese history. This goal was to be achieved by adjustment to the Tao. Such complete adjustment was not for the common man but for the saint (*sheng*) who so identified himself with the Tao that he could do naturally what the Tao did. The saint was placed above the gods in China as in Hinayana Buddhism in India. The saint by his magico-moral power (*Te*) would attract the loyalty of the whole world. The mystics were striving for cultural if not political unity.

Taoism does not belong to the type of mysticism which regards salvation as complete absorption with ultimate reality. It belongs rather to a monism which regards religion not as an escape from illusion but as a means of controlling the relativities of existence.

SELECTED BIBLIOGRAPHY

The Way and Its Power, a Study of the Tao Te Ching. By Arthur Waley. London, 1934.

The Sayings of Lao Tzu. By Lionel Giles. Wisdom of the East Series. London, 1926.

Taoist Teachings of the Book of Lieh Tzu. By Lionel Giles. Wisdom of the East Series. London, 1925.

A Study of Chinese Alchemy. By Obed Simon Johnson. Shanghai, 1928.

Chinese Philosophy in Classical Times. By E. R. Hughes. New York and London, 1942.

Chuang Tzu—Mystic, Moralist and Social Reformer. By H. A. Giles. Shanghai, 1926.

Musings of a Chinese Mystic. By Lionel Giles. Wisdom of the East Series.

Three Ways of Thought in Ancient China. By Arthur Waley. London, 1939.

China's Religious Heritage. By Y. C. Yang. New York and Nashville, 1943.

Hinduism

JOHN CLARK ARCHER

THE term Hinduism is both broad and vague but for want of something better we may use it to designate the religion of the Hindu. The word Hindu itself is an abstract designation of a class more than of any given persons, for there is scarcely any concrete person readily to be identified as Hindu, though we shall have much to say of "Hindus." There are about two hundred and sixty-five millions of them among the nearly four hundred millions counted in the latest government census of the homeland India, and their two-thirds' majority is fairly evenly distributed throughout the land. While numbers may be a matter of the census, Hindu qualities are not fully to be known from written records. Hinduism in its vagueness is first of all an item of the Stone Age, it is so ancient. It comes in fact mostly from the time of man's long infancy, however vast and varied it may be as an accumulation.

Although it is a comprehensive sum of things, it is nevertheless to be distinguished ultimately by some process of exclusion which leaves it as a residue after Indian Moslems, Christians, Parsis, and Jews are counted, as well as Sikhs and Jains. Hinduism as a residue left by this process of exclusion is nevertheless the qualifying substance of all Indian religion. The term as a title and a total represents in the whole field of religion something peculiarly symbolic. A large part of our task is to find whatever unity inheres in the vast and vague Hindu variety in India alone, even though it be often scarcely more than that of the saying, "The camphor and the cotton are 'one,' in being *white*." To which we must add immediately that Hindus are not even one in color, and Hinduism finds coherence and consistency chiefly by sheer abstraction.

Hinduism has had no founder to furnish it a basic message, no early leader comparable with Zoroaster, Jesus or Muhammad—although Muhammad counted himself only a restorer,

44

Jesus declared his mission to be fulfillment, and Zoroaster felt called upon to purge and to summarize what he knew of earlier religion. These at least, each in his turn, inspired a "book of wisdom," a "gospel," and a "writing." Hindus have had no one even like Confucius to edit fully a long, inherited tradition. Strictly speaking, they have had for themselves no such figure as the Jains have in their Vardhaman Mahavira, as Buddhists have in Gotama Sakyamuni, or as the Sikhs have in Nanak. In a sense, the founders of Hinduism are legion, their figures as shadowy as "cloud-messengers" of changeful constitution and fitful errand. Distinguished persons do indeed appear in later times, but the early scenes are conspicuously impersonal. In the earliest deposit of Vedic wisdom no inspired singer stands out clearly as does the psalmist David of the Hebrews. The Indian Kautilya, giver of the Law, is a wraith compared with Moses, and Yajnavalkya, the priest who took to speculation in Upanishadic times, was no such sage and personality as his Greek contemporary Plato.

This kind of survey gives us a valid introduction to the indefinite incoherence which has settled down from precedent to precedent. Consider for a moment how Hinduism has won its way by conversion in a most peculiar sense. It is easier for a non-Hindu to comprehend the faith than to be converted to it. There is almost no provision within Hinduism for conversion as a personal experience, and its expansion has come as a whole rather than by the addition of separate individuals. It represents the sum of penetration, absorption, and accommodation rather than the result of creative evolution, and its totality has been itself exclusive even to the extent of a sloughing-off of variations which disturbed inordinately the loose balance of the general framework. At the same time variants innumerable have occurred within the whole, which being retained have made Hinduism the most confused, confusing, and distinctive of all the world's religions. We hasten, however, to say that we shall in time pick up a clue by which to comprehend the whole. This clue is the major, controlling theory of transmigration which has posited in a universe peculiarly and altogether animate a fixed number of items, entities, or agents known as souls. The Hindu, accordingly, thinks of change within his universe as relative and compensatory. For the soul of any single Hindu there is within the total round of life a series of many births from stage to stage and lot to lot, and his own career is but a manifestation of universal animation.

If we now seek the full perspective on this Hindu total, we must first look in an early age outside of India to a site, whether Asiatic or European, whence not only many Indians but also some of us sprang. It is of interest to us, if merely for an understanding of India, to know of this common heritage and to keep in mind the timeless Indo-European cultural tradition. Even as family trees now grow in Western soil, whose roots suck nourishment from Runnymede, Eire, Etna, the Bohmer Wald, Mt. Zion, and Tai Shan—in the figure, for example, of the Asiatic eucalyptus now thriving in Brazil—so also we are linked with India and Hinduism, as can be proved by archaeology, comparative linguistics, and comparative religion. We may view with special interest, therefore, the human stock of related peoples from whom Vedic, Iranian, Greek, Latin, Slavic, Celt, and Germanic cultures came, however numerous their divisive languages have been.

Two kindred branches of the common stem may have wandered far apart in the third millennium, B.C., some to central Europe and some to Turkistan, but there is evidence in Cappadocia, Asia Minor, that *circa* 1400 B.C. the Vedic Indian deities Indra, Varuna and the Nasatya twins of the Panjab were known there. These divinities of the firmament, the all-investing sky, and the daily sunrise, respectively, were nevertheless but a few of the many factors in the common lot of the two regions two thousand miles apart. In the Panjab itself the Indo-European elements must have found an antecedent culture. Perhaps as early as 3000 B.C. in India before the Indo-Europeans came, the great god Shiva Mahadeva was known and worshiped. There is thus early no record of his name, but there is the relic of a god who must have filled the role assigned to Shiva as Pashupati, "lord of creatures." Therefore, however extensive was the sweep of Indo-European—the so-called "Aryan"—elements, there were antecedents in India and these antecedents were the initial ground for the nurture of the Aryo-Indian or Hindu tradition. Hindus themselves have clung to a purely Vedic heritage—except for acquaintance in modern times with the larger world—and have been indifferent to any outer contacts and especially regardless of any pre-Vedic culture with its international implications. "Back to the Vedas" has been the motto, for example, of the most influential modern movement, that of the Arya Samaj, toward Hindu reconstruction. Hinduism has yet to reckon seriously and reconstructively with a larger realm than India.

Let us get now a nearer view of the Hindu in his own India. Both terms, that of the man and that of his home, were foreign, non-Indian, at the outset. *Hindu* stems from an Indo-European, perhaps an Indo-Iranian, root for "river"—no clan or tribal name, therefore, or something merely local or ancestral, but something, rather, whose origin and volume defied locality. We and they have known it since as the Indus, a stream which rises within the shadow of Mt. Kailasha among the lofty Himalayas, flows first among these mountains northwestward for five hundred miles, turns thereafter southwestward in debouchment, and flows a thousand miles across the plains to empty at the Tropic of Cancer in the Arab Sea, having meanwhile gathered to itself from the east the waters of several other streams which first flowed out from the Himalayan foothills and thereafter made their level way across the Panjab, land of the "five waters."

The moving tribesmen were impressed by the mighty river and called their new home Hindustan, "land of the river," when the Persian word for river had become, probably in post-Vedic times, the Sanskrit *sindhu*. India is short for *sindhu ka sthan*—the same as Hindustan—but it was perhaps the Roman Vergil who first called the whole land "India." Hindus by this and any other designation are *the* people of all India, far more than items in a census, and Hinduism as their common faith is essentially the mind of India.

For the Western student there is no single track into the heart of India, into the core of Hinduism. Our ancient kinsmen, the "Aryans," went by land through the northwest passage. The Portuguese Vasco da Gama took one sea route to Goa and the Englishman Job Charnock took another to Bengal. Perhaps we take a literary passage. And all the while the increasing multitudes live their lives beyond all written records and casual observation.

It soon appears that Hinduism as a social scheme bulks larger than it does as creed. There were in 1945 about 17,000,000 Brahmans, at least 185,000,000 members of the three non-Brahman castes, and some 60,000,000 others, including "God's people" (*harijans*) the "untouchables." These *harijans* are thus identified by most reforming Hindus in whose opinion these former dregs of the Indian social order have come at last to share divine providence as Hinduism has expounded it. Many Brahmans, however, question this version of the matter, and the new opinion has come about by a Hindu change of view and not by the conversion of the outcastes. Obviously something other than pure and undefiled religion is the issue, something separate from creed, if those of the fifth estate, these *panchamas,* these lowest socio-racial elements in the human scale, are to be integrated with the total Hindu order.

What, then, are the tests of the Hindu religion? Literacy and general education seem not to be indispensable among them, although by their presence or their absence they have constituted grounds of wide variety in both belief and ritual. Scarcely a hundred Hindus in every thousand are literate, and they are mostly males. The Shudras of the fourth estate (*ca.* 125,000,000?) are almost wholly without learning and, of course, the panchama harijans are quite illiterate. General education has never been a goal of Hinduism, and custodians of learning have been few. There is no cogent reason for believing that in any former age education was more prevalent than it is in this. This is not to say that creed could not be a test of Hinduism—witness the combination of illiteracy and creed in popular Islam! It is rather to declare that subdivisions of the Hindu multitudes must be classified on other grounds than literacy.

This brings us to the observation that Hinduism is fundamentally a *socio*-religious order, and to the reminder that Hinduism somehow deals directly with the Hindu's total life, including morals, economics, politics, and even music, medicine, military science, architecture, phonetics, grammar, astronomy, and ceremonial. Hindus may include all these in what they call religion. Continuity has been persistent and all-inclusive within the bounds of India for forty and maybe fifty centuries. It becomes clear that something more than mere persistence has been required to account for such longevity in the face of internal reformations and encroachments from without, and that some potency or other has mixed with mere inertia and the force of habit. The Hindu woman's dress, for one thing, has not altered greatly in two thousand years. The village is still the center of the people's life as it was three thousand years ago. The villager still delights as he did of old to hear related, and himself to recite, the myths and legends woven familiarly into the loose fabric of the common faith. Although there may be today in many of the larger towns of India as many as three hundred theaters showing Hollywood and British pictures, the villager still prefers such films as reproduce, however clumsily, the well-worn myths of Shiva and Vishnu-Krishna, and episodes from the Mahabharata, the Ramayana and various Puranas—tales of heroes, gods, and godlings of the classic days. If indeed some other kind of interest has been born among the villages and in many towns, it expresses itself not in films from Hollywood or Britain, but in didactic strips which, against the background of the tragedy and comedy of Indian life itself, seek to teach correction of such current evils as infant-marriage, drink, prostitution, and untouchability, and which promote such goods as the remarriage of widows and a general socio-economic reformation. The Indian order is the Hindu's first concern and any interest he may have beyond it is incidental.

It is not a merely superficial interest. There is a subtle and sometimes explicit consciousness on the Hindu's part of something deeper far than habit and sheer fondness for his order. There is a consciousness that a potency called *karma* operates a round of transmigration for him. Herein is the major clue to the mystery of continuity in the whole agglomeration. It occured, for example, to a certain Moslem author, Mohsan Fani, on his first acquaintance, *ca.* A.D. 1600, with the Hindus, to introduce them to his coreligionists and to the outer world as "believers in transmigration," even while he made much also of their "many systems of religion." He struck a social note as well by referring to "the one principal class of people," the Brahmans, who held dominion over all the other Hindus. He realized the force of the brahmanical role and tradition which had prevailed by his time in theory and in practice for over twenty centuries.

There had been this special "priestly" class of men, these Brahmans, who, although only a fraction of them served actually as priests, had provided the highest type of leadership in education, in current culture, and in sacerdotal service, not the least of their tenets and pronouncements being that of a comprehensive, causal (*karmic*) theory of repeated births. Mohsan Fani could not detect a common creed, nor indeed any such creedal-mindedness as Moslems manifested, or even any universal ritual—no such simple, common ritual, at any rate, as that of the Moslem public and private prayers, but only some elaborate rites for occasional and seasonal observances. He could not discover a brief or simple sacred scripture comparable in any way with his Koran—he didn't hear about the Gita until later on—but only a miscellaneous and confused assortment of jealously guarded, often secreted, writings whose very bulk impressed incomprehensibility upon him, although he spurned them all as falsehood. He was aware of mass on every hand, but not of harmony and unity, except for what he saw of universal karma and transmigration. Their many systems were not, however, many "sects" to him, for he found no sects such as the Semitic and the Christian world had known, sects which themselves are the fruits of varied creed. Hinduism really has lacked sects, creeds, councils, and the like, and has been divided on a theory of universal providence and the circumstance of birth, and not at all on men's opinions.

ONE WORD FOR IT ALL—DHARMA

Hinduism is a frame of mind—a mental attitude within its own peculiar setting, socially divisive, if theologically non-creedal, unused to common worship in a congregational, ecclesiastical, or formal way, and a mood or spirit which has been a substitute for nationality. India has never been a nation under Hindu rule. Political unity, that is, has never been achieved, no Hindu civil state has itself been the framework, or the sponsor, of religion. And yet there is a clue to our ultimate perspective. That clue is—*dharma*. The word represents at once the "law" of life and the destiny which shapes the Hindu's end. *It is the Hindu's own word for Hinduism.* His scriptures and his ritual embody and express it, and his thought and conduct are guided and dominated by it. Its uses range all the way from the stricter sense of law or jurisprudence to the broader, vaguer region which, after the example of Roman *religio,* we have called religion.

Some brief notice of dharma as jurisprudence must be given here. Constitutional administrative procedure has been as noticeably absent from Hindu history as formalized creed. Not only has no nation been achieved; there have been separate states, often dozens of them at a given time, each with its own polity, coinage, and objectives. That each state in modern times had a partial and peculiar sense of law was soon discovered by the English who with their own Runnymede tradition of the Magna Charta introduced themselves to India and undertook one by one the administration of many of these civil units. When for administrative or other purposes they—Warren Hastings, for example, in Bengal—began to study Hindu law, they found it to be what seemed primarily religious custom. Dharma the law meant religion also and required of English justice that it take account of custom; and, as conditions were, to take account of Moslem as well as Hindu custom, with such discrimination in the content and the connotation of the term as good government might require.

There is an ancient Hindu work known as the Arthashastra, with Kautilya's name attached, a sort of legal digest or an epitome of law, which could have been under the circumstances of its time (*ca.* 300 B.C.) no more in itself than a textbook in a school of politics, if indeed it was any more than the author's own private treatise, his own theory of dharma as legal practice. In any case, it puts great emphasis on royal cunning and on the ruler's cleverness in government. It seems to hold the view that jurisprudence springs from sovereignty, not sovereignty from law—the raja wields the *danda,* the "big stick," and exercises *matsya-nyaya,* "fish logic" (by which the larger fishes thrive upon the smaller). And during all the centuries since, whatever limitations were imposed on kings, the importance and the hereditary character of monarchy have been widely recognized. But Hindu history likewise holds evidence of government by common law. In the very era of the Arthashastra, in the palmy days of Mauryan rule this side of 300 B.C., a Greek traveler, Megasthenes, discovered in northern India what he called "republics," even while he observed also that the Hindus "had no laws"! He had discovered the *samitis, sabhas,* or "associations," nonlegislative bodies ("lawless" institutions) which the "Aryans" had introduced to various parts of India. But we should keep in mind the fact that, apart from any such "republics," there were everywhere among the villages *panchayats,* or "five-fold" assemblies, the only bodies which exercised self rule. They named their own committees which exercised control, unless, as was sometimes necessary, appeal was made beyond *panchayat* jurisdiction to the king or governor. Neither the panchayats nor the sabhas or samitis ever united in larger units for administrative purposes or even formed a state. The Hindu masses themselves have always taken pride in qualified dictatorship. Kautilya the "law-giver" (!) himself declared the so-called "republics" to be "nuisances."

This brings us back to the thought that the greater force of dharma has been religious and not legal. It means a broader concept of the law than usual. Actually for the Hindu it covers all that comes within the sphere and quality of the "right," all that Hinduism has commended, in particular, beginning with the Vedic schools themselves which flourished and expounded the Vedic literature as applicable to life. The literature of this early exposition expressing the Vedic "wisdom" is itself often called the *dharma-shastras,* the "sacred scriptures," although there is a lesser portion of the whole, to which this title may be technically applied. It is fundamental to the view of at least the learned Hindu that there is a basic literature of dharma, which during thirty centuries has embodied "honey for all things" as does the honey-comb. Dharma is this "honey" in its "better form," with nothing sweeter and higher than itself. He may even insist that it is the "one only" peculiar element which Brahman the Absolute has made, itself "eternal law" (*sanatana dharma*), itself harmonious virtue which underlies all things and life itself, itself duty and the code of duty, the inner law of men and groups of men, and the destiny of every creature and the very truth of everything.

WISDOM AND ITS SCRIPTURES

But consider now the dharma-shastras as the larger literature of Hinduism. There is no single, simple, indisputable canon of this basic scripture. No councils ever sat to formulate it, nor has any editor issued an edition. Certain tests, however, have been applied to this vast miscellany, the chief of which has differentiated the "revealed" (*shruti*) and the "remembered" (*smriti,* i.e. men's own words passed on orally, etc.). The Rig, the Yajur, and the Sama Vedas represent the basic revelation, and they antedate the year 1000 B.C. being long preserved and orally transmitted until "collected" into written *samhitas* around 600 B.C. It is not until the fifth century, B.C., however, that reference can be found to manuscripts and to the copying of the sacred texts. Meanwhile a "fourth," the Atharva Veda, accumulated in completion of the "original" Indo-Aryan sources. The Rig Veda is the primary exposition of the true religion (*satya dharma*), arranged in ten books of 1,028 hymns in all. These hymns were preserved and handed down by families of priestly singers. They became the hymnal for "chanting" (*saman*) which was called the Sama Veda. Still another adaptation of the basic revelation was made for "sacrifice" (*yajur*) and called the Yajur Veda. While the uses varied, the transmission, we may assume, was fairly accurate. The Vedas may be known rather thoroughly, although men of many different ages have undertaken their interpretation.

The line between revelation and manifest tradition is often vague. Even the Atharva Veda reflects much that seems "non-Aryan," whose quality, therefore, as revelation may be questioned. But in the learned Hindu's view, the post-Vedic Brahmanas also are considered revelation. These textbooks of ritual and exegesis grew directly from the Vedas for use around 800 B.C. and subsequently. The speculative "forest books" (Aranyakas) and the Upanishads, which took shape around 500 B.C., may be on the borderline. They profess to be, and to a large extent they are, commentaries on the Vedas, and to that extent they, too, are revelation. But there are further writings, also, which are clearly *smriti,* and yet share with revelation the prestige of dharma-shastras. Among these are the great Epics, the Mahabharata (including the famous Bhagavad Gita) and Valmiki's Ramayana; the Laws of Manu which are technically the dharma-shastras par excellence; and numerous Puranas and Tantras.

But what about the truly Vedic "wisdom," the basic dharma? We know now that even the Rig Veda itself had roots and antecedents. It is manifestly a continuation of an older order. Although it does not in itself bridge the gap between earlier pre-Indian times and its own time (*ca.* 1250 B.C.), it does indicate and identify some antecedent Indo-European concepts, including the worshipful sky (*dyu, dyaush*), the sky-father (*dyaush pitar,* somewhat equivalent to the Greek Zeus Pater and the Roman Jupiter) who was a true and generous friend of man, his lord and the encompasser of all; and many luminaries known as *devas,* "gods," in the friendly heavens. We would not miss the early Vedic optimism. The Rig Veda gives evidence

54

also that the migrant peoples held some theory of *rita,* "order," whence might have come, had circumstances favored it, the concept of a moral universe. There was even an association in their minds of the god Varuna with rita, whence the notion of a holy god who functioned as the cosmic-moral order. If the people lived in harmony with him, they might become immortal (there was no theory of transmigration yet), living at last with their departed ancestors, the "divine fathers," who had found their way to immortality. Meanwhile these peoples penetrated into India, with such a prayer as this:

> Put us across all obstacles
> As with a boat, thou radiant god;
> For welfare carry us across,
> As in a boat o'er Sindhu's waves,
> Expelling evil with thy light.[1]

Having made their final home in India, they gave prominence to the four gods Indra, Soma, Agni and Varuna, and the goddess Ushas, fair daughter of the dawn. They came as conquerors, led by their warriors, and they sang their battle hymns in the name of these and other deities. The natives of the land they treated with disdain, called them riteless, senseless, inhuman, keeping alien laws, referred to them as ugly, stammering Dasyus, a term that must have had some hostile connotation. Their own gods were conspicuous in distinction from the heathen Dasyus, although we may suppose that the culture of the "godless" Dasyus soon modified the assets of the settlers. Shiva, for example, was already present in essence if not actually in name, and likewise many of his consorts, all of whom betray the flavor of the native order. Vishnu, a more nearly "Aryan" deity who in later centuries has divided honors with the great god Shiva, filled at first a lesser role. Yama, god of the dead in some underworld, was worshiped as god of the *blessed* dead, although in later times he assumes the direful headship of the demons. There were evil powers, chiefly demons of the land, but the settlers believed these could be circumvented.

[1] Rig Veda, I, 97, 7–8.

It is a question, how much to make, in a short chapter, of Vedic Hinduism since Vedism, strictly speaking, is but a portion of the whole. Hymns to the five great gods make up the older parts of the Rig Veda, which may be identified by textual and historical analysis, but Indra, god of the mountain, thunderbolt, and rain, who is celebrated in one fourth of all the hymns, and inspiring Soma, god, and food and drink of the gods, to whom one whole book is dedicated, fade slowly from prayers and the ritual. Gracious, propitious, moral Varuna, lord of the cosmic order, undergoes some magic transformation. The charming Ushas is subject to so many births on endless mornings that she fades into the light of common day. Agni, the god of fire and priestly sacrifice, celebrated in one fifth of all the hymns, enjoys more lasting honor, but chiefly through human sin's persistence and the intermediary character of sacrifice and the sacerdotal priesthood. But Agni in a way transformed himself into an abstraction of the learned, becoming not merely the little flame on many altars but a consuming mystery whence the many flames are kindled.

The more abstract phases of Vedism are likely more important if the "development" of Hinduism is the stake. In the later portions of the Rig Veda and especially in Book x there is evidence of speculation whereby the many gods of the brighter natural order began to be transformed—among the thinkers— into a mystic, somber pantheism, leaving the masses of men to add demons to their own theology. This was the beginning of the construction of the Hindu speculative universe. Hymn 90 portrays Purusha as the universe personified, hymn 121 presents Prajapati as the "lord of creatures" and the "golden germ" whence the universe arose and within whose limits all things are comprehended. In such manner the way is slowly opened for the permanently dominant concepts, which, as we shall see, come to represent the most important elements in philosophic Hinduism.

If, however, the four Vedas are studied a little further, their structure as scripture is more readily seen than is any just analysis of their freely interchanging concepts and ritual practices. We have said above that the Rig is the primary source. The Yajur and the Sama adapt it to the ritual of worship and sacrifice. The Atharva reproduces with or without variations much of the Rig which meanwhile has come to embody later elements. It is not concerned with Soma of Book ix, because Agni meanwhile had become the major deity, his fire cult most prominent. Although the Atharva contains noble hymns to Varuna and to the cosmic "pillar" Skambha who plays the role of Varuna-Prajapati, it portrays far more of the magic which had eclipsed the power of Indra and Soma, and the prevalence of tree and serpent worship. It glorifies the sacred Cow which "hath become this universe," even while it also personifies the "pillar" deity Skambha and identifies it further with Purusha and Brahman. We might here be reminded wisely that many Hindus, including Gandhi, have said that "that which distinguishes Hinduism from every other religion is its 'Cow Protection,' " even though in the long perspective it is obviously the Cow as symbol, rather than as a dumb creature subject to man's compassionate humanity.

Let one further concept serve to illustrate a strain, Rig Vedic to begin with, which tradition has been intent upon preserving to the present, a strain which in itself is both magical and mystical, the concept of Savitar. Savitar, the "stimulator," inspired what came to be the golden text of all the Vedas. This famous stanza [2]:

> May the shining excellence of Savitar
> Be manifest in us
> To his stimulation of our thoughts

has been for three thousand years the morning prayer of Brahmans. The mystical significance of this sacred prayer is considered in the Upanishads but there it has assigned to it the magic potency of OM (aum), another carry-over from the earlier times, whose very letters, the *a, u* and *m,* are held to represent the first three Vedas. These same three letters become in later speculation the theistic triad of Vishnu, Shiva, and Brahmā.

[2] Rig Veda, iii, 62, 10.

RITUAL AND SPECULATION

Tracing the "development" still further, in terms of the sacred writings, we may notice that about 850 B.C. the Brahmanas were composed, those ritual commentaries linked in succession with the Vedas, which have so much to do with "works," as the many types of priests, in particular the Brahmans who had won the leadership in religion and society, define them in the light of Vedic wisdom. Works provided in the priestly view, the first definite *marga,* or "way" of salvation for mankind. Each Brahmana was a commentary to that end on one or another of the Vedas, and thus the Vedic wisdom took the form of intricate and numerous rites and ceremonies apportioned throughout a fixed calendar of worship. Inevitably, some new rites and rules of sacrifice were instituted and quite as inevitably, some priests began to minimize the ritual and calendar and to undertake an inquiry into the function of religion among the thoughtful. By the very example of Book x of the Rig Veda itself they took thought of the character and essence of the universe. There was no ecclesiasticism to prevent this speculation—Hinduism has never been that sort of order—but only such restrictions as the largely illiterate public mind imposed.

With certain priests themselves attending closely to the problem of reality, Hinduism entered upon a new career. The center of gravity of the Hindu faith had been gradually moving southeastward through the "two-river" country of the Jamna and the Ganges and on down the latter stream to the neighborhood of Kashi (Benares) and the time was about 500 B.C. By the same token, Hinduism was becoming more and more Aryo-Dravidian, an accommodation and an amalgamation. Whatever the popular mass-cult that would flourish extensively in the later centuries, a "philosophy" was destined to arise among the thoughtful few. Indeed it was a time of intellectual flood, of idealistic-realistic struggle, and of social reformation. Many thinkers began to emphasize in writings called Upanishads a new "way" of salvation, the *jnana* or "knowledge" way, not a way of scientific knowledge, but one of meditation more effectual than rites, ceremonies, and other kinds of priestly "works." These Upanishads were by no means systematic in any sustained way, and their prominence in Hinduism was destined to come from what was later made of them by certain schools and commentators such as Shankara—and their prominence in the West outside of India is somewhat analogous to that of Plato beyond the bounds of Greece. The burden of their meaning is that, while the Absolute cannot be known, the magic of esoteric wisdom devoted to the quest of it is more powerful than the magic of the sacrifice, and that human thought and knowledge are necessary supplements, at least, to the gods' own providence.

A widely current agitation among high and low alike arose from the doctrine of ahimsa, "non-killing" (no shedding of blood), proposed first and emphasized most by the Jains but gradually accepted by the great majority of Hindus. But it was Gotama the Buddha and the Buddhist gospel which, as a social reformation, subjected Hinduism to its severest test. It offered Hindus new lessons in economics, government, warfare, and the theory of soul or "self," and the contest went on for several centuries. That Buddhism did not supplant, or at least gain supremacy over, Hinduism in this long era may be due to Hinduism's own inconsistencies which were socially reconciled by its theory of "caste." Buddhist thought was intellectually difficult, its order eventually exclusive even though it disregarded caste, and its adoption of ahimsa too positive if not altogether arbitrary. Buddhism failed to cope successfully with the social arrangement then in the process of formulation among Hindus under the guidance of their Brahmans, a scheme which recognized great diversity of occupation. In Hinduism as a whole this reconciled warfare, conquest, and ahimsa.

The Hindu dharma was becoming at the time a unique social demonstration for which their scriptures, Vedas, Brahmanas, and Upanishads, made provision. And the subsequent literature of Hinduism assumed all the major premises whatever variations were proposed. The epic legends, the book of laws, the systematic darshanas, or "philosophic demonstrations," took for granted karma and transmigration and the speculative ideas of both priest and thinker. But for what it would be worth in later centuries there was noticeable, although vague, divergence between the speculative and the practical.

CASTE IN THEORY AND IN PRACTICE

Hindu caste is in itself an impressive lesson in persistent diversity within the scope of a congeries of faiths. It looms large in the Hindu dharma. The term "caste" is not Hindu, nor Indian. It comes of the Portuguese misnomer *casta*. But what the Portuguese—and others after them—failed to understand is something altogether, essentially, and exclusively Indian, and on the whole unlike any social manifestation of the West. It has come to judgment often during twenty centuries, and decisions and practices have varied with regard to it, sometimes almost breaking up the order. But Hinduism as a whole has insisted on its operation in perpetuity. It is in itself evidence of societal religion, of a compartmental social structure, authorized and sponsored by religion. Its many subdivisions are Hinduism's equivalents for sects. Its influence has pervaded all of India, not Hinduism alone. Its hundreds of divisions are not merely such groups, communities, and classes of men as are common in human history when race, color, conquest, servitude, title, occupation, and property are concerned. Caste is more than all of these, with an inner essence of its own.

It originated in India in post-Vedic times; there are no traces of it prior to the entrance of the "Aryans." Its development began during the transition from Brahmana theology, *ca.* 850 B.C. and following, to the era of Upanishadic theory. Its first ingredient was *varna,* or "color" of the skin, with psychological and racial connotations. Assuming that the "collection" (*samhita*) of the Rig Veda reflects that Veda itself, we find that a color line was drawn in Rig Vedic times between the immigrant *arya* stock and the native *dasya* stock, who are designated *dasas,* "slaves." The "Aryans" applied this color test for many centuries, while an increasing intermixture of the population of those regions under the sway of the sun produced varied shades of pigmentation—and of blood and disposition. The book of laws, the Code of Manu, of about 200 B.C., uses the term *varna* in a complicated context with something other than a rigid color connotation. Varna by that time was no longer, as it once had been, a sole consideration in a marriage bargain, and there had appeared an economic factor in what was said to be a just provision for the offspring of a proper marriage.

A second determining ingredient appeared in Manu's time, that of *jati,* "birth." To be well born had come to be essential among the classes, and good birth was stressed especially by Brahmans who in their preeminence condemned mixed marriages as something on a level with adultery. Although shades of color were then common in every major group or class, marriages could somehow be controlled and births thus regulated. It was determined that *jati* should not be promiscuous, nor "births" intermingled. Off to the south, far below Benares, Hinduism had to face a situation in which birth and color tended to be uniformly one, and the contrasts of color and of birth were culture contrasts. One chief consequence was this : that as South India became brahmanized, the people of the lower non-brahmanic culture became in Brahman eyes untouchable, with not only intermarriage but tactile association banned. From this came, in part, at least, the *harijans* of progressive Hinduism's recent reconsideration. But birth, rather than color, had come to be the chief criterion in the brahmanic program.

Then comes a third ingredient into play, the theory of many births in the longer span of any Hindu's life. The soul was subject to rebirth, according to the tradition of *punarjanman,* "still another birth," a round in which not only men but all other creatures were involved. What had taken place in the mind of Hindu men ? Had they noticed death and resurrection in the world of nature ? The seeds they sowed decayed and renewed themselves in mother earth, and resemblances and traits often renewed themselves in human generations. If Dravidianism was largely responsible, as we may well believe it was, for this new phase of doctrine in the Hindu order, the result was clearly a combination of the Dravidian cult of mother spirits, with its rites to guarantee fertility in women and the fields, and to safeguard crops and the mother's life, with the "Aryan" theory of eternal rest among the "fathers." There had been since Vedic times a search for the means of longer life on earth and for the assurance of immortality. Death, resurrection, rebirth, and immortality unite in a single theory which comes to be the property of all. The theory, in fact, becomes the full-blown dogma of transmigration when there is combined with it the principle of karma, and the whole creation is its field of operation, with all life sacred and, in the Brahman's view, at least, subject to the conservation of ahimsa. The tendency increased to think that the process which was creating caste was that by which the universe itself was constituted.

Such was the magic potion brewed of many elements in the hot cauldron of groping minds and restless times—with some disposition, whether by fate or circumstance, to look upon the worldly state with gloom, so great had been during these times the tragedies of famine, flood, pestilence, and war. The social situation came to be in man's own thought something predetermined, and his own lot was incidental to the process as a whole. Life went on by karmic repetition, deeds and rebirth being causally related. While no individual in a single lifetime could register any radical adjustment, his religion told him to accept his lot and live at his best within it in the distant hope that the round would eventually be broken and his spirit would escape to another, agreeable portion of the fixed universe, whence he would not come back again to birth.

The full Hindu dharma, we now see, is both a way of life and a form of thought but the role of the former is far the stricter, being the very ground of any coherence and continuity which Hinduism has maintained for these twenty centuries. Those Hindus, however, who appeal to prior, strictly Vedic, sources as authority in all life's phases can justly question caste, can find in it flexibility, at least, and deem it alterable. The full course of Hinduism is rightly subject to historical analysis, they insist. Even where they find karma in full control, they may detect its creative as well as its causal character, and plausibly suggest that if it be brought under the influence of education, it may become productive of social reformation and may promise men some role of their own in personal redemption. But meanwhile what may become of caste is difficult to estimate, while India is India, where life and thought have been coextensive and mutually interactive and dependent in the total dharma. Caste need not disappear with religious reformation, or with economic and political adjustment. The Brahman in himself might even continue to be, however greatly altered, a living symbol of the continuing identity of life and thought.

But what of caste in recent times? It is not to be considered as a theory alone. It is not enough to say that upper castes are class divisions of the Hindu order and lower castes were of tribal constitution, the *panchamas* being the dregs of tribalism. Nevertheless, the four-fold or five-fold structure stands in all its subdivisions by whatever lines divide the major bodies. Class and character have somehow predominated, although Brahmans have not always been priests and learned men, ruling chieftains have not always been of Kshatriya, or "warrior" stock, and men of lower castes have sometimes entered the professions.

Brahmans constitute about seven per cent of the total Hindu population. They have been for many centuries the highest class, the elite of Hinduism, preeminent for their devotion on the one hand to ritual and on the other hand to learning. Scarcely a million and a half of them, however, are occupied today with priestly ministries while yet another million fill minor temple posts or roam far and wide as mendicants. There are also non-Brahman priests in Hinduism although Brahmans exercise control. Brahmans who are not priests may be land-owners, clerks in business and commercial offices, assistants on the railways, professional and governmental servants, or teachers and educational administrators. All, however, share the common Brahman attitude and are generally jealous of their traditional prerogatives. Although Brahman prestige has often been assailed, in south India in particular, it has endured—not least because sixty of every hundred Brahmans are literate.

The Kshatriyas may outnumber Brahmans two to one, but the percentage of their literacy is less than twenty-five. Their prestige has come from rulership, since the ruling chieftains from earliest times have come mostly from their ranks. Politics and war have been their prerogatives for thirty centuries although they have employed in these pursuits many members of other castes besides. As rulers of the native states which have existed periodically, they have exercised a qualified despotic rule such as the Indian temper seems to have demanded of them. Politics and warfare have not entirely absorbed them nor have all Kshatriyas been thus engaged—most of them, in fact, have been men of industry and peace—but the peculiar status of the caste has often given rise to vexing issues when statecraft has demanded some reorganization of the government. Other Indian communities, also, the Moslem and the Sikh, for instance, have been concerned with government and war. The status of the Kshatriya is not only a Hindu question but something national. Within the total Indian scene caste and communalism make strenuous demands of one another in anticipation of any unity in national government.

There are many Vaishya groups, also, in the Hindu social system, with a membership of at least twenty millions, or maybe thirty millions, if the small village tradesmen be included. The title itself means "vassal," but Vaishyas are the trader-folk, many of them agriculturists, and from their ranks some have come into professional careers to compete with Brahmans. As a class they are more literate, perhaps, than the warrior-folk, having more to do with figures and accounts. Many of them, of course, are highly literate, but on the whole they unite with all ranks to keep the percentage of Indian literacy low. Among all Hindus scarcely fifteen per cent of the males and three per cent of the females are literate.

Brahmans, Kshatriyas, and Vaishyas make up Hinduism's upper castes—we may say varnas, for varna and not *casta* is the proper term to use. These three groups are classified in the Hindu scheme as *dvijas,* or the "twice-born," and they wear— or have the right to wear until they reach a certain variable age

—the thread which symbolizes the "second birth," attained by an initiation ceremony during boyhood. Females have never worn the thread nor experienced this second birth until quite recently when some have claimed the privilege. The initiate may wear the thread thereafter throughout life, unless he scrupulously observes the traditional Hindu *ashramas,* or "stages," four in number, and becomes in the fourth stage a *sannyasi* (if he is a Brahman) or a *sadhu* (if he is a Kshatriya or a Vaishya). In this fourth stage the discarding of the thread betokens complete separation from home, family, and any business or professional occupation—for the sake of being free to renovate his soul and justify its true career.

The Shudra—"clean" in the ritual sense—is the fourth estate among the Hindus, one hundred and twenty millions, at least, in number. Their status is again one of birth, or rebirth, in the longer round of karmic transmigration, but not in the sense of second birth by any initiation symbolized by the wearing of the thread. They are apparently within the pale of Hinduism by necessity, providing society with servile classes. Their major occupation has been agriculture and such offices, chiefly artisan, as village life requires. They have usually had temples, a priesthood, and a worship of their own although they live in association with the *dvijas.* They have been very conscious of caste limitations, in matters of food and marriage in particular. Their only opportunities to share in a casteless life come not by way of any formal stage of their career—the *ashrama* provision does not apply to them—but are occasional, during certain seasons of religious celebration and at times of pilgrimage to certain centers where caste lines fade for a time and the pilgrims of all castes attend a common ministry.

The fifth estate, *panchamas,* pariahs, *harijans,* and others, are a great multitude whose total may exceed sixty millions and whose distribution is country-wide. If they are hard to reckon with, statistically and otherwise, it is partly due to the fact that their station has been somewhat uncertain during all the centuries, shifting often with the changing scene. The lines of caste are themselves seldom clear and rigid and the line between caste and *out*-caste has frequently been vague. There have been and still are "mixed castes" (varna-shankara) within the pale, intermixtures by a "marrying-down" of Brahmans, for example, and by some "marrying-up" among the lower castes. As a rule, however, any given Hindu, and especially any *panchama-harijan,* knows precisely where he belongs by birth and residence, hereditary occupation, and the necessity of observing regulations with respect to food, drink, and marriage. The most rigid line of demarcation has been that between the four major communities and the fifth estate, although some Brahmans still hesitate to take either food or drink, even from the Shudras.

The status of the outcaste is a vivid illustration of the Hindu state of mind. There is reason to suppose that the numbers of this fifth estate have tended to increase by more than natural reproduction among themselves. Their numbers have often increased in staggering proportions as tribes were added to the list, and the total would be far greater nowadays if so many of them had not become Moslem, or Christian, or Sikh. Many centuries ago many of them became Buddhists. Or it could be affirmed that outcastes would not be so numerous today if Hinduism had made some better provision for their reception within the range of operation of the Hindu dharma. Many Hindus, including many Brahmans, now begin to understand that their own numbers would be vastly larger and their religion's social and moral value higher if untouchability had been itself taboo. Measures have been proposed by many, not so much for the conversion of outcastes to Hinduism (we have seen how little Hinduism has provided for such a process as we understand it) as for their elevation within Hinduism, affording them higher rating in labor, education, and suffrage as well as in religion. The *harijans,* in fact, have already won the right of suffrage, not to vote as a separate community but in constituencies with other Hindus. Although the Vaishya Mr. Gandhi is their greatest leader they also have leaders of their own. The outcaste's lot, however, may prove to be for Hinduism more critical an issue than any other phase of caste before the socio-political reformation is complete.

TWO SEATS OF DEMONSTRATION

Two illustrations, from Puri and Benares, may serve us best at this point as we follow Hinduism further as a socio-religious structure.

Puri in Orissa beside the Bay of Bengal is the site of the shrine of Jagannatha, "lord of the world," and the chief seat of his worship. The town is far in miles and years from the Vedic Hinduism of upper Hindustan. Whatever Vedic original it may still reflect, it serves rather to show what original Hinduism may have become when once the hinduizing of non-Vedic elements had set in. Almost every element of the Indo-Aryan and the Aryo-Dravidian accommodations during the accumulation of the larger Hindu whole is reflected there. Jagannatha fills, to some degree, just such a role as the earlier Varuna the "encompasser" and Prajapati the "lord of creatures" played in Vedic times when there was some good prospect that an ethical monotheism might be realized in India. But Jagannatha for want of auspicious circumstances and a great advocate is scarcely more than a shadow of this theme. In the long interval between him and the ancient, encompassing lord of creation, the moral aspects of dharma became affected, qualified, and conditioned by the karmic-rebirth theory and the process which grew under priestly and speculative inspiration. Environmental pessimism repressed and almost obliterated Vedic optimism. In the lower Ganges valley an era of darkness, the inexorable *kaliyuga,* was fashioned in which men lost their sense of moral freedom and responsibility. Now Jagannatha, still further on and down, seems but an echo of what was lost in gradual transmission. The joyful disregard of caste in his presence is that echo while still the mood of Hinduism everywhere without is predominantly that of *kaliyuga,* contemporary darkness, division, sin, and evil, as the gods themselves have predetermined.

67

Jagannatha, after all these centuries, is a composite figure; an epitome of Hindu history. Jainist, Buddhist, brahmanical, Puranic, and Tantric elments, with incidentals of a sun-cult, have been deposited in the primordial, animistic setting. From this ground the cult of Shiva at first and thereafter the cult of Vishnu have flowered, choking most of what had grown before them. When, in modern times, the cult of Shiva the "great god" gained the ascendancy, its emphasis was feminine; it lay in the female consort Kali, the "dark" mother-goddess of Bengal. When the cult of Vishnu took the lead, the priesthood of Puri continued to be chiefly Shivite, but the Krishna-avatara of Vishnu became prominent as Jagannatha, the universal lord. His image has since received extravagant attention twice a year, once during the "bathing festival" (*snanayatra*) and again during the famous "car festival" (*rathayatra*). During the former it is subjected to devout libations and during the latter it is moved about on a huge-wheeled platform. As in the Shiva-cult, Kali herself was "mother of the world" (Jaganamata), so also in the Vishnu-cult Krishna's consort Radha has filled a similar capacity as the mother of mankind.

The Krishna who is known as Jagannatha and identified with Vishnu in Puri is, of course, the higher, nobler Vishnuite incarnation—for Vishnu has a dual personality. There is a legend, quite circumstantial, which accounts for him at Puri: Krishna in some form or other once wandering in those parts was slain —unwittingly?—by a native archer who left his body to beasts, birds, and decay. Some pious persons were prompted to preserve the bones for which they made a little casket. When at the bidding of a local chieftain an image of Vishnu as Jagannatha was fashioned for the Puri temple, the casket with the bones of Krishna was deposited within it. The image, they say, had neither hands nor feet; but it had by divine provision two penetrating eyes and a potent soul, and was a most impressive figure. By whatever circumstance the local cult of Vishnu was established, however, the Jagannatha-Krishna-Radha combination became most popular. As the ruling deity it (he or she) could be approached and worshiped by all "clean" classes—offal-eaters, fishermen, liquor-dealers, prostitutes, and criminals were barred—and in the holy presence men of all castes might eat together in brotherly communion the food which had been offered to and sanctified by Vishnu. This was a rare fellowship, therefore, although it was purely temporary and lingered only in the memory beyond the bounds of Puri. Nevertheless, Puri epitomizes in its contradictory way the whole of Hinduism—in being within itself inclusive, as Hinduism is so largely a phenomenon of India. Or, to put it another way, whereas caste distinction is temporarily lost in Puri, the Hindu who traveled outside of India "lost caste" entirely and became technically an outcaste who had to submit to cleansing and restoration on his return—somewhat similar to the ancient Hebrew theory by which only the one land was considered holy and its inhabitants one with it. In such a sense India has been to the loyal Hindu what might be called Dharma-stan, the true "home of religion."

It is Benares, however, which may be cited as the center most typically and fully Hindu in all its various ingredients and its penetrative atmosphere. Its own emphasis, somewhat in contrast with Puri, is on Shiva. The title of Vishveshvara, "universal lord," is there applied to him exclusively, although Brahma and Vishnu, also, have borne the name. His temples, many of them with gilded pinnacles, crown several of the flights of spacious steps called ghats which lie against the high, sloping left bank of *Ganga-ma,* or "mother Ganges," the holiest of Hindu waters. His, too, is the Golden Temple in the city, in whose compound are the famous Well of Knowledge, a companion shrine to Shiva's consort Durga (counterpart of Kali), and yet another shrine to him in the role of Mahadeva, Great God. Indeed the Ganges throughout its course is peculiarly his stream even though by some theological accommodation the toe of Vishnu was its heavenly source. Its waters are most sacred at Benares although they are more transparent upstream, under the shadow of the Himalayas at Hardwar where Shiva caught them on his brow and broke their fall from heaven.

Benares may be Shiva's city, his seat as universal ruler of tri-loka, the "three worlds," and the Ganges his peculiar stream, but by the very genius of the Hindu faith the city's site is all-inclusive, is virtually anything to any Hindu devotee, commemorative of any deity that has a following. Vishnu's shrines are there—although the legend is that Vishnu first came to do Shiva homage—and even Shiva's devotees may properly greet one another there with a "Ram, Ram" (the name of an *avatara* of Vishnu). When the Moslem Mughal Aurangzib razed one of Vishnu's temples on the highest ghat and built a mosque instead, all good Hindus felt outraged—and many Hindus, both Vishnuite and Shivite, persist in their worship in the very courtyard of the Moslem mosque. Benares is usually crowded with people, a combination of resident custodians of varied rank serving various gods and goddesses, of visitors on pilgrimage to the golden temples, of pillared shrines, consecrated platforms, hallowed tombs, burning-ghats, memorial towers, sacred trees and groves, of carved and molten images, magical relics and holy waters—to mention only the more respectable items in the total situation.

HINDU REACTION TO REFORMATION

Of the two major divisions of modern Hinduism, the Shivite and the Vishnuite, each has some prerogatives of its own, and has its own gods with their peculiar powers, qualities, associates, and festivals. For example, within the huge framework of caste bitter quarrels have sometimes broken out between Shivite and Vishnuite Brahmans, either over the sacred literature and temple ritual or over changes of ownership and administration of temples, temple lands, and temple income. In theory, at least, temples of the "twice-born" are not strictly, exclusively, either Shivite or Vishnuite. The distinction is rather that between (1) what is *smarta,* or more orthodox, with its Vedic ritual and liturgy in the name of Shiva, Vishnu, Devi (goddess), Surya or Ganesha (son of Shiva) and (2) what is more sectarian, with a religio-magical Tantric ritual and liturgy based on more recent Vishnuite and Shivite literature and conducted in the name of one or more sectarian or local divinities. In actual practice *smarta* temples with their five deities are few. Some Shivite *smarta* groups have insisted on an independent, personal worship of the lingam, Shiva's own peculiar symbol, but south Indian Hinduism has not permitted this individual observance; it has provided at each temple a priest, a *pujari,* for the worship, *puja.* Most modern temples (there are, of course, no real parishes or congregations) are more nearly sectarian in the religiomagical sense, no matter in whose name the worship is conducted, and there is much liturgical laxity among both devotees and priests. But it seems wise to defer our final account of current, sectarian Hinduism until we have seen more of the historical development from Upanishadic and Epic times on down. The Hindu thinker's contribution, in particular, must be traced amidst the socio-religious situation which has been depicted, and, in addition, some effects of the coming of the Moslems after A.D. 1000 must be seen.

The fifteen centuries from 500 B.C. to A.D. 1000 provided Hinduism its intellectual substance—and Hindu thought at least has been consistently nonsectarian. The Hinduism of these centuries might be rightly represented by the figure ✕ on its side, as the Romans once wrote it to signify 1000. This might represent two highways intersecting, with an indefinite space for rotary traffic at the intersection, both highways coming from antiquity and both leading toward the present, with much interchange of traffic. These would indicate, for example, the two great strains of brahmanism and of popular religion meeting at the very heart of India, Benares, and leading on by whatever interchange into modern Shivism and Vishnuism, either destination being for the devotee reminiscent of both highways from antiquity. The figure will put us on our guard against any strictly sectarian interpretations of the Hindu order and will keep us mindful of some indiscriminate interpenetration of the thoughtful and the popular.

We may take account of a criticism before 500 B.C among leading Hindus with reference to the sanctity of the Vedas, the specific requirements of the sacrificial and the dominant role of the Brahmans. Two of the radical reformers, Vardhaman

Mahavira the Jain and Gotama Siddhartha the Buddha, rejected the Vedic-brahmanic system and proposed man's virtually atheistic self-dependence for the realization of human
destiny. Both men, the Buddha in particular, offered a *jnana,*
or "knowledge" way, not wholly instead of, but as effectual in
contrast with, the karma, or way of "works." The two ways
were virtually in opposition. Some Brahmans and others, to be
sure, had themselves proposed a higher value to knowledge, but
Buddha made it ultimate. He and Mahavira denied, as no Brahman did, the reality of God and refused to translate Vedic
revelation into any metaphysical theology. That is, they would
not work their way to a philosophic Absolute through theism.
No mere intellectual proposal, however, could have a popular
appeal as religion. The success which greeted Buddhism came
of its social gospel—a gospel which was doomed to failure in
the face of caste. Hindu philosophy, on the other hand, kept
within the brahmanical framework and thus did some leavening of the whole lump before Hinduism felt the disconcerting
shock of Islam. As a result of this leavening Shivism gave increased emphasis to *shakti* (power, producing principle) and
the mother-goddess cult, and Vishnuism emphasized the way
of *bhakti* (devotion) to Krishna and to Rama.

If Hinduism had its "golden age," it was the unusual era
prevailing midway through these fifteen centuries—during the
first Christian centuries. For popular Hinduism it was an epic
age transmitting the lore of the Mahabharata and the Valmiki Ramayana, rehearsing the innumerable folk tales (e.g. the
Panchatantra), and a legal age abiding by the Code of Manu.
For the higher Hinduism it was epic, legal, and much more.
It witnessed the formulation of the "six demonstrations of
schools" (*sad-darshana*) of thought: (1) the esoteric, realistic,
logical Nyaya of Kanada; (2) the companion of Nyaya, the
atomistic Vaisheshika of Gotama (not the Buddha, of course),
which also recognized a God; (3) the atheistic Samkhya of
Kapila; (4) the theistic Yoga of Patanjali, which together with
Kapila's Samkhya, rested upon a dualism of the natural order
to which all castes belonged, and a realm of soul, to which indi-

viduals might have access by an isolation (*kaivalya*) of themselves from the realm of nature; (5) the "former inquiry" (*purva mimamsa*) of Jaimini; and (6) the "latter inquiry" (*uttara mimamsa*) of Vyasa, both of which inquiries may be included in the general term Vedanta, i.e. the "end or object of the Vedas," although the latter is more strictly *the* Vedanta.

These philosophies, especially the two "inquiries" set the intellectual goal of the "twice-born" castes, without provision for Shudras or *harijans*.

The basic stock of these six schools is Vedic by way of the Brahmanas and the Upanishads, though also influenced by the subsequent epic-legal variations. They are not in disagreement among themselves in fundamental theory. Rather, they are mutually complementary with some variance of emphasis, and what they hold in common is the ground on which all succeeding Hindu thought has rested, from the "nondualistic" school (*advaita*) of Badarayana and of Shankara through the "modified nondualistic" school (*vishishtadvaita*) of Ramanuja on to the realistic or pragmatic idealism and the common-sense empiricism of the present time. The theory became general that the phenomenal world is transitory and unreal, that the religions of mankind are themselves phenomenal, that there is something universal and unifying underlying all religions, and that phenomenal variations are merely different steps and stages to ultimate, ideal reality, the truth of Brahman, which is the Absolute. The six schools exhibit a consistency of connection between mind and soul, and are disposed to provide for the *thoughtful* soul within the realm of karma a freedom of action by which the final goal of truth and goodness is attained. The schoolmen themselves have not emphasized the currency of the *kaliyuga* "age of darkness," as the masses of Hindus have done more or less inertly; but to them, as to the masses, the present order of things is impermanent. All of which might be best, but not exclusively, described in terms of the "latter inquiry" of Vyasa—or whatever unknown "arranger" it was which gained preeminence among the schools through the commentator Shankara about A.D. 800.

73

SCHOOLS OF WISDOM: SHANKARA

Shankara's formulation of the Vedanta is the most idealistic of all and the most distinctive in comparison with Western realism. It has been, perhaps, more interesting to idealists of the West than any other Hindu thought has been, even to the point of monopolizing the Western view of India. Its introduction to the West by the Hegelian idealist Paul Deussen was somewhat faulty, since Deussen assumed that he had come upon pure, unvarnished Upanishads which were characteristic of the whole of Hindu thought. Shankara himself was not conscious of preempting the entire range of Hindu speculation but was intent upon offering such a summary of it all as could be made from selected Upanishads, from those least sectarian, and from Badarayana's commentary on the Vedanta-sutras which were themselves an arrangement of many Upanishads. Nevertheless the Vedanta which Shankara expounds is actually old, as it professes to be, representing a typical strain whose origin was Vedic but which reached its "culmination" during the long, eventful centuries which followed.

What Shankara made of the Vedantic tradition is that the All, whether known as Atman, Brahman, or Ishwara, as God or the Absolute, is One and that its essential Unity is real, whereas duality and plurality are phenomenal illusion (*maya,* with a peculiar connotation of its own). He called his exposition *a-dvaita,* "non-dualism," an apparently negative designation, although he did not deny philosophy the power to reach and to know the Absolute. He was not, in fact, providing pure philosophy. He made more than a mere gesture toward religion (dharma) which, he conceded, operated in the immediate environment. He was himself a lifelong devotee of Shiva Mahadeva, without leaving the highway that ran directly from the Vedas. He may have wished at the same time to challenge thoughtful Hindus to seek the One immediately, not as one among the many gods, but as the All, the only One without another, the authoritative Absolute demanding men's direct devotion. He could not push any theory of the Absolute to the obviously absurd extreme of an abstraction which disregarded all experience, even though he was emphasizing altogether spiritual reality, with all else sheer illusion (*maya*).

His typical name for the All, the Absolute, is Brahman, nor would he insist that it was altogether name. It was the end of wisdom, and there were means by which to reach it, the chief means being "knowledge." There were grades of knowledge, especially a higher and a lower. The latter, *avidya*, which by comparison is "ignorance," yields some fruit by sense perception in the transitory world. The higher (*vidya, jnana,* or *vijnana*) ultimately comprehends the All beyond experience. Thus the world and personal experience are both minimized but not denied. Provision was amply made for thoughtful men to reduce manifest confusion in themselves and in all about them to harmony and order, and to see the whole of life in due perspective, although indeed by something of a process of abstraction, Shankara's theory would not obliterate the individual. He plainly stressed the individual's own responsibility by making him the observer, at least, of his own acts, and to a large extent the judge of them. However, Shankara did deny the individual the power of passing judgment on a good-and-evil situation, since he afforded no place at all for anything as positive as evil. The judgment was really a distinction between the karma which could be (and was) the force of good, and the karma that was at most indifferent. He assumed, however, the force of dharma which operates in part by prohibitions. Dharma itself was positive, was the provision whereby men might be released at last from the negative and transient in their quest of the positively truthful and the good, or might be led from the unreal to the Real, as the Upanishadic phrase had put it. Karma itself had a moral value for the individual and for the social order which would utilize it. In so far as dharma embodied karma, it too had moral connotations—although the net result of Shankara's discriminations was a minimum of ethics. Certainly Shivite morality itself to which Shankara tacitly subscribed has been naïve, even in the *sannyasi* stage which Shankara had adopted.

It should be kept in mind that Shankara's method, together

with that of the thinkers in all the schools, was *scriptural;* and his regard for the scriptures may have been itself a handicap, although his loyalty did not prevent a selection of his sources. His originality was confined, it seems, to this limited selection which allowed for some personal assumptions, although he may actually have made assumption equivalent to revelation. Where his sources sought the One by inquiry, experience and demonstration, he himself assumed It. He scarcely reconciled the godly, worshipful Ishwara and the impersonal, attributeless, absolute Brahman, but simply gave them the relationship of the lower and the higher Brahman. A great deal of his emphasis upon idea seems to come by virtual detachment from experience. He emphasized the mind without allowing that men's minds had already thought about the Vedic gods, though he does not imply the nonexistence of these gods and the unreality of men's devotion to them. He seems merely to leave no place for "faith" (*shraddha*) as a positive experience. His method is rather the cessation of the idea which men have of separateness, individuality, variation, and plurality; and of distinction from gods, God, and the Absolute. His emphasis is, after all, on the idea of identity with the Absolute.

All this represents what the comparative religionist might call orthodoxy—adherence to scripture and tradition. Shankara is the last and greatest of the scholastic commentators. His *bhashya,* "demonstration," effectually modified and largely nullified the *dvaita,* or dualistic realism, which had lingered in Hinduism after the era of the Upanishads and of Buddhism. Under the influence of his nondualistic *advaita* the pantheistic trend grew more pronounced. Some minor idealisms appeared which were more extravagant than his; and some of these gained attention in the West as if they were altogether the true Vedanta. Hindu thought, however, was not destined to become unqualified abstraction. Certain theisms have competed with it vigorously. Not long after Shankara's time India and Hinduism underwent sore trials, were disturbed more widely and with greater violence than they had ever been before. Hindus were required not to deny the world but to reckon with it. It is not

surprising that great numbers of them questioned the suffi-
ciency of Vedanta or of any philosophic demonstration and
put increased reliance upon the efficiency of ritual, liturgy, and
the gods.

VEDANTA PROPOSED AND MODIFIED:
RAMANUJA AND TULSI DAS

The most effective modification of *advaita* itself in the days
of storm and stress was proposed in the twelfth century by
Ramanuja, a Brahman and an heir of the Vedantic tradition.
He proposed an *advaita*-with-a-difference, one less strictly a
knowledge-way (*jnana-marga*) and more emphatically devotional, a *bhakti-marga* of devotion to a personal God. This, he
insisted, would more effectually control or nullify the force of
karma, bring rebirth to an end and guarantee men immortality.
Instead of Shankara's God Shiva, his God was Vishnu—a
change of highways, let us say. Nor was Vishnu to Ramanuja
a "lower Brahman" as Shiva was to Shankara; he was truly
Brahman. For Ramanuja rejected the intellectual distinction
between the higher and the lower Brahman, even as he denied
also by qualification the impersonal, attributeless Absolute. This
is theism instead of pantheism. Vishnu-Brahman was Ishwara,
God, at once personal and supreme, the universal Lord dwelling
eternally in his heaven, Vaikuntha, whither he would welcome
any man of any caste whose piety and devotion had saved him,
had brought him release from the perpetual round. This was
salvation by devotion, rather than by any distinction in the
realm of knowledge. Salvation was available to any man, although to such an end Ramanuja did not propose to ignore or
to repudiate caste. He would only modify the scope of it, as
certain Hindu reformers since his time have likewise done,
while recognizing it in operation.

Ramanuja by no means denied the reality of the world in
which men live, but gave it an existence of its own, even while
another world existed. Men lived thus in two worlds and their
salvation was a process between them rather than an identification of themselves with Brahman and an assumption that this

77

world is something phenomenal, an illusion (*maya*). *Maya* itself was interpreted by Ramanuja as the will of God—or an aspect of God's will—operative in man's world. God manifested himself in other ways besides, as Ramanuja could show from the Hindu scriptures; for he, also, was but a "commentator."

Ramanuja is a symbol of transition in the socio-religious order. His is not the full-fledged "way of devotion" He may indeed have overemphasized the knowledge factor in the very stress he put upon the state of ignorance in which, he said, men lived in this world. His gospel had a highly intellectual content beyond the grasp of many to whom he offered it. He virtually taught that man must add to his works knowledge and then to knowledge faith which would be expressed in devotion to his Lord. Few of the common people ever find this sequence easy and effectual. Ramanuja, nevertheless, made a distinctive contribution to the development among the Hindus of this third, or *bhakti,* way of release and destiny. He sought to take account of a changing order but did not realize its full extent. Thus he himself conformed punctiliously to the requirements of caste even while he journeyed here and there in India to see what the new days were bringing forth and to preach his gospel to the multitudes.

Something of an effectual symbol of the later transformation may be found in a sixteenth century figure, Tulsi Das, who took up the burden of the *bhakti*-gospel for the common people in particular. He had recourse not to the Vedas, the Upanishads, or to any school of philosophy, but to the Epic tradition, mainly to legend and to folklore. He took the theme of the ancient Ramayana, the heroic tale of the princely Rama and the banished Sita, and added profusely to it, thus fashioning a poetic bible for the masses according to the Vishnuite tradition. Tulsi had much to say of the dark age and lauded Rama as the one to save men from it. He appealed to men to remember Rama and thus attain their heart's desire, and suggested, somewhat in contrast with the ascetic way, that "he will shave his head and leave his home in vain who does not worship Rama and love him and Sita better than himself." Tulsi expresses real heart devotion for Lord Ram and since his day the most popular of all the couplets which circulate among the people are those of Tulsi Das. He sang of "one trust, one strength, one desire and one hope," none other than Lord Ram. A man, said he, might have scant clothing, eat his meager food without salt and yet not be poor, if the Lord dwelt in his heart.

HINDU-MOSLEM INTERACTION

We might now look briefly at what Hinduism became in its struggle with Islam. In the sectarian Hindu's coat of many colors are strands of Moslem warp threaded through the woof. Indeed many threads of the woof itself are Moslem, although the pattern continues to be predominantly Indian. The Moslem's own devotion to religion varied from doctrinal fundamentalism to a theological liberalism and even to a radicalism whose advocates were strict adherents of Islam. These component parts are represented in Indian Islam which began at the dawn of the eleventh century and moved with such increasing force throughout five hundred years that a continuous empire, that of the Mughals, was built to endure more than two hundred years (1525–1757). During these centuries of war and politics theological issues were often most acute. The enthusiastic devotion of the Moslem as "the slave of Allah" was most intense, usually even more intense than any Hindu *bhakti*. The Moslem religion, with all its dogma, was far more concrete than any or all Hindu dharma. There was challenge, however, to both in certain aspects of the times, e.g. in certain theistic tendencies. Islam was itself a challenge to Hindu theism and the personal religion of the Hindu was a challenge to Islam.

Moslems in India, in general, believed God to be either numerically One "without a second" or else mystically One, but no Moslem contemplated a correlation of Islamic theological Unity with Vedantic "nonduality." Moslems were intolerant of Hinduism, being keenly conscious of what to them was "association" of another power or deity with God, and the "associator" was worthy, in Moslem eyes, of nothing less than

79

death at Moslem hands unless he repented and became a Moslem. Nevertheless, as time went on, there were Moslem Sufis who found in Hinduism certain tenets in common with Islamic dogma. It remained for Moslems as a whole to learn by reasonable apologetic—by a principle of the Koran itself—that Hindus as a "people with a scripture" might be as tolerable as Christians, Jews, and Sabians with their New Testament, Law, and Holy Bible, respectively (for Moslems had not called these three peoples "associators"). Yet, they were puzzled by both the quality and the content of the Hindu scriptures. The literature of popular Hinduism was seemingly far too full of magic, folklore, gods, and goddesses, even as the temples were too full of images.

Islam could welcome Hindus to its fold even while Hinduism was not attractive to the Moslem. Many low-caste Hindus and *panchamas* were converted. (Nothing entered Hinduism from Islam, however, except certain Moslem theological ideas.) But Hinduism gave Islam more than converts; it affected Islam through caste, and something analogous to caste appeared among the Moslems. Moslem theology did induce some Hindus to revise their catalogue of gods, and Hindu syncretism appealed greatly to the Moslem Mughal Akbar. Hindu syncretism and Moslem idol-smashing induced many Hindus to question their own idolatry. The very modern Hindu Arya Samaj, a nineteenth century movement which still continues, has shared with Islam an antipathy toward idols.

The most of what Islam and Hinduism found in common lay in the realm of other-worldly mysticism, in the informal, spiritual reliance which the *bhakta* and the Sufi placed on God. The *bhakta* could possibly be even more theistic than the orthodox Sufi. However, some Sufis were pantheistic heretics. Orthodox Sufism, al-Ghazzali's type, was quite acceptable to many *bhaktas,* for example, in the time of Ramanuja. Possibly Shankara himself, had he known Islam, would have welcomed Sufi pantheism, for there is close resemblance between the heretical Sufi's Allah and the Brahman of Vedanta. Certain it is that Islam was eventually a channel into India of phases of semiticohellenic culture which in days subsequent to Ramanuja affected Hindu *bhakta*.

Now at last against the background of the total setting we have sketched we may look at the highway ends of Hinduism in our own time; at what Shiva and Vishnu are as facts and symbols. Only certain radical intellectuals nowadays deny these gods and have renounced allegiance to them and to what they represent. They are both very real by one means or another to the great majority. They are the two of the modern triad who are supreme. The role of the third, Brahma, that of creation, as the theist has described it, was long since fulfilled. The remaining two are responsible for the recurrent processes of destruction, preservation, and renewal. Nor would the philosopher who holds the theory of an uncreated, endless universe have any place for Brahma, the Creator. Shiva has usually symbolized for all Hindus this present, destructive age of evil however contradictory it may be to hold that this great god of tragic circumstance has power to save men from it. Vishnu stands in fairer view although the round of life is likewise tragic from which he by divine, personal intervention (through an incarnation) provides his devotees release. It is mainly this element of saving intervention which differentiates Shiva and Vishnu. A two-party providence does indeed exist, giving rise to not a little rivalry, although in general the two gods mutually supplement one another, allowing their devotees ample opportunity and some occasion for alternative allegiance. Let Puri, Benares, and many another center give their witness to this.

Shiva, by his characteristic title Mahadeva, Great God, represents after the many centuries a grand agglomeration, his own personality somewhat vague amidst it. Perhaps, if the unnamed, horned divinity chiseled cross-legged on the Mohenjo-daru relic, probably in the role of Pashupati, "Lord of Creatures," is really Shiva, then his age may reach five thousand years. Mingled in him are Vedic elements, mostly male and paternalistic, and pre-Vedic Dravidian maternalism. His very name may have been an adjective before it became a noun. Shiva, meaning "auspicious," was often applied to any god men feared, even when they sought boons of him. Rudra, for example, the minor Vedic deity of the "red" braided hair, a slayer of cattle who was ever ready to slay men also, and a god whom other gods saw fit to placate on occasion, was called auspicious (*shiva*) and may have been one of Shiva's many antecedents.

Whatever his lineage was, Shiva became, in the brahmanic priestly era of the eighth century B.C. and following, the most popular of gods, the chief of the sacerdotal order. In time his special seat was fixed at Benares on the river Ganges, where he has since been known as Vishveshvara, "Lord of All." His consort and counterpart, Mahadevi, Great Goddess, early joined him and virtually acceded to all his powers, taking to herself most of his own personality and leaving him once again a name, a symbol of a state of mind expressive of rather indiscriminate devotion. He is not represented by an image, but by the lingam, a sometimes most realistic figure of the male organ of generation fixed in contact with the yoni, the female organ of conception. But Mahadevi herself appears in graven images and many sorts of prints as chief of the mother-cult within whose scope not only humble villagers are enlisted, but also men of prominence, e.g. Shankara, Rabindranath Tagore, and Gandhi. She may be known simply as Devi, or variously as Uma, "light," Gauri, the "brilliant," Parbati, "mountaineer," Durga, the "distant, inaccessible," and Kali the "dark" mother. Poets have sometimes asked if she were father or mother, have glorified her as the Supreme Principle and have worshiped her even under the names of Krishna, Rama, and Shiva, for she also is an agglomeration. She takes by association, at least, the form of any village goddess whose powers play especially in seasons of distress among the herds and the people.

Shiva in his more paternal role developed on the one hand as *mahayogi* (great ascetic) and on the other hand as *viyoga* (abstraction). As the great ascetic he is dear to yogis, sadhus, sannyasis, and those whose dependence is on works. On the other hand, he is dear to any who indulge in abstract thought in his name and engage in penitential meditation as a means to union with his universal spirit. To devotees of this latter sort, as to Shankara, he is the All-god of scholastic speculation. Although most of these consider themselves heirs of Vedic and brahmanic tradition, others question the Vedas as revelation and the brahmanical order as the ruling caste. Some of them, for example, condemn infant-marriage and, in defiance of brahmanic injunction, sanction the remarriage of widows. Some devotees of the Great Ascetic not only prohibit bloody sacrifice but deny themselves both meat and liquor, whereas some others practice bloody sacrifice and indulge in meat and liquor on occasion.

Not Shiva himself, but either his abstraction—whence ascetic imitation—or his "shakti," feminine "energy or power," is the ruling principle. Shakti, in fact, dominates the stage, and that in a somewhat dual role. There is a "right-hand," and there is a "left-hand," type, both of which have sometimes been contiguous as in Bengal. Right-hand shaktism exhibits clean, unselfish, maternal mercy of an unstrained quality from which certain devotees, e.g. the notable Bengali saint Ramakrishna and his faithful disciple Rabindranath Tagore, professed to draw their satisfaction, even to the realization of perfect union with divinity. Tagore and many another have found Kali's "grace" rewarding and her "name" a channel of salvation, with life at this Mother's "feet" in worshipful humility of greater worth than formal acts, austerities, and pilgrimage. They have sought the exercise of goodness rather than any formal, mechanical adjustment, have emphasized affirmation and not ascetic self-denial, have idealized pure and positive performance instead of mere cessation of the karmic process of rebirth.

Left-hand shaktism is of quite another sort, even exhibiting wantonness, intrigue, and vengefulness in the Goddess's name. One may see at Kalighat, beside Calcutta, something of the merely gross and bloody cult of Kali. Human sacrifices once were offered to her there, and now it is the blood of goats. The murderous "thags" of a former time who operated over many parts of India practiced in her name a ritual of robbery by deceit and strangulation. And her worship by whatever name,

Kali, Durga, or another, has included indecent, orgiastic rites magical in meaning and effect, accompanied by the use of wine, animal flesh, fish, grain, and women. This is Tantric *shakti,* for the most part, a form which has been slowly disappearing, but which has not yet become extinct. It may be seen in some central and south Indian villages at the time of "Durga-puja" (*shakti*-worship), an extensive, seasonal observance with special household rites. Lower shaktism is yielding, nevertheless, to education, radio broadcasting, and the circulation of the public press.

Vishnu, the other great divinity, represents a more definite personality than anything in the Shiva-cult. He has an image of his own and there are idols of his *avataras.* He has had—and yet has—his female associates, his wives, but no one of them has infringed on his prerogatives. They have remained subordinate. The *avatara*-process is altogether different from the Shivite *shakti*-demonstration, although, as has been mentioned, certain Vishnuite and Shivite elements do interchange. The analogies appear chiefly on the lower round of each. Vishnu's own consorts, his wives in his own right, Lakshmi and Saraswati, in particular, are altogether estimable morally. There is some moral difference, however, among his *avataras.* Sita, wife of the gentle, heroic Ramachandra-*avatara,* is most exemplary. There are two types, however, of the Krishna-*avatara,* a higher and a lower, with a corresponding ethical distinction to be seen among their consorts.

Vishnuism, like Shivism, is a *bhakti*-way. Vishnuism is distinctively a *bhakti*-way, however, by the *avatara* method. Nine *avataras* of Vishnu have "descended" from time to time, and a tenth, the Kalki-*avatara,* has long been expected. Kalki is the object of expectant hope for all who desire the destruction of such oppressive alien orders as Islam and Christianity, and who are anxious for improvement in the Hindu order. This is in keeping with the theory of the current *kaliyuga,* the "dark age." The nine *avataras* appeared, as legend has it, in the early years of Hinduism, each on its own occasion for its own specific object: there was the *matsya-avatara,* the "fish incarnation," to rescue and preserve the primal, eternal wisdom at a time of overwhelming flood; then came *kurma,* the tortoise, *nar-singha,* the man-lion, *varsha,* the boar, *vamana,* the dwarf, *parashurama* (Rama-of-the-axe), *ramachandra* (Rama whose symbol is the moon), Krishna, and—Buddha! The Rama and the Krishna *avataras,* the seventh and the eighth, respectively, are the most important of the nine. They all—note the Buddha—indicate the flexibility and absorbent power of the Hindu *dharma* and exemplify the development of theism and personal devotion.

Krishna may be actually older than Rama in the literary records although theology disregards their sequence. Both are ancient and both were early heroes later deified. The higher Krishna is doubtless prior to the lower, in time as well as in character. He is known as Krishna Vasudeva or Bhagavata, the adorable warrior-priest and the adorable God of the subsequent Bhagavad-Gita. A religious movement in his name was successful and he became identified with the very God to whom he himself had first directed worship. The Gita as early, perhaps, as the fourth century B.C. thus sings of him as Bhagavata, the divine. His worship continued unabated, although devotion to him as reflected in the eleventh century A.D. expressed itself in a higher and a lower form.

The higher Krishna of the Gita, itself indistinct because it is composite, became clear-cut through systematic commentary. Krishna as Bhagavata-Vasudeva is thus commended as the goal and refuge of the man of knowledge and devotion. He is the supreme, the absolute, the All, the universal savior who minimizes works, takes no account of caste, sympathizes with men whose very status he had himself assumed, and takes men's works upon himself and rewards men by his grace. The implication is always that what is done in and by his Name is mightier than works and more effectual than knowledge. The intellectual appeal, nevertheless, is present. Men must set their minds on Him. The Krishna of the Bhagavata-Purana, on the other hand, is regarded more emotionally, even without reflection on his morals, and he affords men greater satisfaction, for they may laugh and weep in his presence, sing hymns to him soulfully, and gaze raptly on his image or lapse into long, finally unconscious trances. All this provides a rather speedy means of interruption to the karmic-transmigratory round.

There is, however, a Krishna whose morals may be questioned. He is the Gopala Krishna, a youthful, musical, mischievous, amorous cowherd. His names, Go-pala and Go-vinda, mean "keeper of the cattle." He lives chiefly in Vrindavana or Mathura (the modern Mattra) on the Yamuna river, among the cow-girls (*gopis*) who are led by the goddess Radha who wears a moral cloak of many colors. These cow-girls of Krishna's adventures are, of course, both symbol and reality, as is their leader Radha. They represent either the erotic or the mystical, the sexual or the sexless. In parts of the Bhagavata-Purana, Radha is a gopi who "pleases" Krishna and wins his special favor by her pure devotion, but in the Gita-Govinda, Jayadeva's popular twelfth century rendition, she is a creature of sex-pleasure, the chief companion of the amorous Gopala who dallies with all the gopis in an expression of sensual passion quite similar to the Shivite left-hand *shakti*. Many Vishnuites, however, see Radha in a higher role, as the very incarnation of the pure and estimable Lakshmi and as a mystic symbol of the human soul itself. Radha is as dear to the Vishnuites as is the estimable Lord Krishna; she is not Krishna's mistress but a pure and loving female spirit.

The Ramachandra-*avatara* stands at a uniformly lofty level and holds an equal place with the higher Krishna in Vishnuite esteem. There is a cult of Rama, which is definitely modern. Rama's career, however, began in ancient times, being mentioned first in the Mahabharata. In the companion epic, the Valmiki Ramayana, he is the ideal hero ready to do homage to any one or to all of the people's gods. He came by a theological process into *avatara*ship, holding firm meanwhile the noble qualities of his *kshatriya* heroism. While the older Vedic gods, including Indra, Soma, and Varuna, were giving way, and Vishnu was coming into prominence, Rama's transformation issued in a share of Vishnu's own honors. Vishnu himself became the god-preeminent of metamorphoses and soon thereafter the god-distinctive of the *avataras*. He acquired the whole round to which Buddhists themselves had made some contribution when through their Jatakas, or "birth" stories, gods became not only men but animals. Vishnu perpetuated through the Ramachandra-*avatara* the glory of the marital *kshatriyas* amidst the persistent Brahman priestly heritage; and Rama, who represents him, became himself an acknowledged object of devotion.

Rama's distinction rests on his quality of life. He is never unchaste and impure, as is the lower Krishna. Rama's consort, Sita, is herself as admirable as Vishnu's wives, Lakshmi and Saraswati, and is far more real and influential than they. She is personally more substantial even than the higher *bhagavati* Radha. Hindus generally accept her as womanhood's ideal, and no story is more loved among them than the Tulsi Das Ramayana rehearsal of her chaste devotion while suffering the severest risks of her husband's banishment and of her own abduction—she was never even jealous or suspicious as her husband was sometimes. Rama gains prestige through her devotion.

He came to earth in this evil age, as Tulsi Das narrates, to wage exterminating warfare on all the demons (*rakshasas*) of whom the arch-demon Ravana was chief. They were ravishing all pure women, breaking all the moral laws, and defying every ordinance of the dharma. Although Rama did not dispel entirely the general wickedness, he with his faithful allies, not the least of whom were Hanuman and his dear monkey cohorts, rescued Sita, punished the demons, performed many valiant deeds, and proved himself an example and a savior. He is hailed as God through whom those who trust him and win his judgment and his grace may realize a golden age of wisdom, truth, purity, and joy. Judgment? Grace? There is in Ramaism an interesting duality: Rama's northern followers have emphasized his "monkey-hold" upon them and their clutching of him in turn, while his southern devotees have emphasized his "cathold," themselves yielding meekly to his grasp. Tulsi Das himself has preached the gospel of the monkey-hold, as did his predecessor Ramanuja whose theology was yet more widely

Vishnuite. The cooperative monkey-hold is Hinduism's greatest demonstration of man's own initiative and power in the saving process although they who depend upon it are a small minority in the whole Hindu family.

CONCLUSION: YESTERDAY—TOMORROW

In conclusion, we may remind ourselves that Hinduism as a whole should not be viewed exclusively from literary sources. The basic literature, in fact, is still a closed book to the great majority of villagers who are themselves the vast majority of Hindus. The ideas and the institutions which we have reviewed have, of course, affected all the people, but the villager's appeal in matters of religion is still to "custom" (*dastur*) mainly. The dharma of the more highly privileged is the *dastur* of the common man. Both the literature and the common man are themselves the products of India's own peculiar genius. The writings are a record of Hindu experience, whatever the sequence of practices and thoughts. The Hindu attitude has been mainly pessimistic and provincial with reference to the world and men's institutions, idealistic with reference to the universe. *Dastur* is local and dharma a closed order, with only heaven a permanent reward.

Hindu pessimism will long continue for many reasons, but deterministic karma can be modified, can become creative, realistic. There is such provision in the very root of it. Only thus can karmic Hinduism become the religion of practical, aggressive men, making for basic moral probity and having due regard for human welfare. Even pessimism with a realistic interest has affected speculative idealism and has reduced the emphasis on renunciation and complacency. Hindus in enlarging numbers are busy in physical as well as in mental and spiritual activities through which to renovate their order; and, it may be, to share in a larger-world activity. Whatever transformations come, however, through education, engineering, increased economic production, and popular consumption, and whatever the share acquired in international affairs, Hinduism will continue to be typical of India, and India will continue to be typically

Hindu. Hinduism as religion will remain theistic, with the tendency persisting to view all theories and forms as aspects of one eternal truth and substance, even though Hindu religion has never yet disclosed within itself a cloudless summit to which its many paths may lead. There is nothing in Hinduism, in its consciousness of an all-pervading essence exhaustlessly demonstrating its wisdom and its power in nature, men, and things, which will necessarily prevent Hindus from cooperating with men of other faiths in the discovery and use of paths which must lead eventually to the cloudless summit, symbol of what all men seek in their quest of the highest good.

SELECTED BIBLIOGRAPHY

Legacy of India. Edited by G. T. Garratt. London, 1937.
History of Indian Literature. By H. H. Gowen. New York, 1931.
Insights into Modern Hinduism. By H. D. Griswold. New York, 1934.
The Ramayana of Tulsi Das. By J. Macfie. Edinburgh, 1930.
Hindu Ethics. By J. Mackenzie. London, 1922.
Hindu View of Life. By S. Radhakrishnan. New York, 1926.
Contemporary Indian Philosophy. By S. Radhakrishnan and J. H. Muirhead. New York, 1936.
Outline of Hinduism. By F. H. Smith. London, 1934.
Rites of the Twice-Born. By M. Stevenson. London, 1920.

Buddhism

AUGUST KARL REISCHAUER

BUDDHISM, like Christianity and Islam, is a world religion. While confined largely to Asia it has nevertheless made its appeal to many different nations and races. In its expansion it underwent great changes, sometimes even in the fundamentals of religion, so that Buddhism as a whole is really a family of religions rather than just a single religion. It usually won its way by stages of easy compromise with the local cults and this often resulted in a syncretism of varying shades in which the distinctively Buddhist element is difficult to discover. Moreover in countries like China and Japan many of the adherents of Buddhism at the same time give allegiance to the original national faiths, making it all the more difficult to know just what Buddhism really means to them. In view of all this it is, of course, impossible in one short chapter to do more than give the barest outline of this protean religion which down through the centuries has influenced, more or less, so many of Asia's millions.

BUDDHIST ORIGINS AND EARLY DEVELOPMENTS

When Buddhism arose at the end of the sixth century B.C. India had already passed through a long religious evolution and had reached a certain maturity of thought about the nature of human life and its meaning. Vedic religions, with their conception of the divine in terms that were all too human and which sought the good life largely in the "here and now," were no longer satisfying the more thoughtful. In fact, the Aryan invaders who in the vigor of their youth had overrun India were beginning to undergo a profound change. The life of action was slowing down. Doing things became more difficult and seemed less necessary or even desirable. More important was the meditative life and finding out just what it all meant.

90

And as they meditated they became more and more impressed with the evanescent character of man's life. How quickly the vigor of youth ebbs and gives way to bodily ailments, old age, and death! How much of life is but sorrow and suffering! How insecure is the very foundation of man's physical life and how utterly futile, in the end, are man's efforts, ambitions and hopes! Is life really worth living? Why does man cling so tenaciously to life when so much of it is but suffering and disappointment? Is there a way to end it all, or can one achieve a state of mind indifferent or superior to life's vicissitudes? And if life is incurably evil, is there a way out and, perhaps, a true and better life beyond the present?

These and similar questions thoughtful Indians were asking. The unquestioning acceptance of life and the vigorous pursuit of things that make for physical well-being, prosperity, power, social prestige, and the like gave way to a great doubt. This doubt turned their quest into a new direction, away from the outer life to the inner and spiritual, away from the "here and now" to the beyond and the eternal.

One clear index of this profound change is seen in the wide acceptance of the ascetic ideal as the highest. This rests on the belief that the physical life and physical well-being cannot be the core of the truly good life; rather are they the very antithesis of the spiritual and higher life. Because of this belief, Indians in ever greater numbers were turning away from the normal life of the world to become hermits and recluses in forests and caves in order to gain their freedom from the "bondage of the flesh" and the entanglements of human relationships. They were in quest of an inner peace and security, something that is permanent and truly satisfying.

It was in such an atmosphere that Buddhism had its beginnings. It was one of many similar movements. Most of these soon disappeared or were absorbed by the older brahmanic religion as this evolved into the amorphous and all-inclusive Hinduism. Buddhism, however, achieved a status as an independent religion and for several centuries was the dominant religion of a large part of India. It, too, finally blended with Hinduism.

But long before this merging took place Buddhism spread beyond the borders of India to areas where it has continued as a separate religion to this day. In fact, in its expansion across most of Asia it became the great cultural bond which has bound these lands together in many ways and which may in the future play a considerable role in that capacity.

The Buddha. The founder of Buddhism is known best as "The Buddha," meaning "the Enlightened." This is but one of many titles by which he has been known to his followers; e.g. *Bhagavat,* "Lord," *Sakyamuni,* "Teacher of the Sakyans," or just "Teacher," and *Tathagata,* a title whose meaning is obscure but points to his superhuman qualities.

The Buddha was born about 560 B.C. in the land of the Sakyans, a small aristocratic republic located just south of the present Nepal border. His personal name was Siddhartha and the family name was Gautama (Pali Gotama), hence the title "Gautama Buddha." His family belonged to the Kshatriya or ruling class, his father being a raja, not a king as some of the sources state in their attempt to stress the great sacrifice he made when he forsook the world. As the son of a noble family he was reared in a way befitting his station in life. He was married early and had one son, some sources adding that he had several concubines. In short, he belonged definitely to the privileged class of his day and had the best that life offered. There came, however, a day when he decided to give up this comfortable life to seek something more truly satisfying. Legend seeks to account for this change, telling how one day driving in Lumbini Park, his place of birth, he met in succession a decrepit old man, a sick man, and a funeral procession; one source adding a mendicant. This awakened his sensitive nature to the darker side of life and he is quoted as saying later, "I also am subject to decay and am not free from the power of old age, sickness, and death. Is it right that I should feel horror, repulsion, and disgust when I see another in such a plight? And when I reflected thus, my disciples, all the joy of life which there is in life died within me."

It is natural that much is made of his great "renunciation";

there are many touching references to his departure from his sleeping wife and infant son and of the grief of his parents who had other ambitions for him. The kernel of truth in all these stories is in the sober statement, "He went out from his household life into the homeless state." This expression, "went out," became the favorite expression in all Buddhist lands for entering upon the life of monkhood, for the predominant emphasis in Buddhism has been on the renunciation of the world and the normal life of man living in a family.

After the young Siddhartha had made his great decision he joined himself to two hermits who were noted for their life of contemplation and their skill in the art of inducing trance states, but he soon discovered that while the contemplative life had great merit his teachers really had little to offer in the way of a deeper insight into life's values and meaning. He therefore left them and next joined a group of five ascetics for, as stated above, the ascetic ideal was making its appeal to many. He followed this "hard way" with zeal and determination to the point of almost starving himself to death. "When I touched my belly I felt my backbone through it . . . so near had my back and belly come together through fasting. And when I rubbed my limbs to refresh them the hair fell off."

But all this castigation of the flesh, he found, yielded nothing in the way of spiritual enrichment. So he abandoned the ascetic life as an extreme but he did not abandon his quest. Remembering how once he had a flash of unusual insight and rapture while sitting in meditation, he decided to make a new start along that line. He found a quiet spot under a big tree where he was free from the distractions of the world and as he sat in silent meditation the great experience known ever after as "the enlightenment" came to him. "In me thus set free the knowledge of freedom arose and I knew 'Rebirth has been destroyed, the higher life has been led; what had to be done has been done. I have no more to do with this world' . . . ignorance was destroyed, knowledge had arisen, darkness was destroyed, light had arisen, as I sat there earnest, strenuous, resolute."

Whatever the Buddha's real experience and insight in this

hour of "Enlightenment" may have been, there can be little doubt that to him it was tremendously real and deeply satisfying. He seemed ever after absolutely certain that he had discovered the meaning of human life and a way to live which brings freedom from all bondage and gives the deepest satisfaction. He was never tempted to return to his former way of life, for no matter what pleasures it might have it could never yield what he had found. The one temptation that came to him was to keep his secret to himself and not tell others about it. He knew all too well how hard it is to renounce the world and how strong is the downward pull of sense indulgence. "With great pains have I acquired it. Enough! Why should I now proclaim it? This doctrine will not be easy to understand to beings that are lost in lust and hatred." The Buddha did not, however, yield to this temptation. He devoted the rest of his long life till he died at the age of eighty to going up and down India teaching men how to gain release from their bondage and to attain the state of true enlightenment.

He had remarkable success almost from the beginning of his mission. As the story unfolds we see him winning followers from all classes of society, a surprisingly large proportion coming from the more privileged classes. In fact, one record has it that his followers from the rich merchant class were so many that complaint arose from fathers who had other ambitions for their sons and who did not want the old order of things disturbed. The Buddha met this with the calm statement: "It is by means of the true doctrine that the Tathagata leads men. Who will murmur at the wise, who lead by the power of the truth?" Even rulers sought to do him honor, inviting him and his disciples to meals and then listening respectfully to his discourses. He seemed to impress all who heard him as one speaking with authority.

Among his first converts, apparently, were the five recluses with whom he had practiced the rigors of ascetic discipline. They had scorned him when he gave up this way but apparently were later convinced that he had found the truer way. Among his earliest followers were also some of his own kin such as his cousin Ananda, the "beloved disciple" of Buddhism. Like other wandering teachers, he had a group of disciples whom he instructed more thoroughly in the way and who began to share with him the work of spreading the teaching. He sent them out usually one by one rather than in pairs or groups for Buddhism stresses the solitary life, or as the refrain in a scripture has it, "He wandered lonely as a rhinoceros."

Those followers who were really serious in taking up his way of life, he organized into an order, the *Sangha.* These lived under definite rules and regulations which were gradually formulated as occasions arose and which finally became the well known *Patimokkha,* Monk's Rules, constituting an important part of the Buddhist scriptures. It became the custom of the order to gather twice a month, and later weekly, for a check-up on the progress or lapses of the members. A sort of confessional was developed setting up certain standards, and as this was read before the assembled group each member was expected to examine himself and if he felt himself guilty he was in honor bound to make confession before his brethren. If he failed to confess he was made to feel that "he is no longer in communion" and too open a violation of the rules led to expulsion from the order.

At the instigation of the "beloved disciple," Ananda, the Buddha consented to admit women to an order of nuns but the record makes it clear that he did so with great reluctance and grave doubts. He seemed to share the common Indian view of woman as an inferior being and the Monk's Rules give unmistakable evidence that woman was regarded as the monk's chief obstacle to making progress in the holy life.

While the inner group of his disciples received the Buddha's continued guidance and instruction he nevertheless gave much of his time through the long years to preaching to the multitudes, thus winning many who, though not ready to take upon themselves the vows of the monk's life, heard him gladly and followed at least "from afar." As a matter of fact, the Buddha often accommodated his message to his hearers and as one text has it, "he talked about morality, about *Nirvana,* about the evils, the vanity and the sinfulness of desires, and about the blessings of the abandonment of desire."

His daily and yearly routine is pictured in the scriptures. Rising before dawn he would spend much time in meditation. Sometimes he would call on some monk in the neighborhood. Just before noon, accompanied by some disciples, he would go from house to house with his alms bowl accepting whatever was offered. After this meal, usually only one per day, he would give a discourse on some subject and catechize his disciples, following this with a period of rest and meditation. The late afternoons and evenings were again devoted to instructing his disciples or larger groups. The three months of the rainy season, he spent usually with disciples in one or another of the places bestowed upon the order by some wealthy layman. The remainder of the year he spent in journeying from place to place spreading the teachings. This he kept up to the day of his death for it was on one of these long journeys that he finally died, his body worn out by his arduous labors.

The Essentials of the Buddha's Teachings. What was it, then, that constituted the essentials of the Buddha's message?

While it is exceedingly difficult to answer this question authoritatively because of the nature of our sources and while scholars, including leading Buddhists, differ rather widely in their answers, there are, nevertheless, a few major teachings which can be accepted as characteristic.

The first thing to note is that the Buddha does not put into the forefront of his teachings what is so characteristic of the great theistic faiths or even of religion in general, namely, thoughts about the divine and man's relationship to the divine. He claimed no revelation from above nor did he speak as a prophet proclaiming the will of God to men or bringing them a message of divine mercy and redeeming grace. He spoke rather as a seer who through his own efforts has discovered the truth —truth about the nature of things and especially the nature of human life, the cause of its misery, and the way to achieve freedom from its bondage and sorrows. He seemed absolutely self-reliant and self-sufficient. He meditated much but there is no record of his ever praying or of his teaching his disciples to pray. It is true that the so-called "Three Refuges," namely, "I take refuge in the Buddha, the Doctrine, and the *Sangha,*" are a sort of confession and prayer which the common believers used in expressing their allegiance to him, but the Buddha himself seemed to acknowledge no Being above himself. "I have overcome all foes: I am all-wise; I am free from stains in every way; I have left everything; I have obtained emancipation by the destruction of desire. Having myself gained knowledge, whom should I call my master? I have no teacher; no one is equal to me; in the world of men and of gods, no being is like me. I am the holy One in the world, I am the highest teacher. I alone am the *Sambuddha* [Perfectly Enlightened]; I have obtained coolness (by extinction of passions) and have obtained *Nirvana.* To found the Kingdom of Truth I go to the city of the Kasis (Benares); I will beat the drum of the immortal in the darkness of this world." These words ascribed to him may not be his but they convey the impression he made on others and give the flavor of much that he did say.

As a matter of fact the Buddha had little interest in metaphysical matters and scorned the philosophers of his day for their speculations about the Brahman, the Absolute, and man's relation to the divine. There are, however, certain assumptions in his teachings which have metaphysical implications. Thus he accepted the commonly held view about the *Samsara,* the world of innumerable individual beings which are ever passing from one stage of existence to another, some higher and some lower than the human stage. All these beings are under a law of cause and effect, the law of karma, which the Buddha interpreted ethically rather than physically. He was too much of a realist to hold that all this flux of phenomenal existence is *maya,* an illusion of the unenlightened mind. He accepted it as real and believed that this process of "birth and death and again rebirth and death" would go on indefinitely unless the karma energy, the blind "will-to-be," is stopped. Just how the universe came to be what it is or whether there is some great purpose in it all, he did not pretend to know. "The world of transmigration, my disciples, has its beginning in eternity. No origin can be perceived, from which beings start, and hampered by ignorance, fettered by craving, stray and wander."

But while he claimed no knowledge of the ultimate origin of things, of their meaning and destiny, he believed he had found a way to free man from this "round of individual existences." His conclusions about the nature of man's life and his practical solution of life's real problem, he formulated in the famous "Four Noble Truths." That these "Truths" constitute much of the core of his teachings is indicated by the fact that over and over again his message is represented as an exposition of them.

In the famous sermon of Benares, the Buddha, after warning against the two extremes of self-indulgence and self-mortification and recommending the "Middle Way," proclaims his "Four Noble Truths." The first is that human life is predominantly an existence of suffering. "Birth is attended with pain, decay is painful, disease is painful, death is painful. Union with the unpleasant is painful, painful is separation from the pleasant; and any craving unsatisfied, that, too, is painful. In brief, the five *skandhas,* 'aggregates' [conditions of individual existence] of clinging [to existence] are painful." The Buddha did not deny that life had some pleasures and satisfactions but these are overshadowed by sorrow and suffering. The best in life is fleeting and impermanent. "Which think you are more— the tears which you have shed as you strayed and wandered on this long journey, grieving and weeping because you were bound to what you hated and separated from what you loved— which are more, these tears or the waters in the four oceans? A mother's death, a son's death, a daughter's death, loss of kinsmen, loss of property, sickness—all these have you endured through long ages."

There was no real consolation in the thought of a future life in one of the heavens of popular belief for, even if there were such heavens, existence in them, the Buddha said, will also come to an end some day as does all individual existence.

The second "Truth" offers an explanation as to the cause of human suffering. "It is the craving thirst that causes renewal of becomings, that is accompanied by sensual delights, and seeks satisfaction now here now there—that is to say, the craving for the satisfaction of the senses, or the craving for a future life, or the craving for prosperity." Suffering thus has its roots in man's passionate desire for things which cannot really satisfy. The very pleasures of life become fetters, for desires grow with what they feed on. Desires are a consuming fire. "Everything, O Monks, is burning, and how is it burning? . . . It is burning with the fire of lust, the fire of anger, with the fire of ignorance; it is burning with the sorrow of birth, decay, grief, lamentations, suffering, dejection, and despair." Not only do lust, anger, and ignorance, the three chief evils, cause suffering, they are also the fetters that bind man to the endless "rounds of existence" in this incurably evil world.

In the third "Truth," the Buddha introduces a note of hope, namely, that human suffering can be ended and man set free by ending that craving thirst which is rooted in ignorance. This is the heart of his message. "Just as the ocean has only one taste, the taste of salt, so has this doctrine and discipline only one flavor, the flavor of emancipation."

The fourth "Truth" states how man is to conquer his craving thirst and achieve his release. "Now this is the Noble Truth as to the way that leads to the passing away of suffering. Verily it is the Noble Eightfold Path, that is to say: Right views, right aspirations, right speech, conduct and mode of livelihood, right effort, right mindfulness, and right rapture." This states succinctly what is explained in greater detail in many of the Buddha's discourses.

It is noteworthy that the "Path" begins with "right views," for a true understanding is basic in the Buddha's teachings. While knowledge as such is not sufficient nor an end in itself, it nevertheless is indispensable to true "enlightenment." "Right views" include above all else the "Four Noble Truths" but also certain views about the nature of the self and the destiny of the enlightened self in the *Nirvana* state. These we shall consider briefly after indicating the meaning of the other aspects of the Noble Eightfold Path.

"Right aspirations" require the renunciation of the life of pleasure and the nurturing of a spirit which bears no malice or harm to any creature. "Right speech" is to abstain from all falsehood, slander, harsh words, or foolish chatter. "Right conduct" covers the whole range of moral living but special stress is laid on abstaining from taking life, from taking what is not one's own, from all forms of immorality and sense-indulgence. "Right livelihood" involves entering only such occupations as will bring no harm or danger to any living being. Such occupations as those of caravan traders, slave-dealers, butchers, publicans, and dealers in harmful drugs are specifically proscribed.

With "right effort" the "Path" becomes more positive in tone. It calls for a resolute suppression of all evil states of mind or the arising of such states. Sloth and torpor must be replaced by resoluteness of spirit and the mind must be occupied with a quest for the truth. To the thought that "as a man thinketh in his heart so is he" the Buddha adds: "All that we are is the result of what we have thought; it is founded on our thoughts, it is made up of our thoughts. If a man speaks or acts with an evil thought, pain follows him as the wheel follows the foot of the ox that draws the carriage. . . . If a man speaks or acts with a pure thought, happiness follows him like a shadow that never leaves him."

"Right mindfulness" is to keep the bodily life under strict discipline and demands complete self-control, for "Self is the lord of self; who else should be lord? With self well subdued, a man finds a lord such as few can find." "If one man conquer in battle a thousand times a thousand men and another conquer himself, he is the greatest of conquerors."

The last section of the "Path" is "right rapture," or rather a concentration of mind and meditation ending in an ecstacy of spirit. This is the complete opposite of those "wandering desires" seeking for pleasure through things that cannot really satisfy. It is to be free from all passions and fetters binding one to this life and it is to enter a state of peace, the peace of *Nirvana.*

And now let us return to "right views," especially the view

about the nature of the self and the meaning of *Nirvana,* or the state which the enlightened self is to achieve.

The Self. One of the most important but perplexing teachings of the Buddha is the *Anatta,* or non-ego doctrine. On the surface it appears as if the Buddha denied the very existence of the human self, or at least denied its permanency.

We can understand his teaching best if we consider it under three aspects. The first is what we ordinarily call the "lower self" or the self expressed in our physical passions. This self, the Buddha held, must be suppressed; the whole import of much of his ethical teachings concerned itself with its suppression.

A second aspect is what is involved in the ideal of self-denial, that is, when one, under the impulse of loving service to others, denies himself and suppresses the "selfish" self. This, too, finds many expressions in the Buddha's teaching about the self. Neither this nor the first mentioned aspect is difficult to understand.

There is, however, a third aspect to his teachings about the self which is perplexing and with which the *Anatta* doctrine concerns itself. Thus in the Four Noble Truths reference is made to the so-called "Five aggregates," *Skandhas,* which constitute the conditions of individual existence. These five are the bodily organism as such and four psychic aspects, namely, sensation, perception, predisposition, and consciousness. The meaning of these is fairly clear, except, perhaps, "predisposition," *Sankhara.* It seems to stand for one's general characteristics, inherited or acquired, which condition one's actions and reactions. Now the Buddha denied that the empirical self made up of these "five aggregates," and usually regarded as the self, is the self. "The body, O monks, is not the self. . . . Sensation is not the self. . . . Perception is not the self. . . . Predisposition is not the self. . . . Consciousness is not the self." All these are in constant flux and nothing is more so than consciousness, he maintained. Furthermore, at the death of the given individual these five elements fall apart and cease to constitute an individual being. They are like the parts of a wheel—the hub, spokes, and rim—which for a while constitute a wheel but fall apart and the wheel as such ceases to exist. But there is something which survives the death of the individual, the Buddha goes on to say, namely, karma, and this mysterious psychic force, perhaps best defined as a "blind will-to be," will assemble another "five aggregates" and constitute a new individual being. This new individual, while not identical with the old, is nevertheless conditioned by the old because karma carries over the characteristics and especially the moral qualities of the old to the new. This process goes on indefinitely unless it is stopped. It can be stopped but only as the individual becomes enlightened and realizes that this life of the "five aggregates," or this empirical ego, is only a quasi-self.

Is, then, karma, which alone carries over from one existence to another, the real self in the Buddha's view?

The correct answer seems to be both *No* and *Yes*. Karma apparently carries no consciousness of identity from one existence to another. On the other hand, the Buddha ascribes moral qualities to karma which persist and he speaks of both good and evil karma. Furthermore the individual is held morally responsible for what he does even though the fruits of his deeds may not be reaped until the next rebirth. Likewise the individual's own life reaps the fruits of the previous individual being whose karma has assembled the "five aggregates" which now constitute the individual in question. In fact, if the Buddha's ethical teachings are to make any real sense it can be only on condition that there is some degree of identity between the various individual beings in the causal series. Other considerations point in the same direction. Apparently in spite of the *Anatta* doctrine which seems to deny the existence of anything but a quasi-self the Buddha did believe in a higher self. He definitely rejected views of the self held by his contemporaries, e.g. that the self is an "unchanging and self-existent" spiritual reality, one in essence with the philosopher's *Brahman-Atman*, that Absolute Self about which some talked so glibly but about which, the Buddha felt, they really knew nothing. To him the self was apparently an ever-changing reality. In this very fact that it could change he saw an element of hope, for it could change for the better, become enlightened, and so gain release from the "rounds of existence" in this evil world. The enlightened self could attain to *Nirvana*. Whether this enlightened self is then a truly higher self and is an immortal spiritual reality, in the Buddha's view, depends on the meaning of *Nirvana,* and *Pari-Nirvana.*

Nirvana and Pari-Nirvana. Nirvana in general means the state which the enlightened one attains in this life. *Pari-Nirvana* is the state beyond the enlightened one's death. The primary meaning of the word *Nirvana* is emptiness, or the void. And one who has attained the *Nirvana* state has emptied himself of all that makes up the life of the quasi-self and feels assured that he will never again be born into this world. "Looking for the maker of this tabernacle [empirical ego] I shall have to run through a course of many births, so long as I do not find [it], and painful is birth again and again. But now, maker of the tabernacle, thou hast been seen; thou shalt not make up this tabernacle again. All thy rafters are broken, thy ridgepole is sundered; the mind approaching *Nirvana* has attained extinction of all desires." Thus *Nirvana* means first of all release from and an emptiness of all that makes up man's life of desires and the things that enslave him but that can never satisfy.

Secondly *Nirvana* is spoken of in more positive terms such as freedom, joy, happiness, the deathless and the changeless, and above all as a state of peace where all desires have ceased. But all this is the state of mind which the enlightened one has attained in this life. What happens when the enlightened one finally dies as the Buddha died? Does he continue to exist as a personal being, a higher self, and what is the nature of that existence?

It must be admitted that the Buddha was reluctant to speak on such matters. As with all metaphysical problems he seemed to regard discussion of this problem, too, as "not conducive" to what is really profitable. His own disciples were at times annoyed with him for being so reticent in the matter. We read of several occasions when they confronted him with a demand that he tell them plainly whether the enlightened one exists after death; if he did not know the answer they entreated him to admit that he did not know it. To these demands the Buddha usually replied that speculations about such matters are not helpful in solving the problems that lie nearer at hand, such as obtaining release from rebirth into this evil world. When pressed for an answer he replied that their questions "do not fit the case." "The Arhat who is released from what is styled 'form' is deep, immeasurable, hard to fathom, like the ocean. It does not fit the case to say either that he is reborn, not reborn, both reborn and not reborn, or neither reborn nor not reborn." That seems to mean that the enlightened one continues to exist but that the nature of his existence so completely transcends all that man experiences in this life, even its higher spiritual aspects, that it can neither be expressed in any positive terms nor denied in such terms, even the terms "existence" and "nonexistence." Thus even though the Buddha made the achievement of an ethical personality the core of his ethical teachings and regarded this achievement as the one way to obtain release from the "rounds of individual existence," he was not willing to define the state of existence beyond death, or *Pari-Nirvana* in terms of ideal personality or in any other positive terms. Naturally one who had nothing to say about a Supreme Personal Being could hardly affirm a belief in the personal existence of the enlightened one beyond death.

Among the last words he spoke on his deathbed are these: "All that is born, brought into being and put together carries within itself the necessity of dissolution." "It may be, Ananda, that some of you may think the word of the Master is ended. We have no more a teacher. But you should not think thus. The Truth and the rules which I have declared and laid down for you all, let them be the teacher for you after I am gone." He did not say that he would cease to exist but neither did he comfort them with the thought of his continuing spiritual presence with them. The Truth he taught them was to be their guide and comfort.

Is, then, Truth the abiding and ultimate reality? If so, does not this imply the existence of something like a Supreme Mind which thinks the Truth? The Buddha was never confronted with the question in this form but he spoke of the Dhamma, or Dharma, the Truth, as something absolute and not merely what the finite mind thinks. And in Buddhist thought after his death much is made of Panna, Sanskrit Prajna, which is the collective name for the higher states of mind which alone can comprehend absolute truth; and this Prajna is actually personified and as such is one source for the conception of the Eternal Buddha or Buddhas so prominent in later Mahayana Buddhism.

Layman's Religion. Teachings about the self and *Nirvana,* though difficult to understand, were embedded often in contexts which could be more readily grasped by the ordinary layman. In any case, much of the Buddha's message dealt with the practical problems of the moral life and was cast definitely in terms applicable to man's personal life. It was the achievement of an ethical life that was the important thing. In fact, he interpreted the law of cause and effect which is operative in all things primarily in ethical terms. What a man sows that shall he also reap either in this life or in the beyond whatever the nature of that "Beyond" may be.

This could be understood by the multitudes who heard him gladly and relied on him as a trustworthy teacher. They would take at least the first step in the Way which would guarantee them a more favorable rebirth into this world and then by persisting they would pass from one existence to another, each a little better, till finally they would reach *Nirvana* which they interpreted as a happy personal existence.

The layman, though with his mind at times fixed on *Nirvana* as a distant goal, remained primarily a citizen of this world. As such he had his responsibilities which he expected to discharge under the guidance of certain ideals of conduct. Thus he was expected to observe the five precepts forbidding the destruction of life, theft, unchastity, falsehoods, and strong drink. Each particular station in life had its peculiar duties. Thus parents must guide and protect their children and children honor their parents and maintain the family traditions. Teachers must instruct their disciples and in turn receive due respect. Husbands were to be courteous, faithful, and respectful to wives while wives should show fidelity and be diligent in their home duties. Friends were to be courteous, generous and benevolent to one another, observe the "golden rule" and keep the faith. Masters should assign just tasks to servants, feed and clothe them, provide recreation and occasional luxuries, while servants must rise before and retire after their masters, be content, work well, and praise their masters to others. Laymen should show affection to monks in act, word and thought. Monks must teach laymen and restrain them from evil ways.

These and similar teachings make up much of what the Buddha had to say to the common believers. Much of it is cast in negatives as is the case with commandments and precepts of all the older ethical systems. Sometimes one finds real heights as in the words, "As a mother watcheth over her only child, so let your hearts and minds be filled with boundless love for all creatures, great and small!" And there is gentleness and warmth in the passage, "If there be one of you who would wish to cherish me, let him go and cherish his sick comrade."

The whole process of salvation is summarized as follows: "From birth comes suffering; thence faith in the Buddha, the Law and the Order, thence lightheartedness; thence zest, thence confidence, thence pleasure or contentment, thence concentration, thence the intuition of the truth."

MAHAYANA AND HINAYANA BUDDHISM

It is not strange that after the death of the Buddha his followers differed among themselves as to their interpretation of the Master's teachings. According to tradition several great councils were held to settle matters under dispute. One of these was conducted under the patronage of King Asoka in the third century B.C. By that time at least eighteen different schools had arisen, each with its own interpretation and having even different versions of whatever canonical teachings had been handed down. In fact, the extant Pali Canon, now generally accepted as the best source for early Buddhism, is the canon of only one of these schools. The chief matters under dispute pertained to questions as to the nature of the Self, the *Arhat's* survival after death as a personal being, and whether the Buddha was more than merely human. There were also differences in matters of discipline, some schools being more lax than others. Buddhism was adjusting itself to fit the demands of man's life as a citizen of this world and this together with other external influences started trends which changed the religion of the Buddha, sometimes almost beyond recognition.

By the beginning of the Christian era this trend had developed a type of Buddhism centering especially in northwest India which called itself Mahayana, "Great Vehicle," in contradistinction from the older and more conservative type designated Hinayana, "Lesser Vehicle." Mahayana claimed to represent the true and fuller teachings of the Master and held that Hinayana was only elementary and provisional in character. There can be no question that there is a real difference between the Buddhism of the Pali Scriptures which roughly is the Hinayana type and the Buddhism calling itself Mahayana and having its literary deposit in a much more voluminous canon of scriptures. The latter is, of course, related to the former and germs of its characteristic teachings are present in the older Buddhism but it owes much to other influences. These influences are partly Indian in origin, such as the renascent Hinduism, but some derive from the religions and cultures of the peoples who invaded India from the north.

The main features of Mahayana are briefly indicated below though it should be remembered that Mahayana underwent further changes as it spread across Central Asia, China, Tibet, Korea, and Japan.

There is first the prominence of the *Bodhi-sattva* ideal which carries with it a change of emphasis in other important matters. The Bodhi-sattva is a divine being who having started as human has perfected himself through countless incarnations until he has the right to enter *Nirvana* but who out of compassion for all creatures foregoes this right and continues to be born again and again into this evil world in order to help others. He may even descend into the depths of the lowest hells to rescue the hapless victims imprisoned there. Only after he has provided a way of salvation for all will he enter the rest and peace of *Nirvana*.

While the germ of this ideal is present in the older Buddhism there is here nevertheless a new turn. There is a more altruistic ethical ideal. This ideal introduces the principle of vicarious suffering. It also lays the basis for the principle of transferable merit which became so prominent in later Buddhism. And finally it stresses the personal continuity of the Bodhi-sattva from one rebirth to another even though he may appear in various guises in his loving ministry to helpless creatures.

A second feature is the prominence of the Eternal Buddha or Buddhas who seem much like the God of theistic religions. This is specially true of Amitabha, the Buddha of eternal life and light who saves all who turn to him in simple faith, in his "Land of Bliss." At least in the popular presentation the Amitabha doctrine is couched in the language of theism and salvation in his paradise is a happy personal existence. It is true Buddhist philosophers treat this as a mere "accommodation" to the finite mind but nevertheless the trend is definitely in the direction of theism with its implications of man's personal survival beyond death.

Almost equally prominent is the Buddha Vairocana who seems to have close affinities with certain non-Indian sun deities. He is, on the one hand, a personification of Absolute Truth, eternal in its nature and apprehended only by the enlightened but illuminating all finite minds like the rays of a Central Sun brightening all things. On the other hand, he is represented as the dynamic source and Ultimate Reality from which all phenomenal beings emanate and to which they return. This gives the basis for the characteristic Mahayana doctrine that every man has the Buddha nature at the core of his being and is able to become enlightened and to return to his eternal home.

A third feature is the prominence of metaphysical speculations. Mahayana philosophers have developed great systems of thought, usually of an extreme idealistic type and often quite arid. However, they stress the thought that man is a citizen of eternity and in his true being belongs to a world that is real though its nature is beyond human concepts. In fact Mahayana developed theories of knowledge which characteristically make much of the basic distinction between Absolute Truth and relative or "accommodated" truth. Only the Enlightened One can know Absolute Truth. For finite minds and the unenlightened this truth is "stepped down" and "accommodated." Even the ordinary teachings of Buddhism itself belong to this category. It is this conception of truth which has made Buddhism so tolerant of other beliefs and teachings and which has enabled it to incorporate as its own things of real value from other sources. "Every thing that is well said . . . is a word of the Buddha," as King Asoka had put it. But this relativity of truth can be carried too far and this, too, is a marked characteristic of Mahayana. It all too easily "accommodated" its teachings to the level of its hearers and frequently made its conquests by stages of easy compromise which tended to obscure its own essential message.

But even more fatal is the concealed agnosticism and skepticism that runs all through Mahayana theories of knowledge and systems of philosophy. Granted that man's knowledge of the truth is fragmentary and only partial, we must, nevertheless, hold that in this fragmentariness man has real truth. Mahayana Buddhism all too easily accepts the widest contradictions as fragments of the all-inclusive truth and too often cuts the foundations from all and every truth man lives by with its constant insistence that all teachings of any and all religions and philosophies are in the last analysis but "accommodations" to man's limitations and ignorance.

Mahayana differentiates itself from the older Hinayana most of all in its canonical scriptures, so that as one ancient Buddhist scholar put it when he tried to define Mahayana: "A Mahayanist is one who reads Mahayana scriptures." We must now discuss this difference in respect to the Buddhist Canon.

CANON OF SACRED SCRIPTURES

The sacred literature of Buddhism is voluminous and varied in its contents. There is no single canon of scriptures accepted by all branches of Buddhism. There are rather various canons which though having some things in common nevertheless differ also materially.

Pali Canon. The most clearly delimited canon is the Pali Canon which is accepted by the Buddhists of Ceylon, Burma, Thailand and Cambodia. It embodies roughly what in the preceding section is mentioned as the teachings of Hinayana Buddhism. Though, on the whole, the best source for the Buddha's life and teachings it also includes a record of the historical development and changes which the faith underwent before this canon was reduced to writing about 20 B.C.

The various scriptures included are arranged in three major divisions called Pitakas, "Baskets," hence the common term Tipitaka or Tripitaka for the canon as a whole. These divisions are: (1) Vinaya-pitaka, "Discipline Basket," containing the rules and regulations for the monk and nun orders together with accounts of the circumstances under which the rules gradually were formulated, and accompanied often with important teachings. (2) Sutta-pitaka, "Discourse-Basket," containing discourses and sermons of the Buddha and his disciples. This division is subdivided into the five Nikayas, which arrange the material according to length of the discourses or their subject matter. (3) Abhidhamma-pitaka consists of philosophical elaborations and interpretations of the teachings. It is admittedly of later date. These divisions are more or less arbitrary and there is considerable overlapping in content.

The Mahayana Canon (or canons), accepted by the Buddhists of Nepal, Tibet, China, and Japan, is much more voluminous than the Pali Canon. Standard editions of the Chinese canon contain upwards of 1,600 different works in more than 5,000 volumes. These canons are based on an older Sanskrit canon of which only a few books and fragments are extant, by far the larger portion existing only in translations such as

Nepalese, Tibetan, and Chinese. Portions of these Mahayana canons, especially the Chinese, represent original works in the respective languages mentioned and are of varying dates, some being quite late. In fact, many of the translations from the Sanskrit are rather free and inaccurate translations and have interpretive material added. The truth is, Buddhism, and especially Mahayana, lays little stress on the fixed and unchanging Word "once for all delivered," and believed *semper, ubique, et ab omnibus.*

The Mahayana Canon includes many scriptures which are roughly identical in content with the corresponding sections of the Pali Canon, for it is the very genius of Mahayana to be all-inclusive. On the other hand, the leading scriptures of Mahayana and those which are most widely used have no parallels in the Pali Canon. This fact alone shows what wide differences there are between the various religions that come under the name of Buddhism.

The canon in Japan, where Buddhism has had some of its most remarkable developments and where it is still a real force in modern life, is the same as the Chinese canon. However, in actual practice various writings by Japanese Buddhists, particularly founders of schools and sects, are used fully as much as the canonical scriptures. There is also a trend among the more liberal elements in recent years to include these books as a part of the Japanese canon.

The Tibetan Canon, consisting of two great collections, corresponds roughly with the Chinese Canon. It has, however, less of what in the Chinese Canon corresponds with the Pali Canon while, on the other hand, it contains a good many books that represent a late development of Indian Buddhism and as such is more akin to Hinduism than to the older Buddhism. A goodly portion, dealing with various subjects only indirectly related to Buddhism as a religion, seems to be original with the Tibetans.

The very bulk of the Mahayana canons and the variety of their content, sometimes amounting to contradictions on the essentials of religion, created problems. One was the problem of harmonization, at least for those who believed that all this literature represented the teachings of the Buddha. Another problem was the practical use to which so many books could be put. While a few learned monks do actually read this veritable library and have worked out some scheme by which every book and teaching is fitted into a sort of mosaic whole, it has been a more common practice to select a few books and make their contents the basis of the religious life. Thus the various schools and sects of Mahayana Buddhism in China and Japan usually have based their teachings on one, two, or three of such important scriptures as the famous Lotus Scripture or the Three Amitabha Scriptures, even though theoretically they accept the whole voluminous canon as authoritative. And at least one important school of Mahayana Buddhism, the Contemplative school, lays little stress on any scripture, holding that truth is transmitted from heart to heart or that each man must find the truth within his own heart.

HISTORICAL EXPANSION AND DEVELOPMENTS

Buddhism, though Indian in origin and reflecting an outlook on life that is characteristically Indian, has stood for certain values which have universal validity. The Buddha regarded his message as a message for mankind and not merely for his own people; and as a matter of fact, Buddhism rather early in its history became a missionary religion, first to the millions of India and then beyond the borders of India.

India. As we saw, the Buddha's teachings received a wide hearing during the founder's lifetime. While little is known about Buddhism during the century after Buddha, by the middle of the third century B.C. it had achieved a large place in Indian life. The great Buddhist, King Asoka, not only gave it patronage throughout his extensive realm but even sent missionaries to other lands. Thereafter Buddhism gained steadily in strength and influence in spite of occasional setbacks until the fifth century A.D. This was particularly the case in the Ganges

Valley and northwest India. Southern India seems never to have been so much under its sway. We get our best light on Buddhism's place in fifth century India from the report made by the famous Chinese pilgrim, Fa-Hsien. He found it in a flourishing condition as the dominant religion in northwest India and the Ganges Valley. Hinayana and Mahayana existed side by side in friendly relation and each had numerous monasteries, some of which were of rather magnificent architecture. All in all, things looked most promising.

However, not long after this India came under the heel of the White Huns (A.D. 470–530). Previous invaders had been rather friendly to Buddhism since they themselves had come under its influence in their home lands, but the White Huns were definitely hostile. They ruthlessly looted and destroyed many of the monastic centers. This had a most disastrous effect, for the strength of Buddhism lay more in its monks than in its lay followers. Under the patronage of Emperor Harsha (606–648) Buddhism recovered somewhat from this setback, but the general trend of life in India was rather against it. Emperor Harsha's patronage, for example, though helpful, at the same time stirred up the non-Buddhist communions into action and he was forced to extend to them equal recognition. The truth is, Buddhism was meeting increasing opposition from a renascent Hinduism and this more than any other factor accounts for its gradual decline in the land of its origin. This adverse trend is indicated in the report made by another famous Chinese pilgrim, Hsuan Chuang, who visited India in the seventh century. He states that while Buddhism was still strong in Magadha, he found many monasteries in ruins or deserted. In northwest India a mixed faith prevailed in which the Buddhist element was giving ground steadily to the rising tide of Hinduism. I-Ching, another Chinese pilgrim writing at the end of the seventh century, reports a further decline. The fact is that Buddhism, especially in the faith of its lay followers, had all along compromised with Hinduism and did not stand clearly for the things that were central in the Buddha's message. The lay followers clung rather tenaciously to the worship of the old Hindu deities and to the belief in rebirths into their various heavens. Just because the Buddha had so little to say about the divine and the real nature of existence beyond death, or was misunderstood in what he did say about such essentials of religion, his followers filled the vacuum with gods and heavens of their own imaginings and even made the Buddha himself over into the image of the older deities. The monks may have been fairly true to the teachings of the Master but they did little to check this natural trend in the religion of the laymen. They were too easily satisfied and as long as the laymen supported the order with their gifts and followed the ordinary moral precepts they let them go their own way. It was enough if they subscribed to the common confessional, "I take refuge in the Buddha, the Law, and the Order," but what that meant was left largely for each man to work out for himself. In short, the lay followers were never really expected to understand the deeper things of the Master's teachings nor were they ever made a real part of an organized Buddhist fellowship binding them together into a definite communion. Really, they had much more in common with their fellow citizens, whether Buddhist or non-Buddhist, than with their own monks who lived too much aloof from the world. That is the chief reason why Buddhism gradually lost its identity as a separate religion in India and was merged more and more with Hinduism.

The coming of Islam in the twelfth century with its uncompromising and militant spirit hastened the process of Buddhism's disintegration. By the fifteenth century it had virtually disappeared from the land of its birth and thereafter only vestiges of its former glory remained. How much of its influence survives in Hinduism is another matter. Probably more than appears on the surface, for some of the great leaders in renascent Hinduism were accused of being really Buddhists. In any case, the Buddha is still regarded by intelligent Indians as India's greatest son and his passion for truth, his deep sympathy for his fellow creatures, and his ethical interpretation of the karma law are all regarded as a part of India's great spiritual heritage.

But while Buddhism after a thousand years of great influence gradually faded out in its original home, it won a more lasting place as a separate religion beyond the borders of India. Beginning with the third century B.C. it gradually spread across much of Asia. One stream moved southward into Ceylon and eastward into Burma, Siam, Cambodia, and the Malay Archipelago. Another stream flowed northward into Central Asia and then eastward, into China, Korea, and Japan. A subsidiary and later current, representing a rather decadent Buddhism, entered Tibet and from there reached Mongolia and China. Though early in its history Buddhist missions are said to have been sent to western Asia and north Africa, no lasting results were achieved. Apparently the bulwarks of the great theistic faiths—Zoroastrianism, Judaism, Christianity, and Islam— were more insurmountable than were the mountain ranges separating India from Central and Eastern Asia.

DOMAIN OF HINAYANA BUDDHISM

In its conquest of Ceylon and the countries of southeast Asia Buddhism gained a permanent domain, for these peoples have been followers of the Buddha for centuries and remain loyal to this day. The Buddhism of these lands is predominantly of the Hinayana type though elements of Mahayana and other Indian influences are a part of the accepted religion. In fact, Buddhism came to these peoples not simply as a religion but as the vehicle of the higher Indian civilization, thus bringing them much that is not strictly Buddhistic.

1. *Ceylon.* Buddhism was first planted in Ceylon by a relative of King Asoka. Apparently it won its way rapidly and soon great monastic centers sprang up, often under the patronage of the native rulers who claimed Indian descent and seemed to take pride in Buddhism as the flower of their ancestral culture. Ceylon not only received much from and through Buddhism in the way of religious values, art, literature, and general culture; it contributed much in turn. It was in Ceylon that the Pali Canon was first reduced to writing and so fixed in a more permanent form. The Ceylonese Chronicles have transmitted much

of early Buddhist traditions and history, and in this way have strengthened the faith. It was in Ceylon that Buddhaghosa wrote his great expositions of the teachings which were ever after accepted as standards throughout the Hinayana world. In many other ways Ceylonese Buddhism has been a fountainhead and seat of authority for the faith. Though there have been times of weakness and decline so that once it had to be revived by Burmese monks, Ceylonese Buddhism has continued fairly true to the Master's teachings and remains to this day the dominant religion of the island.

2. *Burma.* The history of early Buddhism in Burma is obscure. Hinayana may have reached southern Burma early in the Christian era if not before. Certainly by the sixth century it was well grounded. Northern Burma first came under Mahayana and other Indian influences. It came also in contact with Tang China when Buddhism was in its prime in China. Chinese annals imply that the Burmese were ardent Buddhists. But whatever the earlier history may have been, by the eleventh century Hinayana had become the recognized religion of the Burmese people and it has remained such to the present. During the twelfth and thirteenth centuries Burmese Buddhism was renowned for its great centers of learning and for its magnificent architecture, of which latter the impressive Shwe Dagon of Rangoon is a worthy successor. In spite of its all too easy compromises with the lower native cults it has played a very significant role in Burma's history and the vast majority of the Burmese people have been and continue to be decidedly under its influence.

3. *Siam.* Like the Ceylonese and Burmese, the Siamese or Thai are loyal adherents of the Buddha. It is possible that the Thai people came under the influence of Chinese Buddhism before they migrated from the north to their present home some time in the fourteenth century. However soon after their settling they came increasingly under the influence of Burmese and Ceylonese Buddhism and so came to constitute the third leading member of the Hinayana domain.

4. *Cambodia.* Buddhism may have reached Cambodia as early

as the sixth century. Apparently up to the fourteenth century Cambodia's religion was really a mixture of Mahayana Buddhism and Hinduism. In the latter part of that period one great expression of this mixed faith was a magnificent style of architecture, the outstanding example of which is the ancient city of Angkor and above all the majestic Angkor Wat which preserved best this ancient glory. After the fourteenth century Cambodia came increasingly under Siamese Buddhist influences and thus the Hinayana type gradually supplanted the older faith.

5. *Malay Archipelago*. Buddhism also found its way into the Malay Archipelago, especially the island of Java where is found one of its greatest architectural monuments, Boroboedoer. The reliefs of this great structure are a "veritable catechism in stone where every clause teaches the believer something new." Buddhism was brought to these islands largely by Hindu colonists, many of them coming apparently from areas where the Mahayana type prevailed and hence Javanese Buddhism was a mixture of Mahayana and Hinduism, though Hinayana characteristics were not lacking. The coming of Islam gradually forced Buddhism out of the picture.

There are, of course, variations in the Buddhism of these different lands, for in each country it has taken on some local coloring and made its practical compromises with the ancient native cults. Thus the average Buddhist layman of Burma fears and seeks to propitiate the *Nats* (nature and ancestral spirits) and *Nat* worship and festivals have long been a part of the regular Buddhist Calendar. Siamese Buddhists in the same way worship their *Phis* and retain other elements of their ancient primitive faith. But while there are these variations caused by the admixture of local cults, one is struck with the remarkable similarity that prevails in the main features of religion throughout the Hinayana domain. Hinayana has remained much the same through the centuries in all these different lands.

Thus all Hinayanists from Ceylon to Cambodia have virtually the same canon of scriptures, the Pali Canon. These scriptures are studied faithfully by the numerous monks, and portions of them are read to the lay followers on stated occasions, sometimes in the vernacular and so with real profit. Secondly, in all Hinayana lands the monks play a real role in the life of the people. Though there is a marked distinction between the monks and laymen, as has always been the case in Buddhism, there is nevertheless a feeling of real interdependence between the two. The very number of monks is indicative of Buddhism's hold. Among Ceylon's 3,000,000 Buddhists, 8,000 are monks. For Burma the respective figures are 11,000,000 and 90,000, and for Siam, 9,000,000 and 50,000. Since the monks are largely exempt from the ordinary tasks of life and must be supported in matters of food, clothing, and shelter it might seem that these tens of thousands would be regarded by the populace as a burden. This is, however, not the case, for they are usually held in high esteem for two main reasons. One is that they are looked upon as holy men who have forsaken the world to walk in the Way of the Buddha. While the layman may not be ready to forsake the world himself he admires the man who has done so and he feels deep down in his soul that some day, either in his old age or in some future rebirth he, too, will take this important step. In the meantime it behooves him to do the next best thing and loyally support those who have taken the Buddha's teaching seriously, for he believes that by so doing a certain amount of merit will accrue to his account. A second reason for the layman's esteem of the monks lies in the fact that they perform certain tasks which are of real value to the layman quite apart from their distinctively religious tasks, the most noted of which is, of course, their function as teachers. For centuries the Buddhist monk in these Hinayana lands has been the guardian of learning. In Burma, the rather high degree of literacy of the population is due almost wholly to the work of monks. This situation may change and in fact has begun to change already, for according to recent statistics the number of monastic schools in Burma has decreased from 3,092 to 928 during the last two decades. But on the whole the

Buddhist monk still occupies a real place in the life of all these Buddhist lands and there are other reasons for saying that Buddhism is still accepted by the vast majority of the population as its faith.

Perhaps nothing expresses better what Buddhism in these lands means to the intelligent layman than a few paragraphs from a statement made by a Ceylonese Buddhist and published in *The Daily Express,* London.

"Yes, I am a Buddhist. I was brought up as one. My people are Buddhists. . . . My parents are pious people. They worship the three Refuges—Buddha, Teaching, *Sangha;* and they keep the *Silas:* not to take life knowingly, not to steal, not to be adulterous, not to lie, slander or chatter, not to go where strong drink is drunk. That's what we profess, you know, when we say we are Buddhists. . . .

"We respect and support the monks; we give them alms when they pass our houses on their alms-rounds; we give in other ways; we go to hear them recite from the scriptures. . . .

"When the monks tell us things out of our scriptures they always tell of the better way of the men who are monks, the better fate for the man who is a monk. We value the monks and their way of life, not because we want to be monks ourselves, but because we believe that to take care of monks is the surest way to avoid a dreadful fate after death. Care of them will be all to our credit then. . . .

"We believe that he [Buddha] was not just a man; he was extraordinary, he was a wonder being. And we believe we others cannot well enter into what he thought. . . . We believe he is no more in any world, either earth or any other, as reborn. It is impossible even to imagine him. We can and do pray to him; we can and do try to meditate on him, on what we are told about him. But we never look for an answer. We believe we shall be somehow better if we meditate and pray. . . .

"Our Buddha spoke of the good life as a Way, and the monks teach it as an Earth-Way, that is, how rightly to walk in this life. But then life, they say is very, very long; and beyond this little bit of it we seem to have no good way. We are in the dark." [1]

Then, after expressing the feeling that perhaps Buddhists have not been quite true to what the Buddha really taught on such matters, the statement proceeds: "Perhaps our Buddha did not want men to let him go into such utter blankness when he left the earth. . . . Don't you think the perfect teacher, the helper greater than the gods, would be always helping men—at least till they could themselves see with him the end of the long way approaching?"

There is more than a little pathos in these words expressing, as they do, man's deep need for certitude about the ultimate issues of life and for personal communion with God or the "Eternal Buddha," of whom Hinayana Buddhism has little to say that is positive and assuring.

While Buddhism has been the dominant religion for centuries in Ceylon and the countries of southeast Asia and while during all that time it has undergone comparatively few changes, the impact of the modern world on these peoples is creating a new situation. Just how successful Buddhism will be in holding its own or what part it will play in the future remains to be seen. There is a growing secularization which runs counter to the monk ideal and which is drawing this generation's interest away from the "other-worldliness" of Buddhism to a greater emphasis on finding the good life in the "here and now" and seeing the good life more in terms of things which modern science makes possible. This does not mean, however, that this generation is turning away from Buddhism in favor of some other religion, or that Buddhism is unable to adjust itself to the new situation. It may require a rather radical change of emphasis and in this Buddhism may itself undergo a great change. As a matter of fact there are signs that this is happening. Buddhism seems to be less of a spiritual force than it has been in the past

[1] This statement is quoted in the Report of the Jerusalem meeting of the International Missionary Council, 1928, Vol. 1, "The Christian Life and Message in Relation to Non-Christian Systems of Thought and Life," p. 112 f.

but there is a sort of resurgence of Buddhism as a political force. The awakening to the modern world has as one of its aspects a growing nationalism and this carries with it a pride in the national heritage. Naturally when these peoples think about their national heritage they must think about Buddhism, for no other force has contributed half so much as Buddhism has. To be a loyal Ceylonese, Burmese, or Siamese is to be a good Buddhist. In fact, Buddhist monks, especially in the larger centers, are taking more and more interest in politics and in the affairs of the modern world. So much is this the case that older and more conservative monks are expressing concern lest "true Buddhism" will not survive.

DOMAIN OF MAHAYANA BUDDHISM

Buddhism, as we said, spread also northward and eastward. It reached the Tarim Basin probably in the second century B.C. if not earlier. Numerous archaeological remains show that this area was once a flourishing Buddhist domain. Its greater significance for Buddhism lay, however, in that it transmitted the faith to China whence it was transplanted to Korea and Japan.

1. *China.* Buddhist influences probably reached China before the Christian era. The date of their official introduction is usually placed at about A.D. 65 when the first Buddhist missionaries from Central Asia were given residence at the capital under royal patronage. Though beginning under such favorable circumstances it required many years before it won a real footing in Chinese life. For several centuries it was propagated largely by foreigners, mostly monks from Central Asia and India. These monks devoted most of their energy to the task of translating numerous Buddhist texts, both of the Hinayana and Mahayana type. The latter gradually overshadowed the former in number and importance with the result that Mahayana became predominant in Chinese Buddhism.

One reason why Buddhism was so slow in getting a hold was the simple fact that China had her own high culture. Whatever Buddhism gave China later, it did not at the beginning appear in Chinese eyes as the representative of a higher civilization as

121

it did to many other peoples. But an even stronger reason was that Buddhism represented an attitude toward life which differed radically from the Chinese. Its view of man's life as an existence of suffering and vanity and its central message of "release from the dread cycle of rebirths" ran counter to the typical Chinese view which regards human nature as inherently good and this life as meaningful and worthy of prolongation. In short, there is no greater contrast than between India's "other-worldliness" and China's "this-worldliness," Buddhism's "denial of life" and China's "affirmation of life," the Buddhist monk ideal requiring "going out into the homeless state" and the Chinese family ideal and love of the natural life. Instinctively the Chinese felt and continued to feel even long after Buddhism had made many concessions that its real spirit undermines the very foundations on which Chinese civilization is built. This has been particularly the feeling of those steeped in the ideals and traditions of Confucianism. As a stone inscription puts it: "Who would feed and clothe the Buddhist monks if there were no Confucianists? And if all became monks and celibates who would be the fathers and mothers of the Buddhists of the future."

On the other hand Buddhism had something which Confucianism lacked, especially the extremely rationalistic Confucianism of the Han period. It had more of a really religious message and filled a deep need, especially for the common man whose life was hard and far from good. It had a peculiar appeal in times of political instability and social insecurity. Such periods have been all too frequent in Chinese history. One of these followed the overthrow of the Han dynasty in A.D. 221 and lasted until the fifth century. During this period the Confucianist's neatly regulated world was shattered. Foreign peoples were irrupting into northwest China and were establishing themselves there while the rest of the country was divided among warring kingdoms of short duration. Some of these foreigners had been under the influence of Buddhism and so helped promote it in their new home. Government restrictions were removed and Chinese were at last allowed to enter monasteries and seek the consolation of this "other-worldly" religion, especially in Amitabha Buddhism with its message about the Eternal Buddha and his "Land of Bliss," and in the Bodhisattva of Mercy (Kuan Yin) or other ministering angels. By the end of the fourth century it is claimed that the vast majority of the populace in northwest China had become Buddhists and as far east as Korea Buddhism was being accepted as the flower of the higher Chinese civilization. By the beginning of the sixth century it had made such strides in other parts of China that the zealous Buddhist ruler, Wu-ti, in 518 ordered the first great collection of Buddhist scriptures to be made, thereby setting a precedent which subsequent rulers saw fit to follow. Six similar collections were made during the next two centuries and, all together, Chinese monarchs have sponsored twelve major collections, published in numerous editions, some of which contained upwards of 1,600 different works in more than 5,000 volumes.

Buddhism reached its highest influence during the great Tang dynasty (620–907). In 740 the capital alone had sixty-four monasteries and twenty-seven nunneries. It had not only become the dominant religion among the masses but had achieved great influence in court circles and with the intellectual classes in spite of the fact that Confucianists continued to control the affairs of state and jealously guarded their position of eminence as the scholars of the land. In the field of art and literature Buddhism wielded a tremendous influence and China would have been much poorer without its inspiration.

But in spite of its popularity and growing strength Buddhism frequently met with decided opposition from the hard-headed Confucianist who continued to regard this imported religion as inimical to China's best interests. Taoists, too, though having borrowed extensively from Buddhism, both in its popular teachings and in matters of ecclesiastical organization and ritual, used every means they could to down their rival. Repeatedly government restrictions were imposed—instigated either by Confucianists or by Taoists. The most severe one in 845 amounted to a real persecution. It is claimed 4,600 large and

40,000 smaller Buddhist structures were ordered demolished and 260,500 monks and nuns were forced to return to secular life.

These persecutions seldom lasted long for they were unpopular with the common people and Buddhism usually recovered rather rapidly. However the great blow of 845 had a more lasting effect, at least on Buddhism's outward power and wealth. Its spiritual hold was too deep to be easily eradicated. In fact, during the Sung period (960–1227) it achieved some of its greatest triumphs, especially in art and philosophy. In the latter field this is shown by the fact that Neo-Confucianism, which claimed to be a restatement of Confucius' teachings, pure and simple, shows decided Buddhist trends. This is even more marked in the writings of the great Confucianist Wang Yang Ming (1473–1529). Thus it may be said that while Buddhism made few new conquests outwardly and even lost some of its former prestige, it had nevertheless become so much a part of Chinese life and thought that even Confucianists could not adequately express their philosophy of life without borrowing heavily from their rival.

During the Mongol period (1280–1368) Tibetan Buddhism, or Lamaism, came into great favor with the rulers. This exerted a considerable influence on Chinese Buddhism, not always for the better. The Ming period (1368–1644) represented on the whole a resurgence of things Chinese and thus Confucianism was specially fostered while Buddhism was placed under certain restrictions. The Manchu dynasty (1644–1911) was in certain ways even less favorable to Buddhism though some of the rulers extended certain favors as good policy since many of their subjects were after all faithful Buddhists. In fact, Buddhism had so long been a vital factor in the life of the people that it could not be safely ignored or too openly restricted. As one of these more tactful monarchs put it: "From of old time the emperors and rulers of our land have modeled their methods of government upon Confucian principles. But Confucianism is not the only doctrine; there is also Buddhism. These two doctrines are like the wings of a bird: each requires the cooperation of the other."

Buddhist Schools of Thought. After Buddhism became more or less indigenous to China various schools of thought developed. Most of these were introduced from India but underwent great changes as they adjusted their teachings to Chinese life and ideals. Ten or more such schools had developed by the eighth century. After this no others arose but instead new developments took the form of brotherhoods, laymen's organizations, and semireligious secret societies which have played quite a role up to the present.

Of the ten schools two or three were Hinayana, making the monk ideal central and promulgating the cardinal doctrines of the older type of Indian Buddhism. The other schools were Mahayana in type. Though they differed rather radically from each other when first developed, they blended later, especially in the religion of the ordinary believers.

One of the most important of these schools was the *Chan,* or Contemplative school, originating in the teachings of Bodhidharma, who came from India in A.D. 520. Bodhidharma (Tamo), supposedly the twenty-eighth Patriarch of this school, was in many ways nearer the Buddha's real teachings than most others, especially with his emphasis on the thought that the deepest truth must be attained through intuitive insight. To find the Buddha nature in one's own heart is the supreme wisdom and greatest good. Good works, ascetic discipline, and laborious study of the voluminous scriptures are all futile unless they lead one to the ultimately real. All these other things are merely "the tracks of the bird which the hunter would catch but not the bird itself."

This type of Buddhism has close affinity with Taoist philosophy. Both are kinds of mysticism. Taoism is more of a Nature Mysticism than Dhyana Buddhism in its Indian form, but as the latter became more acclimated to China it became more like Taoism. Thus it not only saw the ultimately real in man's own inner nature, in good Indian style, but saw also that man's life is grounded in Nature, in good Chinese style. This close affinity was well demonstrated in the Sung period when both Taoism and Buddhism became sources of inspiration to the great Sung

painters. It was in the quietness of some monastery in the mountains far from the bustling world that the artistic monk not
only found his own soul akin to the Buddha nature but also felt
himself akin to the beauty of nature that surrounded him, and
conveyed this to paper or roll of silk with his brush.

In the Tien Tai school founded by the scholarly Chih-kai we
have a very different emphasis. Chih-kai had been a pupil of
Bodhidharma and while he regarded his master's teachings as
valid he felt there was more to be said. As a typical Chinese he
had a high regard for books and knowledge acquired through
formal learning. Man is ignorant and needs instruction. He
needs to profit by the experience of others handed down through
literature, the voluminous scriptures of Buddhism in particular.
And from his studies Chih-kai learned that different ways may
be taken to reach the same goal—silent meditation and mystical
communion with the eternal; ascetic discipline and meritorious
work; and simple faith in the mercy of the all-compassionate
Buddha—all these are valid ways, each being fitted to meet the
needs of a particular temperament. One important result of this
broad-mindedness was that Tien Tai, and its off-spring Tendai
in Japan, stood for a comprehensive type of Buddhism and as
such became the mother of various other schools each of which
developed more fully certain aspects of this all-inclusive
teaching.

The school which in many ways represents the greatest departure from original Buddhism and which has had the greatest
following in East Asia is the so-called "Pure Land School"
whose teachings center around the Eternal Buddha Amitabha
(*Omito-fu*) and his "Pure Land of Bliss" to which he leads
all who put their trust in his name. This school does not deny
the validity of other ways of salvation or the existence of other
Buddhas but holds that for weak and sinful man the best and
easiest way of salvation is not the way of self-reliance or philosophic wisdom but the way of faith and trust in the divine
mercy of the Buddha. It is perhaps not strange that this school
had many adherents and in the course of the centuries its teachings were more or less appropriated by all the other schools.

A fourth major school that must be mentioned is the Chen-Yen or Mystery school. The ultimately real is beyond the power of words to express and is best communicated through symbols and mystic signs. It stands, however, for a sort of pantheism in which the Eternal Buddha Vairocana is represented as the Universal Idea and the source of all finite thought. Vairocana is also the dynamic source of all things, the Ultimate Reality from which all phenomenal existence emanates. Thus man as an emanation from the Infinite Being, the Eternal Buddha, has the true Buddha nature and therefore can himself become a Buddha or return to the Source from which he came.

This line of thought has close affinity with Indian Vedanta and in fact represents a late development in Buddhism when it was being merged more and more with Hinduism. In its more popular aspects it embraces much that is far removed from original Buddhism or India's higher philosophies, especially in some of its symbolism, its love for magic, and its tendency toward the erotic. This symbolism and magic finds expression especially in connection with funeral ceremonies which in Chinese religion have always been so prominent. Certain ceremonies are believed to have magical effects. Thus the spirit can be rescued from hell and brought into the realm of the saved by a ceremony expressing that idea. It is not that the ceremony merely symbolizes a reality but it magically creates the reality if properly performed. And what is done for the fortunes of the deceased can also be accomplished for the living through appropriate signs and ceremonies.

There were several distinctively philosophical schools which had importance for a few intellectuals but never affected the religion of the people very much. One of the last schools arising was a sort of resurgence of the older monastic ideal and a protest against the whole trend of Chinese Mahayana by which Buddhism moved even further from its original basis and became one with its general environment. In this process Buddhism gained and lost. As it came to terms with the better aspects of Taoistic philosophy and Confucian ethics it became more truly a religion fitted for the Chinese. But, on the other hand, it all too often made easy compromises with the superstitious beliefs and practices of the masses and as a result Buddhism in its popular form would hardly be recognized by its original founder.

How much of a real force Buddhism is in present day China is hard to say. Outwardly it has definitely deteriorated in recent years. There are still a few great monastic centers and in certain parts of south China and the lower Yangtze Valley temples are kept in fairly good repair, but in most parts of the country Buddhism seems to be losing out. It must, however, be added that there are a few great leaders who are trying to bring new life into this ancient faith. There is also a sort of revival of layman's religion here and there but it is too early to say how significant it is.

2. *Tibet.* Tibetan Buddhism, better known as Lamaism, is in so many ways such a radical departure that it can hardly be included in this chapter. Furthermore, it would require far more space than can be allowed to present it even in barest outline and so we mention merely a few characteristic features.

Lamaism is, on the one hand, a form of Tantric Mahayana which originated in India when Buddhism was definitely degenerating and when an elaborate symbolism and magic formulas were overshadowing the Buddha's real teachings. On the other hand, it perpetuates much of the native Tibetan religion which is largely a belief in innumerable spirits and fierce demons controlling man's life and whom, out of fear, man seeks to propitiate or control by magic spells and formulas. In Lamaism therefore even the Eternal Buddhas of Mahayana function less as benign beings than as powerful spirits who by their superior might subdue demons and force them to serve rather than injure man. This function of the Buddhas finds frequent expression in Tibetan art portraying the fierce aspects of the Buddhas and thus making them appear more like superdemons than benign and peaceful Buddhas. The aid from the divine is most effectively invoked by use of sacred texts, endless repetitions of certain prayers, and ritualistic formulae believed to have magic power. Thus the prayer or potent spell, *Om mani padme hum,* is on everyone's lips, graven or painted on rocks and walls, printed on flags and perpetually revolved on countless wheels. Its exact meaning is not clear but no one doubts its efficacy against the forces of evil.

Tibet, to be sure, has received something of the purer Buddhism and its great monastic centers have at times been great seats of Buddhist learning where accurate translations of sacred texts have been made, where an approximation to a theistic theology has been developed in its Adi-Buddha doctrine, and where some monks live pious lives. And there is also something of the Buddha's teachings transmitted to the common follower. But all too often even the sacred texts are more valued for their supposed magic power over evil forces than for their guidance to truth and the higher life.

One other striking characteristic of Lamaism that must be mentioned is the virtual identification of religion and the state. Tibet is a sort of theocracy in which the Dalai Lama, enthroned at Lhasa, is supreme in both spiritual and temporal affairs and in which the grand lamas of the various monastic centers, together with their thousands of lamas or monks, virtually rule the nation. In no other land is such a large per cent of the population engaged in the "business" of religion. From the beginning of Buddhism in Tibet the monks took rather lightly the vows requiring a renunciation of the world. The celibate ideal was largely ignored, as was perhaps natural since even the great Buddhas in this Tantric Buddhism are represented as each having his *Shakti,* or female consort, which in Tibetan art receives an all too realistic presentation.

In some monasteries the very qualifications of the grand lama to hold his place as head do not depend upon his spiritual fitness, as the position is purely hereditary. In monasteries of the "reformed" branch where the celibate ideal prevails, it is held that the grand lamas, or abbots, are successive incarnations of some Bodhi-sattva or that each abbot is the reincarnation of his predecessor. This principle holds also for the Dalai Lama who is regarded as an incarnation of the Bodhi-sattva Chenrezi (*Avalokitésvara*), and thus is often spoken of as the "Living

Buddha." All this close linking of religion and the state naturally gives divine sanction to the rule of the Dalai Lama and that of the various grand lamas; and this in a very large measure accounts for the great influence Lamaism has had not only over Tibetans and Mongolians where it is the dominant religion but at times even in China where it was fostered by the Mongol dynasty and even by the Ming as an effective instrument of state.

3. *Korea.* Buddhism entered Korea in A.D. 372 where it was received as a part of the much admired Chinese civilization. As such it flourished for centuries in the peninsula. Great monastic centers were developed, and temples were built in cities and towns where the masses worshiped or took part in religious festivals. Even court circles celebrated these festivals with great splendor and came under Buddhism's influence. But while Buddhism thus became a real force in Korean life it was more as a part of a borrowed Chinese civilization than as a religion standing in its own sovereign right. Korean Buddhists faithfully preserved and reproduced what they had received but it cannot be said that Korean Buddhism added anything original in literature, interpretation of doctrine, or even in art and the externals of religion. Because of this comparative sterility it was perhaps natural that when a new wave of Chinese civilization came to Korea in the thirteenth century in the form of Neo-Confucianism, Buddhist leaders were unable to cope with the problems created. The upper and ruling classes turned to this Confucianism as similar classes in China had always done. While Buddhist monks sought to play a role in the new situation they failed, for they had forfeited their position as spiritual leaders through their worldly mindedness and in the repeated political conflicts they were usually on the losing side.

Beginning with the fifteenth century Buddhism was being definitely restricted, monasteries in the capital and other cities were being closed, and other measures were taken against it by the government. This resulted in a rather rapid decline and today few of the old temples and monasteries remain except in some country districts or remote mountain fastnesses. During recent decades Japanese Buddhists have made attempts to re-vive Buddhism on the peninsula but without much success.

4. *Japan*. Buddhism reached Japan from Korea in A.D. 552. The king of Paikche, one of the three kingdoms into which Korea was then divided, seeking an alliance with the ruler of Japan sent him presents including Buddhist scriptures, images, and ceremonial articles. He recommended Buddhism as "the most excellent of all teachings, though difficult to master and hard to comprehend," but added, "it brings endless and im-measurable blessings, even the attainment of the supreme enlightenment."

Buddhism received due consideration and while there were factions opposing the new religion it early gained a hold, espe-cially in the upper classes. In fact, Shotoku Taishi, the Prince Regent (593–622) became a zealous Buddhist, promoting it in various ways and actually declaring its teachings a fit basis for the state. The truth is, Buddhism was not only far superior to the native Shinto cults as a religion but as the vehicle of the higher Chinese civilization it brought much in its train which was new and interesting to the unlettered and simple Japanese of that day. Buddhist monks and artists, both Korean and Chi-nese, during the following two centuries played a big part in educating the Japanese people and making Japan a part of that great East Asia cultural area which has China as its center. Thus Japan's first great capital, Nara, was largely a Buddhist city and to this day one can see in its surviving temples and art treasures the place Buddhism had made for itself by the eighth century. To be sure, its influence was not yet very great in the provinces or among the lower classes, and it took about four more centuries before it became really the dominant religion of the people.

As in other countries, Buddhism in Japan made its conquests in part by easy compromises with the local cults. The huge bronze statue of the Buddha Vairocana, erected at Nara in the eighth century and still an object of veneration, is an outstand-ing example. It was erected with the explanation that Amate-rasu, the chief Shinto deity, and this Buddha are one and the same. This was soon followed by making room for the myriads of Shinto deities as emanations of the Eternal Buddha and as the Japanese forms of the various Buddhas and Bodhi-sattvas of Mahayana Buddhism. In the practical working out of this syncretism Buddhism became and remained for centuries the dominant intellectual and spiritual force in Japanese life, especially in the upper and more intelligent classes while the primitive Shinto cults continued their hold particularly in the villages and among the ignorant masses.

With the ninth century Buddhism made, as it were, a new start. This time the moving spirits were no longer foreigners but Japanese monks who had studied at the great monastic centers of China. Two men stand out especially, namely, Dengyo Daishi and Kobo Daishi, the founders of the Tendai and Shingon sects respectively. These two sects soon overshadowed the older six Nara sects and dominated Japan's cultural and religious life up to the twelfth century. While they were importations from China and as such represented a new wave of Chinese influence they nevertheless evolved along Japanese lines.

Tendai, like Tien Tai in China, stood for a comprehensive type of Buddhism making use of the voluminous Buddhist canon and stressing the many-sidedness of Truth. This broadmindedness made Tendai's great monastic center on Mt. Hiei near Kyoto the fountainhead of Buddhist studies and the mother of new Japanese sects. In this it ran true to form. There was, however, in Tendai a little more recognition of the practical in religion than in the Chinese Tien Tai. That is why, in spite of its broad-mindedness which sees truth as many-sided, many monks went forth from this sect to form new sects that stood for more specific things.

Shingon transmitted the "Mystery teachings" of the Chinese Chen Yen school but its founder in Japan, Kobo Daishi, was far too original to be a mere transmitter. In fact, he worked out a remarkable scheme of religious harmonization covering the whole gamut of East Asia religions arranged in an ascending scale. Thus as a practically minded Japanese he made room first of all for man's physical needs at the lowest end of the scale, then for moral values as expressed in Confucianism, for cosmic spiritual realities as stressed in Taoism, and for the various degrees of spiritual insight in the different schools of Buddhism, ending with his own Shingon, "True Word," as the crown of all. This highest he defined as a vision of the cosmic mystery in which one realizes that all things are divine. Not only has man at the center of his being the Buddha nature, but all phenomenal existence—when seen in its true nature—is a manifestation of the Eternal Buddha who transcends all concepts and is best expressed by mystic rites and symbols. This may seem like an impractical sort of mysticism but Kobo Daishi and other Buddhists of his day gave their teaching a very practical turn in true Japanese style and Buddhism soon clothed itself in the garments of man's worldly interests. As Kyoto, called *Heian,* "Peace and Tranquillity," grew into a great city it became studded with magnificent temples and halls in which elaborate rituals and ceremonies were conducted to impress the populace. Even emperors who supposedly are descendants of the Shinto Sun Deity, Amaterasu, became ardent Buddhists and added to its worldly splendors. Some became so enamored with it that they abdicated their throne to become monks and regarded it an honor to receive the title *Ho-O,* "King of the Law" (of Buddha). Buddhism's dominance of the intellectual life may be seen in the fact that the literature of these centuries was largely the product of monks who wrote in Chinese, the language of the sacred scriptures. And what there was of secular literature shows a strong Buddhist flavor. Through it all runs the note of the evanescence of life. Life is like the running stream ever changing in its seeming sameness, or like the cherry blossom soon to flutter to the ground.

While Buddhism thus dominated the life of the capital and the upper circles of society and gained in outward power and prestige, it did not gain correspondingly in inner resources as the centuries passed. In fact, it became too much like the effeminate culture of the circles in which it had its main following. However, when in the twelfth century the center of Japanese life was shifting to the crude but vigorous life in the provinces a change for the better came over Buddhism and it at last became the religion of the common people all over the country.

This change was marked by the rise of three new types of Buddhist sects which differed rather widely from each other but which had in common the characteristic that they were all thoroughly Japanese and not merely extensions of Chinese Buddhism.

First in time and extent of influence is Amida (Amitabha) Buddhism. This had been a minor strain in the older Tendai teachings but it now found expression in four distinctively Amida sects, two of which, namely the Jodo, "Pure Land" and the Jodo Shin, "True Pure Land" sects won a great following and have remained powerful influences down to the present. This Amida faith has much in common with the Pure Land school of Chinese Buddhism in that it, too, bases its teachings primarily on the Three Amitabha scriptures of the Chinese Canon making the worship of the Buddha of Eternal Life and Light and salvation in his Pure Land central. However, these Japanese sects and particularly the great Jodo Shin sect, make these teachings far more explicit and practical. Thus Shinran, the founder of the Jodo Shin sect, regarded man as above all a citizen of Eternity and held that he is made such not through profound philosophic insight or by lifting himself to that high plane through his own moral achievements but by simple trust and reliance on the mercy of the all-compassionate Amida Buddha. Let him utter in simple but sincere faith the prayer, *"Namu Amida Butsu,"* "Hail Amida Buddha" or "I worship Thee, Thou Buddha of Eternal Life and Light," and he shall be saved. Good works have their place, to be sure, but they are expressions of the believer's gratitude for Amida's gift of salvation rather than a way of earning one's salvation.

Man is, however, also a citizen of this world and must do his share in the normal life. Shinran therefore stressed "household" religion as more important than "temple" religion. Though reared as a Tendai monk himself, he gave up the monk's type of life, married, reared a family, and lived in other ways like a normal citizen of Japan. This naturally shocked the more conservative elements, but it explains why this sect became so popular and why in the modern world it holds its own.

A second type of Buddhism is Zen. This had its roots in the teachings of the Chinese Chan school and in some ways seems nearer the teachings of the Buddha, but it became thoroughly identified with Japan. When first introduced by Japanese monks who had studied in China it represented a new wave of Chinese influence bringing with it much of the Neo-Confucian philosophy and Sung art but it soon took on a decidedly Japanese coloring. It had its chief center at Kamakura, the capital of the Shoguns who were becoming the real rulers of Japan, and it attracted many of the more robust natures including military men. These men rather scorned the "Easy" and "Short Cut" way of salvation proclaimed by the Amida sects as a gospel for weaklings and as mere "wishful thinking." Zen teaches the doctrine of self-reliance and self-discipline though it would add that this is possible because man has the Buddha nature at the core of his true being. And in its deeper philosophy it holds that the Eternal Buddha or the Absolute so wholly transcends man's finite concepts that the truth can be best expressed in paradoxes rather than in straightforward propositions. But all this is for the serious student. The average Zen follower, especially among the military men, saw in it a way of self-discipline steeling one against the hard realities of life and making one fearless no matter what had to be faced.

The third main type of Japanese Buddhism which originated in the thirteenth century and which has played a big role ever since is Nichiren. It takes its name from its founder, Nichiren. In its main teachings it harks back to one phase of Tendai doctrine, especially as it centers around the Eternal Buddha of the famous Lotus Scripture which even Tendai, with all its regard for the whole voluminous canon, had selected as the greatest. In fact, Nichiren thought of himself as a restorer of the pure teachings of Dengyo Daishi, the Japanese founder of Tendai. These teachings, he felt, were being obscured by the new sects that were arising, namely, the Amida sects and the Zen. He denounced these, in most vigorous terms, as false teachings. But Nichiren was not simply an ardent Buddhist, he was even more a patriot. To him religion and patriotism were one. And he saw in the divisions of Buddhism the undermining of the state. As no man has two fathers, no nation two rulers, and as there is only one sun in the heavens, so there can be only one loyalty in religion. His loyalty was to the glorified Buddha of the Lotus Scripture known in Japan as *Hokkekyo*. Nichiren imparted to his followers his passion as well as his intolerance—without unfortunately, the restraints of his intelligence—so that this sect has become the one sect in Japan or in Buddhism as a whole which stands fanatically for its faith as alone true. In fact, the *"Namu Myoho Renge-kyo,"* "Hail to the Scripture of the Lotus of the Good Law" uttered incessantly by Nichiren's followers, especially at festivals, is really more a fanatical battle cry than an intelligent affirmation of faith, for most of these zealous followers worship their scripture blindly rather than read its contents.

These three major types of Buddhism gained in popularity and overshadowed the older sects. In the period of ceaseless wars and internecine strife through which Japan passed between the fourteenth and sixteenth centuries the Amida faith, with its message of salvation in Amida's Land of Bliss, naturally had its appeal. Zen as the soldier's religion and Nichiren's militant faith appealed for other reasons. There was at the same time a revival of the communal Shinto cults. This led to a renewed syncretism in which the Buddhas and Bodhi-sattvas were proclaimed as the originals and universals of which the Shinto deities were the peculiarly Japanese form. However most of the minor Shinto deities faded out of the picture and the vast majority of the people became adherents of one or another of these Buddhist sects. So great became Buddhism's hold on Japan that each of the major sects had extensive properties contributed by the faithful and some temples became veritable feudal states having their own "fighting monks" to defend their temporal possessions. An index of Buddhism's worldly power is seen in the fact that when in the sixteenth century the numerous feudal states were being brought under the military dictatorship of the Tokugawa Shoguns some of the last strongholds to be conquered were Buddhist monastic centers. Thus the religion of the gentle Buddha and his "other-worldly" Indian faith had become all too deeply "grounded" in sixteenth century Japan.

During the Tokugawa Shogunate (1600–1868) Buddhism more or less held its own. For reasons of state the shoguns encouraged Neo-Confucianism but Buddhism continued to be a sort of state religion. In fact, in connection with the suppression of Catholicism during most of that period all Japanese families were required to register themselves as adherents of one or another of the Buddhist sects, so that Buddhism's extensive ecclesiastical organization was used as an instrument of state.

With the abolition of the Shogunate in 1868 Buddhism ceased to hold this position and in other ways it suffered considerable loss of prestige. Certain properties were confiscated by the state and other similar measures were taken. This had, at first, an adverse effect on its fortunes. However, Buddhism has adjusted itself to the new situation. Its 70,000 temples, many of them of wonderful architecture, have usually been kept in good repair, and such new structures as the Tsukiji Hongwanji of Tokyo with the most modern equipment bear unmistakable evidence of Buddhism's continuing place in Japanese life. The destruction of Japan's larger cities in the war took a heavy toll of Buddhist structures and it remains to be seen how many of these will be rebuilt. Each of the major sects has its own educational institutions, publishes its own literature, and in other ways promotes its faith. It is true that in recent years Neo-Shinto has gained in importance but this is due far more to Buddhism's thirteen centuries of influence than to the beggarly elements of the older Shinto. State Shinto tended to dominate the scene in recent decades and the Japanese people seemed to follow its dictates as loyal citizens, but in spite of this they lived religiously and in matters of general culture far more on their Buddhist inheritance than on Shinto. Also, the more intelligent classes add to their general Japanese inheritance much from the religious and cultural heritage of the West. In fact, these latter share in and contribute to our growing common world culture even though this fact may have been obscured by the last world conflict.

CONTEMPORARY BUDDHISM AS A WHOLE

As one surveys the history and contemporary status of Buddhism as a whole one inevitably gets the impression that in many areas where Buddhism once flourished as the dominant faith its strength and influence have waned, if not wholly disappeared. Matthew Arnold's lines in "Dover Beach" seem peculiarly appropriate.

> The sea of faith
> Was once, too, at the full, and round earth's shore
> Lay like the folds of a bright girdle furled;
> But now I only hear
> Its melancholy, long, withdrawing roar,
> Retreating to the breath
> Of the night wind, down the vast edges drear
> And naked shingles of the world.

Two things should, however, be kept in mind which alter the picture a bit. One is, as we have stated in the preceding section, that Buddhism is still the dominant religion in southeast Asia and in Tibet, as well as strong and influential in Japan. The other is that even though it has waned as an outwardly organized and institutionalized power in many lands, in at least some of these it still lives on as a pervasive influence shaping men's attitudes toward life and their ultimate aspirations and hopes far more than appears on the surface of things. Religion is one of the last things to change and "what goes before becomes (or remains) master." In fact, in spite of all the changes taking place in the modern world some things remain painfully the same. This generation's suffering, brought on by the world conflict, seems to give renewed meaning to the Buddha's pessimistic view that man's life is predominantly an existence of suffering and blind struggle. And the Buddhist may quote further lines from Matthew Arnold's "Dover Beach":

Ah love, let us be true
To one another! for the world, which seems
To lie before us like a land of dreams,
So various, so beautiful, so new,
Hath really neither joy, nor love, nor light,
Nor certitude, nor peace, nor help for pain;
And we are here as on a darkling plain
Swept with confused alarms of struggle and flight,
Where ignorant armies clash by night.

This bitter fact about so much of life may lead many even in "this-worldly" China to follow the recent example of certain political leaders who, failing in their ambition to unify and strengthen their nation, retired to Buddhist monasteries to find consolation and peace of soul.

On the other hand, the very growth of race and national consciousness so marked in many Asiatic countries works to the interest of Buddhism, though for a very different reason. This new spirit carries with it an intense pride in a nation's spiritual heritage and while Buddhism has seldom stressed national interests as such it is recognized in all these lands as having made great contributions to the national heritage. Furthermore, Buddhism, especially in its Mahayana form, has a genius for adjusting itself to new situations and what has already taken place in Japan may be duplicated in other lands. In fact, there are a good many of the better educated and liberal leaders who claim that the very essence of true Buddhism is not a fixed or unchanging doctrine but rather a certain attitude of mind, a spirit of free inquiry and passion for truth. Thus they would make room for all that modern science has to offer and some would even claim that the Buddha, more than any other religious leader, laid the basis for the scientific approach. They would make room also for any insights offered by other religions, especially by Christianity, in so far as these promote man's practical interests. As for the more ultimate issues of life, these liberal Buddhists are rather reticent, as the Buddha had been. They hold, however, in a general way that man, in his true nature, is somehow akin to the Ultimate Source of all things, call this source what you may or conceive of its nature as suits your fancy or level of intelligence.

How successful either the older or the newer type of Buddhism will be in winning or holding the rising generation remains to be seen. It is quite likely that in the immediate future the next development in the Buddhist world will be along two main lines. One will be the acceleration of the present trend toward the secularization of the masses who in the past sought the "good things of life"—largely material blessings—through religion but who will look more and more to modern science and technology for such gifts. The other is the semi-Christianization of Buddhism itself, a trend already seen in the Amida sects of Japan. Which of these two trends will gain the mastery depends in no small measure upon modern Christianity's own vitality and depth of spirituality.

SELECTED BIBLIOGRAPHY

Sacred Books of the East. Vols. x, xi, xii, xvii, xix, xx, xxi, xxxv, xxxvi, xlix. Compiled by M. Winternitz. Oxford, 1910.
  Reissued under title: A Concise Dictionary of Eastern Religion.
Buddhism in Translations. By H. C. Warren. Cambridge, Mass, 1900.
Hinduism and Buddhism. By Sir Charles E. Eliot. London, 1921.
Buddhism, Its History and Literature. By T. W. Rhys-Davids. London, 1926.
The Life of Buddha as Legend and History. By E. J. Thomas. New York, 1927.
Buddhist Philosophy in India and Ceylon. By A. B. Keith. Oxford, 1923.
The Pilgrimage of Buddhism. By J. B. Pratt. New York, 1928.
Truth and Tradition in Chinese Buddhism. By K. L. Reichelt. Shanghai, China, 1927.
History of Japanese Religion. By M. Anesaki. London, 1930.
Japanese Buddhism. By Sir Charles E. Eliot. London, 1935.
Studies in Japanese Buddhism. By A. K. Reischauer. New York, 1917.

Shintoism

DANIEL CLARENCE HOLTOM

SHINTO draws attention to itself for various reasons. Two of them are of paramount interest. First, it calls for special scrutiny because it lies at the center of an intense nationalism. Japanese writers affirm almost unanimously that it is the main inspiration and manifestation of their national unity. For some two thousand years it has furnished an interwoven system of beliefs and ceremonies whereby the Japanese people have dramatized and supported the chief interests of their national life. In so far as Nipponism constitutes a threat to the peace of the rest of the world, Shinto must be subjected to a particular examination by all who would deal realistically with Japan. The conditions necessary either to the elimination or the redirection of some of its aspects must be made plain, for it is impossible to think of its continued existence in a world of intelligent and free men without important change. Just as Nazism and Fascism have called for special measures of control on the part of the democratic powers of the West because they are dangerous instruments of political and psychological unification, so also must Shinto be dealt with as the focus of an exclusive and in certain respects unassimilable Japanese nationalism.

The directive issued on December 15, 1945, by the allied headquarters in Tokyo disestablishing Shinto from its favored position as the state religion of Japan and the emperor's renunciation of divinity that followed two weeks later set up new conditions of control over some aspects of this situation, but not over all. The sponsorship and dissemination of Shinto by government agencies and officials were prohibited. State support, by taxation or otherwise, of the shrines and their priests was terminated. All propagation of Shinto in the public schools was banned. The official use of Shinto as the chief inspiration of militarism was debarred. Forced participation in ceremonies at the shrines as a test of patriotism was annulled. Most significant of all, the traditional claim that the emperor's right to rule was a supernatural, and hence inviolable, inheritance from the ancestral gods was abandoned in favor of the understanding that it was derived from the will of the people.

Over against all this, however, not a single shrine was closed. The organization of Shinto was changed but its continuity was unbroken. The operation of the cultus in fostering sentiments of loyalty and patriotism was shifted to a new basis but not destroyed. Emperor and people alike retained the right of participating as private citizens in the worship of the traditional deities. Domestic veneration before the god-shelves of the homes was untouched. Shinto was disqualified as a state religion but not abolished as a national faith.

Shinto further invites consideration as the only example on earth today of an ancient tribal faith that has survived the vicissitudes of the centuries and lived on into the present as the national religion of a contemporary state. As the thoughtful Westerner takes a long look backward across the years and contemplates the dim areas out of which his own communal life has come, he may perhaps at times be impressed with the fact that the religion of his remote forebears lies scattered through the centuries as broken fragments of myth and ceremony or concealed, often almost beyond recognition, as curious folklore and legend. At times he may try to construct a picture of what the religion of his European ancestors might have looked like if it could have lived until today. He may even be tempted to wonder if his own nation might not have been stronger and richer if the old streams out of the faraway past had never dried up. Yet, in spite of occasional endeavors to quicken nationalism by the revival of old tribal rituals, this reaching back for ancient religious forms must always remain for the Occidental essentially a work of the imagination and the emotions—either the antiquarian research of a few specialists or a passing nostalgia on the part of those who after all is said and done are obliged to let the dead past bury its dead.

It is to the Orient that the Westerner must turn if he wishes to find living suggestions of what his ancestral faith might have looked like had its unity never been destroyed. In Japan he will find surviving as vital social and political entities, institutions and ideas that are only ancestral memories in the Western story. In a real sense he can here look in on the life of contemporary ancestors. In Shinto he will have opportunity to attend ceremonies to tribal gods that were coeval with Wodin and Thor. We will return later to this subject of the unique continuity of Shinto. It is mentioned here because it is one of the special reasons why the study of the indigenous religion of Japan is both attractive and profitable to anyone interested in tracing the origins of human institutions and ideas.

Shinto is extraordinarily composite in its make-up. Confusing heterogeneity is one of its marked characteristics. Bewildering multiplicity and dissimilarity of parts have been fostered by the complications of the god-world with its "eight hundred myriads of deities"; by the changing fortunes of a long history that has been cut up by much internal strife; by the unique geographical position of Japan just off the coast of a culturally rich continent from which profoundly influential movements like Buddhism and Confucianism have found ready entrance along with a vast array of other forces; and finally by the remarkable persistence of local variation within Japan proper. Isolation of small parts behind mountain barriers and on hundreds of scattered islands has led to what amounts to almost a national genius for diversification. The much-vaunted modern unification of Japan has been achieved with great difficulty and, in many directions, is more formal and external than inner and spontaneous, accomplished as it is by police pressure and governmental fiat rather than by true growth from within. In religious affairs all this has found expression in a prolific sectarianism. Japanese Buddhism has branched out into fifty-six forms. Shinto has a multiplicity of sects and subsects, large and small, national and local, estimated at close to a hundred.

So much of a problem did this tendency toward particularism become even early in modern times that beginning with the 'eighties of the last century the government was obliged to take legal measures to keep the sect-making propensity of Shinto within control. In 1882 all institutions calling themselves by this name were divided by law into two classes, those of the national cult centering in the traditional shrines (*jinja,* "god-houses") and those of popular faith centering in a multitude of so-called "churches" (*kyokai,* "propaganda societies"). The meaning of what is here designated "shrine" should not be colored by the fact that this word is employed in English to indicate a small receptacle containing a sacred object, such as a box holding a relic, or a wayside image. The Japanese usage may be best understood as an attempt to distinguish all edifices and properties of the national religion, whether large or small, from the temples (*tera*) of Buddhism, and the churches of both Christianity and lay Shinto, as indicated above.

Thus there are two kinds of modern Shinto which must be carefully distinguished from each other. Failure to do so has often resulted in much confusion and misunderstanding. The one branch is commonly known as State Shinto, sometimes as Shrine Shinto, or again as National Shinto; the other as Sectarian Shinto, sometimes as Religious Shinto. Until disestablishment at the close of 1945, the state form was subject to national management through a Bureau of Shrines in the Department of Home Affairs; the sectarian form, through a Bureau of Religions in the Department of Education. This distinction in control furnished the government with a legal basis for its recurrent assertions that State Shinto was not a religion. That is to say, no matter how truly religious the actual content of ceremony and underlying belief might be, the shrines were not classified by law as religious institutions.

Thirteen sects of Shinto have been accorded government recognition as independent bodies. Subsects and lesser groups are given official control by management through the offices of recognized sects, particularly through one of the largest of the authorized bodies, the so-called Shinto Honkyoku or "Shinto Main Office," an agency which acts as a sort of clearing house for the mediation of government oversight to as yet unrecognized Shinto organizations.

A comparison of the two branches of Shinto would have to take note of certain points of difference as well as of some important likenesses. Sectarian Shinto depends entirely on the voluntary contributions of adherents and income from properties for maintenance; prior to disestablishment the state cult received a certain degree of support from national, prefectural, and local governments, supplemented by income from properties, shrine offerings, and fees from the sale of charms. Religious Shinto is not permitted to make use of the edifices of State Shinto as meeting places. The former has depended mostly on the influence of historical founders for organization and teaching, and each sect requires a minimum of doctrinal uniformity from its followers. The latter boasts that, since it is the spontaneous creation of the Japanese spirit, it is naturally without special founders and that it makes no creedal demands from participants in its ceremonies. Formal attendance and obeisance before the altars alone are required.

This is far from saying, however, that the national faith is devoid of underlying doctrinal presuppositions. It is the fact of inner religious beliefs that gives cogency and meaning to the rites: the immortality of the soul, guardianship over the nation by the eternal ancestral spirits, the efficacy of prayer and offering, the presence of the invisible gods at the shrines, community between the seen and the unseen worlds, a special manifestation of sacredness in the person of the emperor and his biological connections in unbroken line with the ancestral gods, and a divinely ordained national destiny. To fail to accept beliefs such as these is to fail in the primary obligations of loyalty to the state. And while it is true that the priests of the official cult were supposed to take no special measures for the indoctrination of worshipers, yet every school under the control of the national department of education was an agency for the propagation of Shinto doctrine. The deities worshiped in the two forms of Shinto are largely the same. As a matter of fact one will not be far from the truth if he thinks of State Shinto as just another sect, one that was singled out by the government for special protection and propaganda, thus legitimatizing a claim of the emperor on the allegiance of each and every subject.

Taken as a group the Shinto sects are the manifestation of the religious aspirations of the common people of Japan, frequently the creation of the peasantry. Here and there Buddhist and Confucian influences are apparent, but the fact that on the whole the movements have come up from the soil justifies their classification as Shinto. The faith-healing motive is prominent in some. As is to be expected the nationalistic emphasis is prominent throughout. The largest and most aggressive of the sects is Tenri Kyo, the "Teaching of Heavenly Reason," founded by a remarkable woman and proclaiming a teaching that suggests that of Christian Science. This church claims over five million followers and has sent its missionaries to practically all the countries bordering on the Pacific Ocean. The total number of adherents of the Shinto sects as a whole is something over seventeen million. No figures for the adherents of State Shinto are published, the assumption being that the total population is included. Priests of the state cult number sixteen thousand and shrines of all grades total one hundred and eleven thousand. Small rural shrines frequently have no resident priests. A group of such shrines is often managed as an administrative unit under one priest. On the other hand a large shrine may be served by an entire corps of priests.

The ensuing discussion is confined to the account of National or State Shinto. The pattern is largely that which existed prior to the disestablishment of 1945.

NATIONAL SHINTO

The most concise statement of the meaning of the system of ritual and belief that we now have before us is to be found in the word Shinto itself. The term is the Sino-Japanese reading of two ideograms, borrowed long ago from China, the first of which has frequently been rendered into English by the word "gods" and the second by "way." Thus Shinto has often been called "The Way of the Gods." The pure Japanese reading of the original is *Kami no Michi* (*kami*, "gods"; *michi*, "way" or "road"; *no*, the genitive particle). But this descriptive title, simple and explicit as it seems on the surface, covers a multitude of obscurities. As a "Way," the underlying idea of Shinto is undoubtedly a reflection of the *Tao* of Taoism. The *Tao* of the latter and the *To* of Shinto are written with the same ideogram. The first studies of Shinto made on Japanese soil were by Chinese scholars who were well versed in Taoism. As everyone familiar with the thought of China knows well, the meaning of the *Tao* or "The Way" cannot be written off with a few words of English. It is the Great Principle with which everything in the universe should be in accord. Mencius said that it was like a big road which every man should follow. Man finds virtue and happiness by walking in it. This Great Principle, unfathomable and unknowable, self-existent and eternal, is the unseen pattern of all things in the visible world. It manifests itself as the manifold systems of lesser principles that guide human action and thinking into true and proper forms. With this background it is easy to see that Shinto means the principles of right belief and ritual relating to *Kami*. But what does *kami* mean?

At this point we encounter even more serious difficulties. The truth is that Japanese authorities themselves do not know what *kami* means. The great Motoori—certainly one of the most sagacious scholars that Japan has ever produced—once wrote, "I do not yet understand the meaning of *kami*." In a manner suggestive of the story of the wise men of Ind and the elephant, some Japanese writers have declared that the real meaning of *kami* is "superior being," especially superior men, hence Shinto becomes primarily an ancestor worship culminating in the adoration of the emperor as a living god; others have insisted that *kami* signifies "mysterious being," making Shinto fundamentally a belief in spirits and their worship, in other words, animism; others, that the term sets forth an ancient and persistent tendency toward panpsychism on the part of the Japanese people and that this has made Shinto essentially a pantheism. The interpretations are many and it is sometimes difficult to reconcile the one with the other.

Behind this wide diversity of opinion lies a strange complexity in the nature of the objects that are called *kami*. Nowhere is this pointed out more vividly than in a remarkable passage from the eighteenth century scholar, Motoori, whose modest disavowal of ability to understand the meaning of *kami* has just been mentioned. Immediately following his protestation of ignorance, Motoori says:

"Speaking in general, *kami* signifies in the first place the deities of heaven and earth that appear in the ancient records and also the spirits worshiped at the shrines.

"It seems hardly necessary to add that it also includes human beings. It also includes such objects as birds, beasts, trees, plants, seas, mountains, and so forth. In ancient usage, anything whatsoever which was outside the ordinary, which possessed superior power or which was awe-inspiring was called *kami*. Eminence here does not refer to the superiority of nobility, goodness or meritorious deeds. Evil and mysterious things, if they are extraordinary and dreadful, are called *kami*.

"It is also evident that among human beings who are called *kami* the successive generations of sacred emperors are all included. The fact that emperors are called 'distant *kami*' is because from the point of view of common people they are far-separated, majestic and worthy of reverence. In a lesser degree we also find, in the present as well as in ancient times, human beings who are *kami*. . . .

"Furthermore, among things which are not human, the thunder is always called 'sounding-*kami*.' Such things as dragons, the echo, and foxes, inasmuch as they attract attention, are wonderful and awe-inspiring, are also *kami*. In popular belief the echo is called a mountain goblin. . . .

"In the *Nihongi* and the *Manyoshu* the tiger and the wolf are also spoken of as *kami*. Again, there are the cases in which peaches were given the name, August-Thing-Great-*Kamu*-Fruit, and a necklace was called August-Storehouse-shelf-*Kami*. There are further instances in which rocks, stumps of trees and leaves of plants spoke audibly. These were all *kami*. There are again numerous places in which seas and mountains are called *kami*. This does not have reference to the spirit of the mountain or the sea, but *kami* is here used directly of the particular mountain or sea. This is because they were exceedingly awe-inspiring." [1]

Motoori's analysis of the remarkable variety of objects included in the meaning of *kami* could be extended and illustrated at considerable length from other sources. What has just been

[1] Motoori, Toyokai (ed.), *Motoori Norinaga Zenshu* ("Complete Works of Motoori Norinaga"), Vol. I, pp. 150–152; Tokyo, 1901.

given must suffice for present purposes. It seems plain that *kami* cannot be translated into English with any degree of completeness by the word "god" or even by the word "deity." Shinto must be something other than merely the "Way of the Gods."

A term that comprehends within its wide array of meaning: fearful animals like the wolf, the tiger, the serpent, and the dragon; mysterious and awe-inspiring natural phenomena like the echo, the thunder, mountains, seas, the flowing water of rivers and springs, plants, and in particular, trees; old mirrors, swords, spears and beads that were full of wonder-working force; the magic of the phallus and the vulva (represented in Motoori's account by the peach); evil and demonic agencies that brought famine and pestilence from out of the dark lower world; spirits; the souls of the dead; majestic, powerful, or wise personages among living men; and a great host of legitimate gods and goddesses—such a term is obviously far from being exhausted when rendered by "gods." It includes gods and much more.

As a matter of fact the very complexity of the meaning of *kami* is the key to its understanding. Had Motoori written today instead of one hundred and fifty years ago he probably would have easily climaxed his remarkable insight by the discovery of the meaning of *kami,* that is, its psychological origin. The guiding hands of anthropology and the history of religions, made sensitive and sure by the keen insights of recent decades of world-wide research, would have opened to him the door. Indeed, when he declared that anything whatsoever which was outside of the ordinary, which possessed superior power, or which was awe-inspiring was called *kami,* and again that evil and mysterious things, if they were extraordinary and dreadful, were all *kami*—when he had come thus far he was almost through the door. For in these words Motoori had practically defined *mana,* the term which modern anthroplogy has borrowed from the Melanesians and established as the scientific name for the conception of occult force emanating from whatever preliterate man sensed as awesome, weird, inspiring demonic dread, overpowering with fascination, manifesting strange and incomprehensible power, thrilling with the disclosure of majesty, or saturated with *mysterium tremendum.*

This is a suggestion of the age-old psychology that called the Japanese term *kami* into existence. Here again, as in many other cases, we are reminded that our difficulty in accounting for "things Japanese" lies in no small measure in our failure to travel sufficiently far back along the historical stream to enable us to tap the primitive reservoir wherein the true explanation lies concealed. *Kami,* like *mana,* is fundamentally a word that distinguishes between a familiar, "profane" world of everyday things and a "holy" or "sacred" world of special events and personages believed to be filled with occult, mysterious force, and under certain conditions with benevolence. A *kami*-object is a holy or a sacred object; a *kami*-person is a holy or a sacred person. Shinto, properly understood, is the Way of the Holy or the Way of the Sacred. In correct Shinto usage a deity is not properly designated when merely called *kami.* Regard for the primitive matrix out of which gods and goddesses have been born requires the prefixing of a descriptive phrase that indicates some primary function or outstanding characteristic, thus telling what kind of "sacredness" is involved. The sun goddess is the "Heaven-shining Great *Kami,*" the storm god is the "Great Impetuous Male *Kami,*" and so on throughout the entire pantheon.

In saying that Shinto means the Way of the Holy, there is involved the further observation that the kind of religious experience discovered in the examination of the meaning of *kami* (and the notable array of similar terms that have been identified in other cultures) is undoubtedly more significant for the evolution of real value in human society than the idea of gods and goddesses. The latter come and go in a cycle of life and death that parallels the mortality of man himself, but without a sacred world to challenge his utmost loyalty man would cease to be truly man. We may accept the opinion of Söderblom when he says: "Holiness is the great word in religion; it is even more essential than the notion of God. Real religion may exist without a definite conception of divinity, but there is no real religion without a distinction between holy and profane." [2]

While we may admit that this statement sets forth a profound truth, we must at the same time be prepared to recognize that the grounds on which the attribute of holiness, or *kami*-nature, is assigned to various significant events in Japanese experience vary greatly with the changing cultural levels of national and individual development. At the earliest level it is an unreflected primitive emotion, a dread and awe in the presence of mystery and power. Over against this the modern educated Japanese finds nothing of the feeling of the "holy" in the fear of the wolf or the magical fertility of the phallus. He finds his sacred world in the values of moral living. He discovers his holy, *kami*-relationships in the highest interests and supreme personages of the national life, in the deep emotions that they call forth, and in his participation in the powerful sentiments and habits that are associated with tried and true tradition.

Nevertheless the primitive survives as a powerful influence even in the present and mingles strangely with the new in shaping ideas and practices that are associated with the sacred. Thus it comes to pass that composite and often incongruous elements of belief and feeling enter into the foundations upon which the structure of the sacred is reared. We may list some of the most important of these without any special attempt at order, since they are pretty well jumbled in the Japanese experience itself: the magical efficacy of sundry personal and household charms, dispensed by the Shinto shrines as a major business; the emanation of mysterious power from the persons of the great and the mighty—it is by the "virtue" of the emperor, that is by his *mana,* that the armies of Japan win victory in battle; the oversight of human affairs, both national and personal, by the spirits of the dead; the transcendent, superrational authority of the "unbroken line" of emperors; the absolute obedience of subjects to this divine authority; a peerless national structure; a superior race, innately endowed by the gods with unique psychological qualities; the conviction of a great national destiny—

[2] "The Idea of the Holy," *Hasting's Encyclopaedia of Religion and Ethics,* Vol. 6, p. 731.

the duty to spread the glory of Japan throughout the world and thereby "save the world from injustice and wrong"; and—prior to surrender in World War II—a sacred land that had never once been invaded by a foreign foe and a people who had never been defeated in war and had never endured a foreign insult. The picture would not be fairly drawn without the suggestion of the presence of higher and more universal forces that feed the sacred fire. The enumeration of these would have to include: the elation of participation in approved sentiments and habits; emotional expansion arising out of dedications to the highest interests of the common life; the thrill of communion in great ceremonies; conviction of the supreme worth of causes that demand obedience to the death; pride in racial achievement; and, finally, the sense of majesty and exaltation in the presence of the great personages and events of the national life and in the contemplation of the peerless character of the all-powerful state.

These are some of the elements that have intensified the conviction on the part of the Japanese people that a sacred quality inheres in their personal and national experiences. It is the presence of sentiments, emotions, and beliefs such as those just named that have made Shinto the Way of the Holy. Not all of these elements of Shinto as a national religion can be reconciled with one another; some of them cannot be accorded either rational or ethical justification for continued existence in a world of universally valid truth; some are dangerous for the maintenance of peace among nations. They point to a major problem in the Far East, namely, the direction and progressive refinement of the meaning of the sacred to the Japanese people.

THE DEVELOPMENT OF SHINTO

While the general significance of *kami* is as outlined above, the specific content which it enfolds will vary from cultural level to cultural level and from age to age. To be understood it must be examined against the background of its total historical evolution. No contemporary scholar has done more to contribute to our knowledge of Japanese religion in this connection than Dr. Genchi Kato, for many years the professor of Shinto in the Imperial University of Tokyo. A summarized statement of his analysis follows.

Considered in its broadest historical sweep there are three main cultural stages in the evolution of Shinto. There is, in the first place, the stage of primitive nature worship or polydemonism; secondly, the stage of higher nature worship or sheer polytheism; and thirdly, Shinto as an advanced cultural religion wherein beliefs and practices relating to *kami*-objects have come under the influence of ethical and intellectual influences of a high order. It is at this last named stage that Shinto shows its most definite political pattern.

The earliest discernible stage of Japanese recognition of the existence of an overhead *kami*-world takes us back to remote beginnings at a preanimistic level in which certain objects of nature such as fire, wind, sun, moon, rivers, mountains, and trees are immediately, and in and of themselves, regarded as endowed with marvelous power. Baffling the understanding by their mystery, and constituting the source of sharply registered emotions of wonder and awe, they are *kami*. This is not personification, nor is it belief in controlling spirits modeled on the idea of the human soul. It is primitive animatism. To illustrate: there is at this stage no distinction between fire and a god of fire or between the wind and a god of the wind. Wind and fire are each immediately experienced as *kami*. The peak of Mount Fuji is itself the manifestation of a mighty *kami*-power that guards the land.

At still an early period of development—but one that has not as yet passed beyond the stage of primitive nature worship—this simple naturism grows into a complicated polydemonism which registers a belief in the existence of an uncounted host of invisible superhuman beings dwelling in and controlling the visible objects of nature. In this state the *kami*-idea has not yet advanced to that of true gods and goddesses. The *kami* are mere spirits, good and bad, often the rather indefinitely personified powers that animate the manifold objects of the natural world. This is the genuinely animistic stage of early Japanese belief. It finds expression in an unbelievably complicated nature worship, wherein everything from clod to comet is believed to be controlled by its resident spirit.

In the second stage of development this extraordinary polytheistic tendency pours forth in a vast array of authentic gods and goddesses. *Kami* may now be translated by "deity" in the strict sense. These superhuman beings are regarded by their worshipers as possessing sex and procreating offspring like human beings, as engaged in manlike occupations, and as entering into various mutually beneficial relations with men, even to bargaining like sharp tradesmen for good deals in rewards and offerings.

In the third stage of evolution we reach the level of a higher cultural religion and, in spite of the dominance of nationalistic patterns, certain tendencies toward universalism both in ethics and philosophy now manifest themselves. In arriving at this result the natural and independent growth of intelligence and moral perspective in the Japanese people is enriched by liberal borrowings from Buddhism and Confucianism. In a very real sense the former gave Shinto a philosophy; the latter, an ethic. Before this Shinto was mainly ritual, mythology, and magic. In this process of the gradual refinement of cruder and more irrational mytholgical elements into higher manifestations, various local guardian spirits and *kami* of diverse origin are amalgamated into single objects of worship, a tendency for lesser *kami* to be absorbed into greater *kami* appears, and under the influence of more advanced ethical and philosophical insights sheer polytheism tends to pass into pantheism.

Examples of the character of these new ethical attainments appear in many directions, nowhere perhaps more definitely than in the symbolical interpretations of the three sacred objects of the imperial regalia that now arise. An outstanding example of that direct survival in Japanese affairs of primitive folkways, to which attention has already been drawn, is to be found in the preservation out of an unknown past of an ancient mirror, a mysterious sword, and a necklace of stone beads (*magatama*) as the sign and seal of imperial authority. Their custody is vested in the emperor himself and they are handed on from sovereign to sovereign as the inalienable certification of the right to rule. In their original meaning they were mighty fetishes that carried the *mana* of the kingship across the dangerous break of death. They were all *kami* and are so named in the early Shinto literature. Under the influence of widening ethical horizons they have become the symbols of the chief virtues of the upright Japanese. The mirror stands for wisdom, the beads for benevolence, and the sword for courage. Signs of this moral evolution appear in other directions. There is space here for only one additional example. The import of the transition from the earlier naturism to the enlightenment of the new culture religion may be gauged by the vastness of the distance that lies between an old naïve regard for the efficacy of phallic rites and even human sacrifice and the sublime insight of the thirteenth century "Shinto Pentateuch" when it declares: "The gods desire not material gifts, but offerings of uprightness and sincerity."

These three cultural levels do not represent hard and fast chronological divisions. They merge into one another and, like the contacts of land and sea along an irregular coast, they interpenetrate to deep distances. The old survives in the new; higher insight is discernible here and there in the old, like the sparkle of gold in the sand. Even today if one leaves behind him the sophisticated urban areas and pushes into the more simple rural byways, he will discover much evidence of the survival into the present of an old nature worship with its accompaniments of belief in spirits, fetishism, and even phallicism.

Dr. Kato whose outline, supplemented when deemed necessary by explanations of our own, has just been followed is of the opinion that ancestor worship appeared early in the national story and independently of Chinese influence. Not only were exalted personages who possessed extraordinary power and courage, or unwonted skill and intelligence, or majestic mien, regarded as living *kami,* but evidence is found for the existence of genuine ancestor worship as early as the reigns of Jimmu Tenno and Sujin Tenno. And while it is evident that Dr. Kato himself does not accept the governmentally prescribed chronology which places the accession to the throne of the former of these rulers at 660 B.C. and assigns to the latter an impossible reign of sixty-eight years beginning at 97 B.C., yet his conclusions would give to Japanese ancestor worship an age of approximately two thousand years. Japan is called "a classical land of necrolatry or the worship of the spirits of the dead and of ancestor worship."

The insistence on a central core of ancestor worship running through Shinto from early times to the present is thoroughly typical of the vast majority of Japanese interpreters. The position which they attempt to maintain calls for a good deal of qualification and correction. It was probably not until after the influence of Confucianism had made itself felt beginning with the opening of the fifth century of the Christian era that genuine ancestor worship appeared on the Japanese scene. By the time the rituals of Shinto were committed to writing in the tenth century it is sufficiently definite to constitute an observable phase of the national religion, but even then relatively inconspicuous as compared with the still dominant worship of nature gods. It is plain that Shinto did not grow out of ancestor worship. If the indications of origin which we have already examined are accepted, then Shinto has its beginnings in the emotionally founded, primitive belief that occult force or *kami*-power emanates from mysterious objects of nature as well as from the personages of exceptional men. This immediately leads to the establishment of a precautionary religious etiquette or taboo in dealing with power-wielding men, and the necessity for this kind of procedure continues after their death, is, indeed, augmented by the passage of the soul into the mysterious spirit world. This may be the seed of ancestor worship, but it is far from being the grown plant. Moreover the great deities with whom we become acquainted in the pages of the Kojiki (A.D. 712), the oldest extant historical writing of the Japanese people, are nature forces. They are the personifications of aspects of earth, sky, sun, moon, and storm, or mysterious and benevolent agencies that preside over growth and food. The sun goddess of Ise is, it is true, magnified as the "great ancestress" of the emperor, and for a Japanese subject openly to avow disbelief in this doctrine was once treason; but no amount of official coercion can make the sun goddess an authentic ancestor in the records of real historical science. So also for a multitude of other deities included in both state and family genealogies. So-called Japanese ancestor worship is largely nationalistic rationalization on a grand scale.

We may return to the summary of Dr. Kato's studies long enough to permit him to tell us how Shinto attains its highest fulfillment under the influence of political patterns. In this matter he writes:

"Shinto has culminated in Mikadoism or the worship of the Mikado or Japanese Emperor as a divinity, during his lifetime as well as after his death. . . . Herein lies, even at the present day, in my opinion, the essence or life of Shinto, inseparably connected with the national ideals of the Japanese people. Japanese patriotism or loyalty, as you might call it, really is not simple patriotism or loyalty as understood in the ordinary sense of the word, that is in the mere ethical sense of the term. It is more—it is the lofty self-denying enthusiastic sentiment of the Japanese people towards their august Ruler, believed to be something divine, rendering them capable of offering up anything and everything, all dearest to them, of their own free will; of sacrificing not only their wealth and property, but their own life itself, for the sake of their divinely gracious sovereign. . . . All this is nothing but the actual manifestation of the religious consciousness of the Japanese people."[3]

The religious basis of authority in the Japanese state is herein set forth without reservation. It is not easy to see how the great gulf by which all this is separated from religious and moral universalism can be bridged over. We must postpone final appraisal until we get certain other matters before us.

If we wish to supplement the above account of cultural stages with more exact chronological references, we find ourselves again resorting to the idea of three main periods. The first is that of Old Shinto, dating from remote origins in the indefinite mythological twilight of two thousand years ago and ending with the beginning of Buddhist ascendancy at the opening of

[3] Genchi Kato, *A Study of Shinto: The Religion of the Japanese Nation,* pp. 206–207; Tokyo, 1926.

the ninth century of the Christian era. The first and second of the cultural phases which we have already noted, while not limited to these chronological boundaries, have nevertheless left their clearest traces within them.

The second period extends from the beginning of the ninth century to the middle of the nineteenth. For more than a thousand years now Shinto goes to school to Buddhism, or to use what is perhaps a more apt figure, is married to it. A so-called "Two-sided Shinto"—Ryobu Shinto—part Buddhism and part the old religion of the land, is gradually furnished with doctrinal coordination by the comprehensive device of making Shinto deities the avatars of original Buddhist divinities. Thus the sun goddess of Ise is made to stand as the temporal manifestation of the cosmic Buddha—the Maha-Vairo-cana—the transcendent, nonobservable source of all things. So also, in graded scale and emphasis, for all the other national deities. This was a lesson in self-interpretation that Shinto was never to forget. In spite of all the changes that were to come in the following centuries, Shinto, whenever pressed for a philosophical account of herself, has always fallen back on the affirmation of an essential unity beneath her polytheism. The many gods and goddesses are merely the different modes of operation of the Great Life of the Universe.

At the same time Buddhist control over the ceremonies and properties of the shrines was steadily extended. Generations of Buddhist priests, some of them men of extraordinary ability, presided over the fortunes of Shinto. Likewise powerful influences were received from Confucianism, especially in the latter part of the period. Thus the inner quality of Shinto improved notably in the manifestation of higher ethical consciousness and philosophical worthiness, notwithstanding the persistent survival of magic and polytheistic confusion.

The final period extends from the overthrow of the Tokugawa Shogunate and the restoration of direct imperial rule in 1868 to the present. This is preeminently the period of *saisei itchi*, "the oneness of national ceremonies and government" or the union of church and state. Shinto was made the official religion of Japan and, the oft-repeated governmental assertions to the contrary notwithstanding, never once relinquished this favored position until forced to do so after Japan's defeat in the Second World War. At the same time all connections with Buddhism, in so far as they were within the control of official regulation, were cut and this great faith was thrown out to depend henceforth entirely on the devotion of adherents for support and propagation. In private realms, however, it is a noteworthy fact that the ingrained practices of century-long association between Buddhism and Shinto have persisted in spite of all attempts to pry the two apart and millions of Japanese find it possible to accept both without feelings of inconsistency. They like to say that Shinto looks after their religious needs in this world while Buddhism provides for the world-to-come.

DISTINCTIVE CHARACTERISTICS OF SHINTO

We have thus far noted the fact of the composite character of Shinto that comes to such clear expression in the distinction that must be made between the state cult and sectarian movements, and have examined the underlying nature of Shinto revealed in the meaning of *kami*. To this has been added an indication of the major cultural phases and chronological periods through which the national religion of Japan has passed. In our discussion thus far we have acted on the belief that the most important gateway to the understanding of what Shinto is opens from the side of its own conception of nature and mission, and that this aspect of the scene comes to clearest outline in statements made by Japanese writers who have explored by personal faith and special knowledge the inner resources of their national religion. In fact such men, operating on the principle that an outsider sees only the outside, have never been over-diffident about protesting that they alone know what Shinto really is. Reserving the right to qualify their statements by our own observations when necessary, it may be worth something to our study if in the paragraphs that immediately follow, we continue to let some of these men speak for themselves even though they are unnamed.

The next matter, then, concerns the special characteristics

which Shinto manifests when compared with other living religions. These are commonly asserted to be the creation of the inner genius of the Japanese people which supposedly rests ultimately on the possession of peculiar psychological qualities. First is a unique *continuity*. It is true that other vital religions of today have century-old continuity of a sort and that they have grown out of roots that are deep in the soil of the past. Shinto is not guilty of the absurdity of claiming that it alone has a history. It does assert however that it has a unique history and that this appears in the possession of an inseparable and unbroken identity with the national life extending across two thousand years. A few comparisons make this plain. The national religions of ancient Greece and Rome ceased to exist along with the overthrow of the states which they served. They are dead religions, moving only as ghostlike memories and shadows in the background of the Christianity that has displaced them. It is the Vatican that stands as the symbol of life and power of religion in Rome today, not the ruins of the temples of Jupiter and Apollo. Not one of the old folk religions of Europe, faiths that once strengthened the purposes of brave warriors and enriched with colorful ceremonies the assemblies of mighty tribes, has survived into the present. It is true, again, that the Jewish people, though dispersed to the four quarters of the earth, still cling tenaciously to an ancient Judaism. But the Jewish state is only a memory of the past. A Jewish people exists but not an independent Jewish nation, and the historical religion of the Jews lives on not as a national faith but as a racial ceremonial and doctrine.

When we turn our attention to the Far East and consider the story of China, the same kind of picture comes into focus. Taoism may be called the racial religion of China, but no one would claim that the course of Taoism lies along the same road as that of the State Shinto of Japan with its headship in one unbroken dynasty of emperors and its continuous existence for two thousand years as the national religion of one and the same people. Taoism bears the scars of the predilection of the Chinese people for revolutionary upheaval and dynastic change. State Shinto has existed continuously throughout all of Japanese history as the national religion of one people who have always had over them a single unchanging dynasty of emperors. Nowhere on earth today, then, can we find another living national religion which like Japanese Shinto has come down in unbroken line out of a remote past as the sign and seal of the unity of a single people.

Not only does Shinto possess a unique continuity; it also manifests a peerless *inner quality.* "The fundamental character of the Japanese national structure lies in the fact that authority is vested not in a mere man but in a god revealed as man, namely, in a divine emperor." [4]

It is the special function of Shinto to preserve and protect this divine authority as the essence of the state religion of Japan. In thus speaking of Shinto as the state religion of Japan there is an important distinction from so-called "established" religion as it has existed in European history that must be noted with special care. State religion in Europe for the past many centuries has meant Christianity. This Christianity is really a foreign religion which invaded Europe out of Judea. It was never indigenous to any country of Europe proper. It was a transplanted affair that had to be legitimatized by adoption. In contrast with this, State Shinto is the blood offspring of the Japanese people. It is and always has been peculiarily Japanese. This national fidelity to essence cannot be reproduced the world over. This is the unique inner quality of Shinto.

A third special characteristic of the national cult appears in the existence of a deceptive *duality* of ethical or ceremonial outwardness and religious inwardness. A ritualistic garb, which is all that many observers—even Japanese—are able to see, covers a body of genuine religion. This fact has led to much confusion and calls for careful consideration. It has furnished the grounds on which Japanese civil authorities have repeatedly proclaimed that State Shinto is not a religion. Many Japanese have repeated this misunderstanding and it has found constant reiteration in non-Japanese expositions.

There are several reasons for the appearance of this error. The first is theological. It exists in the fact that State Shinto

[4] Genchi Kato.

is an anthropocentric religion emphasizing the unity of gods and men. The Japanese emperor is a god-man; and regardless of actual origins the great deities of Shinto are considered to be the spirits of deified men. Over against this a religion like Christianity which emphasizes the vast separation of God and man is theocentric. God is "the absolutely other." When attention is focused solely on the man-centered manifestations of the national faith it is easy to conclude that State Shinto is a kind of humanism, or the Way of the Emperor, and that it is essentially Japanese politics, or national ethics, or a state ceremonial. Strangely enough, Japanese apologists, sometimes of the most narrow and chauvinistic type, and non-Japanese theologians, often Christian missionary propagandists with the broadest international interests, have here discovered common ground. The former have found it politically expedient to insist that State Shinto is purely an affair of patriotic ritual; the latter, conditioned by Christian standards, have been unable to see religion in anything that did not conform to preconceived type. Thus, the members of this extraordinary team have united in substituting appearance for essence and in declaring to the world that the external ceremonial of Shinto is the whole thing.

Another reason for the failure to see in Shinto more than the outward wrappings of an inner reality lies in the difficulty of according full religious significance to a system that does not transcend national barriers. Full weight is not given the fact that the state cult, though admittedly national in scope, is nevertheless a religion. The anthropocentric deities of Shinto do not transcend the boundaries of a single nation. Over against this, both Christianity and Buddhism, when it comes to the consideration of the interests and advantages of particular states, are individualistic and universal. Jesus taught the idea of the vast separation of God and man and escaped from the problem of the relation of church and state by saying that the things of Caesar should be rendered unto Caesar and the things of God unto God. Buddha threw away his position as a prince of this world and became a mere beggar. Both proclaimed that religion transcends the state. In strict contrast with this, the personnel of the Shinto god-world and the interests which State Shinto promotes are thoroughly Japanese. But on this account Shinto does not cease to be a religion. There are other kinds of religion than the personal and universal varieties, and Shinto is one of them. It is a state religion and a national religion. It reveals a defect in one's knowledge of the science of religion to insist that only a world religion can be genuine religion.

Still another cause of the appearance of the mistaken idea that State Shinto is not a religion is to be seen in the fact that it is in essence this-worldly rather than other-worldly. There is a view abroad that only an other-worldly religion is authentic. According to this conception of things the main business of religion is to teach doctrines of heaven and hell and the fate of the soul beyond the grave. Over against this Shinto has as its chief object the promotion of practical, this-worldly affairs like the prosperity of the imperial throne and the welfare of subjects. For this reason it has been pronounced nonreligious, and partly on this account the idea has arisen that it is nothing more than national morality and state ceremony. This again shows ignorance of the science of religion. The experienced student of human affairs knows that the history of religions shows some that are predominantly this-worldly and others that are strongly other-worldly, with various combinations and stresses of these two forms lying in between. State Shinto is no less a religion for being this-worldly. Indeed, there are grounds for believing that the original teachings of Jesus and Buddha, with all their indifference to the destiny of particular states, were very much concerned with the fate of individual men in this world. From such a point of view there is about as much reason for saying that primary Buddhism and Christianity were not religions as there is for saying the same thing about Shinto. To repeat, the science of religion does not permit us to classify State Shinto outside the religious field just because it is mainly concerned with the earthly welfare of the Japanese people and the preservation of the imperial throne.

To these observations concerning Shinto's own conception of nature and mission, for which we are much indebted to Japanese writers, a further word must be added. The most apparent, and at the same time the most disguised, reason for the emergence of the declaration that State Shinto is merely civil ceremony and not religion is political. The subtle exigencies of statecraft have required it. The story behind all this is a long one and can only be indicated in broadest outline here. Japan's two hundred and fifty years of voluntary seclusion during the Tokugawa Shogunate had been inspired largely by a fear of Christianity and when, in the middle of the nineteenth century, she came once more face to face with the nations of the West for better or for worse, she found herself confronted with a tremendous dilemma growing out of the same fear. On the one hand, she knew, in spite of the warnings of her isolationists, that she must arm herself with the skill and knowledge of the West or else go down before it. On the other, she was convinced that the threatened flood from the great outside world would submerge her own national soul forever unless it were buoyed up by the preservation of continuity with her own past. At the center of Western civilization was a Christianity that was feared as the instrument of the dissolution of a national cohesion that had already been strained almost to the breaking point by recent feudal strife. At the center of the traditional national culture was Shinto. The one taught the existence of a universal Father-God who laid on the consciences of his children the duty of a transcendent loyalty that could repudiate even the state and its claims. The other taught the supreme obligation of absolute obedience to a God-Emperor which nothing either in heaven or on earth could be permitted to contravene. The two had in them the promise of irreconcilable conflict. When Japanese statesmen met with the representatives of Western powers for the introductory negotiations, the first decision of the former was in favor of continuing the strict ban against Christianity which had been used to close the story of the earlier Roman Catholic missions. From the Japanese side announcement was made that their state was founded on the Shinto teaching of the divinity of the emperor, that Christianity by its repudiation of this teaching undermined the imperial throne, and that Japan had no choice other than to resist the incoming of Christianity as it would the invasion of a foreign army. It soon became clear however that in actual outward practice some other choice had to be made. Shinto and Christianity, the old and the new, nationalism and universalism, foreign and national, could not be permitted to come to an open clash. If they did, Japan's chances of making favorable deals with the Western powers in her hour of weakness were perhaps irreparably harmed. She quickly saw that her safest play in creating favorable sentiment in foreign lands was to appear as a "modern nation" and that this involved judicious dissemination abroad of the idea that the Japanese people enjoyed full freedom in religious matters. At the same time the special position of Shinto could not be abandoned. Thus, from the point of view of the Japanese authorities the only possible solution of the dilemma lay in the declaration that the national cult was not a religion. The propagation of Christianity within their land had to be risked, but this risk could be taken as long as it was possible to lay on all subjects, regardless of their other religious affiliations, the legal and patriotic duty of participation in the beliefs and rites of State Shinto. That the solution was purely formal has never given too much trouble to Japanese bureaucratic psychology, steeped as it is in conventionality and accustomed to the establishment of truth by governmental proclamation.

This nationalistic claim of Shinto was steadily enlarged with the passing years and extended to whatever territories came under the sway of Japanese arms. Thus Formosa, Korea, and later Manchuria, and the islands of the central Pacific were brought within the unifying spell of the proper worship of the gods. Meanwhile foreign nations have been constantly informed that Japan enjoys "absolute freedom of religious belief," and minority groups within the nation have been held strictly accountable for obeisance before the altars of the national gods as the certification of their acceptance of the right to rule on the part of the members of the imperial dynasty and their bureaucratic and military representatives.

The question has sometimes been debated as to whether State Shinto possesses a sacred scripture. The answer is a matter of definition. If this means a closed canon of books that are regarded as inspired and authoritative for faith to the exclusion of all other writings, then a sacred scripture does not exist. If it means an open and growing national literature in which the roots of patriotic fervor and religious conviction are nourished, then Shinto does possess a sacred scripture. This applies especially to the Kojiki or "Chronicle of Ancient Events" (A.D. 712), the Nihongi or "Chronicles of Japan" (A.D. 720), the Kogoshui or "Gleanings from Ancient Stories" (A.D. 806), the Engi Shiki or "Ceremonies of the Engi Era (A.D. 927), and in particular to the *norito* or rituals of the last mentioned writing. To these should be added the rescripts of successive generations of emperors and the rituals published by the department of home affairs for contemporary Shinto ceremonies.

An important nucleus of this national literature has found direct religious usage in the public rites of the national faith. No sacred scripture of any people could be accorded more reverential treatment either as a liturgical document or as an inspiration to moral conduct than the Imperial Rescript on Education. Issued in 1890 when anti-Western sentiment was running high, it has been magnified ever since as the flawless epitome of a "peerless Japanese nationalism"—this in spite of well recognized indebtedness to Confucianism. The official English translation follows.

"Know Ye, Our Subjects:

"Our Imperial Ancestors have founded Our Empire on a basis broad and everlasting, and have deeply and firmly implanted virtue; Our subjects ever united in loyalty and filial piety have from generation to generation illustrated the beauty thereof. This is the glory of the fundamental character of Our Empire, and herein lies also the source of Our education. Ye, Our subjects, be filial to your parents, affectionate to your brothers and sisters; as husbands and wives be harmonious, as friends true; bear yourselves in modesty and moderation; extend your benevolence to all; pursue learning and cultivate arts, and thereby develop intellectual faculties and perfect moral powers; furthermore, advance the public good and promote common interests; always respect the Constitution and observe the laws; should emergency arise, offer yourselves courageously to the State; and thus guard and maintain the prosperity of

Our Imperial Throne coeval with heaven and earth. So shall ye be not only Our good and faithful subjects but render illustrious the best traditions of your forefathers.

"The Way here set forth is indeed the teaching bequeathed by Our Imperial Ancestors, to be observed alike by Their Descendants and the subjects, infallible in all ages and true in all places. It is Our wish to lay it to heart in all reverence, in common with you, Our subjects, that we may attain to the same virtue.

"The 30th day of the 10th month of the 23rd year of Meiji."
(October 30, 1890)   [*Imperial Sign Manual, Imperial Seal*]

The Shinto foundations of this rescript are more apparent in the Japanese original than in the English translation. While the personal and civic virtues that are emphasized are such as any people might cherish, the source of both the moral teaching and the structure of the state are peculiarly Japanese. Everything stems from the "Imperial Ancestors." The Japanese mind cannot be officially introduced to spiritual powers that transcend these. The most majestic of these ancestral spirits are the great deities of the Nihongi and Kojiki mythologies—a sky father, an earth mother, a moon god, a storm god, a food goddess and, most sublime of all, a sun goddess. With the exception of the storm god, these are "The Great Deities" who are enthroned in the shrines of the Mecca of modern Japan at Ise as the genealogical heads of the national pantheon and the imperial dynasty. Manifestly the state interpretation does not identify these deities with the natural phenomena just specified. The Japanese subject, no matter how well informed and no matter how serious his private reservations on the subject may be, must take his cue from his official mentors and accept them all as bona fide ancestors without qualification.

As just suggested, it is in the sun goddess that the state worship of Shinto came to a head. This is clearly implied in the imperial rescript that we have just examined. Japanese state education began and ended with this theme. Following primitive patterns that have remarkable parallels in ancient state-forms elsewhere, particularly among the early Egyptians and the Inca dynasty of Peru, the Japanese government established the sovereignty of the emperor on the worship of a sun goddess. Amaterasu Omikami, the name by which this deity is known, was proclaimed to be the "great ancestress" who founded the state. The will of this goddess as expressed in the literature of Old Shinto became the primary spiritual bond of national unity and the means whereby the right of the emperor to rule was divinely authenticated. The speech, which the Nihongi puts into the mouth of Amaterasu Omikami when she sent her grandson down from heaven to have dominion over the tribes of the "Reed-plain Land" that was to become the nucleus of the future Japanese empire, was interpreted as the foreordination by which the establishment and continuity of the state were elevated into the realm of the immutable and eternal. If Japanese usage justifies the attribution of sacredness to any words in the entire range of their literature, it does here: "This Reed-plain Land of Fifteen Thousand Autumns of Fair Rice-ears [archaic name for Japan] is the country over which my descendants shall be lords. Do thou my August Grandchild, proceed thither and rule over it. Go! and may prosperity attend thy dynasty, and it shall, like Heaven and Earth, endure forever."

It is to these words that the Imperial Rescript on Education points when it declares that the imperial ancestors founded the state on a basis broad and everlasting. We cannot examine here the details of the circumstances which led the compilers of the Nihongi to put these remarkable words into the mouth of the sun goddess. Suffice it to say that dynastic centralization, consummated in the latter half of the seventh century under the influence of Chinese administrative models, is here at work, and that modern Japanese statecraft found the superhuman authentication of internal unification and of foreign expansion alike in these god-given words. Other passages of the ancient literature were similarly invoked to hallow the institutions and acts of the state with a divinely authorized immutability. These must all be regarded as sacred scripture in a special sense.

The literary resources of State Shinto show their deepest religious coloring in the *norito* or ritualistic prayers which the priests chant before the altars of the gods at all important public ceremonies and sometimes privately in response to the requests of individual suppliants or small groups of people. *Norito* for specified occasions were issued under the authorization of the minister of home affairs and were printed in the government's rules and regulations for the Shinto shrines. Those in use today are based on the texts of ancient Shinto as set forth in the Engi Shiki. The style is stately and elaborate, and the religious motives largely confined to a kind of glorified barter—the enumeration of offerings that are presented in return for specified benefits. These include the protection and fruition of seeds and plants, national and domestic prosperity, deliverance from calamity, success in war, and a long and glorious reign on the part of the emperor.

Just what these *norito* are may best be judged by an actual example. The one given below is from the ritual performed on February 4 of each year at all shrines in the so-called "Service of Praying for the Crops." In this ritual supplication is made to the gods that the growing crops may be protected from wind and water and that the cereals may ripen abundantly. Translated the text reads:

"In the dread presence, before the holy shrine [the name of the shrine is here inserted], the chief priest of the shrine [the name and rank of the officiating priest are here inserted], with trembling makes utterance:

"Now that His Imperial Majesty—about to make beginning of the rice crop for this year—has caused offerings to be presented in abundance, do we, coming cleansed and purified into thy great presence, make offerings—of food offerings: soft rice and rough rice [i.e. hulled rice and unhulled rice]; of drink offerings: making high the tops of the wine jars and arranging in full rows the bellies of the wine jars; of things that live in the blue sea-plain: things broad of fin and things narrow of fin, even to grasses of the offing and grasses of the shore—all these do we offer in abundance. And as the full and glorious sun of this day of life and plenty rises, do thou hear to the end these words of praise, in tranquillity and peace.

"Grant that all things that may be grown—beginning with the late-ripening rice which will be produced by the people by stirring with arms and hands the foamy waters and by drawing the mud together between the opposing thighs, and extending even to the partial blade of grass—grant that they may not meet with evil winds or violent waters. Prosper them with abundance and luxuriance, and bring it to pass that the Festival of New Food [i.e. the autumn thanksgiving festival held on November 23 of each year] may be celebrated with sublimity and beauty. So, with dread, we declare the ending of the words of praise."

This is thoroughly typical of the entire ceremonial life of modern Shinto. The focal point of the rituals is definite prayer to the deities of the shrines. The statement that has sometimes been propagated, both in Japan and abroad, to the effect that adoration of deities is unknown to Shinto appears for what it is: a fundamental error of fact. The source of the error finally traces back to governmental manipulation which has consistently sought to encircle the shrine with a fog-bank of misrepresentation behind which officialdom might operate with a minimum of outside interference. If adoration means an act of profound reverence to a divine being, if it includes prayer and supplication to deities for specific benefits to family, field, and nation, then the fiber of modern State Shinto is adoration.

There is a further important point that calls for clarification in connection with the nature of the worship performed at the shrines. American readers have sometimes been told that the Shinto shrines contain no images or other representations of deities. The same idea has been stated somewhat facetiously in the observation that the visitor at the Shinto shrine will find nothing there and even that cannot be seen. The reason why the visitor at the shrine sees so little is not because there is nothing there, but because what is there is too sacred to be subjected to the contamination of profane gazing. The holy of holies is protected by the strictest of taboos. Every Shinto shrine encloses in its innermost parts a material object in which the deity has residence and from which the mysterious *kami*-power emanates. Frequently the object is intrinsically worthless—an odd-shaped stone, a phallic emblem, a lock of human hair, or a paper wand.

Commonly it is a mirror after the pattern of the sun goddess shrine at Ise; sometimes it is a string of old stone beads, an ancient scroll, or a symbolic sword or other paraphernalia of a warrior hero. Occasionally it is a living tree or even a mountain. In such case, of course, concealment within a sanctuary is impossible. The point to be noted is that no Shinto shrine can exist without this *shintai* or "god-body," as it is called. In origin and essence the *shintai* is a fetish. It is true that the Shinto shrine does not contain an image of the deity in the sense of an anthropomorphic idol, but it does contain as the indispensable condition of the presence of the god, a wonder-working, *kami*-filled, sacred talisman. Shinto does not represent a stage of religious worship that has transcended idol worship; on the side of its most sacred cult-objects it preserves a primitivity that is below idol worship.

We must pass on to the consideration of certain problems that have as yet only been touched on. It is obvious from what has already been said that any account of the relations of State Shinto to modern life—and in the nature of the case this means almost exclusively Japanese life—as well as any review of the elements of Shinto that are a threat to a truly ecumenical civilization must be approached from the side of connections with nationalism. At the beginning of the discussion attention was called to the fact that Japanese authorities with almost complete unanimity turned to Shinto to find the chief inspiration and manifestation of what they liked to call their unique national unity. How then has Shinto fostered nationalism?

The answer, in brief, is: just as any other religion fosters response and dedication to the ideals and objects for which it stands, mainly by deepening sentiment and conviction. At the acme of Japan's preparation for the Second World War this involved a control over the shaping of the mind of youth that amounted to an elaborate state parochialism in education. Every school in the empire became a factory for conditioning national psychology in such wise as to preserve a nice balance between amenability to official direction on the one hand and confidence in invincibility on the other. All of the agencies of propaganda and control of thought open to governmental choice—police regulation, school, press, and public platform alike—mediated this official purpose to all the areas of the national life so that none might escape. The core of this was Shinto. It was from this source that the chief materials of the nationalistic curricula were drawn. It was in the ceremonies of the shrines that the glory of the state and dedication thereto were dramatized and commemorated. This brings us to the point where we must attempt to clarify the distinctive features of Shinto which have contributed to national solidarity.

First is the support which it gives to the absolute sovereignty of the state. This rests on the Shinto teaching of the existence of a superhuman, transcendent authority in the person of the emperor. Questions of whether the emperor is above the state, or himself actually the state, or a cooperating member of the state along with the people need not detain us here. The second and third decades of the twentieth century saw democratic tendencies make sufficient headway in Japan to permit a moderate attack on political absolutism and the law department of the Imperial University of Tokyo was even able to make open publication of the view that while the emperor was the chief member of the state, he was nevertheless only a part of it.

With the rise of the military clique to totalitarian control in the fourth decade of the century, this enlightened liberalism was liquidated and anything less than blind acceptance of the proposition that the imperial throne stood outside of, and above, the state was punished as a disloyal misconception of "the unique Japanese national structure." In the practical outworking of affairs this merely meant that a group of men—most of them high officers in the armed services—had succeeded in setting themselves up as the state and were in control of all the avenues of the mediation of the so-called will of the emperor to the people. The real will of the emperor was never known since he was not permitted to deal directly with the people; and while it was true that "the emperor could do no wrong" in the sense that ministers of state were obliged to take responsibility for mistakes, yet there is room for more than a suspicion that "imperial rescripts" were secured repeatedly by the ministers to suit the convenience of their own purposes. From the point of view of the military control of the nation this meant that soldiers were able to make their own authority inviolable by sanctifying it with the fiction of the absolute infallibility of the throne. As long as the mind and faith of the nation could be kept at a level where fiction could not be distinguished from truth the scheme was workable. This is where Shinto fitted into the picture: it gave superhuman, and therefore conclusive, authenticity to military command.

Questions have been raised in America regarding the sense in which the divinity of the emperor was promulgated in Japan and whether all Japanese subjects accepted it or were forced to profess belief in it. In answer, two different views of the sacredness or divinity of the emperor should be noted. The one may be called the orthodox view, the other, the progressive view. The former is called orthodox because it is the common presupposition of Japanese tradition. Its main outlines have already been suggested.

It will be recalled that, according to this conception, Shinto attained its highest development in the exaltation of the emperor to the rank of a "living god." The written constitution of 1889 declares that the emperor is "sacred and inviolable." The most important commentary on the constitution that has yet appeared declares that the sovereign is "heaven descended, divine and sacred." One of the outstanding Japanese authorities on Shinto tells us that it is true to the correct line of Japanese belief to regard the emperor as the equivalent of Jotei among the Chinese or Jehovah among the Jews. Japanese literature frequently speaks of the emperor as *Aki tsu Kami* ("Manifest *Kami*") and as *Ara Mikami* ("Incarnate Great *Kami*"). The national government itself took the responsibility for the promulgation of this usage and, while no state shrines were dedicated to the actual worship of the living ruler, nevertheless the ceremonies of obeisance before the imperial palace and in front of the imperial portraits enshrined in the schools, the practice of hallowing national moments of silence with group bowing in the direction of Tokyo, and the profound taboos with which all public appearances of the emperor were protected all pointed to his membership in the ranks of divine beings. Most important of all, his unbroken line of descent from the great *kami* of the misty past preserved in him an essence that made him something more than mere man. He had a god-nature as well as a human nature.

It would be useless to look for logical clarity in this interpretation. It must be taken for what it is—the political exploitation of an old emotionally engendered belief that occult power emanates from the persons of mighty men. For such reason they are *kami* or sacred.

The progressive view still sanctions the use of *kami* in speaking of the emperor but shifts the basis of sacredness from the supernatural to the natural world. In 1937 the national department of education issued a book which deals with this problem. In it the meaning of *kami* when used of the emperor is given the following official definition: "The Tenno [emperor] is a visible *kami* who rules over the country in accordance with the will of our Imperial Ancestors. This visible or manifest *kami* revealed as man is entirely different from *kami* with the meaning of Absolute God, the omnipresent and omnipotent Deity. It means that the Imperial Ancestors are revealed in the emperor, who is their sacred offspring, that the emperor is of one body with the Imperial Ancestors, that he is eternally the source of the growth and development of the land and the people, and that he is forever a supremely exalted and majestic personage."

This manifestly does not call for the worship of the living emperor in the sense of supplication to him or adoration of him as a superhuman or supernatural being, yet it would be a great mistake to believe that by distinguishing between the Japanese ruler and the Absolute God of religious faith it disposes of the religious problem of the throne. We will have to pass by the preposterous condescension manifested in the amazing willingness of the Japanese government to draw a line of distinction between the omnipresent and omnipotent Absolute God of religion and their emperor, and come to the ultimate

174

issue. Whether we follow the orthodox view or the progressive view this is always the same, that is, the basis of authority. Complete state absolutism, manifested and sanctified beyond all human contravention in the person of the emperor, demanded unquestioning obedience from the individual subject. There was no room whatsoever in National Shinto for prophetic criticism of the state or for the nonconformity of an enlightened conscience or for large public service growing out of the mutual cooperation of morally responsible and intelligent men and women. The individual had but one duty—to obey. This explains why the Japanese high command so loved Shinto. Whatever satisfactions the individual enjoyed were found in the consciousness of being merged in the national destiny as determined by his betters, or else in innocuous hobbies or otherworldly pieties where the state laid out no claims. The force of these remarks is well indicated in the following statement by a former professor of the Imperial University of Tokyo. "Sovereignty in Japan is vested in a single race-father—a form of government without peer among all the nations of the world. It is, therefore, not to be tolerated that an authority should be accepted that is respected above and beyond the emperor and the imperial ancestors. Our national structure makes it impossible to permit the acceptance of a 'one true God' above the emperor." [5]

The final balance sheet for State Shinto leaves most of the entries on the deficit side of the account. Shinto glorifies war and makes every appeal to arms that has been sanctified by the will of the emperor a holy crusade. It fosters convictions of racial and national superiority such as have their counterpart in Western racial arrogance at its worst, and in this respect stands squarely across the line of march of true human brotherhood. It frustrates genuine international cooperation by making Japanese national sovereignty absolute and complete, an inviolable entity sanctified by superhuman authority. It makes the chief end of education the inculcation of unquestioning

[5] Hiroyuki Kato.

obedience, thus destroying at its foundations any prospect of building a cooperative human society on intelligent personal responsibility. It stands for a vested reactionism in high places that tolerates neither discussion nor criticism of its own irrational and mythological roots. It inculcates the idea that every good thing of life which the individual possesses is received by him as a benefaction from above, thus sterilizing all personal initiative and making the Japanese subject exactly what he often calls himself, "the little child of the emperor"—the docile tool of statecraft and militarism. It prostitutes human dignity and equality by setting up in the place of God the authority of a "god-man" who can claim to own the bodies and souls of millions of subjects while he himself is above all law. In the end Shinto undermines the very unity which it sets out to achieve as the primary condition of a lasting state structure, for with all their protestations of peerless devotion to country and emperor, among themselves, in their ordinary social relationships, the Japanese people tend to be suspicious, jealous, and uncooperative. The reason for this is plain: the inner, spontaneous motives of conduct dry up where everything, including the idea of truth itself, comes as superimposed regulation from without.

On the credit side of the balance sheet Shinto partisans point to the unique support it has given to the state in a world of bitterly competitive nationalisms. The Japanese passion for Shinto is vindicated as the registration of their determination to guard the continuity of their own national existence in the face of the threat of destruction. This, of course, is only to reiterate the apology for nationalism. Beyond this, in respect to fitness to contribute to an enduring world civilization founded on mutual cooperation and understanding among men, Shinto has pointed often to its emphasis on sincerity. Just as the ethics of Christianity revolve about universal love and those of Buddhism about universal compassion, so also Shinto is declared to cherish at its heart a capacity for comprehensive sincerity. But sincerity alone is not enough. Sincerity unguided by universal ideals may be merely a rationalization of fanaticism; misdirected to the purposes of external authority, it may be merely a sterile legalism. Both of these perversions are illustrated all too well in the story of Japanese Shinto.

At the same time it is no more reasonable to anticipate that in order to make Japan worthy of participation in a fellowship of civilized nations everything in Japanese nationalism must be eradicated than it is to assume that everything in American nationalism must be destroyed. Preservation of national continuity by the dramatization of the significant achievements of the past, commemoration in shrine and ceremony of the devotion of those who have served well both in life and death, the deepening of reverence for ancestors whereby the sense of social responsibility may be refined and quickened, ministration to national health and education, and the fostering of a legitimate pride in the capacity to contribute to a peace-abiding association of nations—these are some of the possibilities that suggest themselves when we consider roads that are open to a Shinto that has been purged of its mythology, sheared of its militarism, set free from racial arrogance and bureaucratic legalism, and made responsive to the utterances of the universal human spirit.

SELECTED BIBLIOGRAPHY

The Religious Life of the Japanese People. By M. Anesaki. Tokyo, 1938.

History of Japanese Religion. By M. Anesaki. London, 1930.

Shinto: The Way of the Gods. By W. G. Aston. London, 1905.

Nihongi, Chronicles of Japan from the Earliest Times to A.D. 697. By W. G. Aston. 2 vols., London, 1896.

Shinto: The Unconquered Enemy. By Robert O. Ballou. New York, 1945.

The Kojiki or Record of Ancient Matters. By Basil Hall Chamberlain. 2nd. ed., Kobe, 1932.

The National Faith of Japan. By D. C. Holtom. London, 1938.

Modern Japan and Shinto Nationalism. By D. C. Holtom. Chicago, 1943.

"The Meaning of Kami." By D. C. Holtom. *Monumenta Nipponica.* Vol. III, nos. 1 and 2, vol. IV, no. 2, Tokyo, Sophia University, 1940–1941.

A Study of Shinto: The Religion of the Japanese Nation. By Genchi Kato. Tokyo, 1926.

Islam

EDWARD J. JURJI

One night near the end of the month of Ramadan, about A.D. 610, Muhammad, according to the belief of his followers, was seized by the mighty grasp of an angel and heard a Voice saying unto him:

> Cry in the name of the Lord!
> Who created man . . . !
> Cry, for the Lord is most generous!
> . . . who taught man
> What he did not know (*Koran* 96: 1–5).

That was the fateful "Night of Power," celebrated among the faithful as the Night of Destiny, when amidst the clash of empires and nations, the wild cries of race and clan, and within the confines of pagan Mecca, the Book was opened to the Prophet's thirsting soul, calling him to preach the God of Nature, who had written His law in the heart of man, and who was now about to restore and perfect the knowledge of His truth, revealed by the true prophets and seers of preceding generations.

In the story of its architects and interpreters down the ages are revealed both the creative impulse of Islam, once it touches the lives of men, and the varieties of religious experience engendered by it. Like the representatives of other historic faiths, these men demonstrate, each in his own way, as William James has aptly put it, "that the visible world is part of a more spiritual universe from which it draws its chief significance"; and what is even more remarkable, they all possess "a new zest which adds itself like a gift to life."

In a sense, however, there has always been but one founder of Islam. To the devout believer, the name of Muhammad—ever to be followed reverently with the mystical formula: God bless him and grant him peace—is high above every other earthly name, designating one whose flaming passion for the truth and luminous presentation of God's purpose has ever inspired the hearts of his followers with rapture and adoration, assurance and faith. This consummate allegiance to the Prophet springs from the breast of the twentieth-century, often sophisticated, Moslem as it did from that of his spiritual forebear in the days of untarnished piety long ago. Let Dr. Muhammad Husayn Haykal, the distinguished Egyptian author, statesman, and critic of today, express the position of his coreligionists on this crucial subject: ". . . the career of Muhammad, though thoroughly human, has, nonetheless, ascended the highest summits ever attained by any man. Upon the Moslems he desperately sought to impress that his humanity was like unto theirs, inspired though he surely was. He knows no miracle save that of the Koran. . . . No other life can match in sublimity and power his own achievement in all the phases of existence. No words can adequately portray the penetrating depth of his communion with the life of the cosmos in its infinite meaning, extending from eternity to eternity, as he communed with the Creator of the universe, thanks to His everlasting mercy and forgiveness. Were it not for this communion, and Muhammad's own veracity in the transmission of his Lord's message, subsequent ages might well have rejected his affirmations. Yet thirteen hundred and fifty years have now gone whereas the message which was delivered unto Muhammad by his Lord remains the wonder of truth and enlightenment. Suffice it to cite one corroborative example, namely, the truth revealed by God to Muhammad that he is the seal [last] of prophets and messengers. Fourteen centuries have now elapsed and no one professing to be a prophet or a messenger bearing a divine mandate has truly captured the imagination of men. Prior to Muhammad, prophecies were successive and divine messengers not unknown . . . though scarcely any one of these proclaimed a universal message intended for all mankind, neither declared himself the seal [last] of the prophets and divine messengers. Only Muhammad makes these assertions, and the centuries believe him. . . ."

Through its reflections on the decisive historic movements in the Prophet's career, the Koran, above everything else, magnifies the one pivotal point in his character—his unwavering conviction. His constant and abiding faith in the divine origin and righteousness of the cause to which he was called marks Muhammad as a unique figure. His firm belief in those invisible things which form the content of many an exhortation is the thread of meaning upon which his entire preaching is strung. As a result the message regarding God's transcendent sovereignty begins to acquire a pregnant urgency. This is the core of that celestial message, delivered unto Muhammad, without which Islam's monotheism would be well-nigh unthinkable.

Deep in the heart of that core is an unmistakable eschatology. One may go so far as to say that if all the details of his life, prior to the emergence of solid faith and conviction within his soul, were to be discarded as biographical embellishment, his prophetic role in the history of religion would still remain intact. Indeed the real opening stage of his ministry at Mecca begins with the hour when his voice rings unequivocally with the words of warning, and his speech bears the accent of eternity and the Last Day, the Day of Judgment and Retribution. It is perhaps symbolic of the profound sense of urgency attached to this teaching that the use of the Arabic imperfect tense—a grammatical device not only indicative of futurity but suggestive also of the ever present imminence of the events foretold—is invariably in evidence when the hereafter is discussed.

". . . All that is in the heavens and in the earth praiseth God, for He is the mighty and wise. His is the kingdom of the heavens and the earth. . . . He hath power over all. He is the first and the last, the seen and the hidden (57: 1–3). Verily those who recite the Book of God, and are steadfast in prayer . . . shall not come to nought (35: 26–7). . . . O ye who believe! Shall I lead you to a merchandise which will save you from grievous woe? To believe . . . is better for you if ye but did know! He will forgive you your sins, and bring you into gardens beneath which rivers flow (61: 11–12). . . . Verily the day of decision is an appointed time; it is a day when the trumpet shall be blown and ye shall come in troops; and the heavens shall be opened. . . . Verily hell is . . . a reward for the outrageous. They shall not taste therein cool nor drink (78: 17–24). . . . Verily for the God-fearing there is a blissful abode—garden and vineyard and girls with swelling breasts, their peers in age, and a brimming cup. There shall they hear no vain discourse nor any falsehood. A recompense from thy Lord—a sufficient gift (78: 31–36)." Starting life an orphan, Muhammad (*ca.* 571–632) knew hardship and suffering at first hand. At about the age of twenty-five, however, his marriage with Khadijah, the rich and noble widow of matronly virtues, brought him contentment and domestic felicity. He could well afford now to give himself to long and assiduous reflection upon the nature and destiny of man. With the approach of his fortieth birthday his mediation began to mellow into a startling spiritual experience whence he emerged with a vast conception of God and His role in history. Mortified by the degrading idolatry of the Quraysh, his own tribe, and its leading aristocracy the sponsors of al-Kabah, a center of fetishism and pilgrimage by means of which Mecca acquired a position of prestige and wealth in Arabia, he roundly denounced the ancient paganism and all its supporters. His first public appearance showed Muhammad as a prophet of God's wrath, a reviler of the people, and a preacher of divine righteousness. Astounded by his audacity, the Meccans at first spurned his message and scorned his call, but, when they became fully aware of his growing influence with the people and the subversive character of his teaching, they turned against him with hate and fury.

Despised and rejected in his native Mecca, Muhammad was now hounded and persecuted. His eyes therefore turned to the north toward Medina, the city of his maternal uncles, to which he fled in the year of the hegira (A.D. 622). The road from Mecca to Medina led all the way from precarious living in the shadow of constant peril to the seat of an august ruler, honored and feared, before whose tribunal disputes between Moslems, Jews and pagans were arbitrated. The state of war, existing between the Prophet and his kinsmen, was brought to an end in the total victory of the Islamic forces climaxed by Muhammad's triumphant entry into the city of his birth to destroy the monuments of idolatry. Prophetic though his career remained, Muhammad had increasingly come to wield the sword of a militant ruler and to head the affairs of an aggressive political state, conscious of its role in history. When his death occurred, on June 8, 632, he bequeathed to his followers a religio-political heritage ever burdened and harassed for many centuries with the task of finding an acceptable caliph (successor) to fill the highest office in Islam. The caliphate (succession) as an issue, aggravated by the uniform silence of the Prophet on the subject of who was to follow him, became the root of much evil, the chief internal misfortune of Islam, the origin of rifts and schisms, and a sad patrimony of tears and blood.

Certain of the divine mandate committed to him and of the Message he was to preach, Muhammad enunciated the new religion as *Islam,* that is, submission and surrender to the will of God. As the movement gained momentum and began to spread in Arabia and the Near East it invited attention to itself as a theism inculcating faith in the one, sovereign and righteous God, and proclaiming a brotherhood of all the believers regardless of class or pedigree. Its professed relation to Biblical tradition and deep roots in the Semitic soil recommended it to many of the followers of Judaism and Christianity, the two older monotheisms which had also originated in Western Asia.

With this measure of initial advantage, Islam was soon to draw the support of the Arab, and later Turkish, conquerors, who carried it westward to the Atlantic seaboard of the Iberian Peninsula, and eastward to the confines of China. Such was the background of medieval Islam when it proceeded to create a gigantic melting pot of races and creeds, out of which emerged a rich culture, unique in the annals of mankind and, in some aspects of its scientific and philosophical contributions, foreshadowing the subsequent Renaissance of Europe. During this period of effervescence, indeed from the beginning of its history, Islam displayed the marked characteristics of theocratic government, embodied in the idealistic relationship between a mighty, absolute ruler—the Commander of the Faithful—and the subservient citizen—a servant of God and the ruler. In this outward setting was laid the foundation of the Islamic state which lasted, amidst many vicissitudes, from the death of the Prophet on June 8, 632 to the abolition of the Ottoman Caliphate on March 3, 1924.

As a contemporary non-Christian religion, Islam is surpassed numerically only by Confucianism. In growth and development it leads every other living religion, with the exception of Christianity, claiming the adherence of about one-eighth of the human race. Mosques and minarets rise as Islamic symbols in a far-flung spiritual empire, stretching from Mindanao in the Philippines to Casablanca in northwest Africa, and from the steppes of Russia to Capetown. The present chapter seeks to describe the core of Islam's religious power, the record and achievements of its founders and interpreters, its world-wide expansion and modern sense of universal mission. A sincere desire to let this religion speak for itself accompanies every line, and the strong temptation to inject elements not peculiar to the inner genius of Islam has been consistently resisted.

THE CORE OF RELIGIOUS POWER

Islam's core of religious power is crystallized in its scripture, worship, theology, and ethics. Beyond the horizon of its history this religion harks back to hoary antiquity and the beginning of time, laying claim to an "authentic" version of the Judaeo-Christian heritage. It pays solemn homage to the true God and is loath to part company with an aggressive doctrinal temper. No Islamic theology can begin anyhere except at the crossroad between polytheism and theism where the edifice of heathenism is shattered and idolatry is made anathema in the name of a pure monotheism.

Muhammad Rashid Rida (1865–1935), founder and editor of the Cairo periodical *al-Manar*, mouthpiece of the Egyptian religious reformation, published in 1927 a commentary on the Koran, based upon the principles of his teacher, the Grand

Mufti of Egypt and chancellor of al-Azhar University, Muhammad Abduh (1849–1905), one of the most enlightened divines of Islam and possibly its ablest advocate in the modern era. In the preface to his work, Rida quotes his former professor: "In the early epoch of Islam, scholars recognized the power of the Koran in captivating the hearts of men, and they came to the conclusion that the faith will not endure without the Koran. To this verdict further confirmation was added when the intermingling of the Arab with other races was under way. Like their Arab coreligionists, foreign converts to Islam came to appreciate the imperative need to retain the integrity of the Arabic language. Accordingly they applied themselves to the study of its literature and reduced its grammar to writing. . . . I, for one, would assert that the Koran is God's miraculous proof of His truthful religion. Islam cannot live without a sound understanding of the Koran, based upon the continuity of Arabic. If Islam has persisted at all in non-Arab countries, it is largely because there was a handful of scholars sufficiently versed in exegetical learning to ward off the doubts cast upon the Koran. . . ."

This elevated conception of scripture is consonant with the claims which the Koran makes in its own behalf: ". . . That is the Book: there is no doubt therein; a guide to the pious who believe in the unseen (2: 1, 2). . . . And if ye are in doubt of what We have revealed to our servant, then bring a chapter like it (2: 21). . . . Lord, there is no God but He, the self subsistent. He has sent down to thee the Book in truth, confirming what was before it, and has revealed the Law, and the Gospel before it for the guidance of men. . . . He it is who has revealed to thee the Book, of which there are some verses that are decisive; they are the Mother of the Book; and others ambiguous; but as for those in whose heart is perversity, they follow what is ambiguous, and do crave for sedition, craving for their own interpretation of it; but no one knows the interpretation of it except God (3: 1, 5). . . . These are the signs of the perspicuous Book. Verily, we have revealed it, an Arabic Koran; haply ye may understand. We shall recount to thee the best of stories, as We reveal to thee this Koran (12 : 1–3). . . . Thou couldst not recite before this any Book, nor write it with thy right hand (29 : 47). . . . A blessed Book which We have sent down to thee that they may ponder its verses, and that those endowed with intelligence may be reminded (38 : 28). Do they not reflect upon the Koran? If it were from any other than God, they would find in it many a contradiction (4 : 84). Had We sent down this Koran upon some mountain, thou wouldst have seen it, humbling itself and cleaving asunder for fear of God : These parables do We speak to the people, haply they may think (59 : 21)."

Intrinsically, the doctrine of the uncreated Koran—the Word of God—strikes one as a singular parody on the Johannine disclosure : "In the beginning was the Word, and the Word was with God, and the Word was God," with possible implications of the ultimate borrowing of the Logos idea from Greek thought or, more plausibly, the concept of God's Word from the Hebraic prophetic tradition. It is not idle to refer here to the repugnance of Islam to any interpretation that makes the Koran a mere Book, or that, being of uncreated origin, the Koran is beyond the spiritual sovereignty of God. Equally abhorrent would be the suggestion that the holy book is a material figure, the one and only idol tolerated in the mosques and covered with honor and artistic embellishment. Ideally, the centrality of the Koran in a mosque has been compared with that of the open Book in Evangelical churches.

This Book is one of boundless spiritual power in the lives of Moslems. Basically, the People of the Mosque, the Nation of Allah, the "Mohammedans" are worshipers of God, but in a real sense also they are "Koranists." No one, save by its authority, may speak about the spiritual realm. Ever since the appearance of the Koran, Islam has come into being, a religion without an ecclesia, without a central see. No one may speak irrevocably for Islam. There is no sacramental clergy, no priestly caste. Anyone, without the laying of hands, or any other form of bequeathing or sharing the sacerdotal office, may become a mosque Imam or member of the conclave of divines.

The net result is that Islam has tightened the legalistic scriptural belt around its body. A great source of power and prestige, this rigid formalism, in the opinion of many honest students of religion, both Moslem and non-Moslem, is a betrayal of the believer's right to direct communion with the Creator. Is not the main purpose of the Koran "to awaken in man the higher consciousness of his manifold relations with God and the universe?" But this complex problem must be understood in the light of Islam's conception of religion and its worship program.

Aside from its communal and legal aspects, religion (*din*) in its simplest essence has a special connotation as a divine institution guiding the rational being, by his own consent, into right relationship with God. In a concrete and vivid manner, religion acquires two principal faculties, an idealistic and a behavioristic one. Within the idealistic prevails the emphasis upon faith (*iman*)—the tranquillity of the soul and its freedom from fear by a complete trust in Allah, His Prophet, and His Book. In the behavioristic realm, a number of characteristics appear, falling under two main classifications: 1. Works, that is, right doing (*ihsan*)—serving God as though He were before one's eyes; 2. Compliance with the five Pillars: profession of faith, almsgiving, fast, pilgrimage, and worship.

Within the sacrosanct orbit of worship a self-disclosure of Islam's spiritual potential is encountered. Whether in the profession of faith, wherein the sole God and last Prophet are confessed; the rendering of alms, an embodiment of charity into law; the fast, an abstinence from food and base thoughts by day; or, the annual pilgrimage, a gathering by multitudes of the faithful from their far-flung habitats, crying *labbayka* (here I come!) at the birthplace of the faith—the worshipful spirit permeates everything, revolving about Prayer—Islam's noblest contribution to moral vigor and spiritual elevation. The Aramaic origin of the word *salah* (prayer) suggests a common ground with Judaism and Christianity.

The standing posture, alternating with kneeling, and prostration, accompanied by Koranic recitation, adoration, and praise, is pervaded by a profound humility and devotion, making for spiritual expansion. Though the face is turned toward Mecca and a fixed order of worship is followed in most communities, the form of prayer was not to become a matter of dispute: "To God belongs the East and the West; whichever way ye turn, the face of God is there. Verily, God is unrestricted, knowing (2: 109)." When intoxicated persons, causing disorder, were discovered at the worship services, the use of wine was restricted, later prohibited. Along with almsgiving, prayer came to be a manifestation of Islamic piety: "Verily the hypocrites try to outwit God, but He outwits them. When they rise up to pray, they rise up lazily to be seen of men, and they remember God but little (4: 141). . . ." The Islamization of the Arab was made possible largely by means of the ritual prayer. Through it today millions of Moslems in many climes—a minority among their people of course—open up their inner selves to the working of a higher life. Whether in solitude or in the congregation of the faithful five times a day—at dawn, noon, midafternoon, sunset, and evening—they seek to express their yearnings in the awful presence of Allah. The greater consciousness of solidarity which communal prayer engenders is enlarged as the armies of pilgrims from distant lands worship together at the annual ceremony around the central mosques of Mecca. Even upon an outsider, the contagious solemnity, decorum, and humility—regnant at a Moslem divine service— leave a profound impression. The cleansing power of prayer is graphically described in a Tradition: "Prayer is like a stream of fresh water, flowing beside the gate of each of you. Into it you plunge five times a day. Thinkest thou that any impurity can cling to thee after so much washing?"

Perhaps the most gracious thing ever said about Moslem prayer is that it is an intimate converse (*munajah*) with God. A creative force in Islam, it has fostered a feeling of equality among the believers, mitigating the rankling sense of race-superiority and caste, and opening a new inlet for the entry of mystical experience into the Moslem heart.

In addition to the scriptural and devotional foci of power,

there is a third, the theological. The whole gamut of Islamic theology is determined by the doctrine of Allah which places the greatest stress on His uniqueness and unity: ". . . say: He is God, one; God, the Eternal; He begetteth not nor was begotten. Coequal with Him there hath never been any one (112: 1–4)." Nor was it an abstract, philosophical concept of God which Muhammad proclaimed when He enunciated the great affirmation: "There is no God but Allah." Rather was it the positive, personal declaration of faith in the Lord over all. Nothing exists apart from Him and His handiwork. The Koranic conception of God includes, among other elements, a clearcut assertion of His Creativeness, Knowledge, Omnipotence, and Eternity.

A clue to God's dealings with men is offered in the formula prefacing every sura (Koranic chapter): ". . . God the Merciful, the Compassionate," handed down from South Arabian antiquity but made to glow with a new incandescence. Before His might and righteousness, man stands destitute and without excuse. God is the Forgiver of man's infirmities and iniquities. His pervasive Ultimate Reality is cosmic like light: "God is the light of the heavens and the earth; His light is like a niche in which is a lamp, the lamp in glass and the glass like a glittering star, lit from a blessed tree, an olive neither of the East nor of the West whose oil would almost give light even though no fire did touch it; light upon light; God guideth to His light whom He willeth; God coineth parables for the people, and God everything doth know (24: 35)." Man's relation to Him is one of complete dependence.

The gap between God's transcendence and His immanence remained a problem of theologians for many centuries. The gradual merging of the world with Allah is largely the product of Sufi mysticism. Meanwhile Islamic thought had gone astray in two different directions: 1. The problem of God's personality exercised the scholastic theologians. Step by step they divested Allah of His creation until it was difficult to discover His relevance to the world. This lamentable fact was further aggravated by their introduction of the doctrine of removal (*tanzih*), the removal of Allah from all qualities of impermanence and the final negation of His knowability by declaring Him to be entirely "other." 2. A quite different mischief played into the hands of the philosophers. With them Aristotelianism and Neoplatonic thought had become an obsession. Their interpretation of the Koran, indeed their whole conception of the Islamic religion, proceeded from the pantheistic assumption that all is Allah. It is to the everlasting credit of al-Ghazzali—the Augustine or Thomas Aquinas of Islam—that he composed and harmonized these contradictory views into a coherent theology. He took the position that Allah is will. Everywhere he cast his glance he caught a vision of His work. Man's kinship to Allah he explained on the basis of sharing in His will through the spirit breathed into every human creature. Thus the soul of man derives its singular role in the realm of beings. It is a spiritual substance (*jawhar ruhani*), created but not shaped, not subject to dimension or locality. Captive upon the earth, man's soul longs for release in order to rejoin its divine maker. With all the touches of pantheism that might be detected in this theology it stands firmly upon the bedrock of orthodox Islam.

Another important phase of Islamic theology relates to the problem of Providence which upon intimate analysis breaks down into two distinct doctrines, that of God's decree (*qada*) and that of His predestination (*qadar*). Underlying the decree is the tremendous assumption of God's creativity and the complete subjection of man to His will. Basically the decree is related to the essence of the Godhead, all Knowledge of Whom must be subject to God's own revelation of Himself. Such knowledge, obviously limited by man's intelligence and the extent of divine disclosure, is nevertheless universal, beneficent, and edifying. In contrast to the conception of the decree, that of predestination envisaged a personal unfolding of divine will in the individual's everyday experience, involving all the aspects of sin and suffering. The impression created by this doctrine of predestination ordinarily came to be one of man's accidental, perhaps even haphazard, exposures to divine caprice and might.

A determinism of this kind reached an all time low when the

divine sovereignty and human freedom were set in mutual opposition. In the end the efforts of philosophers to harmonize free will with predestination came to naught. Add to that the fact that the Moslem spirit, groaning under the unrelenting oppression of secular and religious authoritarianism, was bound to forget its birthright to freedom. Under these circumstances there was no other alternative but unimaginatively to magnify the doctrines of God's decree and predestination, making blind Fate the sole arbiter of man's destiny. In a spiritless and skeptical age, the further deterioration of the once vibrant doctrine of God's sovereignty could sink to the level of *kismet* (lot, portion), especially that of the well-known Turkish brand, which in reality was not an expression of theological doctrine but a practical fatalistic mood which accepted with resignation the slings and arrows of outrageous fortune.

For the source of this dilemma one must go back to the Koran itself. While in no way to be read as a systematic theology, the Book takes a position on predestination which sharpens as one moves from the earlier to the later chapters. And when free thinkers and rationalists began to question the harsh predestinarianism of Islam they resorted to the ethical argument that God's justice must of necessity leave intact the freedom of man's will. But orthodoxy was disposed to frown on such ideas. It subscribed to a view which might be taken as parallel to the persuasive imagery of St. Paul: "Hath not the potter a right over the clay, from the same lump to make one vessel unto honor, and another unto dishonor?" But the nature of the paradox involved in the freedom of man under God's sovereignty never was given a universally accepted interpretation in Islam.

The perennial debate on Providence might have been resolved by a more thoroughgoing appeal to the Prophet's belief in a sovereign, free, and indeterminable God. Implicit here is a full-orbed doctrine of election with far-reaching political, social, and religious significance. For the community of the elect, ruled over by God's absolute sovereignty, has a divine heritage in a geographic, historical, and theological setting which no earthly power can permanently disturb. No one but a believer may fully share in the privileges and responsibilities of a Moslem people or nation. Thus are the hearts of the believers brought together by a divine calling and election. The whole structure of Islamic religion was to be grounded, therefore, in the assumption that it is God who grants or withholds the gifts of faith. In fairness one must admit that in Muhammad's conception of God's sovereign power there is encountered not a weak doctrine but a profound and majestic view of Almighty God and His relation to the world of man. It is with no small measure of certainty regarding the essence of their faith that modern theologians of Islam admonish their folk to shake off an outmoded interpretation of Providence which makes for a depressed condition of social and spiritual decadence.

The ethical character of Islam in its broad, world-wide manifestation seems to follow a set of patterns fixed by the Prophet and amplified later, involving tension between a purely religious motive and one based on the merit and reward principle. Another noticeable form of tension arises between the hedonism bequeathed by both Arab materialistic philosophy and a certain interpretation of the Prophet's sex life and the Koranic picture of a sensuous bliss in paradise, on the one hand and, on the other, the Prophet's austere piety and the ascetic, devotional example of his daily life in keeping with the more spiritual injunctions of the Book. This ethical dualism notwithstanding, man's dutiful response to God's gifts ought to be governed by a profound sense of gratitude. Resignation to one's lot is an imperishable treasure. Other elements in the Islamic ethic reflect an old Arab origin magnified in the cherished virtues—bounty, chivalry, forbearance, hospitality, magnanimity, and patience. The unique position of Mecca as a powerful commercial metropolis, with its established doles for the poor and the sick, might have contributed in part to the early Islamic interest in philanthropy. Few world religions today can boast a greater proportionate wealth devoted to pious purposes than Islam, with its rich philanthropic endowments (*waqf,* pl. *awqaf*), built up through the centuries as a result of innumerable legacies.

The study of the traits of man's moral character (*khulq,* pl. *akhlaq*) was developed into a didactic science permeated by the elements of Greek peripatetic thought on the subject. The underlying assumption here is that certain vices must be weeded out and changed by the right form of nurture. Among the Islamic virtues to which students of ethics give space are delight of the soul, exalted thought, liberality, tenderness, chastity, friendship, and sociability. The moral weaknesses which are commonly recognized include envy, jealousy, anger, intemperance, arrogance, and falsehood. By these and similar standards is the conduct (*suluk*) of the believer to be safeguarded. Moslems have always stood as uncompromising prohibitionists, and the Wahhabi firebrands of Arabia in their inflexible zeal have outlawed tobacco also.

A watchful eye is kept on sexual laxity. Polygamy, rare in urban centers today, is understood as an attempt to curb rather than relax man's inborn lust. It is also regarded by Moslem thinkers as an attempt to grant the surplus women in the community a respected status. The veiling of women and their seclusion, going against the grain of Arabian cutom, represent in reality the restoration of an ancient Semitic practice, reflected in the Code of Hammurabi, and express the desire of Muhammad and the early believers to insure order at public gatherings, and their willingness to catch up with the higher Byzantine and Persian cultures. A similar motive toward Westernization in recent decades makes the continued use of the veil precarious, though Moslems are not altogether satisfied with the position of women in the West. Islamic morality is guided all along the line by the desire to work for the cleansing of one's soul in order that man may thereby be pleasing to God. The ultimate goal of the conscientious Moslem is so to live that the weight of sin may be offset on the Day of Reckoning by one's good works.

This religio-ethical structure is currently discernible in a number of overtones: 1. The fundamentalist, almost fanatical, fervor of Saudi Arabia; 2. The Egyptian rehabilitation of Islamic theology, blending a high esteem for the past with a healthy respect for Western science, in line with the design of Jamal-al-Din al-Afghani (1839–1897), his pupil Muhammad Abduh (1849–1905), and their spiritual posterity; 3. In India, a more liberal, avowedly rationalist (Mutazilite) school of Islamic thinkers, in the tradition of Syed Ameer Ali (1849–1928), Salahuddin Khuda Bakhsh (1877–1931), and Sir Muhammad Iqbal (d. 1938); and 4. A revival of Islamic mysticism, also attaining prodigious scope in India, where more than two-thirds of the faithful belong to one or other of the four leading mystic orders: the Chishtiyah and Suhrawardiyah, the Qadiriyah and Naqshbandiyah. The Province of Sind claims the distinction of being the home of Islamic mysticism (Sufism) in India.

A number of undertones that often pass unnoticed may be said to reflect even more surely the true meaning of ethical revival in modern Islam. Of these two closely related phases may be singled out: 1. A growing dissatisfaction with the theocratic interpretation of Islam which rolls religion, law, and government into one indissoluble unity. Turkey has led the way, and where Mustafa Kemal Ataturk (d. 1938) and his successors have walked, other statesmen of Islam must sooner or later tread. Throughout the vast world of Islam one beholds today the belated repercussions of Turkey's upheaval. The dissolution of the Ottoman Caliphate in 1924 raised a peculiarly Islamic debate on the mooted relation between "church and state." The outcome, vague and indecisive though it may be, is reflected in most of the constitutions which have since been written or amended. 2. A solemn declaration of the universal, primarily humanitarian, and peaceful aspects of Islam is under way. It is patent that the chronic strife and stress of Europe, exemplified in bloody wars and gnawing inner conflicts, have elicited the downright revulsion of the Islamic soul. Today, Islam, with hardly any serious opposition, is being dressed up by its champions as a cathartic for the ailing Western man. Since no frontal attack on Christianity is feasible, Moslem thinkers are constantly reminding the Church of her failure to cope with the recurrent epidemic of war, of her fruitless measures in dealing with the racial issue, and of her current failure to make a contribution to the solution of the economic evils of mankind. Above all, Christianity is taken to task for her seeming inability to tone down the rash imperialistic, materialistic avidity of men and nations within her borders. With perfect logic, therefore, the Moslem presumes to present the claims of his faith. An equally perfect honesty moves him to ask men everywhere, "Why not try Islam?"

This ethical zeal and vitality is shown in the new interpretation of the relation between "church" and state. (Islam, of course, knows no ecclesia in the strictly Christian sense, the word church here denotes established religion as such.) While Turkey staged her upheaval and shattered the Ottoman theocracy she displayed a will militant against the old forms of Islam. She actually showed disdain for the Arab heritage, and declared her intention to become a European commonwealth. In no way did she try to interpret her course of action within the context of Islamic theology. The task of interpretation, which would justify modernization on a large scale, was left for a relatively obscure judge of the Egyptian courts, one whose name would sound insignificant alongside that of Ataturk, but who in the annals of Islamic thought is bound to receive increasing recognition. This man is Ali Abd-al-Raziq (1882–   ) who at tremendous personal sacrifice made an epoch-making contribution which entitles him to a place among the makers of modern Islam. He undertook to show the Moslems of Egypt and the world not only that the institution of the caliphate did not measure up as an integral part of their religion, but that true Islam was a religion in no wise to be confused with the functions of the state.

Although most independent Moslem states today—Egypt, Saudi Arabia, Yaman, Iraq, Iran, Afghanistan, Syria, etc.—in practice recognize a theocratic principle of union between "church" and state symbolized in the almost invariable constitutional stricture that the head of the state must be a Moslem, the voice of Abd-al-Raziq and his ilk has been heard far and wide. Modern Islam may be said to be moving slowly toward his position.

Abd-al-Raziq crystallized his arguments in a book *al-Islam wa-Usul al-Hukm* (Islam and the Principles of Government)[1] setting forth, on the basis of historic and Koranic evidence, that separation between religion and the state is a firmly rooted Moslem concept, disregarded though it has been by the believers throughout the years. Though boldly conveying beyond any doubt the true sentiment of the progressive liberals and most educated Moslems, Abd-al-Raziq earned the censure of his Azharite colleagues who brought about his dismissal from office. The following passages reproduce his thesis in part: "Not only the Koran but the Tradition as well disregard the caliphate. . . . God who has ordained the survival of His religion does not make its rise or fall dependent upon any form of government, or set of rulers. . . . God does not place the welfare of His people . . . at the mercy of any caliph. . . . Islam is a divine message not government, a religion not a state. . . . It is true that the Arabs established both an Arab dominion and government. But Islam, as we believe, is the religion of all mankind. It is neither Arab nor non-Arab. . . . There is nothing in Islam which should stifle Moslems in their efforts to emulate other nations in social and political progress. Nor are Moslems deterred by their religion in their endeavor to destroy the ragged, worn-out structure which enslaves their spirit. They are free to lay the foundation of their power and constitutional system upon the most recent formulations of the human intellect. . . ."

FOUNDERS AND INTERPRETERS

Islamic history bestows upon the austere and resolute second caliph, Omar (634–644), the most illustrious mantle at its disposal, making him the greatest successor of Muhammad. A patrician, he had served his native Mecca in the capacity of a high administrator of justice charged with the settlement of differences arising between the Qurayshites and other Arabs or strangers. An inveterate Moslem baiter, he set out one day to slay Muhammad but, allegedly upon hearing a chapter of the

[1] Third edition. Cairo 1925.

195

Koran recited at his sister's home, he succumbed to the rapturous wisdom and truth of the inspired verses and experiencing a sudden conversion prostrated himself before Allah, dropping the naked sword drawn in his hand. Thus in the grim, dark days of its bitter agony, when its adherents were fleeing to Christian Abyssinia and the Prophet himself, persecuted by his own kinsmen, the Qurayshites, was groping in distress, Islam won the support of a stately personage, the equal of whom is not frequently met with in the annals of its growth.

Thereafter, when the tide had long turned in Islam's favor and the conquest of the Fertile Crescent, Persia, Egypt, and North Africa, was in progress, Omar achieved the reputation of a model ruler, *al-faruq*, that is, divider of right and wrong. His was a consummate piety, blended with the qualities of a born organizer. In all his undertakings he unceasingly strove to emulate the *sunnah* (practice) of the Master. When Jabala— last of the Syrian Ghassanid kings—smashed the nose of a plebeian who had stepped on his cloak in the course of performing a pilgrimage rite, the righteously indignant Omar ordered the arrogant prince to make amends, for Islam has leveled down all believers, be they rulers or beggars. And in 637 while riding triumphantly through the streets of Jerusalem, attended by Sophronius, its patriarch, Omar was invited to perform his devotions in the Church of the Resurrection; but he declined, choosing instead to pray at the steps of the church of Constantine, lest subsequent Moslem generations should invoke his example to violate Christian immunities.

The first Moslem ruler to be styled *amir al-muminin* (commander of the faithful), Omar, with fanatical jealousy, watched over the right of the poor folk to live. His nocturnal tours of inspection in the streets of the capital were carried out incognito that he might ascertain for himself the extent of wretchedness and squalor among his people. A number of constitutional measures, eloquent of statesmanship and fair play, are to his credit, including: (1) the establishment of a cadre of Moslem Arabs, showing the names, according to their tribes, of those who received a stipend from the state treasury; (2) the promulgation of a statute regulating the status of Christians and Jews, who, though forbidden residence in Peninsular Arabia, were to be governed under the terms of a special "covenant" giving them title to protection and toleration in return for submission and tax-payment; (3) the official institution of a Moslem calendar starting with the lunar year in which the flight (hegira) took place.

Omar's noble character and fidelity to Muhammad are illustrated in a terse statement ascribed to him by the renowned historian al-Tabari (838–923) in which the second caliph refers to the privileged function of the Arabs in Islam, and then proceeds to draw a categorical distinction: ". . . we have not gained superiority in the world . . . save through Muhammad . . . if foreigners bring good works and we bring none . . . they shall be nearer to Muhammad on the Day of Resurrection than we."

The spate of religious enthusiasm ordinarily released in Islamic circles upon the mention of Ali's name leaves small doubt in anyone's mind that at least in matters spiritual he ranks second only to Muhammad. And yet the ascent of the man to greatness was largely posthumous, his prestige having suffered eclipse prior to the clarification of events surrounding his mortal life. At any rate, one can scarcely visualize a solid national block behind Ali while he yet lived. A hundred years had to elapse before he actually retrieved his position and in the eyes of a formidable segment of Islam attained permanent standing as the Prophet's vicar by divine will and foreordination. Thereafter, Ali became to his partisans (Shiah) a blessed martyr, a sinless and infallible figure, even an incarnation of God in the opinion of the extremists among them. But the Ali of Shiite faith is something more than a historical figure glorified in and after death. He sums up and symbolizes in himself the political objectives and religious ideals of a broad section of the Moslem world.

Ali (d. 661), the cousin and son-in-law of Muhammad who was preceded only by Khadijah in endorsing Islam and yielding to its heaven-born call, was possessed of a profoundly religious nature, little inclined to worldly matters. The stabbing to death of Caliph Uthman (644–656) so outraged his kinsmen that they broke out in revolt against Ali, the new caliph. The decisive battle of Siffin (657) settled the political fate of Ali, though for a few years he retained a shaky control exercised from al-Kufah in Iraq. His assassination was perpetrated by a member of the notorious, ultra-theocratic faction known as Kharijites (outgoers), who for a long time inflicted heavy damage on the central authority in a feverish assault upon any Islamic government which did not conform to the enigmatic slogan: there is no other arbitration save that of Allah.

According to ibn-Ishaq, earliest biographer of Muhammad, the Prophet once addressed Ali thus: "Art thou not content, O Ali, to be in a relation to me equivalent to that which existed between Aaron and Moses?" A later historian represents the Prophet once as taking hold of Ali by the hand and announcing: "Am I not dearer to the believers than their lives . . . whosoever acknowledges me as lord will acknowledge Ali also. . . ." It is the Shiite contention that by these and similar directions the Prophet specified that Ali was to be his successor. Thus the personality of Ali is of immense meaning in its bearing upon subsequent Islamic developments. It is the watershed, the great divide between Sunnite and Shiite Islam. The Sunnites conceived of the theocratic state as an earthly dominion, headed by a caliph (successor of Muhammad) or Imam (leader) who falls heir only to the secular, temporal office of Muhammad, since the Prophet of Allah, called to his sacerdotal task by divine fiat, could bequeath his charismatic mantle to nobody. Beneath the Shiite insistence on a legitimate Imam, an Incarnation of the Divine, some critics detect the longing of the Iranian soul for the manifestation of God in human flesh, in contrast to which they observe the consistent revolt of the characteristically Arab-Semite who eagerly clung to the humanity of the Prophet and caliphs, repudiating any suggestion of apotheosis.

Shiite theology proceeds from the assumption of Ali's divine appointment, as voiced by Muhammad, and argues to the incontrovertible conclusion that the rule of the three caliphs preceding him is null and void. Then it construes the unalterable proposition that the Imamate (pontificate, according to the Shiite view) of Islam belongs to legitimate Imams (pontiffs), who are Ali and his sons, al-Hasan and al-Husayn. This elaborately constructed dogma of the Imamate, embossed by fold upon fold of Shiite doctrine and tradition, is the heart of a movement which, starting as a despised minority, succeeded at last in working itself into the affection of many. By appealing to multitudes of malcontents, in many generations and widely separated areas, and to the dispossessed and oppressed groups of society, as well as to alien, non-Arab elements conscious of their proud heritage, the partisans of Ali acquired through the years the marks of a colossal schismatic organization, aloof from the main Sunnite body and constituting an autonomous entity within Islam.

The primary concern of the propounders and expounders, who came after the formative era of Muhammad, Omar and Ali, centered for centuries upon the basic structure and doctrinal groundwork of Islam. Their seemingly interminable mission was to wrestle with 1. the Koran, its text and exegesis; 2. the *Sunnah* (practice, custom) of Muhammad and his companions as adduced from tradition; and 3. the *Fiqh* (wisdom, jurisprudence), mainly evolved from the Koran and *Sunnah* and fashioned in keeping with the political and cultural situation, under the impact of external influences and by reason and experience, into law (*shar, shariah*).

Insofar as modern scholarship is able to ascertain, it was Caliph Uthman (644–656) who, out of the several competing codices of the Koran, designated as an authorized version the one then in use at Medina. No definitive text made its appearance, however, till about three centuries later when a standard reading was offered in 933. Almost concurrently with this, the distinguished historian al-Tabari (838–922) compressed the Islamic thought of three hundred years into his prodigious *Tafsir,* commentary on the Koran, to which he brought the results of his assiduous studies in history, jurisprudence, and religion. The rationalist al-Zamakhshari (1074–1143), an adherent of a free-thinking school, employed his *al-Kashshaf* (expositor) to rid the Koran of determinism, anthropomorphism, and supernaturalism. These highly esteemed commentaries, and others, are surpassed by the work of al-Baydawi (d. 1286) which still exercises a leading role in shaping Moslem belief by the favor it enjoys with the classes of scholars and theologians who find its interpretation of the holy book most reliable.

Though most of the exegetes were Persians, they were all of the Sunnite persuasion. The Sunnite-Shiite exegetical line of demarcation soon emerged. It hinged on the principles adopted as an approach to the subject. In its simplest manifestation the cleavage here rested on whether *tawil* (interpretation) was to be made synonymous with *tafsir* (exegesis), following the Koran and the Tradition, as the Sunnites maintained, or to be turned into an allegorical exposition, capable of wringing from the text far-reaching implications concealed from the casual reader, in the Shiite style. There was in addition the open door of *ijtihad*—a uniquely Shiite phenomenon—a free appeal to spiritual and intellectual standards, presupposing a mandate from God whereby the learned commentator might seek to discover and enunciate novel forms of religious truth, though in conformity with an intimate understanding of the Koran and Tradition. In the upshot the Shiites drifted further apart from the Sunnites on this issue also, developing their own commentaries, led by ibn-Babawayh (d. 991/2) and culminating in the determinative exegesis of Tabarsi (d. 1153).

Medina, the capital city of Muhammad and his immediate successors, with its wealth of spiritual lore and prophetic associations, provided the setting for the new science of Tradition, which soon degenerated into a collector's art. Traditionalists assembled the sayings of Muhammad and his friends in accordance with a specific technique. Every single tradition consisted of two parts, the *isnad*—a chain of narrators, concluding in the name of the highest authority who heard the saying from the lips of the Master or one of his associates—and the *matn,* the utterance as delivered. Political leaning, theological bias, personal dereliction, or rank dishonesty militated against the maintenance of high standards in the narrator's art, virtually making the field of Tradition a free-for-all.

Critical care was eventually taken to insure the relative genuineness of Tradition. The first impressive compilation was that of al-Bukhari (d. 870) a Persian Sunnite who traveled extensively in Arabia, Syria, Iraq, and Egypt as well as Persia. His countryman, Muslim (d. 874) is responsible for a similar collection under the same title. The four subsequent collections which were yet to appear never quite attained the distinction of the first two.

The formation of four schools of jurisprudence, on good terms with each other, within the framework of orthodox Islam, significantly took place during an epoch when the fortress of orthodoxy was being assailed. Of the schools, the Hanafite is the oldest, the most liberal, powerful, and widespread, claiming the adherence of about one half of the Sunnite population of the world, and prevailing numerically in the territories of the former Ottoman Empire, Central Asia, and India. Its founder, abu-Hanifah (700–767), advocated in the adjudication of cases the employment of analogical deduction, but sanctioned at the same time recourse to "preference," in certain instances, in order to secure equity. The extreme right wing of orthodoxy was occupied by the Hanbalites, a school committed to the defense of the fundamental faith against the sinister inroads of free-thinkers and heretics. Except for a few adherents in parts of Africa, this school might well have disappeared save for the Wahhabi revival of the mid-eighteenth century in the heart of Arabia. The Malikite school, too, owed its origin to a conservative revulsion against liberalism though never going to Hanbalite lengths. Today it prevails in Eastern Arabia, North Africa, the Sudan, and Upper Egypt. Cairo boasts the tomb of al-Shafii (d. 820), founder of a fourth school; and al-Azhar University is the repository of Shafiite teaching and its disseminator in the world of Islam. Born in Ghazzah, Palestine, al-Shafii was of Qurayshite origin but he spent his life in Iraq and Egypt. His rite is dominant in Lower Egypt, southern and western Arabia, East Africa, Indonesia, the coastal regions of

India, and Palestine. Theologically it is known as a tolerant, moderate school, accepting the speculation with caution. In all these schools the defense of the Moslem faith was undertaken against heresy, represented primarily by the Shiites, and rationalism, of which the Mutazilites were the chief exponents. It is to these two movements that we now turn.

The keystone of the Shiite arch is the martyrdom of al-Husayn (680) under ruthless Umayyad swords. In the shedding of his innocent blood the passion motif, which had been lost to Islam since the breathtaking victories subsequent to the hegira, was restored to a position of cultic significance, reinforced by an emphatic belief in an epiphany of the Divine in the person of the Imam. Muhammad had committed his folk to the Koran as God's uncreated revelation, containing in itself all necessary mediatorial functions and exploding once for all the idea that a personal mediator between God and man is needed. But Shiite belief takes a somewhat different view of the subject. Noting the stormy careers of the Imams in general, the kiss of violent death having visited them all, one is able to discern the religio-historic importance behind the double-edged Shiite dogma of the now-concealed, later-to-return Imam. Both concepts are present in the case of the twelfth Imam, Muhammad al-Muntazar (the expected), who disappeared in 878 at a cave in Samarra, Iraq. He has withdrawn, allegedly, from the visible world but his return as Mahdi to reign in splendor prior to the world's consummation is patiently awaited by his Persian, and other devotees, who meantime recognize the Shah of Iran as vicar of the Hidden Imam, and the ranking interpreters of the faith (*mujtahids*) as his spokesmen.

The triple content of the Sunnite confession is (1) God, the One; (2) the Koran, uncreated from eternity; and (3) Muhammad, Messenger of Allah, seal of the prophets. To these, Shiite theology appends a primary article, belief in (4) the legitimate Imam, bearer of divine being, as the proper guide to religious truth, the mediator between God and man. In other words, the light of divine beneficence that once shone through Adam, then through Muhammad, as all true Moslems believe, is now made to shine also through the holy family. Within the Shiite organization three forms of dissent occur: (1) the extreme form, in which the epiphany assumes the proportions of an absolute incarnation. The mortal Imam is swallowed up in an apotheosis, as a result of which the name of Allah is apt to be obscured; (2) the liberal form which reduces the manifestation of God in the Imam merely to a divine sponsorship; and (3) the mediating form according to which the Imams, though mortal, were created from a preexistent light. Subject to mortal needs and functions, theirs is, nevertheless, an immaculacy and a perfection that set them above ordinary men. Eschewing the deification of Imams in any way, the Twelvers declare them to be after the Prophet Muhammad, yet superior to all other prophets and to angels.

Next to the Shiite heresy in significance was the grand rationalist school which gave birth to a speculative development. Known as Mutazilites (seceders), its representatives forsook the theological arena and sought a neutrality of their own making. Occupying a position midway between belief and skepticism, they followed an independent course based upon the acceptance of man's free will. Though owing its earliest inception to those political currents for which the death of Ali formed the great watershed, the Mutazilite movement gradually transformed itself into a formidable bastion of Islamic religious thought. On the major issue of the caliphate, it held the opinion that the problem in essence was one of expediency, and modern Turkey, with the silent approbation of most Moslems today, seems to have accepted this view when it discarded the caliphal institution. Even more disillusioning to the pious folk was the Mutazilite conception of religion as a body of doctrines, ignoring thereby the value of the zeal and fervor by which men live, and taking little stock in the nonconceptual approach to truth. Above all, these rationalists are reproached for their failure clearly to see that in the domain of religious knowledge, complete independence of thought is ever to be precluded. Orthodox Islam could not forgive their assault upon the centrality of the Koran in the field of sacred learning.

The Mutazilite system harked back to the learned divine al-Hasan al-Basri (d. 728), though its formal founder was his pupil Wasil ibn-Ata (d. 748) who formulated the doctrine of free will, arguing with the aid of Koranic proof texts against fatalistic predestinarianism. He also flung off the belief in God's attributes—Wisdom, Power, Knowledge, etc.—on the ground that it constituted a flagrant denial of His unity. The molders of Mutazilite thinking, many of whom were recent converts to Islam, brought to their task the insights of their former connection with Judaism, Christianity, and paganism. And the unassimilated elements in the newly acquired empire of Islam left an indelible mark upon the emergent rationalism. Among the several influences which determined the course of Mutazilite thought were those of the eclectic Persian school of Jundishapur, with its Zoroastrian, Greek, and Aramaic strands; the logic of Aristotle; and certain patterns of the still raging Christological controversies in Christendom.

Under the Abbasid Caliph al-Mamun (813–833), whose enlightened policy was marred only by his attempt to impose freedom of thought by caliphal decree, the burning theological issue of the day stemmed from the difficulty encountered with Islam's theory of Revelation. The question was whether or not the abomination of Koranic bibliolatry existed under the theological system of Islam. The conservatives were pledged to the doctrine that declared the Koran to be the uncreated Word of God, coexistent with Him from eternity. On the opposite side, the Mutazilites rejected any doctrine of the deification of the Book. They appealed to intelligence and reason, and, with an undeniable intellectual honesty, argued for a theory of Revelation that retained the exercise of understanding, admitting simultaneously that the Koran is God's work, created through the inspired instrumentality of Muhammad. A familiar theme of the Mutazilites affirms that the just God created all things at one time but His divine power did not extend to the realm of accidents, which result from human action. For His creation, He does what is best, but the Almighty has nothing to do with man's evil deeds.

The Orthodox reaction was as immediate as it was forthright. It was spearheaded at last by abu-al-Hasen al-Ashari (d. 935/6) of Baghdad. A native of Basrah, he had started life as a pupil of the Mutazilite school, acquiring the rhetorical techniques and scholarly competence of its disputatious doctors. Then he executed an about-face, and in a public recantation disavowed all allegiance to the Mutazilite school, adopting a strictly orthodox platform with the sanguine determination to wage theological war against his former masters in a fight to the finish. Predestination he accepted, limiting free will to the scope of acquisition, that is, man is free only to acquire what God assigns to him. He accepted the uncreatedness of the Koran and its anthropomorphisms "without asking why" (*bila kayfa*). In him one encounters the final triumph of the Arab clerical spirit over the foreign, critical, and heretical tendencies which had threatened to destroy Islamic theology. He instituted a new dialectic (*kalam*), receptive to Greek reason but thoroughly grounded in Koranic thought and primarily poised to strike at the stronghold of heresy. The Asharite system of theology is the most orthodox in Islam and remains popular to the present day. In revolt against the Aristotelian idea that the universe is fixed, the Asharites advanced an atomic theory of creation whereby the energy of God is in perpetual action, vitalizing the very particles or atoms of all created objects which therefore live and move and have their being by the constant flow of divine life. It is noteworthy that Moses Maimonides (*ca.* 1135–1204), whose is the most radiant intellect in that effervescent Jewry which belongs to Islamic civilization, reproduces this selfsame atomic theory of creation in his philosophical classic, *Guide of the Perplexed.*

The ever-widening breach between the Asharites and the Mutazilites, nevertheless, led to a synthesis personified in the "apostolic" role of al-Ghazzali (d. 1111). He is the distinguished Persian scholar who relinquished a dignified professorship in Baghdad in order to check the rebel sigh within himself. A man of striking sincerity and unbounded knowledge, he plunged into a protracted mystical experience, emerging a chastened and nobler man. With his confusion mastered, he brought his religio-ethical findings together in a series of weighty compositions which stand alone in Islamic theology and firmly establish the primacy of religious thought. A mystic at heart, he recognized the value of emotion in worship and found in the Sufi (Islamic mystical) path a vehicle for religion. He rejected metaphysics and poured contempt on religious doctrines that did not bring the seeker into living contact with Scripture and lead to regenerative results. The concept that doubt is the beginning of knowledge already had been proposed by the Mutazilite al-Nazzam (d. 845), and al-Ghazzali in his *Revivification of the Sciences of Religion* now gave it further amplification within the pale of orthodoxy. That leads him to his primary affirmation that religious knowledge must inevitably and invariably depend upon Revelation.

The full spiritual insights of al-Ghazzali are too tremendous and comprehensive to be given here. He brought about a restoration of Islam's finest qualities of faith. Into the theological blood stream he introduced an intellectual transfusion, and to the Islamic spirit he joined a meaningful mysticism. He reminded his contemporaries of the supreme importance of ethics as the index of religious vitality resorting to the simple demonstration that there is an inseparable relation between man's thought and action, his religious idealism and mundane life, and his faith in God and outlook on human society. To scholarship in general he addressed the findings of his researches in epistemology, summed up in a work entitled "Incoherence of the Philosophers," where he showed that a man might gain the whole realm of human knowledge and yet lose his own soul. To educators he preached the insufficiency of a rationalist materialist system that left out character building and moral discipline. With every means at his disposal he sought to rescue the Moslem soul from the grip of traditionalism, and to rehabilitate a religious heritage that had fallen on evil days.

Although al-Ghazzali's message was directed to Islam, it proved somewhat contagious in the medieval world of the Mediterranean basin. Europe as well as the Near East felt the impact of his teaching. Even as late as the seventeenth century, echoes of his voice are heard in the reflections of Blaise Pascal. And in his discourses on the Christian doctrine and vision of God, as in other phases of his *Summa Theologica,* Thomas Aquinas (*ca.* 1225–*ca.* 1274) parallels al-Ghazzali. Maimonides, an unconscious intermediary between al-Ghazzali and European Christianity, had drawn his understanding of Peripatetic thought from the Moslem thinker. Wherever, in al-Ghazzali's numerous works, the pilgrimage of the penitent soul in its quest after the truth is portrayed, the depths of the human tragedy are plumbed in a manner that is sure to strike a responsive chord in the hearts of men both within and without the confines of Islam.

The defeat of the Mutazilite school seems to have been total. In fact the abiding impact of al-Ghazzali tended in the long run to restore the Asharite fervor of yesteryear, though, as the generations passed, his lofty conception of personal religion and his profound mystical idealism faded. By the time one reaches ibn-Khaldun (1332–1406), the first sociological historian, indeed the greatest until the nineteenth century, Islamic theology has forfeited its patrimony of religious vitality by an undue concern with the scholastic disciplines, which had once served a higher purpose in combating the early heretics, but were really too decrepit now to keep abreast of the times. One thing had been accomplished nonetheless: the overthrow of Greek philosophy, in particular Aristotelianism, with its vaunted excellence. In a chapter headed "The Abolition of Philosophy and the Discrediting of Its Professors," ibn-Khaldun's Prolegomena repudiates Greek thought as a broken reed unfit for the defense and adequate accommodation of religion: ". . . certain wise individuals of mankind pretend that both the physical and metaphysical realms can be grasped . . . by the mental faculties. . . . These are the so-called philosophers, the singular philosopher being Greek lover of wisdom. . . . The foremost authority in this domain . . . is Aristotle the Macedonian . . . a pupil of Plato and a teacher of Alexander. He is reputed to be the First Teacher, that is, teacher of logic which he was the first seriously to cultivate. . . . Now the canons of the Greek ancients, translated into Arabic under the Abbasid Caliphs, have since been perused by many of our brethren, some, whom God led astray [Averroës, ibn-Sina, and al-Farahi, for example] even professed them. . . . Know, however, that the basic contention of the philosophers is untenable in all its implications. Insofar as it attributes all existent forms to the first Intellect, by whose agency it proposes to ascend unto the self-existent God, it fails to take cognizance of the multiple gradations of God's creation that lie beyond the reach and ken of the mind. Nay, the realm of existence is far too complex to be thus encompassed. . . . God alone doth guide men to righteousness and truth. He leads on to Himself. If God had not guided us to the light we would never have been enlightened."

Sir Muhammad Iqbal of Lahore, leading modern poet of Moslem India and one of its notable luminaries, recalls Flint's unforgettable sentence on ibn-Khaldun: "Plato, Aristotle, Augustine were not his peers, and all others were unworthy of being mentioned along with him." In substance he seeks to relate ibn-Khaldun to Islamic theology and world culture, offering four important observations: (1) Only a Moslem like ibn-Khaldun could conceive of history as a continuous, inevitable creative movement in time, not one whose path is already determined. (2) For the source of this conception ibn-Khaldun is ultimately indebted to the Koran whose "alternation of day and night" is a symbol of reality which "appears in fresh glory every moment." (3) As a powerful exponent of this conception of time and history, ibn-Khaldun's primary contribution to Islamic theology lay in his identification of the Islamic genius with a revolt against the hegemony of Greek thought which made time either unreal (Plato, Zeno) or cyclic (Heraclitus, the Stoics). (4) The anti-classical spirit of modern culture not only coincides with the genius of Islam, it stems from it.

Ibn-Khaldun probably sympathized with al-Ghazzali for he too cast off the shackles of speculative philosophy. Taking stock of the forces that make history he looked not only without but also within. Religion, as it manifests itself in behavior, he drew into the orbit of man's social life. And though his orthodoxy remained untainted, he was a true philosopher. His philosophy of history bore no great resemblance to Hegel's theodicy. Steeped in Koranic doctrine, its prevailing affirmation was that things are what they are by God's Providence, though he but faintly flashed the vision of a divine purpose, gradually discernible in the contours of history as the mists lift. Above everything else, ibn-Khaldun conceived of history as sociology, a term first used by the French philosopher of positivism, Auguste Comte (1798–1857) who, however, was not the first to define its scope and meaning.

Having in his own lifetime beheld the last convulsions of eight Islamic centuries, crowded with momentous transformations, and having been the eye-witness in northwest Africa and the Near East to startling happenings, ibn-Khaldun acquired the necessary historical perspective to compose a monumental work of interpretation. He began therefore to assemble the phenomena of Islamic history under general principles and to propose, perhaps for the first time in world literature, a comprehensive philosophy of history embracing the whole mass of relevant facts, yielding a reasonable explanation of the laws that govern progress and revealing a plausible goal. Hence his universal stature as an Eastern Montesquieu, and the foremost culture historian of the Moslem peoples. Nowhere before this great Tunisian had the conception of history as a special science appeared, embracing all the known phenomena of life. He treated the different forms of human society, ranging from the conditions of savagery, nomadism, and tribalism, down to agricultural, cattle-breeding, and urban society. Differences in mores and social order he explained on the basis of physical environment, habitat, climate, soil, and diet. He proposed the law of causality in its manifold connotations, and depicted its relevance to human society in the domains of science, art, and religion. His views on war and slavery were strikingly in advance of Aristotle's. Deprecating the antisocial nature of absolute authority and blind obedience, he observed that if some did not command as masters and others obey as slaves war would be impossible. Yet he did not definitely come out against either war or slavery.

With the recognized novelty of his ideas, ibn-Khaldun managed to retain an enviable position as a primarily Moslem thinker, and a strict theologian at that. His law of natural causality should not be mistaken for a new determinism or pessimism. His highest ambition did not go beyond the attempt to evolve a political theory in terms of Islam, and to build a philosophy of history that rested on a solid theological foundation. The reconciliation of the ideal demands of Islam with the facts of history formed one of his deepest concerns. Nor did he ever lose sight of that central theme, to which he invariably returned, namely, that history is what it is because of man's chronic transgression of the divine law. It is man's blind defiance of the Almighty, therefore, that brings woe upon himself and the race, and involves him in the tragic cycle of rise and fall of civilization. Instead, God intends that the mutual association of men should be a means of grace and happiness.

With this necessarily condensed appreciation of ibn-Khaldun's thought our analysis of Islam's founders and classical interpreters reaches its logical end. Due consideration must now be given to the propagation of Islam and its contemporary sense of mission.

EXPANSION OF ISLAM

The stage is geography in general, all the known continents on earth; the time is history, after the seventh century of the Christian era; the dramatis personae are a multiplicity of the races of man, Arab, Persian, Turk, Indo-European, Mongol, Negro, Hindu, Malayan, and Indonesian—brown and black, yellow and white—colors of every shade and hue; the title role goes to the Arab, but the leading character is better symbolized ever and anon by Islam herself; the thrilling story is cast in the forms of diverse tongues and nationalities, Syrian, Persian, Hindustani, Urdu, Javanese, Malay, Chinese, Tartar, Hausa, Turkish, and of course, always the sacred Arabic. If this four-dimensional scope of Islam, in space, time, race, and tongue, means anything it is that the religion of Allah has played a dynamically "humanistic" role in the corporate life of the world.

Neither time nor space, neither tongue nor race has seriously impeded or impaired the onward sweep of this faith. With a startling ease of movement, the transfer of cultural and moral values proceeds in one gigantic swing from Peninsular Arabia to the Iberian Peninsula. Eastward, the intangible wares of Arabia flood that other great Peninsula—the subcontinent of India—borne by wave upon wave of doughty settlers, confident in the knowledge that they have come to stay. Thus in widely separated regions, and under the stimuli of varying factors, Islam captured the imagination of men and succeeded in implanting itself beyond the influence of society's ebb and flow. It erected lasting monuments ever resisting the onrush of the centuries.

Invaded in A.D. 711, the Iberian Peninsula was almost immediately overrun, with the exception of the Cantabrian and Pyrenean highlands. The two most effective forms of intimacy between peoples, war and peace, provided the Arabs with ample means of contact with the indigenous stocks down to the fall of Islamic Granada in 1492. In the course of those centuries Islam flourished within the gates of European civilization and entered into the makings of Western culture. And while Christendom experienced an age of comparative darkness, the stars of Baghdad, Damascus, Cairo, Seville, Toledo, and Cordova glittered. From the ninth to the eleventh century, the major civilization of the world was Islamic. The last word on science, art, politics, culture, and refinement proceeded from Islamic sources. Islamic Spain gave the world a galaxy of philosophers, astronomers, mathematicians, mystics, poets, and historians. Arabic and Romance were both spoken by the inhabitants regardless of race or creed, the former among the cultured, the latter by the masses. Salvador De Madariaga in a brilliant volume titled *Spain* writes that the mighty and refined caliph of Cordova must have looked down on the petty warring kingdoms of

Northern Spain much as the President of the French Republic looks down upon the Moroccan tribesmen.

About the same year that the conquest of Spain was initiated (711), the Arab conquerors, long enamored of the wealth of India, launched an attack upon her, led by the intrepid general of the Umayyads, Muhammad ibn-al-Qasim. But the Islamization of India did not mature till after the tenth century when a Turkish warrior, Mahmud of Ghaznah (999–1030), whose father had originally been a slave, rose to the occasion, achieving a fame that belongs to the greatest figures in Islamic history. In a series of raids he ravaged India, acquiring permanent foothold in Lahore. The short-lived Ghaznid dynasty was overthrown by fierce Afghan highlanders from the region of Ghor in the western portion of modern Afghanistan, who subsequently were subdued by a succession of Islamic powers known collectively as the Sultanate of Delhi (1206–1526).

Islam attained its highest peak in India under the Mogul dynasty (1525–1857), founded by the energetic and cultured Babar, in whose veins flowed the blood of the Mongol Chingiz Khan, mingled with that of Tamerlane the Turk. At the Indian metropolis of Agra, once the Mogul capital city, Emperor Shah Jahan erected the Taj Mahal (distinguished abode) as a mausoleum in honor of his favorite wife, Mumtaz-i-Mahal (d. 1631), mother of fourteen children. The Moguls lost their power upon the death of Aurangzib in 1707, although the semblance of sovereignty did cling to their representatives till 1857, the last three emperors having been pensioners of the British crown. Under Akbar (1556–1605), whose prestige with the Hindus was enhanced by his high regard for their religion, the Mogul Empire extended over northern and central India, as well as the Afghan territories about Kabul and Qandahar. But even though the Moguls are solely credited with giving Islam its golden prime in India, the Arab traders, ever since the eighth century, had made the preaching of Islam in the heart-shaped peninsula their special concern, beginning at the Malabar Coast and penetrating inland. In the early nineteenth century an Islamic revival in Bengal owed its primary inspiration to the appeals of Wahhabi reformers, followed in a few decades by an independent large-scale spiritual awakening within Indian Islam.

The naturalization of Islam in India has not been easy. It has been hampered by the country's rich and noble heritage, by the firmly established brahmanical priestly institutions, and by the stratified social structure. The acceptability of Arabia's religion was made contingent upon its being Hinduized. Nevertheless, India is no exception to the rule that the national character of any people undergoes a transformation when the Crescent appears on the horizon. Nowhere does the formative power of Islam seem more effective than in its mediatorial function between different races and cultures, banishing the boundaries and barriers that hold men apart. In a more profound sense Islam has turned the eye of the Hindu from caste rigidity to a democratic ideal rooted in submission to the Almighty. In the field of religion it has sought to switch off that deep concern with impersonal Being, on which Hindu thought has dwelt so long, and it has drawn attention instead to the significance of the human soul in the sight of God. Thus it has discredited world flight and breathed a new spirit of comfort and reality into the philosophies of India. To this the noted German thinker and founder of the School of Wisdom at Darmstadt, Hermann Keyserling (1880–1943), in *The Travel Diary of a Philosopher,* bears testimony: "Even the faces of the faithful, who belong unmistakably to the blood of the Hindus, betray the self-conscious, calmly superior expression which characterizes the Moslem everywhere. . . . How right are Englishmen in regarding and treating the Islamic element in India as the decisive one! . . . Islam is an expression, among others, of the western spirit. . . ." [2]

The constitutive role of Islam on a world-wide scale is brought to light by the brilliant insight of Arnold J. Toynbee. One is reminded that the Hellenic civilization is in a parent-child relation to Christendom in its Western and Eastern branches. Between the vanished Hellenic civilization and the modern Christian arise the intermediary phenomena of the Roman Em-

[2] Vol. i, New York, 1925, pp. 203, 213.

pire, the Christian Church, and wandering peoples. Likewise Islamic civilization is an heir to an antique parent, the Syriac, which became resplendent in the time of King Solomon and Hiram of Tyre. It also branched out into the affiliated Arabic and Persic civilizations. And between the current Islamic and the ancient Syriac appear the intermediaries of the Baghdad-centered Abbasid Empire, the Islamic "church," and the wandering peoples. In the Arabic-Persic complex one sees not only the Sunnite-Shiite sister groupings, but also the Arab and non-Arab peoples within Islam. Saudi Arabia, Egypt, Iraq, Syria, Palestine, North Africa, the Sudan, and al-Yaman fall into the Arab sphere. In the non-Arab orbit are Turkey, Iran, Afghanistan, Turkestan, Moslem India, Malaya, and Indonesia. An outer ring of non-Arab Moslems is constituted by Moslem Negro Africa, Moslem Russia, and China as well as by isolated, though not always inconsiderable, communities in Europe, the Philippines, Japan, and the Americas. All in all this is a world of some two hundred and seventy-five millions. Moreover, the persistent, world-wide character of Islam manifests itself on the political, ethical, and religious fronts.

Though Ottoman Turkey declined in the seventeenth and subsequent centuries, her impressive period, extending from before the conquest of Constantinople in 1453, and for more than a century thereafter, was not easily forgotten in Europe. The Ottoman civil, military, and religious administration centered in a school, connected with the royal palace, where surprisingly modern curricula and techniques were in use. At the outset of the nineteenth century, following a long lethargy, Sultan Mahmud II (1808–1839) of Constantinople and Muhammad Ali (1805–1849) of Cairo were typical Moslem rulers wide awake to the sore needs of Islamic society. Therefore they instituted many reforms and created a disposition in favor of Western technology and initiative. Sir Syed Ahmad Khan (1817–1888) founded Aligarh College in India, into whose charter he wrote: "Modern science and oriental learning are not mutually exclusive and Muslims must make an effort to combine them."

All these trends were translated into action, despite the tragic fall of the Ottoman Empire. On the field of battle a brilliant record was set for Islam by Turkey in 1919, when Ataturk won among his people the sobriquet "Victor of the Dardanelles" through his victory over the British-French fleets and forces, as well as when he prosecuted to a successful conclusion the war against Greece (1919–1922).

In the political-military arena the publicized transformation of Turkey is symptomatic of what is in store for all Islam. The gains of the Kemalist revolution (*inkilap*) remain untarnished by the stolid neutrality of Turkey in World War II. The disreputability of a decrepit Turkey has now been erased by the modern offspring of those who were strong enough to conquer Constantinople in the fifteenth century. By all means at their command, the makers of modern Turkey have sought to keep fresh the achievements of their ancestors who in their prime beat at the very gates of Vienna, heart of Europe. Those same Turks, who in 1943 asked the United Nations for larger lend-lease deliveries as a condition for joining the Allies against the Axis, were aware that in the sixteenth century their forebears had scored victory after victory because theirs was the strongest military machine of the time.

CONTEMPORARY ISLAMIC MISSION

In its self-respect, self-maintenance, and realistic zeal, in its fight for solidarity against racist and Marxist ideologies, in its thirst for mastery over the common Western philosophies, in its vigorous denunciation of imperialism and exploitation, in its bold revindication of the Koranic faith against the incursions of critics and the peaceful competition of other religions, as in the preaching of its own message to a wayward, bleeding humanity, Islam faces the modern world with a peculiar sense of mission. Not confused and not torn apart by a mass of theological subtleties, nor buried beneath a heavy burden of dogma, this sense of mission draws its strength from a complete conviction of the relevance of Islam. It assumes the consonance of the Islamic faith with the spirit of the times. And it reproduces its passionate, historic claims as the product of a clear contemplation of power and truth.

Only through such an approach is it possible for one to comprehend the amazing tenacity and robust steadfastness of Islam, for instance in the alien soil of the Far East. Save for the overwhelmingly Moslem majority of the Netherlands Indies, Islam in the Pacific area consists in a set of minority groups, considerable numerically though some are, dispersed among other religions, in China, the Philippines, Malaya, and India. As a rule these scattered Moslem communities have experienced the usual tribulations which foreign elements defying assimilation encounter in any land. Even in the modern era, the Moslems of China, for example, have not been left alone. About twenty million strong, they had already received the doctrines of two twentieth-century revolutions—the far-away Turkish and nearer home, the Chinese—when upon them burst the Russian Communist tide, desecrating their mosques and holding their religious beliefs in contempt. The Moslem Mutual Progress Association, founded in 1911 with the backing of an active press, and later also the radio, aided the Moslems to withstand these ravages. The doors of constructive citizenship in China, opened to all races and creeds under the revolutionary regime (1912–   ) of Dr. Sun Yat-sen, founder of modern China, led subsequently, through the enlightened policies of Chiang Kai-shek, to the improved status of Moslems. The Generalissimo translated his good will toward Islam into action in the appointment to key positions in the government of Moslem leaders of the caliber of General Pai Tsung Hsi of Kweilin. Their sense of national mission has been twice demonstrated by China's Moslems in recent decades: (1) in their unflinching resistance to the Commintern and eager expression of loyalty to the Kuomintang; (2) in their outright rejection of Japan's repeated offers they consistently withheld support of the discredited East Asia Co-Prosperity Plan.

To the Philippine Moslems belongs the distinction of living in the midst of the one officially Christian country of a definitely non-Christian, non-Moslem, part of the world. Their impressive settlements in Mindanao and Sulu form the only big Moslem community ever to come under the American flag. Their name "Moros," that is, Moors, they owe to the Spaniards with whom they struggled for some three hundred years, a sequel, as it were, to the seven-centuries-long war of the Iberian Peninsula between the followers of Muhammad and Christ. Hardly to be reckoned as sympathizers with the vagaries of modern nationalism, the Moros—a minority of half a million—view the prospect of Filipinization with pronounced apprehension. An aggressive element in the life of the archipelago, they are not likely to surrender their local autonomy without a showdown. The introduction of Islam into Mindanao in A.D. 1475, via Johor in Malaya, ushered in literacy and the caliphal forms of political and constitutional government. The Arabic alphabet was applied to local dialects. The Koran and other Islamic texts were translated into the vernacular. But the relative harmony between the Moros and Filipinos has been made possible through American vigilance entailing Army action, since Admiral George Dewey took Manila in 1898. Among the several United States ranking officers who distinguished themselves in the pacification of the Moros, the name of General John J. Pershing is the most illustrious.

The influx of Chinese and Indian nationals into British-ruled Malaya was accelerated by the exploitation of the tin mines and rubber plantations. The indigenous Moslems finally discovered themselves a minority in their own homeland. Nationalism, with its concomitant religious and cultural awakening, was the sole refuge of the native stock, already chafing under alien tutelage. Their Sunnite Islam had been imported from India at a time when Persian was in the ascendancy as a language of letters. Contemporary reformers in Malaya are determined to rid their faith of heretical, mystical, and magical accretion. In this endeavor they naturally look to Egypt and Arabia for inspiration. The Malayan states normally send one of the largest annual pilgrim contingents to al-Hijaz, some 30,000. Accorded a free hand in their respective domains by the British authorities, the sultans of both Federated and Unfederated states have given their sanction to certain changes in the Islamic law of the land. In 1933, ibn-Ahmad al-Hadi, a Malayo-Arab jurist, pupil of the late Muhammad Abduh of Egypt, reached the somewhat radical conclusion, though not without social implication, that interest from banks, stocks, and cooperative bonds is lawful.

Fifty-eight times the size and nine times the population of Holland, the Netherlands Indies has from the early seventeenth century down to the latter half of the nineteenth been exploited in unjust fashion. Toward the end of this period the Netherlands Government started to rethink its Moslem policy. A group of Leiden professors, among whom were Snouck Hurgronje and C. Van Vollenhoven, formulated a new approach to the Indies problem, with the recommendation that it be left free from state interference. It was based, in the main, upon a profound understanding of Islam. Sarikat Islam and Muhammadiyah are the two outstanding Islamic organizations in the Indies. The latter, still the most influential Moslem society, was founded at Djokjakorta, Java, in 1912. In order to check the rising power of Christian missions, it bestirred itself to nationwide endeavor after 1923, making a strong impression upon the lower middle class of Java and Sumatra. Toleration of the Muhammadiyah group by the Indies government is explained on the ground that it is less subversive than the out and out secular nationalists. Sarikat Islam founded four years before its sister organization, has had a more definitely nationalist history. The leading plank in its platform was intended to thwart the ever-growing menace of the Chinese middleman. It was transformed, however, into a veritable political party, willing to do business with the communists. It acquired an anti-capitalist complexion throughout the archipelago. In the long run it has been considerably weakened by the obvious incompatibility between Islam and the Marxist philosophy.

In the Pakistan movement of India, a special contemporary type of Islamic nationalism, manifesting the features of religious mission, is evident. The demand for an independent Moslem state, uniting the Panjab, Northwest Frontier Province, Kashmir, Sind, and Baluchistan, was first given definitive form in 1933 by C. Rahmat Ali. The same leader declared in 1942, "we must do all we can to recover our lost position in the world by saving our people from the serfdom of 'Indianism.' . . ." Any suggestion that the movement carries implications of a military design on a large scale is dismissed by the spokesmen of Pakistan. Sirdar Iqbal Ali Shah wrote in 1940 that Islam identified itself with the British war aims. He gave emphasis to the view that Islam's political morality derives its principles from the Prophet's last sermon in which the lives and property of all people are held inviolable.

The credo of Islam's new nationalism may be understood in the following summary of a poem by the sociologist Ziya Gök Alp (1876–1924), intellectual father of modern Turkey: "In order to create a really effective political unity of Islam, all Moslem countries must first become independent, and then in their totality they should range themselves under the caliph. Is such a thing possible at the present moment? If not today, one must wait. . . . In the international world the weak find no sympathy; power alone deserves respect." Having cited with approval Ziya's words, Sir Muhammad Iqbal, seer of India's contemporary Islam, adds this comment: "These lines clearly indicate the trend of modern Islam. For the present every Moslem nation must sink into her own deep self, temporarily, focus her vision on herself alone, until all are strong and powerful, to form a living family of republics. A true and living unity . . . is truly manifested in a multiplicity of free independent units whose racial rivalries are adjusted and harmonized by the unifying bond of a common spiritual aspiration."

That Indian Moslems, who support the Pakistan movement, are inspired by this principle is self-evident. On March 23, 1943, Muhammad Ali Jinnah (1876–   ), president of the All-India Muslim League, issued from Delhi a message in which he said: "Never before in the history of the world has a nation rallied round a common ideal in such a short time as the Muslims have done in this vast subcontinent. Never before has a

nation, miscalled a minority, asserted itself so quickly. . . .
Three years ago Pakistan was a resolution. Today it is an article of faith, a matter of life and death with Muslim India. It is
not mere sentiment. . . . It is really the justice of our cause . . .
and our birthright to self-determination, by which today we are
proud to stand and for which we are willing to die. We have
embodied our goal in the famous Lahore Resolution . . . as the
only solution of the political problem of India. . . . We . . . must
rely mainly on our natural potentialities, our own internal solidarity and our own united will to face the future." In achieving
her national independence—especially after Great Britain's determined effort toward that end began early in 1946—India felt
the impact of political Islam on a grand scale. This impact,
channeled through the Pakistan movement, assumed international significance, becoming a major concern of world statesmen in the highest level.

Beginning with Russia's expansion in Transcaucasia, early
in the nineteenth century, and ending with Italy's annexation of
Tripoli (1911), a number of assaults on the doddering Ottoman Empire led to Islam's political and spiritual retreat. Irri-
tated by the Mandate system and other imperialist designs, the
Zionist impasse, and the alleged violation of pledges, the Moslems of Western Asia and North Africa responded with a
marked passivity to the Allied cause in the Second World War.
But those who went so far as to read in this passivity the death
warrant of Islam made too hasty a judgment. For meanwhile
a leaven of entirely different forces was also at work, preparing
the Moslem mind for a better and stronger future. Among these
mention may be made of the stimulating occupation of Egypt
by Napoleon (1798–1801); the cultural, moral and spiritual re-
freshment due to the labors of Christian missionaries in the
Near East, India, the Netherlands Indies, and elsewhere; the
literary and scientific radiation from foci of enlightenment in
Egypt, Syria, India, and Syro-American communities; the inner
revivification of Islam in several forms, especially the Wahhabi Arabian; the vitalizing example of Turkey in her ambi-
tious and bold onward stride; and the rise of the rationalist-

nationalist school of thought in Egypt, but even more remarkably in India. To the new imaginative mentality may be ascribed numerous developments in recent years such as the call issued by al-Shaykh al-Zinjani of Iran, with the concurrence of the chancellor of al-Azhar, for a congress to reconcile the standing differences between the two historic divisions of Islam—the Sunnite and Shiite. And in Soviet Russia, where Bolshevist legislation had been prejudicial to Islam, al-Mufti Abd-al-Rahman Rasulev, nevertheless, could call upon his Moslem coreligionists in 1941 to support the national effort against the Nazi invaders. In 1944, for the first time since the Red Revolution, Russia was represented by a contingent of Soviet Moslems at the annual pilgrimage to Mecca.

Islam's sense of mission is manifest in its readiness to see the world as a whole and in its prescriptions for the promotion of the religious life. Al-Shaykh Muhammad al-Maraghi (d. 1945) of al-Azhar sent a message to the meetings of the World Congress of Faiths held in London, July 3–17, 1936, which reads in part: "The appeal for the development of the common religious consciousness should be preceded by the establishment of fellowship between the heads of religions themselves. They . . . are more capable of understanding that the menace threatening humanity does not arise from the differences between religions, but through atheism and . . . materialism. . . . It is deplorable that followers of religions should mobilize their forces to attack one another. . . . This has weakened them before their common foe. . . . I now propose . . . (a) Creation of a body to cleanse religious consciousness of hatred . . . by 1. preaching in each religion a human trend based on its own standards; 2. assembling all religious ideals . . . kindness . . . love . . . ; 3. religious propaganda to be based on pure reason, love of truth . . . avoiding . . . unscrupulous means . . . and confining it to the proclamation of the beauties of some particular religion. The function of this body is to settle . . . differences . . . arising from the aggression of propagandists. (b) Creation of a body . . . to strengthen the religious consciousness particularly among the intellectual classes. This body should support the position of religion in regard to scientific investigation and free thought. This support must necessarily depend on . . . proof . . . and the avoidance of coercive and misleading measures as well as reliance on arbitrary spiritual authority."

Beneath the surface of its contemporary program of world mission, Islam shows the signs of real enlightenment, promising progress in new directions. Often suppressed and denied self-expression, the liberals include a dynamic though small faction of men and women who harbor no illusions as regards the inadequacy of the old Law to cope with the needs of modern society, or to inspire a generation groping for democratic institutions and striving for fuller participation in the councils of the nations. In the Middle East, Moslem Arabs have demonstrated, under the Arab League, their ability to create, together with their Christian countrymen, an entirely secular, political front. Even more startling and revolutionary is the call for social and legislative reforms, sharpening the break with the conventional theocratic pattern which has hitherto restricted groups and individuals to moral, cultural, and spiritual categories bequeathed by a long dead past, making little allowance in practice for personal judgment and initiative. What is crucially at stake, therefore, amounts to nothing less than the very meaning and soul of religious liberty. For it is becoming increasingly clear that no religion, claiming a divine mandate to serve the purpose of God for mankind, can long endure unless it leaves man's conscience absolutely free to choose the kind of spiritual worship and religious affiliation which best agrees with his inmost understanding of the eternal truth.

SELECTED BIBLIOGRAPHY

The Spirit of Islam. By Amir Ali. London, 1922.
Mohammed: The Man and His Faith. By Tor Andrae. Translated by Theophil Menzel. London, 1936.
Arab Heritage. Edited by Nabih Amin Faris. Princeton, 1944.
Encyclopedia of Islam. Edited by M. Th. Houtsma, *et al.* London, 1913; Supplement, 1938.
History of the Arabs. By Philip K. Hitti. London, 1940.

The Reconstruction of Religious Thought in Islam. By Mohammad Iqbal. Oxford, 1934.

Islam: Beliefs and Institutions. By Henri Lammens. Translated by E. Denison Ross. London, 1929.

The Koran. Translated by E. H. Palmer, Oxford, 1928; Richard Bell, Edinburgh, 1937.

Legacy of Islam. Edited by Thomas Arnold and Alfred Guillaume. Oxford, 1931.

The Moslem World Quarterly. Edited by Samuel M. Zwemer and Edwin E. Calverley. Hartford, Conn.

The Muslim Creed. By A. J. Wensinck. Cambridge, 1932.

Judaism

ABRAHAM A. NEUMAN

JUDAISM is the religion professed by a small people, the Jewish people, who numbered no more than sixteen million souls at the zenith of their numerical growth before World War II and are now reduced to about ten or eleven million through the maniacal fury of a clique which set out to destroy the religion and the people, root and branch. They numbered less than a million in the days of their nationhood, when according to tradition David composed Psalms and Solomon wrote epigrams and parables of wisdom; and probably not more than four to five million when their political fate as a nation was sealed in the year 70 and they set out upon their historic career as a global people with a religion and a Bible to live by and to defend, if need be, even unto death. At the height of the Middle Ages, during the thirteenth century, when Judaism had reached its full rabbinic development and was exerting a great influence upon the emerging European civilization, the Jewish population in Europe did not much exceed one million souls.

This people, one of the smallest and oldest historic nations—now scattered over the globe—out of the depth of its own experience, attained to a lofty and unique vision of God, man, and the universe, and translated that vision into a program of living. That vision and that way of life constitute the philosophy and the precepts of Judaism.

The relationship between the people and the religion is unique in Judaism: for the religion is inconceivable without a continuous, living Jewish people. By the normal process of religious conversion Judaism can absorb and assimilate individuals and even nations within its fold, and it has indeed done so. But were the Jews of the world to disappear, their religion would inevitably disappear with them. Other peoples who had no historic connection with the Jewish past could under such circumstances become heir to the universal teachings of Judaism; but the precepts, ceremonials, and observances in which these principles are incorporated and which make up the body of Judaism would have no relevancy for those whose ancestors did not "go out of the land of Egypt," and who were not born to the tradition that their fathers stood at the foot of Sinai and that they and their descendants were forever to be a kingdom of priests and a holy nation.

The indissoluble bond between the people and religion is a basic part of Judaism. Judaism was not given full grown to the Jewish people as was Christianity to the pagan nations. To its adherents, the Jewish religion in essence is not the distillation of the tears and sorrows of others, freely given them by an act of divine grace or acquired through the mysteries of faith. Slowly and painfully over the course of many centuries it was beaten out of the historic experiences of the nation, illumined by the vision of its prophets and sages. The prophets of Israel, profound mystics, who envisaged God the Infinite, who perceived that His Spirit filled the universe, and who spoke in His Name with the warmth, intimacy, and conviction of personal revelation, were not detached individualists or universalists. They were essentially national heroes of the Jewish religious genius. The problems, sins, failures, and sorrows of their people were the starting-point of their spiritual brooding. However universal and far-reaching the resulting prophetic vision may have been, its light was focused upon Israel and, through Israel, its rays were diffused round the world.

Secondary only to the people was the relationship of the land to the religion during the early stages of its development. In the Abraham covenant, the promise of the land follows closely upon the choice of Abraham's descendants as "a blessing to all the families of the earth." The possession of the Promised Land was not merely a national goal; it was not only the vehicle of a divine covenant and an instrument by which God's pleasure or displeasure with the people was manifested; it was the medium for a system of agricultural and land legislation which gave meaning to the ethical character of the religion. Rooted in the land are the Biblical laws for relief from the curse of poverty, precepts to prevent land concentration in the hands of the few, provisions for a program of social justice. Even after the forcible separation of the Jewish people from their land, the skies and the soil of Palestine, the rain and the dew, the trees and the fruit of the Holy Land have continued to be mirrored in the prayers and festive days of the Jewish religion to this day.

Judaism therefore appears under two aspects: the universal and the national. As a system of religious thought it is transcendent and universal. As a religious cult, it is characterized by historic associations and even geographic coloring. Its ethical principles embrace all mankind; its religious discipline binds only its adherents. Through its own votaries in the Graeco-Roman world and later more effectively through its daughter religions, Christianity and Islam, it won the pagan world over to the Hebrew God of justice, mercy, and holiness. But even when the world was the prize at stake, Judaism would not surrender its distinctive historic ties. It could not abandon its religious system of law, rite, and ceremony any more than it could compromise with its conception of pure monotheism.

It may well be said that Judaism views theology through the eyes of history in contrast to Christianity, for instance, in which theology is primary and history is secondary. Basing itself on the record of the Pentateuch, the Prophets, and the oral tradition, Judaism beheld the gradual and manifold manifestation of God's Being and His active Will revealed variously in its history, in the forces of nature, in prophetic utterances, and in a program of divinely inspired legislation. In the drama thus unfolded historically, the Jewish people was the chief instrument of the divine revelation. Having revealed Himself through the instrumentality of Israel he was called the God of Israel, as formerly he was called the God of Abraham, Isaac, and Jacob. But the God of Israel was the Father of mankind, the Creator of the universe, the Source of all life and the Ruler of all His creatures. He was clothed in Holiness. His chief raiments were Justice, Love, Truth, and Mercy. These attributes of God were manifested in the historic experiences of the people and were revealed in their divine light to His prophets. They were channeled into human life as an activating force for conduct through the Law, written and oral. The Law, therefore, has an exalted place in Judaism. No distinction divides so-called ceremonial or ritual laws from ethical precepts, as both drew their sanction from the living God. However detailed any part of the Law may be, it speaks the language of the universal God. "Blessed art Thou, Oh Lord our God, king of the Universe" is the introductory invocation to the performance of all religious precepts in Judaism.

In this conception, Israel is the custodian of a religion the essence of which belongs to the world. It lays no claim to a monopoly or the exclusive possession of God's truth. Rather does it proclaim itself to be the God-appointed trustee of religion in the interest of all mankind. This is the meaning which Judaism gave to the verse: "And ye shall be unto me a kingdom of priests and a holy nation." As the priests served their people in the Temple of God, so must Israel serve mankind in the Kingdom of God on earth. As the priests, serving in the Temple, observed a priestly code to fit them for their special functions, so must the Jews observe a special code, the Torah, written and oral, to fit, or sanctify, themselves for their world ministration.

The attitude of Judaism toward other religions is therefore unique and distinctive, following therein too a historic pattern. The stern religious discipline of the Law, which grew out of the very history of Israel, was requisite for this priestly people, but not for the general redemption of mankind. Indeed, according to rabbinic tradition, God made a covenant with the human race which long preceded the covenant with Israel, and in that early covenant was laid the basis for a universal faith of mankind. The foundations, or principles, of this early universal religion were described as the "Laws of the children of Noah." These religious "Laws," or ethical principles, were elementary in character but not different in kind from the advanced religious-ethical principles which Israel was destined to develop under prophetic tutelage. They were the embryonic stage in the evolution of that religion which Judaism envisaged as the ultimate faith of mankind. Undoubtedly, the rabbis reconstructed imaginatively the "Laws of the children of Noah" with an eye to paganism. Their purpose was to construct a program to lead the nations away from the glaring moral and religious delinquencies of paganism. The nations were therefore bidden to abandon idolatry and blasphemy. Incest, murder, theft, cruelty to animals, as practiced in the eating of limbs torn from living animals, are the negative precepts of the moral law. The covenant to administer justice is the seventh and final commandment of the universal faith. On these minimal conditions, so the rabbis taught, the moral order of the world could be sustained and human well-being maintained. But it was the function of the priestly people to lead the nations to nobler heights of moral and religious perfection. How was this to be accomplished? Judaism never developed a religious army of missionaries. The driving impulse of an exclusive gospel, which would be the sole key to salvation, was utterly lacking. For salvation was open to all who honored even the minimum standards of the universal faith. The formal conversion to Judaism of the nations of the world was not part of the divine program. Rather was it the function of the priestly people by its life and its work to establish moral and religious standards which would of their own attractive powers draw the nations to the road of moral perfection and closer communion with God.

This ideal relationship between Israel and the nations, between Judaism and other faiths was not an isolated concept limited to one period in the evolution of Judaism. It pervades the entire course of Jewish history. In glowing and poetic metaphor, the prophets pictured the fulfillment of the vision "in the end of days." The rabbis, in turn, gave voice to this hope in homily and legend. Through prayer, chant, and song, the Synagogue kept this faith and hope active in the hearts of the people from generation to generation down to our own days.

In the Jewish dream for the future of humanity, Christianity and Islam play a divine role. Notwithstanding the inhospitable spiritual atmosphere of the Middle Ages, Judaism, although oppressed by its own daughter religions, recognized its spiritual kinship with them. It regarded these dynamic conquering faiths as carriers of divine truth to the nations of the world. Without deviating from its uncompromising monotheism and its consequent opposition to the trinitarian conception of God, the divine nature of Christ, the worship accorded to saints and images, and other Christological features of the Church, Judaism freely acknowledged the divine mission of Christianity, and equally that of Islam, whose theism was pure and unblemished. According to Jewish teaching, they were unconsciously—but by God's design—Israel's apostles to the heathen nations. They were the active agents spreading the basic truths which God revealed to Israel, in forms which were more readily assimilable to the nations because of their pagan background. The very elements in Christianity which separated it from the mother religion—the conception of God in human form, the priest as an intermediary between God and man, the profusion of images with supernatural attributes, the worship of saints, the dogma of mysteries or sacraments, were interpreted as pedagogical means for drawing pagan multitudes to the true God who revealed Himself to Israel as the One God, the Creator of the Universe, the Father who created man in His image, who inspired him to a life of holiness, through compassion, love, and justice. Precisely during the period of medieval scholasticism, when Christian dogma was being crystallized in rigid concepts, Jewish philosophers interpreted sympathetically, as means to an end, Christian teachings which were unacceptable to them but which were effective psychologically in bringing about the mass conversion of heathen nations to Christianity. This enlightened attitude impressed itself also on Jewish canon law.

With the rise of Christianity and Islam, therefore, Judaism, in its own view, was not superseded. It remained more than ever "a light to the nations." Unwillingly, Christianity and Islam were profoundly influenced for good by the continued existence of Judaism. Christianity in its expansion from a Jerusalem sect to a world religion absorbed foreign pagan elements which needed purification. Judaism preserved the vision of God in its purest Hebraic form. Furthermore, the greater the expansion of a religion and the greater its secular power, the greater becomes the temptation toward worldliness, toward more power and wealth, and finally to the use of force in the defense of its institutions. Thus, inevitably, the worldly success of a religion, be it the Church or Mosque or Synagogue, is bound to carry with it dangerous germs of spiritual decay. Because Judaism during the past two thousand years has been dissociated from worldly power, it has carried a moral admonition of great historic import for the religions of mankind. Its defiance of worldly power, its loyalty to the God of Israel, its sacrificial devotion to religious truth, could not help but excite the imagination of mystics and daring religious spirits in their independent search for God in their own conscience and in the words of the Hebrew Scriptures. Above all, the defiant existence of Judaism as a protesting, or a Protestant religion, was a challenge for freedom of conscience, the most prized possession of free men throughout the world.

Viewed from a historic perspective, therefore, it can be seen that the ideal role which Israel cast for itself in the human drama that was mirrored in its own soul was reflected realistically in the course of human events. Whatever new interpretation Jewish religious thinkers may give to individual Biblical and rabbinical concepts and however they may view the entire development and evolution of the Jewish religion as a result of critical historical methods, there is fair unanimity among all schools of Jewish thought as to the broad aspects of the historic role of Judaism in the religious evolution of mankind. That Judaism is still in the vanguard of the march of the human spirit, that the world must yet rise to the cosmic ethical concept of God upheld by Judaism, that the ancient faith contains within itself the seed of unlimited development that may prove as great a blessing to mankind in the future as in the past is the conviction which inspires its adherents today as in years gone by.

II

Because the source of the Jewish religion is to be found not in abstract dogma but in the historic experiences and insights of the Jewish people, its outlook upon the world of nations and other faiths is warmly realistic. By the same token, the ideational contents of the Jewish religion—its vision of God, and the ritual through which its relation to Him is expressed; its teachings of justice and holiness; its ideals of love and brotherhood which will pave the way to the happier world of the future—are to be explained introspectively in terms of historic experience, not by the artifices of prefabricated theology.

It is necessary to bear this in mind if one is to resolve the seeming paradox presented by Judaism in its theological aspects. On the one hand, every aspect of Jewish religious life is charged with the consciousness of God from the prayer at dawn to the prayer when the eyes close in sleep. Every detail of life is related through Jewish law to its divine origin and sanction. Through prayer, precept, and religious discipline, God's immanence is impressed upon the Jewish consciousness in multitudinous ways even in the prose of daily living. In the spiritual beauty of the Sabbath and the holidays, in the study of the Torah and in mystic prayer, the religiously sensitive person may soar to heights of religious ecstasy. The Talmud like the Pentateuch is not only a book of law but also a fountain of religious thought and inspiration. Such a religion is manifestly rich in the essence of theology; and yet it is singularly lacking in formal theology, in the systematic presentation of its theological principles. Some writers have indeed sought to read formal philosophy and theology into the thoughts of the Biblical prophets. But such anachronism can hardly be taken seriously. In the main, modern writers on Jewish theology wonder at the surprising dearth of Jewish works on theology. Viewed in the light of historic perspective, however, the reason for the paucity is not far to seek. The rigid formalism of thought which the very term suggests is alien to Judaism. The Jewish people did not learn to know God through either syllogism or dogma. They happened upon God. As a sensitive child who awakens to the mysteries and wonders of nature, so were the early spirits in Israel in their awareness of God. Their God-perception was the result of intuition rather than reason and it unfolded as a psychological process.

With the race as with the child, there comes a period of self-consciousness. Growth and experience gradually widen the horizon of understanding and cause deeper penetration into the mysteries which are at first felt with childlike intuition. Thus stage by stage the vision of God expanded as the historic horizon of Israel widened. The tribal deity of its early history became the God of the nations. He became One and there was none other. In turn, Israel, conscious of the burden of its own religious genius, was committed to a fateful destiny as "a kingdom of priests and a holy nation." As God revealed His purposes through the extraordinary experiences of the nation and its prophets, His attributes became manifest to them. He was seen to be the Creator of the Universe, the Father of man, the universal Ruler and Judge. He revealed Himself merciful, long-suffering, and compassionate, but also under the aspects of truth and justice, so that nations as well as individuals are held accountable by these standards. This was natural theology.

To the ancient Hebrews, then, the knowledge of God was not a matter of transmitted knowledge to be classified or codified, but a growing awareness of His Being through growth and experience, a spiritual sensitivity which eluded definition. To know God in the Biblical sense did not mean intellectual perception or cognition, but a soul-stirring emotional reaction due to the impact of His Will on the human being. The knowledge of God thus understood and thus acquired obviously does not fall into the convenient metaphysical categories so dear to the heart of a theologian.

Israel's feeling toward nature and man was part of its God-perception, a mystic, intuitive awareness. Thus as the nation through its prophets became increasingly God-conscious, the world itself was spiritualized, for it was filled with His presence. Its forces were visibly the instrument of His Will. As man was led to probe deeper into his soul, he discovered within himself the image of God in whose form he was created. He discovered that he was born noble and free, with the power to emulate God Himself through the practice of holiness. At an early stage in their history, a divine law was given to the people through the medium of Moses, the greatest of all prophets, to guide them in the paths of social righteousness and personal holiness.

A series of prophets, seers, and sages, unparalleled in the history of any other nation, followed one upon another. National life took on dramatic, tragic aspects. The nation prospered, sinned, repented. God-conscious prophets stirred the souls of their people with searing tongue and flaming eloquence. Conquering nations trampled over the little country. Exile followed and then religious regeneration. The process continued during the Second Commonwealth and thereafter in the lands of the Diaspora. Every age, every new experience was transmuted into deeper religious values. One can thus witness the rise of angelology, the stirring of Messianic hope, the dawn of the belief in the hereafter. There was no pause in the process of growth and development as Judaism passed from the prophetic to the rabbinic period, from Palestine to the Diaspora. Nor was there any disposition within Judaism itself to halt the free and manifold expression of the God-consciousness in the storm-tossed souls of the people during their historic transitions and forced migrations. Only when Judaism was challenged by a sectarian revolt from within or when it was forced by conflict with other religions or civilizations to clarify its own religious conceptions did Jewish teachers formulate their positon on the specific issues under challenge.

Mountains of theology have been reared on Bible foundations but it would be difficult to point to any avowed formulations of a metaphysical doctrine in the Bible, save "Hear, Oh Israel, the Lord is our God, the Lord is One," which indeed has become the cornerstone of Jewish metaphysics. This proclamation of monotheism, originally an affirmation directed against polytheism, remained to challenge the dualism of the Persians and stands to this day a protest against trinitarianism or any conception which beclouds the pure prophetic vision of God as the One and Only Being. Simultaneously with the rise of Christianity there are to be found in Judaism some traces of creedal doctrines as recorded in an early Mishna. These affirm the Jewish belief in resurrection, in divine revelation of the written and oral Law, and in the guiding control of Providence; and their creedal nature is indicated through the denial of a share in the world to come to those who negate these beliefs. Obviously, those were lingering issues of the old controversies between the Pharisees and the Sadducees. Strangely enough, early Christianity and the New Testament, which produced such grave political and social strains between the new sect and the mother religion, were not sufficiently provocative on the intellectual plane to force the rabbis to formulate a creed in opposition to the new tenets of faith.

Talmudic literature is replete with discussions and opinions on theological themes and doctrines. Flashes of thought and brilliant comments illumine a wide range of subjects that come under the heading of theology: God, His Kingdom, the Election of Israel, Revelation, Prophecy, the Law, Holiness, Sin, Forgiveness, the Messianic Hope. But nowhere in the Talmud and its cognate literature was any attempt made to reduce these thoughts to a formal system, the prevailing feeling being, as it would seem, that "the true health of a religion is to have a theology without being aware of it." The characteristic talmudic teaching concerning God, like that of the Bible, is derived from experiencing God. It is of necessity direct, simple, personal. Formalism is alien to its essentially intuitive, warm, mystical nature.

It was under Moslem influence and later in opposition to Christian scholasticism that Judaism was led to systematize its own views according to an established pattern which would readily reveal its points of agreement and disagreement in relation to the dominant rival faiths. Beginning with the ninth century there was a continuous development of philosophic-theologic literature within Judaism till Spinoza broke out of the bounds of religion into the area of pure philosophic speculation. Within these centuries lies the period of classic Jewish philosophy which, like contemporary Moslem thought and later Christian scholasticism, was primarily theological in content. It was a period of stirring theological ferment within Judaism. The basic beliefs of religion were subjected to rigorous critical analysis and opposing views and tenets were held by many writers. Parallel to the rational theology of the philosophic schools there was a deep undercurrent of mystic speculation which found its Bible in the Zohar (a mystical commentary on the Pentateuch) and its ultimate development and locale in the Holy Land in Safed during the sixteenth century. As the mystics eschewed transparency of thought, "systematic" theology must be sought in the writings of the rationalist schools.

These were the problems which agitated the minds of the Jewish thinkers during that classic period: What were the proofs of the existence of God? What is the nature of His Being and what are His attributes? In what sense is the Infinite one when there can be no plurality? Wherein lay the act of Creation: was it *creatio ex nihilo* or did matter coexist eternally with the Creator? Are miracles reconcilable with the laws which God implanted in nature? Has God withdrawn from the universe He created or does Providence still control the world? Is Providence general or collective only or does it reach out to the individual?

Most of these problems were basically philosophic questions and they were resolved according to the established thought patterns of Aristotelianism or Neoplatonism. But, as can be seen, they were also intermingled with theological issues which were rooted in the Hebraic thought of the Bible and the Talmud. Thus the Jewish philosophers struggled with the problem of divine revelation which was complicated by the anthropomorphic passages in the Bible. What were the means of divine communication with man? Wherein was the revelation on Sinai unique and how did it determine the role of Israel among the nations? In particular, they stressed the prophetic primacy of Moses, the father and greatest of all prophets. Hence the problem: What is prophecy and what are the criteria for gradations in prophecy?

With Moses' prophetic primacy was bound up the Law of Moses—the Pentateuch—or, more comprehensively, the Torah. The word of God, revealed through Moses, was divine and immutable. A number of philosophic-theologic problems followed in its wake. Is retribution, or reward and punishment, of this earth or also in the hereafter? What is the hereafter and what is the nature of the divine retribution deferred to the hereafter? Reward and punishment implied free will. How then was this to be reconciled with God's omniscience? Was resurrection of this world or in the world to come? When is the longed-for Messiah to come? How is the true Messiah to be known? Is he mundane or supernatural?

It is readily apparent that the problems, though related to Hebrew thought and scriptures, did not flow naturally and spontaneously out of the current of Jewish religious consciousness. Many of the terms of reference belong to another realm of thought, the world of Greek thought which was resurrected by Islamic and Jewish thinkers and subsequently opened up by them to Christian scholastics as well. Most of the problems and some of the solutions too were common to all three religions. Even those peculiar to Judaism alone were formulated in reaction to the postulates of the other faiths to which Judaism was opposed.

Out of this literature there developed characteristic theological attitudes and tenets in Judaism rather than an authoritative system of Jewish theology. The latter was precluded; for without an authoritarian Synagogue or Synod, the writings of no author carried authority beyond the force of their own logic. More important fundamentally, the sovereignty of reason, or the duty to think, was not only sanctioned but was regarded as a divine mandate in Jewish religious thinking. When there exists such wide latitude of mental freedom regimentation of thought is impossible.

But regimentation of thought, or dogma, was part of the mental equipment of the age. Ineffectual attempts were therefore made also by some Jewish philosophers to formulate a series of cardinal beliefs in Judaism to which in their opinion every Jew had to subscribe or "have no share in the world to come." The nearest approach to an almost universally accepted creed in Judaism was that projected by the famous Jewish philosopher, Moses ben Maimon, or Maimonides, in the latter part of the twelfth century, as an appendix to his commentary on the Mishna of Sanhedrin. It consists of the following thirteen articles of faith: (1) Belief in the existence of God; (2) in His Unity; (3) in His incorporeality; (4) in the eternity of God; (5) belief that worship is due to Him alone; (6) belief in prophecy; (7) belief that Moses was the greatest of all prophets; (8) that the Torah (the written and oral Law) was revealed to Moses on Sinai; (9) that it is immutable; (10) that God is omniscient; (11) belief in reward and punishment in this world and in life hereafter; (12) belief in the coming of the Messiah; (13) in resurrection of the dead. This creed was later formulated as a credo, every article commencing, "I believe." It was also versified, set to music, and admitted to the prayer book. It allegedly inspired a Christian poet to exclaim: "Behold, the Jews sing philosophy and chant theology."

The Synagogue, however, admitted these articles of belief into the prayer book not because they were the creed. Rather may it be said that they became the creed because they crystallized beliefs already held by the people. But though the Synagogue for this reason sympathetically assimilated their contents in the prayers, it was not as dogma but as religious themes that they found such ready acceptance.

Judaism never furnished fertile soil for a dogmatic interpretation of the articles of faith. The concept that there is saving power in holding to a doctrine as dogma is foreign to Judaism. "Thou shalt believe" is a precept unknown in the Jewish religion. At most a dogma in Judaism is to be defined as a fundamental doctrine essential to the nature of Judaism. The attack upon the creedal character of the thirteen principles of faith came from many quarters. Some argued against any kind of differentiation among religious principles and precepts. According to them all the religious precepts, which traditionally numbered six hundred and thirteen, were equally sacred. Others preferred making their own selection in the garden of faith. Critical philosophers expanded or reduced the number of essential principles according to their own more or less arbitrary reasoning, till Moses Mendelssohn toward the end of the eighteenth century, at the dawn of modern Jewish history, made the startling declaration that Judaism was a religion without dogma; in other words, it was a social religion with law as the primary cohesive principle.

Most penetrating of all was the criticism directed at the very heart of Maimonides' formulation by one of the keenest and most original Jewish philosophers of the Middle Ages, Hasdai Crescas, who has been characterized as a forerunner of Spinoza. Of keen analytical mind, he pointed out that Maimonides tended to confuse important doctrine with cardinal dogma. The former are more than thirteen in number, actually sixteen according to Crescas. Of dogmas Judaism knows only seven, he claimed. But far more important was Crescas' difference from Maimonides in the fundamental approach to religion. To Maimonides, religion, in essence, was metaphysics. Its truths were the fruit of the intellect. To Crescas, religion flowed from the heart. Without impugning the sovereign right of reason, he argued that piety was not the product of speculation but the child of love. Goodness was an emotional quality not an intellectual abstraction. The indispensable essentials of religion therefore could not be cast into metaphysical propositions. Thus Crescas sought to direct the trend of Jewish thought away from the artificial circle into which it had been drawn by the centripetal influences of medieval Moslem thinking into the original orbit of the intuitive, emotional religion of prophetic-rabbinic Judaism.

In this general attitude, Crescas did not stand alone. He had both predecessors and successors. But no substitute formula ever succeeded in obtaining universal assent. Maimonides' credo was not displaced from the prayer book, nor from Jewish religious consciousness. It remained a noble affirmation of basic fundamental truths which Judaism upholds in contrast to Christianity and Islam. But at no time did it exercise the curb of dogmatism. Within the general compass of a universe created by a personal God and a moral law to rule the children of man whom He created in His image, the human mind was free to explore the mysteries of religion and to follow the explorations of the soul in its search for the Infinite. Throughout the ages, therefore, it has been possible for Judaism to adapt itself theologically to the changing currents of religious thought and mystic movements whether these influences came from without or were impelled from within by the dynamics of Jewish history.

The Italian Renaissance was reflected not alone in Hebrew works on rhetoric like the *Nofet Zufim* but in the religious emotionalism of the younger Abravanel's *Dialogues of Love*. The shattering experience of the Spanish expulsion in 1492 inspired the most heroic figure of the period, Isaac Abravanel, to proclaim the near advent of Messianic salvation and to build his theology in a series of impressive works round this central theme. The Cabala which held sway for centuries and which ultimately found lodgment in the mystic movement known as Hasidism, or Saintliness, was in its earliest stages a reaction against rationalism which failed the people in the hour of despair, and in its later aspect was part of a social-religious revolution. In the nineteenth century there developed in some Talmudic academic circles a significant religious tendency known as *Musar* (Ethical Discipline) which fostered classes for religious self-cultivation through ascetic and ethical practices, bearing in some aspects a faint resemblance to the Oxford movement.

In all these developments, the basic tenets of Maimonides' articles of faith were not consciously challenged or denied. Some of them were circumvented, or by-passed, as other religious concepts forced their way to the center of Jewish consciousness. A fundamental change and departure was inaugurated with the rise of the Reform movement in Judaism. A product of nineteenth century rationalism, its attitude to religion is that of the advanced critical-historical school. It has disavowed the belief in resurrection and the traditional view of divine revelation, and has otherwise interpreted freely Jewish doctrines that in the opinion of its votaries were not in accord with modern thought. Although this apparent break with a long tradition reaches to the very roots of Judaism and has naturally aroused violent opposition and heated controversy, its leading exponents have always maintained that their position was in harmony with the genius of the Jewish religion and its evolutionary process. Even in the ranks of Conservative Judaism, often called traditional or historical Judaism, there is such wide difference of opinion on basic theological tenets that it has not been possible in fifty years to formulate a theology acceptable even to this school alone. Indeed out of its ranks there has recently emerged a new movement, Reconstructionism, which, from a theological viewpoint, in its concepts of God, revelation, Providence, and every other basic religious idea, holds the most advanced revolutionary position in Judaism. Orthodox Judaism maintains the strictly traditional viewpoint, while in Palestine there has been a marked revival of cabalistic mysticism.

Despite these wide divergences of thought, there has been no schism, no attempt at forced reconciliation, and a broad unity of faith has been maintained by the thread of historic continuity and by the fact that these various modes of religion basically express the religious consciousness of one people, the people with whom the life of Judaism is coexistent. Thus it was in the days of the Pharisees and the Sadducees, in the opposing schools of Shammai and Hillel, in the differences among the academies of Palestine and Babylon, in the varying attitudes of mystics and rationalists, in the conflicts at certain periods between the Karaites (who disavowed the Oral Law) and the rest of the Jewish people, in the conflict between the *Hasidim,* the sect of mystic saints, and the traditional Talmudists, in the internal conflicts with the Enlightened Modernists, the *Maskilim* in the nineteenth century ghettos of Eastern Europe, and in the present day divisions of Orthodox, Conservative, and Reform Judaism. Only when a religious group cut itself off from the body of Catholic Israel or set itself up in place of historic

Israel, was it disowned and regarded outside the pale of Judaism.

From the foregoing it is clear that Judaism is infinitely rich in religious values and responsive to the varied moods of individual souls. The selection by various thinkers of what constitutes the fundamental doctrines of Judaism makes it evident too that these doctrines do not negate one another. Far from it. The selection has been primarily a question of emphasis. With every fresh wave of thought that would dominate a generation, a shifting of emphasis in religious values would cause some doctrines to recede to the background and others to assert their primacy.

III

Among the doctrines that held a relatively fixed position in the center of Jewish consciousness was the belief in the coming of the Messiah. This doctrine reaches deep into the roots of the Jewish past and extends far into the future, for it is tied up with Israel's vision of the ultimate establishment of the kingdom of God on earth. As may be expected from its ancient and complicated history, the Messianic ideal is not a clear-cut dry catechismic formula. It voices the varied contradictory moods of a religiously sensitive people, the yearning and aspirations of a religious community that has plumbed the depths of despair and soared to the heights of hope and joy. It is rich in poetic sentiment, lore and legend; it is imbued with the pathos of suffering, and exultant in the faith of the final triumph of Israel, humanity, and the God of Zion.

Although the New Testament concept of the Christ was patterned verbally and figuratively upon the older prophecies of the Hebrew prophets, the consequent deductions of Judaism and Christianity are totally at variance and irreconcilable. The differences are not merely of tense but of consequence. Because the advent of the Messiah is to inaugurate the triumph of God's kingdom on earth, his coming according to Judaism is of necessity an event of the future, not of the past, with its record of wars, violence, greed, and evil. The eyes of the Jew-

241

ish community were always upon "the end of days." They could not possibly have endured their trials and ordeals, if they had not been buoyed up by an unfaltering faith that a new order of peace and justice will prevail "in the end of days" under the rulership of God and His anointed.

That the Messiah was to be a descendant of the house of David not only seemed vouched for by Scripture but it also responded to the mood of a nation that identified the purpose of its very existence with being the carrier of the divine promise to mankind, and who envisioned itself in the vanguard of the universal procession to God in Zion. That the Messiah was to be without claim to deification was never questioned at any stage in the complicated development of the Jewish Messianic ideal. The nature of the Messiah was differently conceived at various stages in the evolution of the ideal. For unlike the Messianic phenomenon in Christianity which was a startling and completely new revelation to the great masses who were won over to the new faith—literally a *fait accompli*—in Judaism the Messianic ideal was throughout the centuries in a process of flux, following the ebb and flow of national experience and responding to the spiritual needs of the nation as it passed from one crisis to another. In the prophetic vision of Isaiah when the house of David still occupied the throne in Judea the Messiah was idealized as a future scion of the royal house, a wise, just, and good king upon whom rested "the spirit of the Law, the spirit of wisdom and understanding, the spirit of knowledge and of the fear of the Lord." In his reign, surpassing peace and justice would prevail even among animals of prey. "They shall not hunt nor destroy in all My holy mountains; for the earth shall be full of the knowledge of the Lord, as the waters cover the sea." Not the personality of the King Messiah was stressed but the era of human brotherhood and peace which would be inaugurated in his reign. In the famous peace-prophecy of Isaiah and Micah all mention of the Messiah is omitted and the rule of God alone fills the framework of that Messianic picture "in the end of days." As political doom and exile darkened the horizon, the brooding spirits of prophet and psalmist depicted the Messiah as a conqueror over the hosts of evil who must be vanquished before lasting peace can come to Israel and mankind. When the nation groaned under the trampling tyranny of Rome, the longed-for Messiah was lifted into the realm of the miraculous and was seen through the dim light of apocalyptic vision.

From that stage the ideal soars into the realm of mystery. The Messianic age is preceded by violent physical and moral struggles, the birth-throes of the Messianic age. Elijah, the harbinger of glad tidings, returns from Heaven to bring inner peace to the heart of the people and to effect reconciliation with God. It becomes more and more difficult to follow the course of the Messiah to come. But certain characteristics stand out boldly: the reunion of Israel in the Holy Land, victory over all hostile powers ranged against God, and an era of supreme happiness, peace, and good will among all men.

Needless to say, those ideals did not always float aloft purely as visions of dreamers and apocalyptic visionaries. Claimants to the Messiahship rose and fell. Bar Kokba, "the son of the star" who waged war with superhuman powers against the hosts of Emperor Hadrian, was acknowledged as the Messiah even by the immortal Rabbi Akiba. The soil of Jewish history is strewn with fallen Messiahs. In bitter disillusionment, some stray rabbinic voices could be heard despairing of a personal Messiah but still believing in the Messianic age, when God Himself would redeem Israel and be acknowledged by all men as sovereign ruler of the world.

Cutting through the fog of mysticism, Maimonides in his twelfth article of faith dealing with the belief in the coming of the Messiah uttered the following conviction: The Messiah will issue from the house of David. He will excel all rulers in history in the exercise of justice and peace. . . . Notwithstanding the majesty and wisdom of the Messiah, he must be regarded as a mortal being and one who restored the Davidic dynasty. He will die and leave a son as his successor, who will in turn die and leave the throne to his heir. Nor will there be any material change in the system of nature and human life; accordingly Isaiah's picture of the living together of lamb and wolf cannot be taken literally. . . . We are only to believe in the coming of Elijah as a messenger of peace and the forerunner of the Messiah, and also in the great decisive battle with the hosts of heathendom embodied in Gog and Magog, through whose defeat the dominion of the Messiah will be permanently established. . . . The Messianic kingdom itself is to bring the Jewish nation its political independence, but not the subjection of the heathen nations. The Messianic era will not be merely one of material prosperity and sensual pleasure, but of general affluence and peace, enabling the Jewish people to devote their lives without care or anxiety to the study of the Torah and universal wisdom, so that by their teachings they may lead all mankind to the knowledge of God and make them also share in the bliss of the world to come.

Noble as was this teaching of Maimonides, its very clarity detracted from the force of its popular appeal. The strength of the Messianic ideal in Judaism lies in the mystic power of its vision to respond to many moods. Its moral texture is a blend of many hues. When the nation found itself chained and tortured in the web of cruel circumstance the vision of the Messiah to come held forth the promise of liberation. To individual sensitive souls, wearied and frustrated by pitiless struggle with the crushing forces of this material world, it was the rainbow at the end of the road. Above all, to the collective Jewish people carrying the message of God, human brotherhood, universal peace and justice as their historic destiny but meeting with affliction, persecution, and frustration, the vision of the Messiah was a mystic light under which their suffering was suffused with a halo of glory. The Messiah was the symbol of national redemption. The restoration of Israel's nationhood in Palestine was to be not only a moral vindication of Israel through a political medium. It was to be a vindication of the reign of God in Zion whose light was to illumine the darkest crevices of the earth and whose influence was to unite all the nations in universal brotherhood under the Fatherhood of God.

Such a vision was necessarily compounded of many elements:

prophecy, history, poetry, legend, apocalyptic hopes. It drew vitality not from the intellect but from the soul. It flourished not in the topsoil of the mind but in the deep, moist earth of mystic faith. It did not grow bare and upright as a poplar, but as a tree with "sinuous trunk, boughs exquisitely wreathed." At times, the personal Messiah was apotheosized as the collective personality of Israel, "the suffering people." Often his symbolic personality silently receded to the background and in his place stood forth the ideal of the Messianic age with God as the Judge and Ruler. Such a vision filled the soul of the prophets of old. It inspired medieval Jewish saints who gloried in martyrdom. It is this matured vision which upholds and in turn is upheld by countless modern Jews who no longer look for the Messiah in human form but look forward all the more eagerly to the more natural redemption associated with the Messianic era. Whatever form the Messianic ideal assumes, however, it is in any event an embryo in the womb of time.

Although the state of the world is far from the Messianic goal, it is a hopeful sign that two corollaries of the Jewish Messianic ideal have impressed themselves upon the advanced religious thinking of our age. They have far-reaching implications for the role which religion is destined to play in the future of organized society. One concerns human nature, and the other is the concept of this world as the theater of the religious drama of mankind. Judaism never wavered in its espousal of these ideals and it may well take heart as this influence is making itself increasingly manifest in the religious conscience of our time.

The Jewish Messianic idea whether idealized in a millennial era or incarnated in a human personality implies the concept of human perfectibility. According to Jewish teaching, man must perfect his own nature to prepare the way for the Messiah. For the function of the Messiah is not to redeem a race which is incapable of redeeming itself. On the contrary, he is the symbol and the triumph of man's self-redemption. The Messiah is the climax of man's ascent to moral perfection. He is the denouement in the human drama of history.

IV

There were fleeting periods in the early centuries of the common era when the story of the fall of Adam cast the shadow of original sin upon Jewish thought. In later cabalistic doctrine, this concept was reflected obliquely in the theory of ultimate human redemption through the restoration of the original soul of Adam. But, on the whole, Judaism did not allow the spell of original sin, this unhappy concept of human nature, permanently to affect its outlook. That man, born in the divine image, was capable through his own endowments to reach heights of infinite self-development remained a basic concept of the Jewish religion. Those who accepted the Biblical narrative literally and the philosophers who treated it allegorically met on common ground in this regard. Neither party tolerated the idea of original sin. They both viewed the Biblical episode in the Garden of Eden as depicting a passing phase in the hopeful development of the human race. Not only was man endowed with divine possibilities, but he was assigned a supreme role in the completion of the work of creation. The cultivation of nature, the harnessing of natural forces, the building of civilization, and above all the fulfillment of man's moral potentialities were incumbent upon man, and within his grasp to achieve. Viewed in this light, every advance in science, in government, in the organization of social justice helps to complete the program of creation and brings nearer the advent of the Messiah. The organization of the society of nations for the assurance of international peace, the recognition of the right of all peace-loving nations to share in the natural resources with which God has dotted the world, the safeguarding of the individual in religious and political freedom and equal economic opportunity— the translation of these ideas into actuality will, in the language of Judaism, hasten the footsteps of the Messiah.

As this faith in man, born pure as a child of God, is the antithesis of original sin, so is the cosmic optimism of Judaism in contrast to the other-worldliness which has dominated Christian thought throughout the centuries. At the heart of Judaism is the vision of God's kingdom on earth. Not in the world to come but on this earth in the hearts of living men and nations is the divine kingdom of justice and righteousness to be established. When religion views life as fleeting, the world transitory, and salvation is referred to life beyond the grave, man is deprived of the great religious incentive to struggle with the social forces of evil and to establish on earth a moral order of justice and truth. Jewish thinkers too were at times profoundly affected by this mood and their reactions left an indelible mark upon Judaism. Indeed, no religion can wholly escape the dilemma raised by such an influence. But the religious genius of Judaism, cast in the robust mold of the Hebrew Bible, successfully averted the paralyzing influence of the ascetic's surrender of this world.

From the opening chapter in Genesis, through the thunderous pages of the Prophets, the agonizing experiences of the Psalmists, and the calm wisdom of the sage literature; in the contemplation of the rabbis, matured in the academies of Palestine and Babylon, and throughout a long history of courageous martyrdom, the Jewish religious outlook upon the world has been one of energizing optimism. "God saw all that He had made and behold, it was very good," is not only the summation of the Biblical narrative of creation; it is the consistent viewpoint of Judaism in many of its historic manifestations. In varied forms, the conviction appears and reappears in Jewish literature that a world created by God must necessarily partake of the nature of the Creator. Not even evil, suffering, and sin are shut out of this consideration; for they too serve a purpose toward a moral end. They are a goad to man's upward struggle toward moral perfection. Far from shunning this world, Jewish teaching made it the central stage of the human drama conceived by God.

In the Hebrew Bible—Pentateuch, Prophets, and Hagiographa—the notion of a hereafter, in so far as it exists at all, is a vague, dim vision without any power of motivation. Human life is bounded by earth, sky, and sea, which are the handiwork of God and are moved by His will. Within this frame-

work amidst the powers of nature through thunder and light-
ning, rain and drought, and in the still small voice of conscience
God speaks to the heart of man. The physical powers of nature
are harnessed to the moral laws of religion. The divine commandments given to man are reinforced by the operations of
the laws of nature. Divine retribution, reward and punishment,
blessings and curses are visible in the physical manifestations
of rain and drought, fertility and sterility, riches and poverty,
freedom and bondage, peace and war. Man's religious hopes and
fears, his joys and sorrows before God, his dreams and visions
of the future were centered in the world of nature and in his
social relations with man and society. "To walk before God in
the land of the living" expressed the highest yearning of the
religious soul.

The earthly concentration of religious hopes and aspirations
did not exclude the belief in a shadowy existence after death
in the nether world (Hebrew, *sheol*). This was a universal belief in the entire ancient world; and the Hebrew shared it with
the Babylonians and Egyptians. But neither law-giver nor
prophet was much concerned with the shadowy world after
death. The goal of their task was to elevate the life of individuals and nations for this world to the end that "the earth
shall be full of the knowledge of the Lord as the waters cover
the sea."

Maturity and experience cut deeply into the moral optimism
of the Bible. After the Jewish people experienced exile, restoration, and finally subjection and bitter persecution, the pious
Saints, predecessors of the Pharisees, many of whom cheerfully
gave their lives for their religion, had to look beyond this world
for the vindication of God's justice. Belief in a future world
and in a life hereafter where justice is meted out for good and
evil deeds committed in this world then assumed overwhelming
importance. It was one of the great issues which the Pharisees
maintained against the Sadducees and on which they scored the
final triumph indicated in the dictum of the Mishna that he
who denies the belief in resurrection of the dead "shall have
no share in the world to come" (Sanhed. 10: 1). The New

Testament in this instance not only followed but intensified the Pharisaic teaching, so that in the Christian tradition the fate of the individual soul in the future world became the prime consideration; the social fabric of society was of secondary importance; and renunciation of the world was the ideal of the holy man. Asceticism, monasticism, celibacy, and the denial of the flesh are only a few of the most significant signs of the surrender of this world in favor of the world to come.

Judaism emphatically rejected this attitude of the renunciation of society and the world. Judaism embraced two worlds, this world and the world to come. The nature of the hereafter, the character of its subdivisions of Paradise and Hell, the timing of the resurrection of the dead, the state of the soul in immortality—all these formed subjects of intense speculation and theorizing among the Jewish philosophers and mystics. The relative importance attached to the two spheres varied with the mood of the individual and the generation. But at no time did Judaism surrender its profound concern with the affairs of men and nations in this world. For it is in the hearts of men and in the lives of nations that the kingdom of God is to be established on earth. The Messianic kingdom will not rest on supernatural foundations in a supernatural world but on a moral order of justice, peace, brotherhood, and truth. It required heroic courage for a people generally disowned by the world to retain such faith in the future of mankind. But Judaism never wavered in its belief in the ultimate triumph of God's will on earth. As crucified humanity in our time struggles to lift the clouds of war and turns yearningly to the distant horizon for the dawn of lasting peace, the Synagogue prays more fervently than ever:

We therefore hope in thee, Oh Lord our God, that we may speedily behold the glory of thy might . . . when the world will be perfected under the kingdom of the Almighty, and all the children of flesh will call upon thy name, when thou wilt turn unto thyself all the wicked of the earth. Let all the inhabitants of the world perceive and know that unto thee every knee must bow, every tongue must swear. Before thee, Oh Lord our God, let them bow and fall; and unto thy glorious name let them give honor; let them all accept the yoke of thy kingdom, and do thou reign over them speedily, and for ever and ever.

To keep before the world and the Jewish people in particular the vision of the kingdom of God on earth and to prepare the Jewish people for moral leadership in the Messianic era, Judaism does not place reliance wholly on emotional inspiration. Prophetic utterances, moral exhortations, picturesque homilies, and parables were incorporated in the prayers and the daily speech of the people. They stirred thought currents and set the pattern of religious idealism. But to carry out the lofty purposes of the Kingdom, a special vehicle, unique and distinctive of the Jewish religion, was created. This vehicle is a social organism, the Torah, the Law of Judaism. It served the double purpose of advancing the progress of the Kingdom and saving the Kingdom for this world. Torah, or Law, in Judaism was both an institution and a faith. It is a theological concept and a legal constitution. Both notions are complementary and interrelated. The Torah is the constitution of a people whose ideal of government is the kingdom of God.

V

A proper understanding of the term Torah is the indispensable key to a comprehension of Judaism. The fatal misconstruction of the nature of Judaism so prevalent in the writings of non-Jewish historians and theologians is due in great measure to a failure to grasp the subtle connotations of this profoundly spiritual concept. Torah, which literally means a teaching, is used in so many senses and in so many gradations that one may easily be led to confuse the part for the whole, the word for the spirit, the literary content for the poetic soul itself. For Torah denotes variously the Pentateuch, the whole of Scripture, the revealed Word, written and oral, wisdom in its most elevated and spiritual sense, and also the entire content of religious thought and feeling as it is expressed in the literature and experience of the ages. Still more loftily, the Rabbis describe the Torah as the premundane plan which existed, as it were, in the mind of God in accordance with which He called the world into being and by which it is governed.

With love and poetic flight of imagination, the Rabbis mystically personified the Torah and invested it with romantic, supranatural character. The Torah was the heavenly bride wedded to Israel at the revelation on Sinai. Nature interrupted its course, the angels refrained from chanting the song of glory, "Holy, Holy, Holy," as heaven and earth witnessed the union of Israel and the Torah. The Torah came down from heaven endowed with humility, righteousness, and uprightness. In her are to be found "peace, strength, life, light, bliss, happiness, joy, and freedom."

Changing the mood of poetic metaphor, the Rabbis exalted the Torah as the manifestation to mankind of God's will. "Whosoever labors in the Torah for its own sake, merits many things . . . he is called friend, beloved, a lover of God, a lover of mankind; it clothes him in meekness and reverence, and fits him to become righteous, pious, and upright; it keeps him far from sin, brings him toward the side of virtue, and gives him sovereignty and dominion and discerning judgment. To him the secrets of the Torah are revealed; he becomes a never failing fountain, he grows modest and long suffering, forgives insults, and is exalted above all things."

This decription of Torah is barely suggestive of the riches of thought and the joyous love which filled the Jewish consciousness of Torah. But it may at least serve as a background for that aspect of Torah with which we are immediately concerned: Torah as the Law of Judaism. To enter into the spirit of the Law, to appreciate its mystic hold upon the Jewish mind for thousands of years, to see it in its ultimate relation to the kingdom of God, it must be viewed not merely as jurisprudence, dogma, or canon law but as the crystallization in human terms and social forms of an ideal drawn from the fountain of mystic faith on the heights of theology.

At the core of Torah are the laws of the Pentateuch. This was the base on which was reared the structure of Jewish law in all its branches. Like the laws of the Pentateuch which cover not only the duties of man toward God but also toward man and society, the system of rabbinic law that evolved out of the basic law of the Bible embraces all possible human relationships, personal, social, national, and international. Many of the laws are prohibitive: Thou shalt not. The greater number are affirmative commandments: Thou shalt. The positive laws, or commandments, regulate the personal life of the individual, his property, his social conduct; they define his duties toward the state and the cult and his ethical obligations. There is no aspect of the life of a nation or a country which is overlooked. The farm, the flocks, the home, the wages of the worker, the very garments of a man are subjects of legislation in the Pentateuch and correspondingly in the more comprehensive and mature development of rabbinic law.

In Jewish doctrine these laws are looked upon not as ordinary legislative enactments. They are divine decrees; they are the laws of God's kingdom. As the Rabbis put it: God said, "You have received my kingdom in love, receive now my decrees." Because they are divine in nature, the potentiality of these laws is infinite. There is no limit to their study or comprehension. Transcendent wisdom, truth, and justice are hidden in the Law, and it is the supreme duty of the faithful to immerse himself in its study day and night. In its ultimate and perfect development the Torah could be regarded as the law or constitution of the kingdom of God on earth.

Translated into modern terms, the Torah is a system of law which was applied by divinely inspired teachers to the conditions under which the Jewish people were living. As the conditions changed from time to time, some of the laws became obsolete and others had to be modified. But these laws embodied indestructible principles of justice and truth which can give rise to ever new legal concepts and social institutions as mankind is striving toward a new and better world. This was the spirit of the aphorism of the famed Rabbi Simeon son of Gamaliel: "The world rests on three pillars: truth, justice, and peace."

The *potential* values and ideals still to be derived from the Law constitute the dynamic element in the Law, or Torah.

The laws of Judaism fall naturally into several categories. There are those which relate to the cult and the ritual. They are interspersed in the Five Books of Moses and considerably elaborated in the Talmudic and later rabbinic literature. They were intended primarily for the adherents of the Jewish religion. Their function is disciplinary, to train the priest-people through a special regimen of life for their historic role of moral-religious leadership. The other laws touching the general life of the people socially, politically and economically, and constituting general Jewish jurisprudence, are also based on the Pentateuch but by their very nature kept closer pace with the inherent evolution of Jewish life and the changes imposed from without by the peculiar political fate of the Jewish people. Both branches of Jewish law influenced the historical development of Western civilization. It is a matter of great moment as to what extent the *potential* ideals imbedded in the entire Law of Judaism, or Torah, will be permitted to develop and to influence the future course of civilization.

As previously indicated, Judaism makes no distinction between the sanctity of religious law, so-called, and the general law covering human relationships. All law is sacred in Judaism. The laws of mine and thine, the laws safeguarding honest weights and measurements, profits and wages, the laws protecting the weak, the underprivileged, the stranger in the land, have the same degree of sanctity as the laws regulating the duties between man and God. In a society that recognizes the rulership of God there is no phase of human life whether of the individual or the group which is outside the sphere of religion. All the infinite threads of human life are woven into one harmonious pattern. The laws which Judaism has in the past developed in theory and in practice are like a blurred mirror which reflects the ideal Torah, the hoped-for pattern of society in the golden age of the Messianic era. The laws of the Torah are to the ideal Torah what the mechanism of a clock is to the eternity of time.

The Torah is reflected in the institutions of Judaism: the Synagogue and its auxiliaries, the Sabbath, the Festivals and Holy Days and the laws of daily religious living. In their growth and development is manifested the ever widening horizon of the Torah and the social vision which permeates the religion of Judaism. This vision is held steadfastly in view not only in the laws of man's relationship with his fellow man, but also in those touching man's approach to God in prayer and worship.

Worship as it was practiced in the Temple of old through animal sacrifices at the hands of priests and Levites vanished completely with the destruction of the Temple and the fall of Jerusalem and the Jewish State in the year 70 C.E. The Synagogue replaced the Temple, and prayer took the place of sacrifices. Child of the Babylonian exile and mother of the Church and the Mosque, the Synagogue was from its very origin and throughout its long history a socializing and democratizing institution. Its character is indicated by the various names under which it was designated in Hebrew: the House of Prayer, the House of Study, and the House of Assembly. Whether the Synagogue had its origin, as some scholars think, in early Palestine prayer-meetings dating back to the days of the First Temple or whether, as others hold, it was organized originally as a meeting-house for social purposes during the days of the Babylonian Exile and gradually incorporated the other features, it is clear that when the Synagogue emerges into the full light of history, whether in Palestine or in the Diaspora, before and after the destruction of the Second Temple, it had the three features of prayer, study of Torah, and public assembly, each reacting upon the others.

Prayer is the most intensely personal expression of the human soul. But just as in the Psalms, so in the general prayers of the Synagogue, the individual worshiper immerses his individuality in the collective soul of Israel. No mediator is permitted to stand between the worshiper and Him to whom worship is directed. But granting some exceptions of prayers of an individual character, the chief prayers are designed for the individual as a member of a human brotherhood, or the household of Israel.

As the Jew bows in prayer before the Lord God, King of the Universe, and pours out his heart before "the God of our Fathers, the God of Abraham, Isaac, and Jacob" he no longer stands before his Maker as a naked soul but as a social personality with hallowed memories. The contents of the prayers are cast in the collective plural. The worshiper in the Synagogue prays not for himself alone but for the common welfare. Petition, in general, is but a small part of the Synagogue prayers. Adoration, praise, and thanksgiving form the major theme of the Hebrew prayers and all living creatures are invoked to raise their voice in songs and hymns of glory. Although prayers may be recited in the home and when "thou walkest by the way" it is believed that they find greater merit when uttered in unison with other worshipers. Some themes, such as the *Kaddish,* the exalted prayer for the coming of the Kingdom of God, are to be recited only when there is a quorum of at least ten male worshipers assembled. Through these and other subtle psychological suggestions, the Synagogue utilized the mystic power of prayer to foster the feeling of social responsibility and community conscience.

Of immense social consequence was the incorporation of study as a function of the Synagogue and as an integral part of the religious service itself. The Synagogue made of the Torah "an inheritance of the congregation of Jacob." What Ezra began so brilliantly, the Synagogue carried on. Ezra inaugurated a momentous spiritual revolution by bringing the Torah to the people. The Synagogue housed the Torah and made it the spiritual possession of the nation. Knowledge of the Torah made the people free from priestly domination. No priestly tyranny was possible as long as the Law was the subject of popular study and understanding. Furthermore, the diffusion of the Torah among the masses paved the way for the success of the revolutionary Pharisees whose innovations were fought so obstinately by the entrenched priesthood and aristocracy. The Church Father Jerome left eloquent testimony of the

255

role of the later Synagogue of his time in fostering devotion to learning among the Jewish populace.

Without interruption, for two thousand years, the Synagogue continued to be a storehouse of learning as well as a fountain of prayer. Piety rooted in ignorance was discountenanced. One of the most popular aphorisms of the Ethics of the Fathers reads: "A boor cannot be God-fearing nor an ignoramus a saint." This attitude of the Synagogue, this program of spreading knowledge and cultivating learning as an act of piety, encouraged religious independence and discouraged many of the antisocial evils to which religion is liable under the excesses of religious emotionalism. It invested Jewish personality with an intellectual cast and a high social conscience which reflected the vision and ideals of the Torah.

The synagogue was not only a place of prayer and study. It was the locale in which all public life was centered. For fifteen hundred years, from the early Middle Ages to the dawn of the modern era, the democratizing influence of the synagogue radiated in all directions, political, social and philanthropic. Here political meetings were held during the long centuries that preceded Jewish emancipation when Jewish communities were self-contained miniature republics. In the councils of these communes which met on synagogue premises democratic principles were pursued in the name and under the sanction of the Torah. Justice was administered by rabbinical courts in the synagogue precincts. Any aggrieved person could demand a hearing and if necessary interrupt the synagogue service till he was assured that his cause would be heard. The synagogue preached and practiced charity. It tended to the needs of the poor and dependent. It housed the stranger and wayfarer in its auxiliary buildings. It fostered a wide range of philanthropic institutions. Two centuries before the dawn of Christianity, the Synagogue taught, in the words of Simon the Just, that benevolence and worship were the pillars upon which human society rested. How fitting and characteristic therefore was the following selection from the Mishna which was incorporated in the prayer book and recited by the worshipers as a prologue to the morning devotions: "These are the things the fruits of which a man enjoys in this world, while the stock remains for him for the world to come: namely, honoring father and mother, the practice of charity, timely attendance at the house of study morning and evening, hospitality to wayfarers, visiting the sick, dowering the bride, attending the dead to the grave, devotion in prayer, and making peace between man and his fellow; but the study of the Law is equal to them all."

With the transition to secularism that is so characteristic of the modern era the Synagogue no longer holds sway to the same degree. The institutions which it created—philanthropic, social, and educational—are no longer housed within synagogue precincts nor can they be said to be under its direct control. But their moral relation to the Synagogue is unbroken. They draw their life and light from its moral sanction and social vision. The prime motivating force within these institutions emanates consciously and subconsciously from the traditional ethical teachings of the Synagogue.

VI

Of all the institutions with which the Jewish religion enriched the spiritual life of mankind, the Sabbath is preeminent. It commences traditionally with the setting of the sun on Friday and concludes with the appearance of the stars the following evening. Notwithstanding its primitive Babylonian origin, the Sabbath is a true creation of the Jewish religious genius. Judaism endowed the Sabbath richly with the poetry of custom and ceremony and deepened the spiritual significance of the day through song, prayer, and precept. At no time was the Jewish Sabbath merely a day of bodily rest. As a covenant between man and the Creator, its purpose was to release man from labor and worldly cares for the sake of moral cultivation and a deeper understanding of his own spiritual personality. Thus the Sabbath not only suffused Jewish life with light and rejoicing, but it also exerted a far-reaching and beneficent influence on human civilization itself.

The Sabbath holds a place of central importance in the Torah: that is to say, Torah as identified with the written and oral law of Judaism and Torah as the ultimate idealized law of the kingdom of God. Its centrality in the Pentateuch is of course indicated by its inclusion in the Decalogue: "Remember the Sabbath day to keep it holy." Its deep religious symbolism is in full consonance with the high place it occupies. For it is not merely a day for the cessation of work. It is a testimony of the Creator and creation itself: "Wherefore the Lord blessed the Sabbath day and hallowed it." Its holiness extends even to the slave in the household and the stranger, who are thereby endowed by the Sabbath with a dignity akin to that of the freeman and the native. This note is stressed in Deuteronomy where the socializing, emancipating influence of the Sabbath is emphasized: "And thou shalt remember that thou wast a servant in the land of Egypt and the Lord thy God brought thee out thence. . . . therefore the Lord thy God commanded thee to keep the Sabbath."

The vagueness of the wide-sweeping prohibition "Thou shalt not do any manner of work" opened wide the door of religious controversy. Its meaning was heatedly debated among the Sadducees and Pharisees, and it remained a subject of sectarian contention throughout the ages as illustrated by the sect of the Karaites who have survived to this day. The Pharisaic rabbis undertook to define the meaning of "work" and, using the analogy of the work done for the tabernacle, divided it into thirty-nine categories, such as sowing, reaping, spinning, weaving, kneading, writing, and analogous forms of labor. Against the background of Sadducean teaching, this was a liberal interpretation on the part of the Pharisees who consistently sought to free religion from the chains of literalism while retaining the essence of the Law under precise definition. The victorious Rabbis safeguarded their conception of the Sabbath through numerous precepts which they derived from Biblical interpretations and legal inventiveness. These constitute a considerable portion of the written and the oral Torah. Two large tractates of the Talmud were devoted to the Sabbath and its laws.

The elaborate framework of the Sabbath which the Pharisees thus constructed, however, did not meet with favor in anti-nomian circles among whom are to be counted the writers of of the Synoptic Gospels; so that the Jewish Sabbath has been a target of sarcasm and irony as well as a cause for complete and utter misunderstanding. Instead of a "gift of heaven," partisan theologians pictured it as a burdensome day of repression, gloom, and sorrow. Because the prohibition of work was defined in such minute legal detail, those who were strangers to the inner warmth and spiritual beauty of the Sabbath conceived of it in negative terms as a legalistic instrument of repression— a grave injustice to one of the noblest creations of the religious spirit.

To the exilic prophet (Isaiah 56, 58) the Sabbath is coupled with justice and righteousness. It is a bond of union between His people and the alien that hath joined himself to the Lord. It is an everlasting memorial, a covenant, and a delight. From a Pharisee, who was one of the younger contemporaries of the Apostles, the Sabbath evoked these words: "Through the love with which Thou, Oh Lord our God, lovest Thy people Israel, and the mercy which Thou hast shown to the children of Thy covenant, Thou hast given unto us in love this great and holy seventh day." The same sentiment is echoed in song, prayer, and hymn composed over many centuries by Hebrew poets in many parts of the world. In the synagogue, the congregation ushers in the Sabbath by chanting:

"Come, my beloved, to meet the Sabbath bride. . . . Though last in creation, yet it was first in the design Divine. . . . Awake! awake! thy light is come, arise and shine forth! Awake! awake! chant a hymn! for the glory of the Lord is revealed upon thee. . . ."

At home the Sabbath is introduced at sundown with the kindling of lights; the children are blessed with Biblical blessings; the wife is praised with the recital of the classic chapter of Proverbs (31: 10–31); and the Sabbath is welcomed with the ministering angels of peace:

Peace be with you, ministering angels,
Angels of the Most High,
Coming from the King who rules o'er kings,
The Holy One, blessed be He. . . .
Bless me in peace, ministering angels,
Angels of the Most High,
Coming from the King who rules o'er kings,
The Holy One, blessed be He.

Every feature of the Sabbath is lighted with hope and joy, even the very meal with its special food and delicacies and the table songs touching God's love, the banishment of worldly cares, the soothing of all sorrows. The Sabbath brings a new soul in its wake, such was the popular belief. Those who probed more deeply sensed in the Sabbath a foretaste, or symbol, of the Messianic bliss of universal peace and brotherhood.

Like the Sabbath, the Festivals of Judaism tended further to spiritualize human life and blended nature and history in a divine pattern. Seasonal festivals associated with nature's manifestations of spring, summer, and fall took on new meaning as they were correlated with dramatic historic events in the life of Israel. Primitive celebrations were thus raised to the level of Holy Days impregnated with deep religious aspiration. Some of the earlier stages in the religious evolution of the festivals are delineated in the Bible record. But much of the poetry and the spiritualizing effect of the holidays was developed later in the Talmudic and medieval periods. As the Church from the very beginning cut itself loose from historic Israel, it remained indifferent to the spiritual content of the Holidays which were so intimately associated with the history of the Jewish people. It is true that the Church retained some of the holidays by name in the Christian calendar. But the names took on a new and strange meaning that had little or no relevancy to their original character. The Biblical holidays remained the spiritual treasures of Judaism and it was through the Jewish people and its literature that their influence radiated throughout the world.

First in time and season is the spring festival of Passover.

From its earliest beginnings to this day, the holiday was surrounded with picturesque ceremonies, and observances which grew out of historic memories and stirred the religious imagination. Many of the customs are traceable to pastoral and agricultural celebrations of spring. But even in the earliest Bible records, they are associated with the springtime of Israel's nationhood and the religious epic depicting the triumph of freedom through a covenant between God and man.

The Passover observances celebrated in our time are among the oldest religious symbols consciously preserved in the memory of man. Feast of Unleavened Bread is the Bible designation for the Passover holiday. To this day, the eating of unleavened bread to the exclusion of that which contains any form of leaven is one of the conspicuous features of the Passover celebration. Over the great span of time, the *mazzah,* or unleavened bread, has stood for one symbol: the hasty flight of Israel from Egypt—the redemption wrought by God in leading Israel out of bondage into freedom: more pointedly, human freedom under the covenant of God. More than a thousand years later, when the Jews lost their freedom to the Romans, they expressed their undying hope by designating Passover "the Season of our Liberation."

In the days of the temple, the Paschal lamb, slaughtered in every household, on the fourteenth day of Nisan, inaugurated the festival in the evening when it was eaten with great ceremony amidst song and psalmody. Among the small dwindling sect of Samaritans in Palestine, the sacrifice of the lamb is still practiced, so that their Passover celebration annually attracts many curious, interested onlookers. In Jewish observance, however, the Paschal lamb sacrifice was abandoned with the destruction of the Temple and the consequent abolition of all animal sacrifices. But with the disappearance of the sacrifice, the name of Passover which formerly had been attached to the sacrifice came to designate the holiday itself. The transference of the name was not an arbitrary act; the meaning of the symbol itself had grown and expanded. In the Bible the Paschal sacrifice and the sprinkling of the blood commemorated the act of God who caused the angel of death to "pass over" the homes of the Israelites. What was more fitting than to attach the name Passover to the holiday itself which perennially commemorated the far greater and continuous miracle of Jewish survival since the dark ages that followed the burning of the Temple and the destruction of the Jewish state?

In ancient days, the inauguration of the holiday celebration centered round the family hearth when the Paschal lamb was eaten amidst symbolic accompaniments. To this day, the most distinctive feature of the Passover celebration is the family ceremony—the Seder ritual—which is enacted on Passover eve around the dinner table with the festive candle lights, the sanctification wine, and the ornamental platter containing the symbolic food items: three *mazzot,* bitter herbs, parsley, other accessories, and the shank bone as a reminder of the Paschal lamb. The Seder ceremony is a pageant: partly drama, partly ritual. Legend and history are woven into its composition. There are dialectic discussions for the learned, fun and humor for the children. The youngest child is encouraged to ask the four set questions concerning the nature of the ritual, whereupon the head of the family, the chief celebrant, commences to narrate: "Once upon a time we were slaves unto Pharaoh in Egypt; and the Lord our God brought us forth from there with a mighty hand and outstretched arm." The recital of the story, loosely woven together from Bible passages and later rabbinic compositions, is complemented by the chanting of psalms. The festive food is served, grace is said, and the service is concluded with chants, psalms, and songs. Throughout the ceremony, questions are encouraged, the symbolic objects are pointed to and explained, so that the Seder ceremony may aptly be described as a demonstration of spiritual pedagogy.

The education conveyed through the Passover holiday had enduring effect upon the soul of the Jewish people. Redemption, freedom, undying hope for the future of mankind became deeply ingrained ideals commanding Jewish allegiance. Jewish sages came to speak mystically of a millennial Passover that will complete the historic Passover of the past. In the days to come, the promise of Passover will be fulfilled in the national redemption of the land of Israel and in an era of universal brotherhood, justice, and peace that will embrace all His creatures. This universal spirit was painted with poetic fantasy in Jewish legend in the scene at the crossing of the Red Sea. On the day of the drowning of the Egyptians, the angels in heaven wished to sing the song of glory to God as is their wont. But God silenced them. "My creatures are drowning in the waters; would ye sing before me on such a day?" The Passover pageant in the Seder ritual opens with the prologue: "Let all who are hungry enter and eat with us; let all who are in need come and celebrate the Passover." This may well be the call of Passover to all the nations and faiths of mankind. It is the everlasting cry for freedom, unity, and brotherhood. This too is symbolized in the midst of the Seder service when the door is dramatically opened for Elijah, the invisible, to enter, Elijah the prophet of glad tidings, the harbinger of the Messiah.

The complement to Passover is the succeeding holiday, known as the Feast of Weeks, or Festival of the First Fruits. This holiday was the subject of protracted controversy between the revolutionary Pharisees and the die-hard Sadducees. While the controversy ostensibly centered around the day from which the count of seven weeks is to be made (Lev. 33 : 15), there is little doubt that a strong contributory factor in the agitation was the fundamental change which had been wrought not long before in the very nature of the holiday itself.

In the Bible, the Feast of Weeks was wholly an agricultural festival with little or no historic association. It marked the completion of the wheat harvest, the beginning of which was signalized during Passover by an offering in the Temple of a sheaf of barley, the *Omer*. On the Feast of Weeks, which was seven weeks after Passover the harvest was completed and the farmer this time brought to the temple some of the first ripened fruits and two loaves of wheat flour from the new crop. This was on the fiftieth day after the *Omer* was offered in the Temple. There was much rejoicing connected with the celebration and always the social-ethical motif was emphasized that rejoicing before the Lord meant that the means to share in the joy must be given to all, without regard to class or station.

Under the influence of Pharisaic teaching, and especially after the destruction of the Temple, the concept of the Feast of Weeks was completely transformed. It became the Festival of the Giving of the Law, a holiday commemorating the Revelation of God on Sinai and the giving of the Ten Commandments. This interpretation was readily harmonized with the Bible account of the Theophany and may indeed have followed an age of long oral tradition. The Festivals of Passover and Weeks were linked in spiritual union to proclaim a new truth: freedom from bondage is not an end in itself but a means to spiritual emancipation. Thus rabbinic Judaism converted an agricultural feast into a spiritual harvest. A Palestine festival became a universal symbol. To this day, the holiday is the occasion of Israel's perennial dedication to the Torah, God's covenant with mankind. The Book of Ruth with its setting in a wheat harvest scene is read on this festival—an idyl of love and loyalty which transcends the bounds of country and nation, presaging the birth of David, the ancestor of the Messiah.

The Feast of Tabernacles, "the Season of our Rejoicing," completes the Biblical cycle of holidays, or pilgrimages. This was the major harvest festival in autumn at the close of the Ingathering season when the people flocked to the Temple in Jerusalem to give thanks and to rejoice before the Lord. Rustic booths, or tabernacles, were set up for seven days and from them the holiday derived its name. The harvest festival was given spiritual connotation in the Bible by associating these pilgrimage booths with God's care of the children of Israel who also dwelt in booths as He guided and protected them during the forty years in the wilderness. Public processions with "the fruits of the goodly trees," palm branches, myrtle twigs, and willows of the brook gave festive color to the general celebration. Great solemnity was attached to a special procession from the silver pool at the foot of the temple mount to the altar in the Temple. Great was the joy at this ceremony of water-drawing for the libation which was offered on the altar in symbolic prayer for the hoped-for autumn rains. Always a note of spiritual aspiration permeated the ceremonies; the libation of water was accompanied by the chant: "With joy shall ye draw water out of the wells of salvation."

Nature's profusion was paralleled at the altar by numerous sacrifices, seventy bullocks in all, which led the Rabbis later to offer this significant interpretation: that the Jewish people offered those seventy sacrifices on the altar of God in behalf of the seventy nations which comprised all the peoples of the world. The universal idealism suggested in this rabbinic thought evidently harmonized with an old tradition of the later prophets. For it was Zechariah who prophesied that the day would come when the nations would go up to Jerusalem from year to year to worship God and to keep the Feast of Tabernacles.

When the Temple was destroyed and the people were uprooted from the land, the Feast of Tabernacles, like the other holidays, had to be adjusted to the new conditions. The ceremonials of the sacrificial cult could no longer be observed; the festive features of the harvest holiday lost much of their significance as the people were forcibly detached from the beloved land in ever increasing measure. All the more did the holiday take on symbolic spiritual characteristics in the new orientation of Judaism under the aegis of the Rabbis whose religious genius proved them worthy successors of the Biblical prophets.

The booth is now the central symbol of the holiday. This is an improvised frail structure like a rustic cabin. It has no roof but a thatched covering of leafy branches and twigs, sufficient as a protection against the sun while allowing the stars to shine through at night. It is customary to decorate the interior with fruits and vegetables as a reminder of the harvest in Palestine. In these booths the faithful are supposed to eat their meals during the seven days of the festival and also to sleep therein. It is a religious duty for every family to have its own booth but as this is not practical nowadays, especially in urban communities, the booth is usually set up near the synagogue premises to which the congregation repair for a brief repast after the regular morning and evening service in the synagogue.

Ethical religious symbolism guides the detailed rules laid down for this quaint construction: the frailty of life, the shelter of God's wings, Messianic hope, the stars of faith that pierce through the darkness that besets the life of individuals and nations. Likewise "the goodly fruit"—the *Etrog,* or citron—and the *Lulab,* consisting of the palm branches, the myrtle twigs, and the willows of the brook which were featured so prominently in the Biblical observances of the festival are endowed with mystical thoughts and are retained as a Biblical precept and a remembrance of Palestine. They are blessed in the home; and in the synagogue, as in the Temple of old, they are waved in concert in all directions, and carried in procession around the altar, symbolizing God's presence in all points of the world's compass. Mysticism and joyousness were blended in the spirit of this festival, and this mood reached a climax on the seventh day known as Hoshana Rabbah when the refrain *Hoshana,* or *Hosanna* was the recurrent theme in the processional service. A similar mood of solemn prayer when the soul is uplifted with joy and exultation in the Law is continued on the day following, the Eighth Day of Solemn Assembly. In the communities outside of Palestine, where an extra day is traditionally added to the holiday, the ninth day is known and celebrated exuberantly as the Day of Rejoicing in the Law.

The Festivals of Judaism are thus history reincarnated and theology in action. This theology is a dramatic living history, not abstract dogma. The voice of God which speaks in the rhythm of nature, the poetry of the stars and skies in Palestine, the music of its hills and valleys—these living themes of Israel's prophets and psalmists—are captured in the picturesque symbolism of the festivals. And as with the prophets and ancient bards, they inspire visions of universal truth and holiness. Nature is blended with moral philosophy and theology is scented with the fragrance of earth and soil, fitting it for habitation in the heart of man.

VII

In contrast to the luxuriant associations of the festival cycle is the chaste atmosphere surrounding the holy days of New Year and the Day of Atonement. On those days, Judaism stands at the highest peak of religious vision. The kingdom of God is clearly visible on the horizon. It is seen peopled with all races of mankind. It is filled with righteousness, holiness, justice, and goodness. To cause the Kingdom to descend upon the earth, to cause it to penetrate the individual soul and also to make it co-extensive with the whole world is the object of prolonged prayer, penitence, and fasting during those holy days.

In the Pentateuch, the first day of Tishri, which is the New Year Day is called simply the Day of the Blowing of the Trumpet. What occasioned the trumpet blowing is not indicated in the Bible. But the Pharisees and the early Rabbis filled the gap with deep religious thought. According to their tradition, the first day of the seventh month (Tishri) was the day of creation, the day when time began. It was truly the New Year Day. The blasts of the Shofar in three groupings proclaimed three divine manifestations: God the King of the world; God the Judge who on New Year passes in review the actions and designs of men and nations for reward or punishment; God the Ruler of history who once revealed Himself to Israel on Sinai through the shout of the trumpet and who will again blow the trumpet on Judgment Day to gather all men and nations under the rule of the Messiah.

This three-fold theme is developed in many prayers. They are intoned in chants which are among the oldest music in Jewish tradition and create a feeling of profound solemnity. The combined effect is designed to make man feel vividly the majesty of God; to stir within him the feeling of repentance and a resolve to put himself in harmony with the Judge on high; and as an Israelite to prepare himself for God's ultimate redemption of mankind with Israel leading the nations to the God of Zion.

It is characteristic of Judaism that the day of judgment is

not deferred to the hereafter but is effective at the beginning of every year in this living world. It may also be regarded as significant that the Jewish New Year is made to coincide with the autumn season when nature is about to be denuded and to enter the decline of winter. It is then that the trumpet blasts blow to proclaim the God of life and the coming of the day when His rule will bring hope, light, and redemption to all who walk in darkness, bowed down and stricken.

The New Year Day marks but the beginning of the Ten Penitential Days which are considered a special time of grace "to seek the Lord while He may be found." The culmination is reached on the tenth day of Tishri, the Day of Atonement, the Day of the Lord, great and fearsome. On New Year Day, according to a poetic rabbinic conception, the actions and thoughts of every living being pass before the Divine Judge and are recorded for judgment in the Book of Life. On the Day of Atonement, after man has been led to the path of penitence, the judgment is rendered; the fate of men and nations is decreed; and the verdict is "sealed." Atonement rather than judgment is the dominant note of the holy day, for the contrite heart has repented and sin is mercifully forgiven. Thus it becomes a day of salvation; a day of moral regeneration; or as the Rabbis expressed it: "On the Day of Atonement, I will create you a new creation."

The growth of this religious concept from the time of the Bible through the Pharisaic-Talmudic period into the days of rabbinic Judaism reflects the widening horizon of the Torah vision vouchsafed the priestly people. In the Pentateuch the theme of human sin and atonement by divine grace is delineated in clear, bold outline. The Day of Atonement is a day for the affliction of the soul when all the people are bidden to fast—from sundown to sundown—and the high priest offers solemn atonement sacrifice: for himself and his household, for the priests, and for all Israel. The priest, the altar, and the sacrifices were the media through which atonement reached the nation, and the eyes and the hearts of the people were upon the high priest throughout the solemn day. Even when the entire system of priest, Temple, and animal offerings ceased to exist after 70 C.E., the ancient Atonement service was reproduced in the form of a dramatic recital in the Synagogue liturgy of the day. Nevertheless a revolutionary advance in religious conception came about inevitably with the vanishing of the sacrificial cult. The mediation of the priest between God and man was gone forever. Mortal man appears before God on the Day of Atonement to confess his sins, to repent with contrite heart, and to receive divine forgiveness without the benefit of priest, altar, and sacrifice. Said Rabbi Akiba: "Happy are ye Israelites! Before whom do ye cleanse yourselves and who cleanses you from sin? Your father in Heaven."

In the rabbinic conception, confession must precede repentance. According to Maimonides, "Repentance means that the sinner gives up the sin, removing it from his mind, and determining in his heart not to repeat the evil action again." Confession furthermore must be expressed in words. Even an offense committed against a human being is not expiated by mere restitution but must be accomplished by confession to the injured person: how much the more when the offense is against God. But the spoken confession is addressed to Him alone. It must be accomplished with a feeling of shame. "To him who commits a transgression and afterwards is ashamed of it, all his sins are forgiven."

Prominent in the liturgy of the Atonement Day, therefore, is the rite of confession. It is a recurrent feature of the Service from sundown to sundown. It is recited with moving lips but inaudibly by the individual and repeated with the congregation in unison. The sins cited in the confession are intended to cover every possible transgression to which the human being is liable, but significantly enough ritual sins are almost entirely omitted. The stress is wholly on ethical sins.

The Day of Atonement cannot, however, even with repentance and confession absolve violations committed against a fellow man. Restitution and reconciliation are necessary concomitants of moral regeneration. On this subject, rabbinic judgment is emphatic: "Matters between thee and God are forgiven;

matters between thee and thy fellow man are not forgiven till thou hast appeased thy neighbor."

To bring into bold relief the ethical demands of atonement, the architects of the Synagogue liturgy selected the immortal utterance of the exilic prophet as the prophetic reading for the Atonement Day.

> Cry aloud, spare not,
> Lift up thy voice like a trumpet,
> And declare unto My people their transgression,
> And to the house of Jacob their sins. . . .
> Is not this the fast that I have chosen?
> To loose the fetters of wickedness,
> To undo the bands of the yoke,
> To let the oppressed go free,
> And that ye break every yoke?
> Is it not to deal thy bread to the hungry,
> And that thou bring the poor that are cast out to thy house?
> When thou seest the naked, that thou cover him,
> And that thou hide not thyself from thine own flesh?
> Then shall thy light break forth as the morning,
> And thy healing shall spring forth speedily.

As the Day of Atonement nears the climax in the hour of twilight, the call to repentance reaching out to distant heathen nations is echoed ringingly in the Synagogue from the book of Jonah. Great and universal is the power of human repentance from whatever source. "It ascends to the very throne of God," say the Rabbis. With mounting intensity the theme of the Atonement Day is developed in hopeful prayer and majestic chants as the sun sets and the last rays come over the tree tops till the Service is finally concluded with the fervent proclamation of God's Unity and Sovereignty, and the seven-fold rallying cry, "The Lord He is God." With dramatic fitness, the fast is concluded with the blowing of the notes of the ancient trumpet blast.

The philosophic and ethical principles of the Jewish religion which are thus poetically portrayed in the institutions of Judaism—in the Sabbath, the holidays and holy days—are developed and expounded in the rabbinic literature. Each of these forms the theme of one or more tractates of the Mishna and the Talmud where the laws and principles pertaining to the subject are fully elaborated. While the Talmud deals primarily with the laws prescribed for the observance of these religious institutions, its pages are illuminated with ethical comments and brilliant interpretations that bring to light the eternal religious values embodied in these observances. These mystic aspects of religion are especially elucidated with flashes of wit and wisdom in the Midrash, a quaint literature that is supplementary to the Talmud and is mostly contemporaneous with it. It consists of loose collections of homilies, legends, ethical discourses, parables, and pithy sayings. The Talmud and the Midrash are thus mutually complementary. They are two faces of the one medal.

Even so minor a holiday as Purim is treated in a special tractate of the Talmud and a corresponding homiletic Midrash based on the Scroll of Esther. This festive day, the fourteenth of Adar, a month before Passover, commemorating the deliverance of the Jews from the plot of Haman is celebrated as a day of popular rejoicing with plays and games, the exchange of gifts, and the giving of bounties to the poor. Underneath the merry-making, however, is the sober realization that Haman's plotting never ceases and that deliverance from such designs and persecutions is both a saddening and inspiring feature of Jewish history.

On the other hand, Hanuccah, the eight day Festival of Dedication, or as Josephus called it, the Festival of Lights, commencing on the twenty-fifth day of Kislev (*ca.* December) and commemorating the victory of Judas Maccabeus over the hosts of Syrians as narrated in the Books of the Maccabees, is glossed over in rabbinic literature; the military victory is ignored; and the triumph of war is replaced by an imaginative tale of a small cruse of pure Temple oil that burned miraculously for eight days during the rededication of the Temple, whence arose the custom to kindle lights for the eight days of Hanuccah. Modern historians have been at pains to explain this apparently studied rebuff to the great heroes of the Maccabean revolt who saved Judaism by their marvelous exploits on the battlefield. But the Rabbis left little doubt as to their religious motivation. For they turned to the book of Zechariah to furnish the prophetic commentary, the Haftarah, on the Sabbath of Hanuccah: "Not by might, nor by power, but by My spirit, saith the Lord of hosts."

The distinctiveness of the Jewish religion is not confined to its sacred calendar or its religious-historic institutions. The nature of Judaism is equally revealed in the daily religious practices, in the ethical studies prescribed for everyday living, in the laws of social justice, and in the emulation of holiness which is the heart of the Jewish religious system. Rabbinic law is co-extensive with life itself. Talmudic law, known under the name of *Halakah,* draws its inspiration as well as its etymological origin from the phrase "to walk in the ways of God." Every phase of life and every human relationship is treated from this standpoint in Judaism, both in its sacred literature and in the detailed system of law and practice.

Only a fleeting view of the duties that circumscribe the life of the religious Jew can be conveyed within the compass of this chapter. Jewish piety begins and concludes the day with prayer. "I accept upon myself the fulfillment of the commandment: 'Thou shalt love thy neighbor as thyself,' " is a preliminary to the morning devotions. And the last words recited before the eyes close in sleep are:

> I place my soul within His palm,
> Before I sleep as when I awake,
> And though my body I forsake,
> Rest in the Lord in fearless calm.

On the threshold of the Jewish home, in an encased bit of parchment known as the *Mezuzah* is inscribed Israel's creed of faith, "Hear, Oh Israel, the Lord is our God, the Lord is One"; also the following verses: "And thou shalt love thy God with all thy heart, with all thy soul and with all thy might." Whatever possible talismanic association the *Mezuzah* may have had,

Maimonides voiced its true meaning in Judaism: "Every time one enters or leaves the house, he meets the name of God inscribed on the door post, recalling to him His love and thereby teaching him that there is nothing true and enduring but the recognition of the Creator. Then he will walk in the paths of uprightness."

Within the home, the feeling of spiritual dedication is accentuated through many precepts and religious practices. Food is treated as a symbol of God's providence. Therefore, to express gratitude to God, the recital of blessings are punctiliously prescribed before and after partaking of food. It is a popular Jewish concept that the table where food is eaten partakes of the sanctity of the altar of ancient days. The laws separating "clean" and "unclean" beasts, fowl and fish, permitting the one and forbidding the other species to be eaten, are the foundation of the elaborate dietary laws which under Talmudic and rabbinic development became one of the most distinguishing marks of personal and home life in traditional Judaism. The rationalist view that those laws were devised as hygienic measures cannot be maintained seriously. In the Bible, they are clearly part of the code of holiness: "I am the Lord your God, who have set you apart from the peoples. Ye shall therefore separate between the clean beast and the unclean, and between the unclean fowl and the clean. . . . And ye shall be holy unto Me; for I the Lord your God am holy, and have set you apart from the peoples that ye should be Mine." The ideal of "separation" for the sake of holiness was immeasurably strengthened under the influence of the Pharisees in their heroic struggle to preserve Judaism against the attacks of Hellenism and the antinomianism of the Christian sects of the times. To the Talmudic rabbis, therefore, the sole purpose of these laws which separated the Jews was moral purification and voluntary submission to the will of "our Father in heaven." They were part of the moral discipline of a priestly people whose eyes were upon the kingdom of God. Morally and physically the need for this spiritual discipline was accentuated during the Middle Ages both as a protest and as a shield of protection. Such was undoubtedly the concept of the rabbinic jurists and moralists; and the Jewish home of today where these laws are still observed bears testimony to this Jewish concept of the ages.

The distinctiveness of Judaism, however, is not to be sought solely in the visible and mystical symbols of religion but even more so in the laws governing the moral and ethical conduct of the individual and those regulating the economic, social, and political relations in organized society. This conception of the function of religion takes on special significance in these days when the eyes and hearts of the nations are set upon creating a new world in which peace shall be secured through justice. The Hebrew Bible, or Torah, is not a testament, old or new. The Torah fundamentally signifies Law, the law as the will of God, the law that is to prepare individuals, nations, and society for the rule of God. Unlike the New Testament, the Hebrew Bible is not primarily concerned with the salvation of the individual soul in the hereafter but treats men and nations as units of a society that acknowledges God as king. Its laws are the crystallization of a lofty conception of God, man, and the universe. Hence they are not limited to the national boundaries of one people alone, but extend to other nations and to relations between nations in war and in peace. Basic to these laws is the concept of the fatherhood of God and the brotherhood of man and their corollaries touching the dignity of man and the inalienable quality of his rights under a universal law of justice and righteousness. The Mosaic law consequently is a program of life and a code of law. It was actually the constitution of the Jewish State in Palestine under the Second Commonwealth. Fifteen hundred years later, in a totally different environment it was recognized in a limited degree as basic law in the Puritan commonwealths set up in Colonial America. Having in mind the universal principles underlying the laws of the Bible, Philo, the Hellenistic-Jewish philosopher at the beginning of the common era declared: "As God Himself pervadeth all the universe, so hath our law passed through the world."

VIII

From the historic viewpoint, the Mosaic law was only one step in the evolution of the Torah. This also accords somewhat obliquely with the fixed tradition that prophecy succeeded the Mosaic revelation, which in turn was followed by the teachings of the Pharisees and the interpretation of the later Rabbis, the fathers of rabbinic Judaism. Thus interpreted, the laws of the Torah are the distillation of a growing, expanding vision of the interrelations of God, man, and society. It is the vision back of the law which is greater than the law itself, and this vision has constituted the religious genius of the Jewish people throughout the ages. It is a living, continuous function which makes itself manifest in the harmonious development of the Jewish spirit over a period of three thousand years. As in the Bible, so in the Talmud, Jewish law was expanded to embrace the totality of human life under those aspects which society then assumed: religion, ethics, morality; and also the government of society: civil, political, and ecclesiastical.

By liberal interpretation of the Biblical law and by new legislative enactments, the Rabbis implemented the social and democratic ideals inherent in the Bible. Law was sovereign and universal. Equal justice for all was its paramount aim. The dignity of the human being was not left as a theme for moral preachment but was safeguarded by laws protecting the inherent rights of the individual and the minority. The rights of property were recognized but subordinated to the interests of society. Labor was protected and commerce was regulated. Slavery was not abolished but substantially humanized through laws guaranteeing even the heathen slaves fundamental human rights, which if violated resulted in emancipation. The status of women, and children during minority, was revolutionized. The laws regulating marriage, dower-rights, and divorce were liberalized to protect the wife and mother from the handicaps of the older codes.

Nor did the living law cease with the close of the Talmud at the end of the fifth century. On the contrary, the post Talmudic Rabbis—the Geonim who later succeeded the Talmudic Rabbis in Babylon and were acknowledged as spiritual heads of world Judaism as well as the European Rabbis from the tenth century onward—continued to develop new principles of law and created moral institutions in order to make the Biblical-Talmudic law keep pace with life. Political and social conditions in the Middle Ages were not as favorable toward a natural evolution of the Jewish system of life as they had been in Palestine and Babylon, respectively, in earlier epochs. The implementation of Jewish ideals and principles of justice was greatly hampered by arbitrary governmental restrictions and the hostility of the populace and the Church. Nevertheless, throughout the Middle Ages, when the Jewish communities were generally granted a measure of autonomy, the Rabbis heroically applied their own standards of law amidst all the complicated relations of the feudal order, aiming consistently to emulate the eternal pattern of a society formed "on truth, justice and peace."

The rise of national states in European countries from the thirteenth to the end of the fifteenth century caused a drastic reversal of the status of the Jews and Judaism. It was precisely in the centuries of the Renaissance and of the exploration of new world frontiers to which the Jews had contributed so heavily that they experienced the misfortunes of wholesale expulsions or segregation into ghettos. This turn in the historic fortunes of the Jewish people brought about temporarily at least a spiritual metamorphosis. The people that had so richly given of its spirit to the world experienced the bitterness of worldly disillusionment. The need for solace and inner compensation gave a strong impetus to the intensive cultivation of the Cabala and the sway of mystic forces in Judaism. Were it not for the moral restraints and the discipline of Jewish religious law, and in particular the robust intellectual vigor with which Talmudic studies disciplined the Jewish mind, Judaism might have fallen into the pitfall of antinomianism and the extravagances of unrestrained mystic orgies. As it was, a forced abortive Messianism in the seventeenth century caused much havoc, but the impetuous current of mysticism was finally restrained and channeled within the bounds of Judaism. Nevertheless, the growth and expansion of Jewish law was retarded. After a dynamic course of thousands of years, the law of Judaism became relatively static during the dark ghetto days of the seventeenth and eighteenth centuries. Within the ghetto the old-time exponents of Talmudic erudition clashed with the new movement of mystic saintliness (Hasidism). Between the ghetto and the outer world, all lines of vital communication were disrupted.

Out of this state of isolation Judaism was forcibly brought back to the center of the world's arena by the political and spiritual storm of the French Revolution and its sequels in the nineteenth century. The physical and mental walls of the ghetto were broken down in all West-European countries. Judaism as a religion was compelled overnight to meet the challenge of history, science, and philosophy with which Christianity had had to contend, none too successfully, over the course of several centuries while Judaism was living a sheltered existence in the ghetto. In the meantime, political surgery was applied to prune off vital limbs from the Jewish "tree of life." For political emancipation which conferred citizenship upon the Jews necessarily involved on their part the surrender of the so-called mundane laws of a civil, political, constitutional character which in the Jewish conception emanated from the will of God. They were the means for implementing the ideals of social justice, righteousness, and holiness in human society. Indeed, it was these laws which were directly related to the vision of the Kingdom of God. But their exercise would be inconsistent with citizenship and the law of the land. This was in great measure true even in reactionary Russia with its unhappy Pale of Settlement. As a result of this dilemma, a process of spiritual self-curtailment was set in motion. Judaism as an over-all program of living gave way to a more limited regimen of piety, spiritual devotion, worship, ritual law, and ceremonialism. The Torah as a law governing the totality of life became more of a theological concept than a living reality.

But this revolutionary course in reverse was not destined to stop midstream. Too many diverse currents, political, cultural, spiritual, had been set in motion. The sudden transition from the medieval ghetto to the modern city produced a feeling of giddiness rather than stability. The lure of Western culture proved intoxicating to the descendants of those who had once been its masters and teachers, but from which they had been rudely separated by the European disciples. The advent of historical criticism, the application of critical methods to the study of ancient texts, the skeptical attitude toward tradition, the effects of which were so disturbing to the established Christian religions, proved even more revolutionary in their effects on Judaism.

Added to this was the confusion brought about by the interplay of political aims upon religious ideals. In the hearts of the emancipated children of the ghetto there burned a passion for political, social, and civic equality. To share in the cultural and civic life of their fellow citizens and to gain their esteem religiously and civically was a permanent goal, especially in Germany, strong enough to override in many quarters the Biblical-Talmudic aim to keep the Jewish people "separate" through precepts and commandments in order to make them a "kingdom of priests and a holy nation."

Out of this spiritual ferment, new religious parties arose, the most radical of which was that of Reform Judaism. This branch of Judaism, which developed principally in Germany and in the United States, represents a complete revision of the philosophy of Jewish history; a modernistic interpretation of religion according to the accepted historical, critical standards of comparative religion; and a break with tradition in its attitude to Jewish law in general and especially in relation to the binding authority of the Bible and the Talmud in matters ceremonial and ritual, which it categorically denies.

Accepting the basic principle that the Messianic ideal is to be the ultimate fulfillment of Judaism and the end-all of Jewish history, Reform Judaism accentuates the principle of the historic mission of Israel as the priest of humanity and the champion of God's truth; it is the historic function of the Jewish people to lead mankind through the ages until the kingdom of

God is established on earth and the highest ideals of a united humanity are realized through the universal knowledge of God and the love of man. Identifying the Jewish nation with the suffering servant of the Lord, depicted in Deutero-Isaiah, Reform Judaism accepted the belief "that Israel, the suffering Messiah of the centuries, shall at the end of days become the triumphant Messiah of the nations."

These affirmations are, as we have seen, part of the religious consciousness of the Jews throughout the ages. What was novel and striking were the negative implications deduced from the concept of the Messianic ideal. Not only was the belief in the personal Messiah formally negated but the entire concept of Jewish history and the destiny of the Jewish people was reversed. The loss of their country and the dispersion of the Jews in exile was not divine retribution for the sins of the people. On the contrary, it was a blessing for it opened to the exiles the gateway to the world and the fulfillment of their Messianic mission. The restoration of the Jewish people to the Holy Land which was vouchsafed them in Biblical prophecy and was cherished in the Messianic dream of the ages was decried as contrary to the philosophy of Reform Judaism and all allusions to such a hope were excised from the new liturgy. To stress the common bond with their countrymen, the vernacular was substituted for Hebrew as the chief language of prayer and the study of Hebrew was either eliminated or subordinated to a minor place in the religious curriculum. Whatever savored of social segregation or emphasized ritual distinctiveness, such as the dietary laws and numerous other observances, was opposed on doctrinal grounds and by the denial of supernatural authority to ceremonial law in the Bible and later sacred literature. The Torah thus lost its realistic meaning as the law of Judaism and retained only its symbolic significance as the divine vision which spurs man on to the ultimate goal of God's kingdom on earth.

Reform Judaism was not at any time a spiritual revolt against moral or religious abuse. It was a movement of so-called enlightenment and in its initial stages was supported by brilliant

Jewish scholars whose works created a literary-historical renaissance in Jewish scholarship and gave rise to what has since been called the Science of Judaism. But these scholars, in the main, came to feel that Reform Judaism violated historic truth by its one-sided trend toward universalism and away from the national, Hebraic character of the Jewish people and its religion. From these ranks therefore grew another school of thought that laid stress on historical continuity and the evolutionary character of Judaism. Thus arose the historical or traditional branch of Judaism, known in America as Conservative Judaism. Sharing with all religious elements in Jewry the belief in the Messianic goal of Judaism, the conservative branch, in contrast to Reform Judaism, emphasizes the distinctive Hebraic contribution which the Jewish religion is destined to make to the world and the need for preserving the Jewish people as a separate and distinct element consecrated by divine commandments through ceremonies and ritual to be a unique nation—"a kingdom of priests and a holy nation." Hebrew is not only retained as the language of prayer, but is also highly valued as a national bond of union, as a vehicle in which the Jewish soul is revealed historically, and as an instrument for preserving the living Hebraic consciousness. Conservative Judaism does not seem committed to a literal interpretation of the Sinaitic revelation, but it does acknowledge the authority of the Bible and the Talmud and deals reverentially with the customs and ceremonies that developed during the later centuries. The Torah is revered as a program of living as well as an idealized concept of divine wisdom. Particular stress is laid on home ceremonies, the observance of the dietary laws, the Sabbath, and the holy days according to the traditional laws and customs. The hope for the restoration of Israel to the ancient soil is vividly retained as a divine promise and a living ideal. With its realization are bound up national salvation and the condition preceding Messianic fulfillment.

The principles of Conservative Judaism have not been so categorically formulated as those of Reform Judaism partly because of an instinctive historic reluctance on the part of many of its rabbinical leaders to multiply religious parties in Israel. The lines of demarcation between Conservative Judaism and Orthodoxy, whose adherents form the third and numerically the largest part of Jewry, are not sharply delineated. The chief theological distinction of Orthodox Judaism is its adherence to the principle of literal revelation and its denial of the principle of historic evolution as applied to the theory and practice of religion. It has been pointed out significantly that the appellation Orthodoxy as applied to Judaism is not only etymologically alien but is also theologically foreign to the historic character of Judaism which has always been hospitable to difference of thought within the bounds of the traditional faith. The term Orthodox was borrowed from the vocabulary of Christian theology to offset the equally foreign name of Reform.

The three religious parties, Orthodox, Conservative, and Reform, constitute what has been felicitously called catholic Judaism. Wide as are some of their differences in belief and practice they are not separatist sects but differing members of one religion. They are united not only by kinship and history and the bonds of a common destiny but also by a deep abiding faith in religious principles which they hold to be immortal and which they cherish for the happiness of humanity.

Common to them all is the belief that Israel has a divine and prophetic role to play in the concert of nations and in the progress of united humanity toward an era of universal justice and peace. The millennial vision abides eternally in the Torah and illumines the hope of all its children. The creative religious genius which has produced the world's greatest prophets and has given the greater part of mankind its religion and ethics still holds great promise for endless generations to come who will build the foundations of "a new heaven and a new earth." Whatever interpretations a religious party or individual may give to this Jewish Messianic faith, its essence is spiritually alive with optimistic faith in God and the future of mankind. Therein lies the strength and the unity of Judaism.

IX

Noble but futile attempts have been made to define in precise terms the future function of the Jewish people in the religious drama of mankind. There are those who see Israel's destiny to be the spiritual mediator between the East and the West. However, the hand of Providence is firm without drawing blueprints. Of certain things there is surety. If there is to be security and peace among nations, this teaching of Judaism must be taken to heart: that religion must deal with nations, not only with individuals; with international law and ethics, not merely with personal salvation and beliefs. A world hungering for peace must recognize the religious axiom of Jewish teaching that the foundation of peace is justice. The tragedy of war and crime vindicate the Jewish conception that the religion of love must also be a religion of law.

Judaism does not however merely seek vindication of its historic teachings. It looks to greater spiritual fruition in the future. The restoration of Jews to their ancestral home in our day and the rebuilding in Palestine of a national home for the genius of the Jewish people may usher in a new epoch of prophetic creation comparable to that of the Second Commonwealth that saved Judaism and ended by giving birth to Christianity. Holding firmly to the past the Seers of Israel fix their vision, like the prophets of old, upon the end of days when many peoples shall go up and say:

> Come ye and let us go up to the mountain of the Lord,
> To the house of the God of Jacob;
> And He will teach us of his ways,
> And we will walk in His paths.
> For out of Zion shall go forth the Law,
> And the word of the Lord from Jerusalem.

SELECTED BIBLIOGRAPHY

Essence of Judaism. By Leo Baeck. New York, 1936.
What We Jews Believe. By Samuel S. Cohon. Cincinnati, 1931.
Judaism. By I. Epstein. London, 1939.

Judaism. The Religions of Democracy. By Louis Finkelstein. New York, 1941.

The Jewish Religion. By Michael Friedlander. New York, 1935.

Judaism as Creed and Life. By Morris Joseph. London, 1903.

The Meaning of God in Modern Jewish Religion. By Mordecai M. Kaplan. New York, 1937.

Jewish Theology Systematically and Historically Considered. By Kaufmann Kohler. New York, 1918.

The Reform Movement in Judaism. By David Philipson. New York, 1931.

Some Aspects of Rabbinic Theology. By Solomon Schechter. New York, 1909.

Judaism as a Religion. By Solomon Zeitlin. *Jewish Quarterly Review,* vols. XXXIV–XXXV.

Eastern Orthodoxy

JOSEPH L. HROMÁDKA

In 1853, one of the leading Russian philosophers, A. S. Khom-yakov, complained, in a reply to Laurentie's pamphlet on the Eastern Church, of the total lack of knowledge and understanding in Western Europe in regard to Russia and Eastern Orthodoxy. The situation has changed. The Ecumenical movement brought, in the era between the two wars, Eastern and Western Christianity into a close cooperation. The representatives of the East and West honestly tried to understand one another in the deepest motifs of their faith and confession. The method of controversy and polemics was replaced by the method of attentive listening and good will. There was a genuine desire to dig deeply into the common ground of Christian tradition and to discover, behind the old-time formulas and petrified prejudices, the burning lava of common faith and hope. We have learned to understand and respect one another more adequately than ever before. Even Eastern Orthodoxy became a living factor in the world-wide community of Christians. It is no exaggeration if we say that the active participation of Eastern Christians in religious, theological, and philosophical discussions has been one of the unprecedented aspects of the post-war era of the Christian Church. This alone makes our effort to understand the Eastern Church urgent and essential.

The rapidly changing political and cultural situation in the East of Europe is another reason for our growing interest in the nature of the Eastern Church. The area of the Soviet Union belongs, historically, to the orbit of Orthodox Christianity. Kiev and Moscow received the Gospel from Byzantium. In the devotional life as well as in theology and church policy, the Christian heritage of the Russian, Ukrainian, White Russian, and Caucasian people has been rooted in the spiritual, moral, and intellectual tradition of the ancient Church of Egypt, Syria, Asia Minor, Greece, and Constantinople. Now, the Church in the Soviet Union underwent a stupendous trial and ordeal in the years after the collapse of the czardom, and the October Revolution of 1917. A distant observer knew next to nothing about what was then going on in Russian Christianity. Was it an agony of death or a new beginning? How should one understand the Soviet Revolution in its antichurch drive? And, furthermore, how should one understand the reorganization and the restoration of the Eastern Orthodox Church in Russia, in the years of 1942–1945? Have we to do with an irrepressible regeneration and growth, a powerful reemergence of Russian Christianity or with a shrewd, tactical move on the part of the Soviet Government? Is the Russian Church going to play an essential role in the spiritual destiny of the Soviet people, or is she just a faithful relic from the past which can be tolerated because she is doomed anyway? All these questions bear on our understanding both of our times and of the way the Eastern Church may exert her influence in the days to come. Yet we can hardly answer them unless we have some notion of the main spiritual and historical issues of Eastern Orthodoxy in general.

THE NAME OF THE CHURCH

The names of the Eastern Church vary in different official and unofficial documents: "The Orthodox Catholic and Apostolic Church of the East," "The Orthodox Eastern Church," "The Eastern Church," "The Orthodox Church." In recent times, the theologians of the East have spoken simply of "Orthodoxy" or of the "Orthodox Church." The term "Orthodoxy" means to them more than right dogma or doctrine; it means the totality of right worship, right confession, and the undisrupted continuity of hierarchy and sacramental communion originating in the apostolic church and going down to the present. The word "Eastern" does not designate any local or geographic boundary of the Church. It indicates the glorious memory of Second Rome, Constantinople, which in the mind of Eastern Christians succeeded the Rome of St. Peter and St. Paul, and became the mother of Orthodoxy and apostolic tradition. After 381 the bishop of Constantinople was granted an honor second only to the bishop of Rome, and the Eastern Church has never questioned the primacy of honor due to the Roman bishop. However, the head of the Roman Church forfeited his privileges and honors by violating the dogmatic tradition and by claiming a jurisdictional and doctrinal supremacy which contradicts, in the judgment of Eastern Christians, the very spirit and freedom of the apostolic Church. The primacy of the bishop of Constantinople is purely historical and symbolic without any jurisdictional implications.

After the fall of Constantinople in 1453, the Russian Orthodox Church became increasingly aware of her actual leadership within the area of Eastern Christianity. Her intellectual representatives developed a philosophy of history in which Moscow appeared as Third Rome, being a legitimate heir both of Rome and Constantinople. "Two Romes have fallen and gone, the Western and Eastern; destiny has determined for Moscow the position of the Third Rome; there will never be a fourth," a Russian monk, Philotheus, proclaimed soon after the fall of Constantinople.

The Church of the East firmly believes that she has been the only truthful heir of the apostles since the West, in both its Roman and Protestant branches, had increasingly corrupted the very nature of the Church of Christ. The Roman Church was infiltrated with the legal and political spirit of ancient Rome. She is, in many ways, the continuation of the Roman Empire. Her hierarchy ceased to be a pure mystical vehicle and channel of the grace of Christ, and adopted a claim of government and compulsion; her sacramental means of grace were transformed into tools of priestly domination; her theology succumbed to the spirit of Greek philosophy, and instead of a humble and silent reverence before the unfathomable mystery of Christ tried to explain what is unexplainable. Roman legalism, imperialism, and rationalism were incapable of protecting themselves from Protestant humanism and subjectivism. In the judgment of Eastern Christians it was the Roman Church that separated herself—way back in ancient times—from the One Apostolic Church. It was the bishops of Rome that had set themselves above the mystical fellowship of faith, and followed their particular interests and designs—against the principle of consultation and common decision. The West also introduced a word "filioque" (meaning the procession of the Holy Spirit "from the Son") without the consent of the Eastern brothers. The spirit of Protestant individualism is a logical reflection of Roman particularism. The Protestants carried the process a step further by declaring that every Christian stood above the whole of the Church and became a law to himself. The Western European disintegration and atomization of life are the climactic stages of the process which started with the particularistic revolt of the Roman Church.

Thus the categories "Orthodox" and "Eastern" express the belief of the Eastern Christian that only the Church of the East is the authentic continuation of the Apostolic and Catholic body of the Incarnate Christ.

ORGANIZATION

The Eastern Church claims to be Catholic, universal, but objects to any centralized, canonical, jurisdictional authority. Historians have explained the absence of a central supreme authority in the Eastern Church on the ground of a quite specific historical situation. Whereas in the West the Catholic Church was, for centuries after the fall of the Roman Empire, the only integrating and unifying force both in religion and civilization, the Eastern Church had had little to say in the realm of secular, cultural, and political life. Her external unity, security, and freedom depended on political factors, primarily on the Empire of Byzantium. After the imperial court of the Roman Empire was transferred from Rome to Constantinople, in the fourth century, the bishop of the new capital reflected, in many ways, the glamour and splendor of the emperor. His spiritual, moral, and doctrinal authority never equaled that of the Roman bishop. He never was in a position to assume a centralizing power or political and cultural influence such as the Roman bishop had assumed. Philosophers of history, again, have pointed to a specific atmosphere of the Eastern area as responsible for the nature of Eastern hierarchy and authority. The spirit of the Roman West was active, pragmatic, legal, political; the spirit of the East more speculative, mystical, and passive. Even the function of hierarchy was of sacramental, mystical character. There was no need of, and request for, a canonical authority and legal discipline. The unity of the Church manifested itself in the unity of liturgical and sacramental life, not in obedience to some visible hierarchical office.

All these historical circumstances had without question contributed to the absence in the Eastern Church of any central office and organizational unity. However, the theologians of the East rightly emphasize the spiritual and theological motives of this fact: The Church as the body of the Incarnate Word of God is a mystical, sacramental fellowship, and exists beyond all legal forms and jurisdictional categories. Ecclesiastical organization, external administration is not at all formed *iure divino* (by the divine law), as the Roman Church maintains of the papal universal episcopacy and infallibility, but merely on the ground of external necessity or expediency. Instead of the divine law we can speak merely of the ecclesiastical law, more often just of historical reasons. In this way were established, in the old church, several patriarchates: Constantinople, Alexandria, Antioch, Jerusalem, and later church units within newly organized national states. Strictly speaking, each diocese, with the bishop as its head, is entirely independent and self-governing, reflecting in itself the very nature and totality of the Church, just as a drop of water contains the nature and essence of the whole ocean. But some organization and coordination is inevitable. The old patriarchates as the remnants of the old, glorious Church, and the new units established within national, political areas (Russia, Rumania, Yugoslavia, Bulgaria, etc.) are called autocephalous (independent) Churches. They are linked together by the consensus of the seven ecumenical councils (325–787), by one Creed (the Nicene) and by the same sacraments. The hierarchy of each autocephalous church recognizes the validity of the hierarchy of all other churches. The primacy of honor accorded to the Patriarch of Constantinople has no dogmatic or jurisdictional nature. It involves the privilege to proclaim the definition of ecumenical councils, and to be a symbolic representative of the unity of the Church.

NATURE OF THE CHURCH

The final separation of the Eastern and Western Church came about in 1054. The Patriarch of Constantinople, Michael Cerularius, closed down Latin churches in his city and also, indirectly, in Bulgaria. The Roman bishop, Leo IX, condemned, in 1053, any criticism of the West by the Eastern Church, reiterated the principle of the jurisdictional supremacy of the Apostolic See (*Summa Sedes a nemine iudicatur*), proclaimed in 865 by Nicolas I, and on July 16, 1054, anathematized the Patriarch of Constantinople. Although he cautiously drew a dividing line between the Patriarch and the Eastern Church, his act sealed the separation for all time. The Church of the East identified herself with the Patriarch.

The officially discussed points of dissension between the West and the East were of minor nature. They had gone back into the days of the patristic era: fasting on Saturday, celibacy of priests, separation of confirmation from baptism, the article of "filioque," all these innovations of the Western church were frowned upon by the East, but would not have resulted in the final and conclusive division had it not been for some more relevant issues. The essential reasons behind the disruption were undefined, inarticulate, often intangible—and still they proved to be the ground on which the Eastern Church has grown into a unique historical form of Christianity. Let us examine some of the primary aspects of Eastern Orthodoxy.

Eastern theology has not defined any doctrine of the Church. Retrospectively, her theologians argue that a definite doctrine of the Church is impossible just as a definition of life itself would make no sense. The Church of Christ is the original, primary reality preceding any human thought and action; the light which enables us to see; the truth which mediates any knowledge of what is true and right; the love which brings us in touch with our fellow men and fills us with human understanding and compassion. The Church as the primordial reality resists any dogmatic definition; the real being exists beyond human abstractions and categories. Unless we share in it, and find ourselves part and parcel of the mystical fellowship embracing all the members of the body of Christ we are incapable of understanding and apprehending the Church. It is senseless to start from a definition or a dogma of the Church. What is essential is to be born in a mystical, mysterious way—in the womb of the Church—and to be continually nourished by her heavenly food. The Church is a living organism of the God-man in which all our knowledge, salvation, love, joy, and blessing originate, grow, and fulfill their purpose. The Church exists before the individual Christians both logically (if it is permissible to use this word) and historically; it exists in us not as an institution or a social phenomenon, but as a new life, as a spiritual certainty, as a living experience—undefinable and unexplainable; it exists independently of its historical origin; or, in other words, what historians describe as its origin is only a visible reflection of the divine mystery hidden behind all historical events.

The theologians of the East like to speak of the Church as the continuation of Christ's incarnation and of Pentecost. Through the incarnation the eternal Son of God entered the realm of history and nature, broke the dividing line which separates the realm of the immortal, uncreated deity from the created, sinful, mortal, perishable world. The incarnation as the reality of the divine regenerating life did not cease to exist within our life and history with the resurrection and ascension of Christ; it is present in its original, real, and life-creating nature within the mystical, sacramental, and liturgical fellowship of all believers, in their mystical love for one another. The life of the Church is the life of the Incarnate Christ, the life of the Truth.

Hence we may understand some of the emphases of Eastern Orthodoxy: First, the Church is only One, as Christ can have only one body. It is useless to argue about the relation of the visible and invisible Church. The Church is both, continuing in the unity of the divine and human nature of Christ. It is a unity of the transcendent and immanent, of God and man, of God and creature, a bridge between heaven and earth. Visible is the Church in her organizational, liturgical, and mystical acts, invisible in the mystical presence of Christ, in the activity of the Holy Spirit in the life of individual believers. Any personal or sectarian self-separation contradicts or violates the very nature of the Church. Just and unjust, sinners and saints grow in sanctity and perfection only as long as they are united in mystical love with the whole of the Church. The moment a saint despises a sinner and separates himself in spiritual pride, he loses his knowledge and saintliness. As some of the modern Russian thinkers put it: Salvation is possible only in love and unity; it depends on the salvation of all. Any separation ends invariably in bankruptcy and death. We are saved in unity, we sin in separation.

Second, the Church has the final norm and criterion of truth in herself. There is no higher authority beyond the Church since the Church is the primary reality, the source and fountain of all redemptive knowledge and life. Not even Christ should be understood and looked upon as authority to which the Church is subordinated. The Church *is* the Incarnate Christ, His life is her life; there is no dividing line between His God-manhood on the one hand and the Church on the other. Christ does not live and act outside the Church. After His incarnation, the Church is the only mode of His existence. The Christ outside the Church, the Christ of modern rationalism or moralism is an artificial construction, without life and without power. An appeal to Christ against the Church contradicts the very reality of the heavenly life. The same is true of the authority of the Holy Scriptures. The Bible of the Old and New Testament has no normative validity outside the Church. It is the Church that created the canon, not vice versa. The Scripture certainly is the eternal revelation of God, and has its unique value. Nevertheless, it is only a part of the living tradition of the Church. The Church lived prior to the creation of the Bible, in prayer, liturgy, contemplation, adoration, and love. The Scripture is the work of the Church as the mystical whole; without the Church, the Bible as a norm seemingly superior to the Church withers away. Without the Church it is like a branch cut off from the living tree. Only in fellowship with the Church, in a direct and spontaneous communion of prayer and love can an individual Christian understand the very truth and meaning of the prophetic and apostolic writings. The criterion of truth, the ultimate court of appeal, the final authority is the Church itself. The truth of the redemptive message can be apprehended only through the internal testimony of the Holy Spirit. But, the Holy Spirit is active through the mystical union of love and faith.

Third, strictly speaking there is no specific office or instrument of infallibility. In the Roman Church either the Pope alone or the Pope with the Ecumenical Council are the divinely instituted channels of infallible authority, of the *Potestas magisterii*. Not so in the Eastern Church. Of course, the believers cannot live without the light of definite dogmatic formulas, liturgical and sacramental order. They must hear and know the voice of truth lest they get lost and confused. The Church has an unambiguous, unqualifiedly valid confession of faith, a doctrine concerning God, Christ, salvation, and eternal life. The seven Ecumenical councils were official gatherings of the Church acting, speaking, and defining the Creed under the guidance of the Holy Spirit. Historically or empirically, these councils of all bishops represented the Church and have been interpreted as infallible spokesmen of the whole Church. Yet, the theologians of the East more and more energetically object to this interpretation, and insist upon the fact that the Church as a whole, is an organic, mystical body of all believers, and has been the medium, instrument, and embodiment of the infallible truth of Christ. True, some doctrines and dogmas were defined and promulgated by the councils; however, it was not until the whole Church accepted, and incorporated, them into the living tradition that they proved to be authoritative, infallible manifestations of the divine Truth. The patriarchs of the East replied to the letter of the Pope Pius IX in 1849 in this spirit:

Only the Church as the living organism of all believers, laymen as well as bishops, can claim infallibility and protect the integrity of dogma and the purity of the liturgy. The Church *lives* the truth, *has* the truth; an individual believer can have a real knowledge of it not by memorizing and accepting the formally promulgated doctrine but by living in communion with the body of the Church.

Here we can understand the meaning of the word so often used by Russian theologians in regard to the Church: *Sobornost* (ecumenicity, catholicity). It expresses the idea that the conscience and consciousness of the Church is super-personal: truth is revealed, not to the individual mind, not to a particular office or group of believers (e.g. council, the bishop of Rome or of Constantinople), but to the unity in love of the Church. The claim of exclusive dogmatic or doctrinal authority by clergy, episcopacy, or the Pope amounts to an arrogant, heretic, disruptive self-separation from the Church.

Hence the conviction that the Church can grow and expand solely in a spiritual way. She has no right and means to force anybody to join her and to accept her truth. She invites into unity and fellowship but without judging or condemning the recalcitrant. The Church rejects any legal form, order and discipline—the law and legal power are at variance with the nature of the Church. The Eastern Church claims to be hierarchic, but not hierocratic, her authority being spiritual and mystical, not legal and jurisdictional.

EASTERN FAITH, LITURGY, AND SACRAMENTS

The core in the intellectual, devotional, and practical life of the Eastern Church is faith in the resurrection of the Incarnate Christ. All historical forms of Christianity have based their theology and confession on the Incarnation of Christ, but none of them has to the same extent made it the central pillar of faith and liturgy. One need only compare the Eastern liturgy with the Roman mass or with the Protestant (Lutheran or Calvinistic) worship in order to realize the specific nature of the Eastern jubilant and triumphant faith. Through the Incarnate Christ

God entered the world of death and corruption and unveiled the mystery of His love and goodness. The separation between God and His creation ceased to exist and the unity of the Creator and Lord with the realm of His creation was restored. Some Eastern theologians say that the original process of creation, thwarted by human rebellion and sin, has been more than restored; it has been perfected. God as all-embracing love and self-humiliating sacrifice has made His relation to the world and humanity more intimate. At the moment of the creation, God stayed beyond the world. God as the absolute did not enter the realm of the relative which had been called forth out of nothing. However, through the incarnation He not only overwhelmed the kingdom of death and evil but opened the inexhaustible fountain of His eternal redemptive goodness and destroyed all the barriers between Him and the created world. Incarnation is more than the restoration of the world as it was before the fall. It is the initiation of the never ceasing mystical and sacramental transformation of the whole cosmos.

The Eastern Church confesses the human and the divine nature of Christ but interprets Christ as the God-man in perfect ontological unity. Some of her theologians and philosophers are more critical of Israelistic transcendentalism than of Monophysitism and monism which stress the absorption by the eternal Logos of the human nature in Jesus Christ. The tremendous emphasis upon the bodily resurrection of Christ in the common worship of the Church is the reaffirmation of the mystery of the God-man, of the miracle of the Incarnation. The risen Christ confirms the defeat of sin, death, and evil. All the departed have been liberated from the abyss of perdition. With an indescribable joy the Eastern Christian proclaims the victory of Easter morning. From the days of the ancient world languishing in skeptical despair and agonizing pessimism, down to the present misery and chaos, the resurrection of the God-man has been the only source of hope and comfort. Christian joy has its source in the real event of the incarnation and resurrection, not in abstract monotheistic doctrines. The resurrection and glorification of the whole man in soul and body, the victory over death, is, the Eastern Christian asserts, the basic and central message of the apostolic, and of any authentic, church. Death and hell have forever lost all power and horror. The God-man is the head of the whole humanity, past, present, and coming, in Him is potentially realized the eternal purpose of the world, the destiny of humanity, the restoration of the corrupted life, and the everlasting Kingdom of love.

The incarnation and resurrection of the God-man, His mystical and sacramental presence, is the meaning of the public worship, of the holy liturgy. The liturgical service is not only a commemoration of Christ; it does not consist only in the preaching of the prophetic and apostolic witness. The meaning of the liturgy is that the event commemorated really happens in the service and in the life of the assembled Christians. During the Eucharistic service not only are the holy gifts consecrated, but the whole mystery of the Incarnation is renewed from the angelic Ave Maria and Bethlehem to Calvary and the Mount of Olives, from the Nativity to the Ascension. The holy drama of the liturgy extends from the Messianic prophecies to the victory of the Incarnate Lord and the miracle of Pentecost. The same Christ whom the disciples met is present, the same drama of salvation and new life that we read about in the Gospel narratives is going on. The liturgy is a manifestation, creation, and reaffirmation of the mystical unity of Christ with His Church. It nourishes the believers with supernatural gifts and unites them with the unseen realm of Eternal Life, Grace and Truth. The mystery of liturgy is the channel of incorruptible divine gifts, of Christ's victorious life within this world of sin, death, and perdition. "Yesterday I was buried with Thee, oh Christ; with Thee today I rise from the dead"—these words of joy and jubilant assurance mean the real presence of the divine creative Life. The Saviour Himself abides—in a sacramental, mysterious way—in the heart of a Christian and manifests His power in all his acts.

The same is true of sacraments. As a matter of fact, the liturgy and sacraments form one organic indivisible unity. The Eastern Church interprets sacraments as divine mysteries. A

Western Christian may miss in the Eastern understanding of sacraments the motif of the divine Covenant, the pledge of allegiance to the heavenly Lord. However, the sacramental life of Eastern Christians fits perfectly into the general fabric of the spiritual tradition of the East. Sacraments are external vehicles of the unfathomable and mysterious presence of the Holy Spirit, of His healing, life-regenerating power. The individual Christian is integrated into the mystical body of Christ and made a direct participant in the life of Eternity and incorruptibility. As some theologians put it, Christ's connection with the world, since His ascension, is realized sacramentally, especially through His real presence in the Eucharist, until He comes again at the end of human history. Christ's glorified body, wholly divinized through its union with the divine nature in the one person of the Logos (Word), embraces, through the mysterious activity of the Holy Spirit in sacraments, all members of the Church and, furthermore, all the created Cosmos. In the sacraments, the incarnation and Pentecost are ever present and ever active, thanks to the apostolic succession of the hierarchy. Although the Holy Spirit is not confined only to the sacraments and liturgy—"The wind bloweth where it listeth, and thou hearest the sound thereof, but canst not tell whence it cometh, and whither it goeth"—nevertheless the church has an immediate, axiomatic certainty of their efficacy: in the sacraments the Holy Spirit *is* conferred upon believers, and the body of Christ lives, through them, in the heart and body of individual Christians.

The Eastern Church has officially accepted seven sacraments: baptism, chrismation (confirmation), penance (second baptism), eucharist, Holy orders, marriage, and Unction of the sick. However, the sacramental power of the church extends beyond these most important manifestations of the incarnation and the Holy Spirit. There are special forms of blessing (e.g. holy water, bread, a church building, cemetery, consecration of icons, crosses) which do not differ qualitatively from the seven sacraments. There is no strict dividing line between sacraments and sacramentalia, since the whole life in the Church has a sacramental nature. Whatever comes into touch with the Church becomes linked to the process of incarnation and divinization. Any personal act of faith and love, compassion and service has invisible roots in the sacramental reality of the Church.

THEOLOGY AND PHILOSOPHY

Eastern Christianity has produced a definite system of thought and world-view. Its mystical and sacramental structure has been integrated and fortified theologically and philosophically; that is to say, its devotional, personal, and corporate life is not just a mass of ritual acts and rules without coherence and deeper meaning. As we have pointed out it is the very nature of the church that manifests itself in a definite conception of hierarchy, liturgy, and sacraments. However, Eastern theology goes still further: The Church is rooted in a specific inter-relation between the world and God. The Church of the East has not been so mechanically ritualistic and traditionalistic as to exclude any theological interest in the deeper meaning and presuppositions of the sacramental communion between God, the earthly Church, and human nature.

There may exist communities and groups in the East which have degenerated into dull and deadening ritualistic cults. But it is not true of the main body of the Eastern Church. As a matter of fact, she has been, for almost a century, an arena of significant intellectual activity. Confronted with the elaborate systems of Western theology and philosophy, and under the challenge of Western antireligious and anti-Christian tendencies, thinkers of the East have made a magnificent effort to interpret adequately the essential and unique fundamentals of what they regard as the true meaning of the Gospel and the Church. They go back to the early centuries of the Christian era, study the writings and liturgies of St. Athanasius, St. John Chrysostom, St. Basil the Great, St. Gregory of Nazianz, St. Ignatius of Antioch, St. Gregory of Nyssa, St. Cyrill of Alexandria, St. John of Damascus, and many other representatives of the Eastern Church, in order to penetrate into the very depth of her thought, and to interpret it as adequately as possible. It has been precisely in the modern era, in the days of profound crisis of the Eastern Church, that its intellectual leaders have distinguished themselves by valuable contributions to Christian thought. They have also challenged the self-complacency of Western Christianity, both Catholic and Protestant. The names of A. S. Khomyakov, V. Solovyov, F. M. Dostoyevski, P. Florenski, the late Metropolitan of Kiev Antonius, S. Bulgakov, N. Berdyaev, S. Tsankov, the Metropolitan of Thyatira Germanos, and many others, bear witness to the fact that the Church of the East represents much more than a museum of antique rites, institutions, and conventions. It may so happen that some insights of Eastern Christianity will bring an indispensable corrective to Western thought and a remedy for the ailing soul of Western spiritual life and civilization.

Eastern theology, more than any other historical form of Christianity, seeks to understand and interpret the common principle uniting God with the world. The theology of the Reformation has stressed the dividing line between God and the creation; Western Catholic thought has coordinated God and the world, revelation and reason, faith and rational knowledge. Eastern thought has accentuated the hidden ground of the incarnation and salvation. How could the Eternal Word of God become flesh? How is the reality of the God-man possible? It is true, indeed, that God created the world and, as the Creator, is qualitatively different from the world. And yet, the world as the divinely created reality must have an invisible, hidden connection with God; there must be some principle which links the world to God and fills up the gap between Him and the creation. The incarnation of Christ, and the activity of the Holy Spirit in the world are ontologically and theologically impossible unless there exists "something" that unites the creaturely world and the world of the Triune God. This unifying principle is continuously under the shadow of sin, death, and corruption. Especially the sinister reality of death manifests the presence of the chaotic, disintegrating, destructive forces in our midst, in the world in general, and in our individual lives in particular. Nevertheless, the world has never ceased to be the creation of

God, to abide in God, and to reflect His wisdom and glory. The end of Christ's incarnation is to raise the human race, and the whole cosmos, to the glory of the original life and incorruptibility before the fall, and, furthermore, to a state of full divinization (theosis). This is possible if the created world in general and human nature in particular are ontologically linked with the nature of God, if they partake of the divine life.

Some Eastern theologians and philosophers (primarily Russian) set up a whole system of sophiology in order to point out in all details how God in His acts of creation used His wisdom (Sophia) as a "between," a link between Himself and the created world. This wisdom is neither exclusively divine nor exclusively creaturely. It is God's nature revealing itself. Manhood—the highest manifestation of the created world—is the created form of the divine wisdom. The incarnation of Christ was, then, not an arbitrary act of the divine power or omnipotence; he was not a *Deus ex machina;* the incarnation had its ground in the essential conformity between the divine and human nature in Christ, in the Wisdom which is both divine and creaturely. The God-Manhood of Christ, e.g. the union of His two natures, is rooted in their original ontological interrelation; and this conformity is understandable if we interpret the two natures of Christ as the two forms of the one Wisdom of God —the one form in God, the other in creation.

The salvation of the human race and of the whole cosmos can be interpreted as a state of full divinization ("God shall be all in all"). It is a result of the incarnation, it is the work of the grace of God; and yet, it cannot be without some ontological ground as well. Our human nature cannot be saved unless it has the capacity prerequisite to receive such a gift. The same is true of Pentecost. The transforming power of the Holy Spirit presupposes the ontological link between His divine nature and the realm of creation. Pentecost is the penetration of the creature by Wisdom, the union of the divine and created Wisdom in the power of the Spirit. Let me quote S. Bulgakov: "In the Incarnation, created Sophia, earthly manhood receives, in the Logos, the personal Wisdom of God. At the descent of the

Spirit the same human nature receives the personal Spirit of Wisdom." [1]

In the same manner the Eastern theologians interpret the ontological background of the eucharistic change taking place in the elements of bread and wine. The change is real; the miracle of the incarnation has its continuation in the eucharistic presence of Christ in the world. And this continuation is possible and understandable because Christ has forged in His own body a link with the whole world of "flesh," and because His Manhood is in a real, ontological manner related to His divine nature.

Not all Eastern theologians and hierarchs have accepted the doctrine of the divine Wisdom (Sophia). Some of them have raised serious objections to Bulgakov's or Florenski's sophiology as a dangerous innovation pregnant with potential heresies. However, it may be stated that Eastern theology and philosophy have laid a much stronger emphasis upon the conformity and "sympathetic" interrelation between God and creation than any of the main historical forms of the Christian West. Over and over again, the West has interpreted some aspects of the Eastern Church as the heritage of Platonic dualism or as a Monophysitic tendency which had never died out in the East. But the Eastern thinkers defend themselves by insisting upon having preserved the genuine spirit of the Apostolic Church. And the authentic Gospel, they say, is based upon the real reunion of God and the world in the incarnate Christ, upon the real (not only symbolic or moral) presence of the Holy Spirit in the Church, and upon the real victory of the God-man over the powers of death, chaos, and sin. The real presence of the God-man in the Church, the liturgy, and sacraments, and his transforming, regenerating power in the whole realm of creation is beyond our rational and moral categories. It defies any theological explanation. It is a divine mystery and a divine reality; it is an unceasing process of divine creativity, not only restoring what was broken by the fall of Adam, but also, as we have pointed out, producing a new life and bringing God and the

[1] *The Wisdom of God,* p. 158 f.

world into a perfect communion of self-sacrificing love. It is such a communion as had never existed, not even in Paradise. But though we are unable to explain and interpret it with adequate formulas and categories, we may say—the Eastern thinkers insist—that a philosophy of an ontological and sympathetic interrelation between God and His creation reflects much more adequately the gospel of the God-man than any of the Western schools of thought.

Furthermore, they insist also that this way of theological or philosophical thinking lays the ground for the creation of a genuine Christian civilization. The Roman Christian tradition failed, in the end, to integrate all the areas of human life, of nature, history, and personal conscience, and to open the divine source of the all-embracing, dynamic, transforming, divine, self-sacrificing love. It separated the realm of nature from the realm of grace, the earth from heaven, reason from mystery— and instead of creating a spiritual basis for the spontaneous growth of a genuine Christian civilization, the Latin Church has tried to unify humanity by the use of external power, by organization and legal authority. It killed freedom and spontaneity. Protestant churches have gone beyond the Latin Church in separating the majestic God from the fallen, corrupted, sinful creation. They have interpreted salvation in exclusively spiritual terms, and by bringing the individual soul into an isolated relation to God they have destroyed the mystical body of Christ and de-divinized the whole realm of what we call secular civilization. Individualistic experience of salvation has produced the spirit of egotism and gradual disintegration of modern society under which we suffer at the present time in an unprecedented way. It is here that the failure of Protestantism is most apparent. It has restored freedom of individual conscience and faith but undermined the ground on which a real fellowship of love and sympathy can thrive, and cut off the area of civilization from the divine creativity. The end can be only the atomization and self-destruction of secularized, egocentric humanity.

The Eastern Church, as the thinkers of the East maintain, offers a healing remedy for our ailing civilization. In her living tradition we are offered a powerful spiritual freedom and genuine Christian creativity. In the sacramental communion with the Church man is free from the destructive forces of self-love and self-isolation. Engrafted into the body of the Incarnate Christ, he becomes a fruit-bearing branch of the mystical Kingdom of God. Whatever he does in science or philosophy, in social or political activity, in literature and art, in family and personal life all reflects the invisible realm of Christ and prepares for His second coming and ultimate victory.

PRACTICAL PIETY AND MORAL LIFE

The Western observer has often failed to understand and appreciate the ethical stamina and resilience of the Eastern Church. He has missed in her life not only intellectual clarity and spiritual vitality but also practical dynamism. The religion of Eastern orthodoxy amounts, he says, to a bleak mixture of rites, cults, and mysteries; the dogma of the East degenerated into unintelligible formulas of yore, and the life of Eastern Christians into a passive, dumb observance of traditional customs and sacred habits; the Christian East has contributed little to a living spiritual culture or to social or political progress.

However, an adequate understanding of the practical life of Eastern Christians is for us, people of the West, as difficult as our insight into their thought and philosophy. Only from a historical perspective can we possibly be just and fair in our judgment. Let us not forget that the area of the Near East and the Balkans was for centuries held under the pressure of Islam, and thus crippled both in its free spiritual growth and in spontaneous ethical vigor. The vast spaces of Russia have had to suffer untold privations and handicaps under the Mongolian expansion and to defend themselves against the conquests of the Teutonic *Ritter-Orden* (religious order of knighthood) to a certain extent also of the Polish and Lithuanian armies. For centuries, the Eastern Church was cut off from the vital stream of the free Christian civilization. Under foreign domination and under a continuous threat of foreign invasions, the people of the Christian East clung to the visible forms of devotional life and to the sacred formulas of faith in order to preserve for future generations the "uncorrupted" heritage of the apostolic and patristic church.

Besides corporate sacramental and liturgical piety the spiritually minded individuals developed a rigid discipline of monastic life—in seclusion, contemplation, and silence. The monastic tradition of Egypt and Byzantium, rooted both in the old Church and in Neoplatonic mysticism, expressed itself with such an ascetic virtuosity as we scarcely find anywhere in the history of Christianity. This rigid and static form of other-worldly asceticism contradicted sometimes the very nature of the cheerful, world-transforming message of the Incarnate and Risen Christ. It was a religion of hatred of the world: God had cursed the world; everything in the world must perish; God and the world are opposites; Christianity is a religion of fear, not of love, a religion of self-mortification; it negates any joy of life, any love of humanity. A Russian thinker, K. N. Leontyev (1831–1891), made a tremendous effort to justify philosophically this form of Orthodoxy as a religion of static, motionless, joyless, loveless asceticism.

However, the practical expressions of Eastern Orthodoxy have been much richer and more vital. The church used to be—in the days of the greatest national and political agony—the only rallying point, the only refuge, shelter, and comfort for the people of Greece, Serbia, Bulgaria, Rumania, and Russia. She was a guardian of national identity and a spiritual mother. The heroic struggle for national freedom and political self-determination was inspired by her silent presence. In many ways we may say that the Eastern Church has been the main history-building factor in the national destiny of the peoples of her spiritual heritage.

The Church of the East produced, in the days of her greatest trial, a type of practical fervor which is unique in the history of Christianity. The sacramental and and liturgical piety never absorbed or overcame a naïve, simple, almost childlike devotion to the humble, poor, and self-sacrificing Son of Man in Whom love and sympathy had reached the deepest abyss of human suffering. Humility, simplicity, and poverty in loving service, toil, and self-denial were—in the minds of Eastern Christians—regarded as a genuine expression of the human communion with Christ. Especially Russian Christians and thinkers would speak of the "kenotic" ("self-emptying") spirit of Eastern Orthodoxy, referring to St. Paul's interpretation of the incarnation: The Son of Glory and Majesty stripped himself of all heavenly splendor, "emptied" Himself, assumed the form of a servant, became poor, entered the life of labor, toil, humiliation, and sacrifice—and did it in silence, patience, endurance, and unqualified obedience.

The historians of Russia point to the "kenotic" spirit of Orthodox monks as the foremost civilizing agency of early Russian history, and of the national revolt against the Mongols. Monks, of high theological education, like Sergius of Radonesh would form small groups of "kenotic" Christians in order to clear forests and swamps, to struggle against unfriendly elements of nature, to conquer the wilderness, to explore unknown spaces of the north and the east, to build wooden churches and to provide spiritual and physical care for the scattered, lost, toiling, and frustrated families. All this was done in a spirit of childlike joy and obedience, with love for nature, with an assurance that the Lord of Glory was present with them in the form of a servant, poor, and still rich, crucified and still victorious, humble in His suffering and still an unceasing help in the struggle against foreign domination.

When, in the nineteenth century, the Russian intelligentsia, revolting against the official neglect of the common people in villages and hamlets, undertook a plan to go to the people, to the most ignorant and poverty-stricken peasants, to teach them better ways of living, to educate them, and to alleviate their burden of misery, historians and sociologists of Russia used to relate this pioneering, missionary activity to the old spirit of "kenotic" Orthodoxy.

Furthermore, the tremendous humanitarian impulse on the part of the modern Russian intelligentsia advocating a collectivistic organization of national life in which all class differences would dissolve in the spirit of mutuality and solidarity can hardly be understood without the heritage of Orthodox Christianity always linking individual salvation to the salvation of all. "We perish individually, but we are saved collectively." Christ came in poverty and weakness, stripped of glory and power in order to help all who are weak, poor, downtrodden, and oppressed. Can there be a better remedy for any misery than a fellowship of brotherly love, humility, and simplicity?

A Western observer of Eastern European events can hardly realize to what extent even the present Soviet social and political structure reflects the spiritual and national tradition of Russian Orthodoxy. It certainly is misleading to interpret the Russian revolution and its results exclusively as a fruit of Marxian ideology. The ideas of Marxian socialism were unquestionably a powerful weapon in the revolt against the old political, social, and ecclesiastical "theocracy" of czarist Russia. Without Marxism, Russian Communism is as unexplainable as the Great Revolution of 1789 without the philosophy of French Enlightenment. However, very soon after the liquidation of the old order and the Civil War, in the period of constructive organization of the Soviet system, many of the old spiritual and national elements of Russian history began to reemerge and shape the life of the people liberated from the shackles of the old regime. At the present moment we clearly see the contribution, often intangible and undefinable, offered by "kenotic" Orthodoxy to the national community. Its emphasis upon self-sacrifice, simplicity, and poverty, its deep compassion for wretched human beings, was in the background of the revolutionary movement of the Russian intelligentsia. And the emphasis upon the organic unity between personal life and the mystical body of Christ has fostered the collectivistic tendency of the Soviet order. What we call Russian Sovietism is unexplainable without Russian Orthodoxy.

After September, 1943, the Russian Church commenced restoration in a full measure. First, the Patriarch of Moscow was elected, then the national apparatus of the Church was restored, religious instruction of children permitted, theological schools reopened, and religious propaganda admitted.

The whole area of Eastern Orthodoxy is undergoing an unprecedented transformation of social and political life. None of us can make any predictions as to the future structure of this part of the world and the leadership of the Eastern Church. We do not know very much about her present spiritual vigor, intellectual and moral stamina. What we do know is that, in the days to come, the peoples of the Eastern Orthodox heritage will come closer to the rest of the world than ever in history and that they will exert an influence surpassing that of any era of their past. An adequate understanding of their spiritual tradition is essential for any post-war planning as well as for any cultural cooperation between the Western world and Eastern civilization.

SELECTED BIBLIOGRAPHY

The Orthodox Church. By S. N. Bulgakov. Translated by Elizabeth S. Cram; edited by Donald A. Lowrie. London, 1935.

The Wisdom of God. By S. N. Bulgakov. London, 1937.

What Is Christianity? By Adolf von Harnack. Translated by Thomas Bailey Saunders. London, 1901.

Soul of Russia. By Helene Iswolsky. New York, 1943.

The Spirit of Russia. By T. G. Masaryk. New York, 1919.

Holy Moscow. By N. S. Arsen'ev. London, 1940.

Lectures on Godmanhood. By Vladimir Solovyev. New York, 1944.

The Eastern Orthodox Church. By Stefan Zankov. Translated and edited by Donald A. Lowrie. London, 1929.

The Greek and Eastern Churches. By W. F. Adeney. New York, 1908.

The Eastern Church. By A. P. Stanley. London, 1876.

Roman Catholicism

GERALD GROVELAND WALSH

As nearly as critical scholarship has determined the date, it would seem to have been in the early summer of the year we now call 27 A.D. that Jesus of Nazareth "came into Galilee, preaching the gospel of the kingdom of God" (Mark 1 : 14). The "kingdom," in the first account that Jesus gave of it, was pictured as a fulfillment and a promise: "The time is fulfilled, and the kingdom of God is at hand"; and two conditions were imposed on all who sought to share in it: "Repent and believe" (Mark 1 : 15). For the first six months of His preaching, Jesus stressed the first condition only—repentance, change of heart, moral renewal, personal perfection. "Come, follow me" (Matthew 4 : 19), He said. "Blessed are the poor in spirit . . . the meek . . . the merciful . . . the pure of heart . . . the peacemakers . . . they who suffer persecution for justice's sake, for theirs is the kingdom of heaven" (Matt. 5 : 3–10).

Only later did Jesus enunciate what we would now call the great paradox of Christianity: "He who loses his life for my sake will find it" (Matt. 16 : 24). For some, the kingdom became a special call, beyond the ordinary power of human nature to accept. A young man who had been faithful to all the Commandments of the old Law wanted to "gain eternal life." He was invited to sell all he had, and give to the poor, and be content with "treasure in heaven," and come follow Jesus. "But his face fell at the saying, and he went away sad" (Mark 10 : 22). For others, the kingdom would be a call not merely to poverty but to the more difficult renunciation involved in voluntary celibacy. "There are eunuchs who have made themselves so for the kingdom of heaven's sake. Let him accept it who can" (Matt. 19 : 12).

But before Jesus fully revealed His Way as a Way of the Cross, He began to speak of a second main aspect of His kingdom. It was a gospel of Truth, a faith, a mystery to be known;

not merely a call to the will but a challenge to the mind. "To you," Jesus said to His followers, "is given to *know* the mystery of the kingdom of God" (Mark 4: 11). And just as His Way led up to higher and higher peaks of moral and superhuman perfection, so His Truth reached down to deeper and deeper levels of spiritual and supernatural mystery. Jesus asked His followers to believe in things that would not happen until the end of the world when, for example, there would appear "the sign of the Son of Man in heaven . . . and they will see the Son of Man coming upon the clouds of heaven with great power and majesty; and . . . his angels . . . will gather his elect . . . from the uttermost parts of the earth to the uttermost parts of heaven" (Matt. 24: 30, 31, with Mark 13: 27). He spoke more mysteriously still when he said: "He who eats my flesh and drinks my blood abides in me and I in him" (John 6: 56). Many of Jesus' disciples, when they heard this, complained, saying: "This is a hard saying. Who can listen to it?" And, like the young man who "went away sad," some of them "turned back and no longer went about with" Jesus (John 6: 66).

In spite of these defections, the number of those who walked in the Way and accepted the Truth of Jesus continued to increase; and the kingdom began to show itself, in its third aspect, as a community, an organized society of men and women living the way and the truth. The kingdom was thus not only a code and a creed but a Church. Jesus, in fact, constituted a rudimentary hierarchy. Twelve men were chosen and commissioned with special powers; and seventy-two were sent to preach in His name. When one of the Twelve, Simon, openly confessed his full faith in Jesus as the promised Messiah, saying "Thou art the Christ, the Son of the living God," Jesus appointed him to a very special position in the hierarchy of the kingdom:

"Blessed art thou, Simon Bar-Jona, for flesh and blood has not revealed this to thee, but my Father in heaven. And I say to thee that thou art Peter [*Kepha*] and upon this rock [*kepha* in Aramaic, the language which Jesus spoke] I will build my Church, and the gates of hell shall not prevail against it. And

I will give to thee the keys of the kingdom of heaven; and what-soever thou shalt bind on earth shall be bound in heaven, and whatsoever thou shalt loose on earth shall be loosed in heaven" (Matt. 16: 17–19).

In many things that Jesus said and did, He implied a fourth and more mysterious aspect of His kingdom. He did not ask men to consent to follow His way by their unaided will, but "with God," by means of Divine help or grace. "With men this is impossible, but *with God* all things are possible" (Matt. 19: 20–26). Nor did He ask men to assent to His truth by an un-aided act of their minds. Peter's faith, for example, had not been possible to "flesh and blood"; it had been an illumination communicated by the "Father in heaven." So, too, membership in Jesus' Church was a matter not only of voluntary enrollment, but of Divine inspiration. "No one can come to me," said Jesus, "unless he is enabled to do so by my Father" (John 6: 66). Thus the kingdom implied more than a code, a creed, and a community; it meant communion with God, a communication of Divine Life.

Deeper and more mysterious still was a fifth aspect of the kingdom. Jesus not only identified Himself with His "king-dom," as code and creed and community: "I am the way and the truth and the life" (John 14: 6); He identified Himself with God: "Before Abraham was, I am (John 8: 58). . . . I and the Father are one (John 10: 30). . . . I am in the Father and the Father in me. . . . All things that the Father has are mine. . . . I came forth from the Father" (John 16: 15, 28). Just before His ascension into heaven, He spoke words which are without parallel in the whole history of religion:

"All power in heaven and on earth has been given to me. Go, therefore, and make disciples of all nations, baptizing them in the name of the Father and of the Son, and of the Holy Spirit, teaching them to observe all that I have commanded you: and behold, I am with you all days, even to the consummation of the world" (Matt. 28: 18–20).

309

THE BODY OF CHRIST

In these last words there is implied still another and, for our present purpose, a most important aspect of the kingdom. Jesus had made it clear that His Church—the community of His followers in communion with God through Him—would continue after His death in historical existence until the end of time: "I will ask the Father and he will send you another Advocate to dwell with you for ever, the Spirit of truth whom the world cannot receive, because it neither sees him nor knows him. But you shall know him, because he will dwell with you and be in you. I will not leave you orphans" (John 14: 16, 17).

Jesus indicated that the Holy Spirit would reveal to the Apostles truths that had not been expressly declared by Jesus himself: "Many things yet I have to say to you, but you cannot bear them now. But when he, the Spirit of truth, has come, he will teach you all truth . . . and the things that are to come he will declare to you" (John 16: 12–14).

Besides promising this continuity and authority, Jesus assured His future followers of a Divinely communicated oneness both with themselves and with God:

"Holy Father, keep in thy name those whom thou hast given me, that they may be *one* even as we are. . . . Yet not for these only do I pray, but for those also who through their word are to believe in me, that all may be *one,* even as thou Father, in me and I in thee; that they also may be *one* in us, that the world may know that thou has sent me . . . I in them and thou in me; that they may be perfected in *unity* . . . in order that the love with which thou hast loved me may be in them" (John 17: 1, 11, 12, 20, 21, 23).

After Jesus was crucified, rose from the dead, and ascended into heaven, the fact of a visible, historical, constitutional Church made up of weak and sinning human beings, ruling and being ruled according to His Way, teaching and being taught according to His Truth, living a social life of prayer, worship, love, sacrifice according to the communication of His Life, and claiming to be in a real, if "mystical," sense His very Body is attested by the writings of the Apostles and first converts.

The greatest of the early converts was Saul of Tarsus. Renamed Paul, and given the high authority of an Apostle, he keeps repeating in his writings the ideas that Christ is God, that the Church is Christ, that all men everywhere are called to communion with Christ and God through the Church:

"As the body is one and has many members and all the members of the body, many as they are, form one body, so also is it with Christ. For in one Spirit we were all baptized into one body, whether Jews or Gentiles, whether slaves or free; and we were all given to drink of one Spirit. For the body is not one member, but many. . . . God has set the members . . . in the body of Christ (I Cor. 12: 12–27). . . . There is neither Jew nor Greek; there is neither slave nor freeman; there is neither male nor female. For you are all one in Christ Jesus (Galatians 3: 28). . . . By revelation was made known to me . . . the mystery of Christ . . . that the Gentiles are joint heirs, and fellow-members of the same body, and joint partakers of the promise in Christ Jesus through the gospel . . . that through the Church there may be made known . . . the manifold wisdom of God according to the eternal purpose which he accomplished in Christ Jesus our Lord . . . to be strengthened with power through his Spirit unto the progress of the inner man; and to have Christ dwelling through faith in your hearts, so that being rooted and grounded in love, you may be able to comprehend . . . Christ's love which surpasses knowledge, in order that you may be filled unto all the fulness of God. . . . I therefore exhort you to walk . . . careful to preserve the unity of the Spirit in the bond of peace: one body and one Spirit . . . one Lord, one faith, one baptism; one God and Father of all, who is above all, and throughout all and in us all" (Ephesians 3: 3–4, 6).

CATHOLIC RELIGIOUS EXPERIENCE

Jesus once said, "The kingdom of God is within" (Luke 17: 21). Looked at simply as a personal, religious experience, Roman Catholicism is the consciousness of membership in a society that, for a Catholic, integrates in a single living whole all the aspects of the "kingdom of God" and the "Body of Christ" to which allusion has just been made. The Catholic is conscious, first, of what seems to him a communication of Divine power, an "inspiration," in virtue of which he feels able, "with God," to "repent," to answer a call upon his conscience to follow, however falteringly, a way of life, a moral code, that seems to him transcendent. The code is transcendent in the sense that neither he nor the society to which he belongs had any part in formulating its basic principles. The Catholic conscience is thus conceived as a guidepost pointing to an objective rule of life, rather than as a subjective categorical imperative establishing a rule of life from within. In this sense, his conscience is not the law, but a light by which the law may be more easily discerned.

The Catholic is conscious, secondly, of what seems to him a communication of Divine light, an "illumination," in virtue of which he finds himself able, beyond the power of "flesh and blood," of natural insight, to "believe," to answer a challenge to his intelligence, to assent, however difficult the comprehension, to an objective body of truth, a religious creed, that appears to him to be a Divine Revelation.

The Catholic is conscious, thirdly, of communion or fellowship with all those others who openly accept the same Way and Truth as communicated to them by the living authority of a visible society that seems to them to have a life that is like the life of Jesus Christ, both human and Divine. The Catholic's sense of communion with God and of communication from God is seldom without some direct relation to his communion with others in the Church, and especially with the ministers of the Sacraments and of the Sacrifice of the Mass. While the conditions for membership in the Church are the same as the conditions laid down by Jesus for membership in the "kingdom," namely to "repent" and "believe," the Church itself, like the "kingdom," reveals itself to him as a fulfillment and a promise.

The Church "fulfills" all that was adumbrated in the Law and the Prophets—and, above all, the ideal of Israel as a community of members united one with another and all with God, a "vineyard" of Yahweh: "My Loved One had a vineyard on a fertile hill. . . . The vineyard of Yahweh of hosts is the house of Israel, and the men of Judah are His cherished plantations" (Isaias 5 : 2, 7). More than a fulfillment, the kingdom seems to a Catholic to be a promise. The life of Grace (to use the language of theology) is, for him, a foretaste of the life of Glory; the Church on earth, a prefiguring of the eternal and indefectible union of souls with the ultimate source of all being and truth, of all goodness and beauty and, therefore, of all (and much more than all) that we mean by happiness.

The Catholic is grateful that after many experiments in over-interiorizing and overexteriorizing Christian life, the Church has "fulfilled" many implications in the Scriptural record in her balanced sacramental system of baptism, confirmation, confession, eucharist, matrimony, orders, and extreme unction, in which outward symbols and inward grace meet and mate and generate the most lasting of the Catholic's religious experiences. The Catholic is, above all, grateful for that sacramental and, therefore, real Presence which is the occasion of his most fervent prayers and warmest consolations, the center of his supreme act of communal worship in the Sacrifice of the Mass, the main source of his growth in holiness.

The Catholic is grateful, too, for that extension of the sacramental spirit whereby the treasures of all the arts—of building, carving, painting, music, singing, writing, preaching—have been allowed to lift on the wings of feeling and fancy, especially in the splendid and dramatic liturgy of the Church, the convictions of the Creed and the obligations of the Christian Code. He is grateful, too, for the Catholic "devotions"—to the Sacred Heart of Jesus (symbol of His love both for the Father and for us), to the Virgin Mother, Mary (in whose womb the Eternal Word was made flesh), to the Saints (who like ten thousand different syllables spell out the full lexicon of Christian love), to the Holy Places (where He, or even she or they, once lived and loved and died). All these, like the cement that binds the bricks together, like the bridge that links the distant banks, are found, in Catholic experience, to aid and not to hinder communion of his soul with God.

The Catholic is only too aware of the human side of the Church, as he is aware of the human nature of Jesus—of His hunger and thirst (Matt. 4 : 2; John 19 : 28), His need of rest and sleep (John 4 : 6; Matt. 8 : 24), His groans, and tears, and love and sorrow (John 11 : 33, 35, 37), the "scandal" (Mark 14 : 27) of His weakness. The Catholic remembers that Jesus said there would be "weeds among the wheat" (Matt. 13 : 24–30). He knows that many in high places in his Church have been moved by greed to betray Jesus as Judas did. And some, in folly, have drawn the sword as Peter did—as though the kingdom could be defended or extended by the use of force. Dante's *Inferno* is a sublime confession of the Catholic's shame in the presence of a long history of all too frequent lust and pride. Yet above the din of all this scandal, the Catholic is conscious, especially after confession and Holy Communion, of a Voice that speaks to him, as Jesus spoke to the Twelve: "Do you also wish to go away?"; and he feels, he does not quite know how, the strength to answer as Peter answered: "Lord, to whom shall we go? Thou hast the word of everlasting life" (John 6 : 68–70).

THE CATHOLIC CHURCH

Correlative to Catholicism as a personal experience of a Call to "repent" and a Command to "believe" is an objective, historical fact, the institutional Catholic Church. This Community seems to every thoughtful Catholic to be a "fulfillment," in virtue of direct and unbroken historical succession, permanent and exclusive Divine commission, and present indwelling of the Spirit of Truth, of the society founded by Jesus Christ, and which He had in mind when He said: "Upon this rock I will build my Church," and again when He gave the commission, "Go . . . and make disciples of all nations . . . I am with *you* all days," and, again, when He prayed for a Divinely given unity "for those who through *their* words are to believe in me, that all may be *one,* even as thou Father in me and I in thee, that *they* also may be one in us," and, above all, when He prayed for a Divinely infused life of *agape,* of love, charity, supernatural grace, "that the love with which thou hast loved me may be in *them,* as I in them."

The warrants for these claims are often summarized in the official title of the Roman Church as "One, Holy, Catholic and Apostolic." Historical and geographical identity, externally and juridically manifested by profession of the same faith as defined in the great Councils, participation in the same worship, communion in the same bloodless sacrifice of the Mass, observance of the same laws under the primacy of a single visible head, the Pope, is only made possible, the Catholic thinks, because of a "divinely given unity by which all men of every race are united to Christ in the bond of brotherhood . . . a fellowship in charity" (Encyclical, *Corporis Mystici*[1]). The Holiness of the Church, as revealed outwardly in an unbroken series of martyrs and other saints in every age and clime, is considered by a Catholic to be an effect of the fact that "the Spirit of our Redeemer . . . until the end of time penetrates every part of the Church's being and is active within."[2]

So, also, the Catholicity of the Church, visible in the diocesan, parochial, missionary organizations throughout the world, is regarded by a Catholic as a fulfillment of the divinely given commission to "make disciples of all nations . . . teaching them to observe all that I have commanded you." The Apostolicity, visible in the direct and unbroken succession of 262 Bishops of Rome, is a guaranty for a Catholic of the more invisible realities of succession to Apostolic doctrine and to the Apostolic power of conferring orders.

The most recent authoritative statement of the Church's conception of her nature and claims is to be found in the Encyclical Letter, *Corporis Mystici,* cited above. The "One, Holy, Catholic, Apostolic, Roman Church"[3] is identified with the "mystical" Body, as described by St. Paul, and with "the society

---

[1] Encyclical, *Corporis Mystici.* It was published in Latin in the official *Acta Apostolicae Sedis,* July 20, 1943.

[2] *Ibid.*

[3] From the English translation. New York: America Press. Page 9.

established by the Redeemer of the human race," [4] in which alone His Way and Truth and Life can still be fully found. It is the main contention of the Encyclical that the visible, juridical organization that has developed in history and now includes over 380,000,000 members can no more be separated from the invisible, supernatural indwelling of the Holy Spirit than any other living body can be separated from its soul, or than the manhood in Jesus Christ can be separated from His Godhead:

"There can be no real opposition or conflict between the invisible mission of the Holy Spirit and the juridical commission of the Ruler and Teacher received from Christ. Like body and soul in us, they complement and perfect each other, and have their source in our one Redeemer, who not only said "Receive ye the Holy Spirit," but also clearly commanded, "As the Father hath sent me, so I send you"; and again: "He that heareth you heareth me." [5]

The visible Church, "constituted by the coalescence of structurally united parts," has been "commissioned by the Divine Redeemer" to continue "Christ's apostolate as teacher, king, priest." [6] As the "mystical" Body of Christ, the Church is a "fellowship in charity" with a "divinely given unity by which all men of every race are united to Christ in a bond of brotherhood," [7] and she is "endowed with the fullest communication of the Holy Spirit." [8]

While the Pope is the visible Head of the historical Church, in the sense of the visible representative, the Vicar, of Christ, there is, of course, only one Head of the "mystical" Body, namely, Jesus Christ. It is He "who grants the light of faith to believers . . . who imparts the supernatural gifts of knowledge, understanding and wisdom to pastors and teachers and above all to His Vicar on earth. . . . It is He who, though unseen, presides at the Church's Councils and guides them. . . .

[4] Page 4.
[5] Page 29.
[6] Page 10.
[7] Page 6.
[8] Page 15.

When the Sacraments of the Church are administered by external rites, it is He who produces their effects in souls." [9]

THE WAY

It has been the experience of the Catholic Church that, in the ever-changing complexities of historical life, the normal Christian conscience needs to have the general Gospel formulation of Christ's Way supplemented by one of three means. It was by Divine inspiration that St. Peter abrogated the ancient dietary regulations (Acts 10). It was by means of an official ruling of the Church leaders that the question of circumcision was settled (Acts 15). Most cases of conscience must be settled by approved spiritual directors; and of such direction there has been a long history. The fourth century, for example, was a golden age of moral theology. It gave the Church such masters as Gregory of Nyssa (d. 395), St. Ambrose of Milan (d. 397), St. John Chrysostom (d. 407).

It was the merit of the Scholastic theologians to make a synthesis of the rational ethics of Aristotle and the Will of God as revealed in the Scriptures. Moral responsibility was conceived as an objective and inalienable attribute of a created human nature intrinsically related to truth and goodness and, therefore, to the Ultimate Truth and Supreme Goodness of God. The *ought* in conscience is as objective, real, and measurable as the *must* in physical gravity.

The greatest of the Scholastics was St. Thomas Aquinas (1225–1274). Looked at theologically, the second part of his *Summa Theologica* is a systematic commentary on Christ's two fundamental commandments concerning God and our neighbor (Matt. 22: 37–40). Looked at philosophically, it is an attempt to consider human virtues and vices under the aspect of the Aristotelian concept of habits (i ii qq. 49–89; ii ii qq. 47–170). But, of course, in treating of God's Law and still more of God's Grace (i ii qq. 90–114) and of the theological virtues of Faith, Hope, and Charity (ii ii qq. 1–46) the theological element is completely predominant.

[9] Page 24.

A typical manual of contemporary moral theology in use among American Catholics is the *Compendium Theologiae Moralis* (in Latin) by Timothy Barrett, S. J. (1862–1935). Based on the work which Luigi Sabetti (1839–1898) had developed from that of the Frenchman, Jean Pierre Gury (1801–1866), each of the thirty-two editions was adapted to changing conditions. Gury's work was itself a skillful modernization of the ninth edition of the work of the Italian, St. Alphonsus de Liguori (1696–1787) which, in turn, was largely inspired by the *Medulla Theologiae Moralis* of the German Jesuit, Herman Busenbaum (1600–1688); and Busenbaum acknowledges his indebtedness to the Spanish commentators on St. Thomas, Francisco Suarez (1548–1617), and Juan de Lugo (1583–1660). The combination of fixed principles, historical experience, and corporate prudence with a keen perception of contemporary and local conditions has eliminated from Catholic "casuistry" the elements of personal improvization, national prejudice, and ephemeral fashion.

Particularly since Leo XIII (1878–1903), the Popes have given an example of moral leadership in the domestic, educational, social, economic, political, and international crises which have tormented the world in the last three generations. The paganization of love and marriage, revealed in divorce, companionate marriage, free love, artificial "eugenic" practices, private abortion, public sterilization, juvenile delinquency, pornographic art was faced in two notable Encyclicals, the *Arcanum* of Leo XIII (1880) and the *Casti Connubii* of Pius XI (1930). So, too, with the problem of education. Leo XIII's *Inscrutabili* (1878) and the *Divini illius Magistri* (1931) of Pius XI accuse secular education of a lack of realism. Pius XI insists that education must look to "man whole and entire, soul united to body in unity of nature, with all his faculties natural and supernatural such as right reason and revelation show him to be, man, therefore, fallen from his original estate, but redeemed by Christ." While approving "a gradually more active cooperation on the part of the child" and the banishment of "tyranny and violence from the classroom," the Pope condemns the Rousseauistic and experimental systems which tend to make the child "the slave of his own blind pride and disorderly inclinations." The educated Christian who "thinks, judges, and acts constantly and consistently in accordance with right reason illumined by the supernatural light of the example and teaching of Christ" is not called upon to "renounce the activities of this earthly life" nor, still less, to "stunt his natural faculties."

The social and economic Encyclicals, *Rerum Novarum* (1891) and *Quadragesimo Anno* (1931) face the fact that a "small number of very rich men have been able to lay upon the teeming masses of the laboring poor a yoke little better than slavery itself." Pius XI warned the world both of "economic imperialism" and of the "no less noxious and detestable internationalism or international imperialism in financial affairs, which holds that where a man's fortune is, there is his country." He feared both the atheism and "statism" of Communism; but praised that mitigated Socialism whose tenets could be reconciled with Christian principles.

In the great political debate of the modern world, the Encyclical of Leo XIII, *Immortale Dei* (1885), insisted on the simple truths that are the sufficient answer both to the naturalistic liberal theory of the State and to contemporary totalitarian practice, namely, that the origin of society is in human nature, that the author of human nature is God, and that, therefore, all public authority is from God and for the people's welfare. The world today understands better than it did in 1885 that "it is a public crime to act as though there were no God"; and the world today, after sad experience of the totalitarian tyranny over souls, is more ready to agree that "it is to the Church that God has assigned the charge of seeing to, and legislating for, all that concerns religion." On the general question of the relations of Church and State, Leo repeated the Gospel and traditional teaching of the Catholic Church: "Each authority in its kind is supreme. Each has fixed limits within which it is contained. . . . Whatever . . . belongs . . . to the salvation of souls or the worship of God is subject to the power of the Church. . . . Whatever is to be ranged under the civil and political order is rightly subject to the civil authority." It was in this Encyclical, too, that the Pope pleaded, in the language of St. Augustine, for the principle of practical religious toleration: "Man cannot believe otherwise than of his own free will."

Especially on the question of war and peace has the modern Papacy offered to the whole world an example of moral leadership. As far back as 1889, in an address to the College of Cardinals (*Nostis errorem*), Leo XIII warned that "nothing is so important today as to ward off from Europe the danger of war." While allowing that it "is lawful to use force in defense of one's rights," he insisted that "for States as for individuals, concord chiefly rests upon justice and charity," two virtues of which the Church, by the command of God, is "the parent and the guardian." While the First World War was at its height and still indecisive, Pope Benedict XV, in a diplomatic note, *Dès le début* (August 1, 1917), proposed seven "bases of a just and lasting peace": the primacy of the moral force of right, reciprocal diminution of armaments, establishment of arbitration, true freedom and common enjoyment of the seas, complete and reciprocal condonation of damage done, reciprocal restitution of territories occupied, settlement of territorial questions, "taking account . . . of the aspirations of the peoples and . . . coordinating particular interests with the general weal of the great human society."

During the Second World War, Pius XII proposed ten Peace Points which attracted much attention. The Five Points proposed in a Christmas Eve address (*Questo giorno*) in 1939 dealt with peace in the international sphere; the Five Points proposed in 1942 dealt with national peace. In both cases there is a synthesis of realism and idealism, of contemporary facts and unchanging principles. In both cases the ultimate appeal is to the sovereignty of God and, under God, to a sense of moral responsibility rather than to treaty-made or national positive law. In both cases, the Pope starts from the most commonly accepted of all contemporary agreements, namely, that "all nations great or small, powerful or weak" have a right "to life and independence" in the international community, and that all persons have inalienable rights in the national community. While the independence of nations must be guaranteed by some such practical method as progressive disarmament and juridical international organization, the freedom of the individual calls for the reconstruction of an economic system in which families can find stable security.

All men of good will, and still more, all men of religious convictions, under the common menace of world chaos have felt an increasing need for some kind of collaboration. The modern Papacy has been sensitive to this need. In his first public utterance, Pope Pius XII spoke sympathetically of "those outside the enclosures of the Catholic Church." Again in the Encyclical, *Summi Pontificatus* ("On the Unity of the Human Society"), he spoke of "those who, though not belonging to the visible body of the Catholic Church, have given noble and sincere expression to their appreciation of all that unites them to us in love for the Person of Christ or belief in God. . . . The . . . trials of the present hour . . . make all believers in God and in Christ share the consciousness of a common threat from a common danger."

In a Christmas allocution in 1940, the Pope offered his prayers in union "with all those who recognize in Christ their Lord and Saviour." In 1941, he spoke of "a universal undertaking for the common good, which requires the collaboration of all Christendom in the religious and moral aspects of the reconstruction of the social order." In 1942, he begged "all who are united . . . by the bond of faith in God . . . to unite and collaborate toward renewal of society in spirit and in truth."

The Papal initiative in welcoming the collaboration of all Christians in the reestablishment of political reason and economic justice as the norms both for national and international life has been seconded by the Catholic episcopate and laity throughout the world. In England, under the vibrant leadership of the late Cardinal Hinsley, the Catholic Sword of the Spirit movement has worked in close collaboration with its counterpart in the Anglican and Free Church communities, the Religion and Life movement. On May 28, 1942, there was issued a notable Joint Statement on Christian cooperation at a meeting of Church leaders sponsored by the two movements. It spoke of the "compelling obligation . . . to maintain the Christian tradition and to act together . . . in the handling of social, economic and civic problems." The field of cooperation was defined as the "broad lines of social and international policy"; and the hope was expressed that the two movements would "work through parallel action in the religious, and joint action in the social and international field."

In Australia, in June, 1943, a joint statement was issued by the Catholic and Anglican Archbishops of Sydney. It noted that "all who profess the Christian faith—without compromising their own doctrines—possess in the virtue of love or charity common ground on which all Christians should adhere." These principles included general ideas of the sovereignty of God the Creator, the dignity and the duty of the created human individual, the obligation to obey "God's law imprinted in the nature of man" and "God's positive law in the Commandments and in the Scriptures faithfully and continuously interpreted by the Christian Church."

In Canada, a joint meeting held in Toronto, June, 1943, proposed that a "Believers' Bloc" should be present at any future Peace Conference. In our own country, October 7, 1943, there was issued a statement on a just peace, consisting of seven points accepted by a very wide representation of Catholics, Protestants, and Jews. The points included the statement that "States and international society are subject to the sovereignty of God and to the moral law" and proclaimed the rights of "the human person as the image of God," of "all peoples, large and small," of "ethnic, religious and cultural minorities," and the necessity of "the organization of international institutions," of "international economic collaboration," and of the "equilibrium and social order of the individual State."

These gestures of Christian charity and these expressions of social hope leave unaltered the dogmatic and liturgical isolation of the Catholic Church. Collaboration in social renewal does not imply complete community of faith nor communication in the sacramental means of supernatural renovation, *communicatio in sacris*. While the basic assumption of the Protestant movements in the direction of the "Reunion of Christendom" is that the unity of the Church is an ideal still to be reached by collective collaboration and individual compromise, the Catholic position is that Christian unity is a fact settled once and for all by the substantially irreformable constitution established for His Church by Jesus Christ. The juridical successors of the Apostles, the Bishops, under the primacy of the successor of Peter, constitute in the Catholic view a perpetual center of unity which no peripheral dismemberment of the faithful can affect. Unity of government cannot derive from a bargain between the sheep but only from appointment by the Shepherd. Reunion, in this view, must take the form of a return of the sheep to the fold (John 10: 1–16; 21: 15–17).

THE TRUTH

In the first recorded Christian sermon after the coming of the Holy Spirit, St. Peter did not merely expose the faith; he *argued*—from prophecy, "miracles and wonders and signs" wrought by Jesus—the historical fact of the resurrection and the visible effect of the outpouring of the Spirit. He ended with a logical conclusion: "*Therefore,* let all the house of Israel know most assuredly that God has made both Lord and Christ this Jesus whom you crucified" (Acts 2: 14–36). The same argumentative form of exposition appears in the first recorded sermon of St. Paul. This, too, leads to the logical conclusion: "Be it known *therefore* to you, brethren, that through him forgiveness of sins is proclaimed to you" (Acts 13: 16–42).

St. Paul was a master theologian. It is an easy task to build up from his Epistles a complete theological system dealing with the Father, the Redeemer, the work of Redemption, the channels of Redemption—Faith, Sacraments, the Church; with the fruits of Redemption—morality, asceticism, Christian perfection; with the "last things"—death, the *Parousia* or Day of the Lord, the Hereafter.

The general character of Christian theology, up to the end of the third century, has been sketched in a remarkable series of chapters in *Die Mission und Ausbreitung des Christentums,* by the Liberal Protestant scholar, Adolf von Harnack.[10] The most general characteristic "native to the preaching of Christianity from the very first" was, in Harnack's view, "unity and variety," that is to say, the characteristic of "Western Catholicism, when surveyed as a whole . . . a *complexio oppositorum.*"[11] Both dogmatic and moral theology, a "crucial message of faith and of ethical requirements,"[12] were involved. "Grace never displaced recompense."[13] Christian theology was likewise both ascetical and mystical: "If the early Christians always looked out for the proofs of the Spirit and of power, they did so from the standpoint of their moral and religious energy.[14] . . . The Catholic doctrine of *praecepta* and *consilia* prevailed almost from the first within the Gentile church."[15]

Harnack notes, too, a characteristic insistence on both reason and authority. St. Paul, he observes, "endeavored to reason out everything, and in the last resort it is never a question with him of any sacrifice of the intellect."[16] There was always a double appeal to "the authority of the letter of Scripture . . . together with that of the Church"; and both the authority of the Bible and the Church were buttressed "by means of rational arguments."[17]

The earliest Christian theology was likewise a sacramental theology: "for although Christian worship is to be a worship in spirit and in truth, these sacraments are sacred transactions which operate on life, containing the forgiveness of sins, knowledge and eternal life . . . the symbols do actually convey to the

[10] Translated and edited by James Moffatt, *The Expansion of Christianity in the First Three Centuries,* vol. 1. New York: 1904.

[11] Pages 102, 103.

[12] Page 105.

[13] Page 116.

[14] Page 258.

[15] Page 271.

[16] Page 277.

[17] Pages 277, 278.

soul all they signify . . . to talk of bread and wine as . . . the body and blood of Christ . . . was quite intelligible to that age. . . . The two most sublime spiritualists of the church, namely John and Origen . . . the great gnostic theologians . . . were all sacramental theologians. . . . The sentence of the later Schoolmen, *Sacramenta continent gratiam,* is as old as the Gentile church, and even older." [18]

In brief, Harnack concludes, "Christianity is a revelation which is to be believed, an authority which is to be obeyed, the rational religion which may be understood and proved, the religion of the mysteries or the sacraments, the religion of transcendentalism." [19]

Of course, almost from the beginning there were heretics. The Gnostics like Saturninus, Basilides, Carpocrates, and Valentinus wanted the "transcendentalism" without the "sacraments." Montanists like Priscilla, Maximilla and, later, Tertullian put more trust in personal piety and "prophetic insight" than in the public "authority which is to be obeyed." Others like Sabellius, Cleomenes and, later, Arius doubted the dogma of the Trinity.

In the fourth century, some of the highest ranking leaders in the Church accepted the Arian heresy. Even when a Council of the Church held at Nicaea in the year 325 defined the dogma in the clear, philosophical words, "One Lord Jesus Christ, the Son of God, begotten of the Father, only begotten, that is, of the substance (*ousia*) of the Father; God of God, Light of light; very God of very God; begotten not made; being one substance (*homoousios*) with the Father," doubts remained; and fierce intellectual battles filled the next fifty years. Moderate and mediocre men, tempted to put peace above orthodoxy, proposed a mitigated divinity for Christ—He was not of the same substance as the Father, but He was like the Father: not *homoousios* but *homoiousios.*

In this crisis, a man of extraordinary moral, intellectual, and supernatural endowment, Athanasius of Alexandria (d. 373),

[18] Pages 286, 287.
[19] Page 299.

realized that the battle was not about words like *genomenos* (created) and *gennomenos* (begotten), *homoiousios* and *homoousios,* but for the soul of Christendom and the destiny of the world. He realized that if Christ is merely a creature and not also the Creator of the world, Christianity is a man-made religion, the Church an ethico-political debating club, and Christian life a pious emotion. Supported by Pope Julius (337–352), Athanasius won; and eight years after his death, the Council of Constantinople in 381 reaffirmed the definition of Nicaea.

Meanwhile a second difficulty arose. As the heretical Arians had attacked the Divinity of Christ in the name of Scriptural simplicity, so the schismatic Donatists opposed the juridical authority of the Church in the name of personal holiness. But again a man of extraordinary spiritual and intellectual gifts came to the defense of orthodoxy. The writings of St. Augustine (d. 430) have left a deep imprint on every aspect of Christian doctrine, discipline, and devotion. He is perhaps best known for his insistence on the dogma of the necessity of grace; but his witness is likewise important on the juridical primacy of Papal authority. "Those who do not love the unity of the Church," he wrote, "cannot have the Love (*caritatem*) of God; that is to say, only in the Catholic Church is the Holy Spirit received." [20] The essential unity of the Church is in this possession of the Holy Spirit and, therefore, in a spiritual bond; but this spiritual bond must be implemented in a juridical organization with a visible head, since in case of doubt there must be a court of last appeal in the Apostolic See: "si opus fuerit ad Sedem Apostolicam scribere ut . . . communi omnium auctoritate . . . firmetur" (Epist. 250). The Pope is the Bishop of the primal see—"in qua semper Apostolicae Cathedrae viguit principatus" (Epist. 43).

To complete the picture of a full dogmatic Catholicism, a third decision was necessary. It had to be made clear that since the juridical unity of the visible Church was willed by a Divine Founder, such a juridical organization is as inseparably one with the Life of the Holy Spirit as the human nature of the son

[20] *De Baptismo,* III, xvi.

of Mary of Nazareth was inseparably one with the Divine Life of the Word.

The victory over the divisive spirit of the heresy of Nestorious of Constantinople was largely the work of Cyril of Alexandria (d. 444), who was commissioned by Pope Celestine in 430 to threaten Nestorius with excommunication. Cyril kept insisting on the ideas that when the "Word became flesh," one "Godhood and manhood constituted *one* Lord Jesus Christ by an ineffable concurrence into unity"; that the "body that tasted death was God's very own"; that the mother who bore Jesus Christ was literally the Mother of God (*theotokos*). And this doctrine was defined in the Council in Ephesus in 431. Only when this was clear could it be fully grasped that, however human the juridical organization of the Church might be, the Church was as "mystically" one with Christ as Christ was "hypostatically" one with the Divine Word. Cyril has nowhere better expressed the closeness of the communion of the members of the Church with God than in his *Commentary on the Gospel of St. John* (Patrologia Graeca, vol. LXXIV):

"When we receive the Spirit we become sharers and partakers of the divine nature (col. 545). . . . He joins our many distinct spirits into unity and somehow makes them one in a spiritual unity . . . the unity of the Spirit in the bond of peace, one body and one Spirit . . . one Lord, one faith, one baptism. And truly if the one Spirit abides in all of us, then the one Father of all will be God within us, and through His Son He will bring into unity one with the other and with Himself those who participate of the Spirit (561). . . . The bond of our union with God the Father is Christ; as man He unites us with Himself, and as God He unites us to God. . . . For when we receive within us, corporeally and spiritually, the true Son who is substantially united with the Father, we have the glory of participating and communicating in the divine nature" (563).

When Cyril of Alexandria died (A.D. 444), the Catholic dogmatic system had, as it were, reached its majority. The great unities were clearly grasped by the whole mass of the faithful: the unity of three distinct Persons in one, unique Divine Nature; the "hypostatic" unity of two natures, human and Divine, in the single Person of Christ; the "mystical" unity of Christ as Head with His Body, the Church; the juridical unity of the multilingual Church under the visible primacy of Papal authority.

At the moment of Cyril's death that authority was in the hands of Pope Leo the Great (A.D. 440–461). Leo's authority was openly accepted in an imperial constitution bearing the names of both the Eastern and Western emperors; and when six hundred bishops, nearly all Easterners, met at the Council of Chalcedon in 451, there was no hesitation in accepting the delegate of Pope Leo, as the President of the Council, and no doubt in any mind that a dogmatic letter which Leo had addressed to the Patriarch of Constantinople was authoritative for the whole Church: "This is the faith of the Fathers. This is the faith of the Apostles. So we all believe.... Through Leo, Peter has spoken" (Mansi, *Conciliorum . . . Collectio,* vol. 6, col. 971).

All subsequent Popes have claimed the dogmatic authority which Leo exercised; but not all Bishops have imitated the Fathers of Chalcedon. Six centuries later, in 1054, almost all the Bishops of the East withdrew their allegiance; and before five centuries more had passed, the Protestant Revolt was triumphant in many of the northern nations of Europe. The Councils of Constantinople II (553), which confirmed the first four Councils; of Constantinople III (680–681), which condemned the heresy of Monothelitism; and of Nicaea II (787), which condemned the Iconoclasts are still accepted by both Roman and Orthodox Churches as Ecumenical; while the Lateran Councils of 1123, 1139, 1179, 1215 and subsequent Councils are not accepted by the East, although Eastern Patriarchs attended the Councils of Lyons in 1245 and 1274, the Council of Vienne 1311–1313, and the Florentine sessions of the Council of Basle in 1439.

It fell to the thirteenth century to present a systematic exposition of the whole of the dogmatic tradition as defined in the great Councils. The genius capable of achieving this task was found in Thomas Aquinas (1225–1274). Inspired by the Pauline conception that the invisible God can be known from visible creation (Romans 1: 20), St. Thomas argues from the movement, causality, contingence, imperfections, and order of created beings to the existence of an uncreated principle of being, to a Being whose essence it is to exist, to a Being whose proper name is "I AM" (Exodus 3: 13), to a God who is one and true and good, infinite, eternal, and immutable (*Summa Theologica* I, qq. 1–13). The analysis of the Divine Life of Wisdom, Love, and Power (qq. 14–26) prepares for the Thomistic speculations on the dogma of the Trinity (qq. 27–43). The "Word," the *Logos,* the Second Person is thought of as "conceived" by the Father somewhat as a concept, an idea, is conceived by the human intelligence; only, of course, the Divine Word cannot be a fleeting, accidental phenomenon that *happens,* but must be an Eternal, Subsistent Person who *is.* The Holy Spirit is thought of as "proceeding" somewhat like the movement of human love; only the procession is eternal, and what proceeds is subsistent Love, a Person.

The Third Part of the *Summa* deals with Christ, the Way by which men may reach Beatitude in God. St. Thomas deals with all the issues raised in the discussions which led to the definitions of Nicaea, Ephesus, and Chalcedon, but with a firmer philosophical grasp than was revealed in the earlier debates. He takes up, first, the nature of the union of the "Word" and the "flesh," (III, q. 2) and then, point by point, the Divine Person (q. 3), the assumed human nature (qq. 4–6), the endowments of the human nature of Christ in the order of Grace (qq. 7–8) and of knowledge (qq. 9–12); and finally the mysterious consequences of this union in regard to such matters as Christ's priesthood (q. 22) and His role as Mediator (q. 26).

St. Thomas next examines in the light of these theological ideas, the Gospel story of Christ's birth of the Virgin Mary (qq. 27–34) and His early life (35–39); His public life of teaching and miracles (40–45); His passion and death (46–52); His resurrection, ascension, and seat at the right hand of the Father (53–59).

Not only in Himself is Christ the Way, but also in the Sacraments He instituted (66–83). It was while writing the section on the Blessed Sacrament that the "angelic" Doctor died. The treatment of Penance was sketched but never completed.

There has been some clarification of Catholic doctrine since the time of St. Thomas. It was the special task of the Council of Trent (1545–1563) to deal with the dogmatic difficulties raised by the Reformers in regard to Original Sin (Session v), Justification (vi), the Sacraments (vii) and especially the reality of the Presence in the Eucharist (xiii), and the Sacrifice of the Mass (xxiii). In the Vatican Council (1869–1870) the wider issues of modern rationalism had to be met (Session iii); and in the face of the multiplication of Christian sects, the Primacy of Papal Jurisdiction and the Infallibility of the Pope's official teaching authority were clearly defined (iv). One other dogmatic decision was reached in the nineteenth century, namely the definition by Pius IX (1848–1878) of the Immaculate Conception of the Virgin Mary, that is to say, her exemption from original sin. On this matter, the opinion of St. Thomas was rejected.

Other less official modifications of Thomistic Scholasticism were suggested during the sixteenth-century intellectual revirescence associated with the Counter-Reformation. Of this movement the Jesuits, Francisco Suarez and Luis Molina (1535–1601) are outstanding illustrations. Suarez's *Metaphysical Disputations,* published in 1597, has been called a "climax of sixteen centuries of Christian philosophical speculation," and his works on the Soul (*De Anima*) and on Laws (*De Legibus*) are marked by an emphasis on personal consciousness and individual existential reality that adapted them to the new needs of modern psychological, scientific, and political inquiry. Molina's work on the *Harmony of Free Will and Grace* (*Liberi 'Arbitrii cum Gratiae donis . . . Concordia*) emphasized, even more than St. Thomas, the freedom of the human will.

Scholasticism dominates Catholic thinking today. It is marked by a complete emancipation from all those forms of Neoplatonic necessitarianism, which St. Thomas so vigorously contradicted in his battle with Averroism. In the Averroistic system man has no more responsibility for culture and civilization than God has for creation. By accepting the idea of a world created by the free act of the Creator, St. Thomas could interpret personal existence and human history in terms of progress and purpose, human and Divine. And by analyzing human intelligence and the Revelation of Redemption, he saw the human person to be the highest value in visible creation. God freely chose to create active and free causes. And such a Creator of such a human nature freely chose a way, a supernatural means, by which human nature could reach a destiny higher than it can understand.

St. Thomas not only rescued man from the slavery of Averroistic and Avicennian necessity; he also saved the autonomy of human philosophy by rendering to human reason what belongs to reason and to Divine Revelation what is due to Revelation. St. Thomas brought an optimism into his attitude to human intelligence that has made modern Catholic thinking immune from every form of philosophical and theological pessimism. This optimism was finally canonized by the Vatican Council in the formal definition of the native power of the human reason to reach a certain (if incomplete) knowledge of God even antecedently to Revelation.

It must be insisted, on the other hand, that man, nature, reason are created man, created nature, created reason, owing their being and all their endowments to God; and therefore modern Catholic thought has been equally immune from the ultra-optimism of Renaissance humanism, eighteenth-century rationalism, and contemporary positivism. Catholic philosophy accepts the power of reason to reach the universal and necessary truth of first principles and the power of conscience to reach the universal and morally necessary obligations of the natural law.

Another aspect of Thomistic thinking is important in relation to contemporary totalitarianism. St. Thomas insisted that the soul of man has a life of its own and not a life that is only for the body, and still less only for society. It is this fact, rooted in the unique character of the human intellect, that makes a human being a person and gives him a dignity higher than anything else in nature. This intellect, in turn, is the root of human free will and therefore of moral responsibility. This conviction of human responsibility has made Catholic thinking impervious to the simplifications of modern materialism. It has also given to the Catholic intellectual system a basis for the defense of law and liberty, progress and democracy, against tyranny and license, which it is difficult to find in any of the totalist or liberal systems which have emerged since the disintegration of the medieval philosophical synthesis.

. . . AND THE LIFE

While "repentance" and "belief," the Way and the Truth, a Code and a Creed, moral and dogmatic theology have formed the banks and given direction to the current of Catholic life, the stream itself has been a confluence of "fulfillment" and "promise," of "age and grace" (or, as the Authorized Version has it, "stature and favor with God"), of historical development and metahistorical life. The Catholic Church is a visible community in invisible communion with God.

As a visible Community of ordinary men and women, the Church has had an historical life like any other community; and she bears today the marks of all the crises she has had to face.

The world in which Jesus first preached the kingdom was a world of Roman civilization, Greek culture, and Hebrew religion; and even today the Codex of Canon Law, the manuals of Scholastic philosophy and parts of the Catholic liturgy are impregnated with those ancient influences. It was possible for Hobbes in the seventeenth century to see in the Popes the "ghosts" of the Roman Emperors; for Paul Elmer More to see in the theology of Chalcedon the fulfillment of Hellenic philosophy; and today no one can take up a missal or a breviary without feeling the continuity of the worship and prayer of the Church with that of the Synagogue. Catholics are, as Pius XII once said, "spiritual Semites." Rejecting the view that a hypothetically "pure" Christianity has been "contaminated" by Hellenism, Latinism, and Mosaism, Catholics hold that an Apostolic Christianity has organically "grown," as its Founder grew, in "wisdom and age and grace," *sophia, helikia* and *charis* (Luke 2 : 52). Catholics recall the parable of the mustard seed (Matt. 13 : 31–32) ; and what our Lord said of being "with" the Church until the "consummation of the world" (Matt. 28 : 20).

The Barbarian invasions, coming after centuries of Roman persecutions, after many intellectual, moral, and spiritual crises, after the hardly less menacing years of imperial favor, overtaxed the human energies of the Church. Nevertheless, in the end, the "Barbarians" contributed enormously to Christian life, to those elements of vigorous feeling and fancy which seem to a Catholic to be as genuinely human and, therefore, as blessed by God as intelligence, conscience, and taste. The humanism of the twelfth-century Renaissance had about it a certain Teutonic roughness mingled with Celtic softness that contrasts sharply with the neo-classical humanism of the fifteenth century. Yet Catholics recognize in Walther von der Vogelweide and in the creator of Parzival, Wolfram von Eschenback, in Hildebert of Lavardin and John of Salisbury, in St. Bernard and Hugh of St. Victor, in Abelard and Heloise, as much as in Marsilio Ficino and Pico della Mirandola, Nicholas of Cusa and Conrad Celtes, Thomas More and Reginald Pole, Raphael and Michelangelo, the children of the same teeming womb. When the temper of the times moved from humanism and romance to Scholasticism and constitutionalism, the Church was fearful only of exaggerations. Medieval Catholic culture at its best was represented in the author of the *Vita Nuova* and the *Divina Commedia,* the *Convivio* and the *Monarchia,* the affirmer of all the values, material, mental, and mystical, of art, philosophy, and religion; the defender of all the fundamental institutions— home, school, State, and Church; the integralist who refused to put asunder what God has joined together—reason and Revelation, nature and Grace, conscience and Law; and what any balanced human being can hold together—ardor and order, love and learning, personal rights and community duties.

Medieval Christendom was the creation of the Catholic Church. Like every other age, it had its tragically human side, its Feudal violences, and its social tensions. The history of the Inquisition tells of ghastly episodes of ruthless cruelty. There were moods of "Augustinian" pessimism that may have overvalued physical asceticism and for a long time undervalued the secular purposes of political and economic life. Nevertheless, the Renaissance illusion of the "Dark" ages has been all but dissipated. In one of the most recent of M. G. Cohen's brilliant and erudite works, *La Grande Clarté du Moyen-Age*,[21] he has summed up the conclusion of all recent research: "The only darkness about the Middle Ages is in our ignorance of them." There could have been no lack of the love of truth and beauty and goodness in an age that produced the cathedrals, the universities, the saints of the twelfth and thirteenth centuries. And when bishops could remind kings that they were "under the law and God," and when a monk could remind the Pope that he must rule by reason and not by will, there was little danger of totalitarian tyranny. Most of the modern movements—nominalism, Renaissance humanism, Protestantism, classicism, rationalism, materialism, and finally totalitarianism—have seemed to a Catholic to be apostasies from the hard duty of mental, moral, religious, and social integration. It was not Occam's interest in the visible, concrete individual that was wrong; but his denial of the equally real, though invisible, universal nature. It was not the affirmations of humanism but only its denial of the supernatural that proved a danger. Even Protestantism, the Catholic holds, has involved a sacrifice of the fact of wholeness for the feeling of holiness, of human nature in the name of Divine Grace and Omnipotence, of Christendom in the name of nationalism and, ultimately, of the Church in the name of the State.

The Church has often enough proved that she has no contempt for the classics, for reason, for matter, for the nation, and the State; but she has been suspicious of a classicism, a rationalism, a materialism, a nationalism, and a Statism that misunderstood either human emotion, or Divine Revelation, or

[21] New York: 1943.

spiritual reality, or human brotherhood, or inalienable personal rights. And she will oppose in the future, as she has done in the past, any such partial interpretations of human life.

And yet her own real life is not that of a human, historical community that is being "fulfilled" in time; it is a life "hidden with Christ in God," that "promise" of Eternal Life which is sanctifying grace, that communion of the soul with God, which is the purpose of all the rest. In her religious Orders and Congregations—Benedictine, Camaldolese, Carthusian, Cistercian, Carmelite, Trinitarian, Franciscan, Dominican, Ursuline, Jesuit, not to mention the more modern foundations—her full life of community and communion is most perfectly realized. Even today prodigies of missionary and educational effort are being wrought by men and women who have joyously renounced the pleasures and prizes of ordinary life for the "hundredfold" of spiritual peace and the promise of eternal life (Matt. 19: 29).

Not all the monks and nuns have been saints; and not all the Catholic saints have been integral humanists. But the average Catholic is inclined to feel that if, after all these centuries of worship in spirit and truth, of contemplation and meditation, of adoration, thanksgiving, petition, and self-oblation to God, human nature still shows every evidence of the wounds of original sin, then no "world of tomorrow" is likely to be a heaven on earth. The Catholic Church lives for the present; but she does not stand still. In the light of her history and in the force of her holiness she moves ever onward in hope—but like a ship on a wide ocean, guided by visible stars to ports, human and Divine, that are still unseen.

SELECTED BIBLIOGRAPHY

The Catholic Encyclopedia. An international work of Reference on the Constitution, Doctrine, Discipline, and History of the Catholic Church. Edited by C. G. Herbermann, *et al.* 15 vols., New York, 1907–1912. Index vol. 1914.

The History of the Church. Edited by A. Fliche and V. Martin (to be completed in 24 vols.). English translation by Ernest C. Messenger. London, 1944 ff.

335

The Lives of the Popes of the Early Middle Ages. By Horace K. Mann. 18 vols., London, 1902–1932.

History of the Popes from the Close of the Middle Ages. By Ludwig von Pastor. English translation by F. I. Antrobus, *et al.* 34 vols., St. Louis, 1898–1938.

Christian Spirituality. By P. Pourrat. English translation by W. H. Mitchell and S. P. Jacques. 3 vols., London, 1922–1927.

The "Summa Theologica" of St. Thomas Aquinas. Translated by the Fathers of the English Dominican Province. 22 vols., New York, 1912–1925.

Dogmatic Theology. By Joseph Pohle. English translation by Arthur Preuss. 12 vols., St. Louis, 1911–1917.

Moral Theology. By Henry Davis, S. J. 4 vols., London, 1938 (rev. ed.).

A Commentary on the New Canon Law. By P. C. Augustine. 8 vols., St. Louis, 1920–1922.

The Lives of the Saints. By Alban Butler. Edited and revised by Herbert Thurston and D. Attwater. 12 vols., New York, 1926–1938.

Protestantism

JOHN ALEXANDER MACKAY

It is an impressive, albeit unhappy, fact that the Christian religion, the most influential and aggressive of the great religions of mankind, has been represented for the past four hundred years by three separate traditions, Eastern Orthodoxy, Roman Catholicism, and Protestantism. These traditions, while they all derive from a common source and are one in essential Christian loyalties, differ from one another in very important respects.

The Christian tradition which took historical form most recently is known by the general name of Protestantism. In its institutional expression, Protestantism is the youngest of the three Christian traditions. To be more specific, it is that Christian tradition which owes its ecclesiastical form, its confessional position, its spiritual attitude to the attempt made in the sixteenth century to give a more adequate expression to Christianity than that which was current at the time. The historic endeavor to restore the Christian religion to its native, pristine glory, is commonly called the Protestant Reformation. This revolutionary movement in the field of religion became the source of a diversified expression of Christianity. Because of its variegated character, Protestantism as a phenomenon in history is difficult to define. "If we are thinking of a purely historical definition of Protestantism," says Ernst Troeltsch, "we soon recognize that for Protestantism as a whole, it cannot be immediately formulated." From the viewpoint of its inner religious spirit, however, as distinguished from that of its outer diversified expression, Protestantism can be readily defined.

Some important facts should be held in mind as we undertake this study. While Protestantism emerged in history at a given time and under special circumstances, its ideas and spirit were not a creation of the sixteenth century. For these it claims high

337

antiquity. It was the contention of the Protestant Reformers and continues to be the contention of their successors, that the religious emphases that began to be made in that century were not discoveries of new truth, but rather recoveries of ancient truth. The Reformers did not regard themselves as discoverers but as restorers. They did not think of their work as opening up new paths, but as reopening old paths, great highways of truth, which in the course of Christian history had been abandoned or grown over. Their emphasis from the beginning was positive, not negative.

The term "Protestant," it is true, suggests, at first thought, a negative attitude. It has been interpreted as an attitude of pure dissent from a positive position. Nothing could be more untrue, historically and etymologically, to the famous "Protest" which was presented at the Diet of Spires in 1529, and which gave its name to the new religious movement. The German princes and the representatives of the fourteen free cities which had embraced the principles of the religious reform did not "protest" against ideas; they appeared in the role of "protestants" because a curb had been placed upon the free propagation of truths which were decidedly positive in character. Etymologically, moreover, "protest" means dissent only in a secondary sense. The essence of the word is to "state as a witness," to "aver," "to make solemn affirmation." As we engage, therefore, in the study of what Protestantism is, it is well that our minds be disabused of the idea that what will engage our attention is a negative dissent from a positive position. The genius of Protestant Christianity is affirmation, not negation.

We begin with a description of Protestantism from the viewpoint of history. Within the perspective of the last four centuries, Protestantism has expressed itself in two main religious types. These may be called (A) Classical Protestantism, (B) Radical Protestantism. By Classical Protestantism we mean the great churchly systems, which, while they revolted against what Christianity had become, retained a catholic sense of the Church. Classical, or churchly Protestantism, has been represented by the Lutheran, the Reformed, and the Anglican Churches. Radical Protestantism is the word used to designate the so-called "sect" phenomenon in Protestant history. It embraces religious groups and schools of religious thought which were formed around some particular emphasis to the right or to the left, which the members of the group felt to be expressive of the essential core of Christianity.

CLASSICAL PROTESTANTISM

Classical Protestantism, toward which, it may be remarked, Protestantism as a whole is steadily moving at the present time, discovers certain common characteristics of a basic kind. Its leaders, the Reformers of the sixteenth century, proclaimed to the world that the Reform movement was not a schism from the Church, but a schism in the Church. They claimed to be heirs of the full Biblical and Patristic heritage of the Christian Church. They were not sectarians. They viewed themselves as men whom God had commissioned to fight His battles and the battles of His Church in a degenerate time. Against the authority of the Papal See, which in the medieval period had come to claim plenary jurisdiction over all Christendom, they made their appeal to Jesus Christ Himself, and to the "next free General Council of Holy Christendom." Classical Protestantism appealed to origins against developments in Christian history. It proclaimed a once-for-allness in the redemptive activity of God, both with respect to what He did for men, and with respect to what He said to men regarding their relationship to Him. It affirmed that Christianity is primarily an individual relation of the soul to God, founded upon the once-for-all redemptive act which God wrought in Christ, and maintained by the abiding presence of the Holy Spirit in the Christian heart. It made its appeal from a religious hierarchy to Christ, from tradition to the Bible, from an ecclesiastical system to the living fellowship which the Spirit created at Pentecost.

I. *Lutheranism.* Earliest among the general expressions of Classical Protestantism is Lutheranism. By Lutheranism is meant that particular Christian emphasis and those particular churches which owe their origin to the activity, spirit, and emphasis of Martin Luther. Lutheran churches are found chiefly in Germany, the Scandinavian countries, and the United States. Following their founder, they have been profoundly concerned throughout their history about two main things: the life of the soul, and the worship of the Sanctuary. Luther's agonizing concern about the problem of personal sin, his dramatic release from its fetters through the Biblical truth of justification by faith, his religious subjectivity and love of song, have left their imprint upon the Lutheran tradition.

It is the supreme function of the Church, according to the Lutheran view, to see to it that the Word of God is truly preached, and that the Sacraments are rightly administered. In the Lutheran communion, questions of polity and order have always been secondary to a concern for the preaching of the Word and the administration of the Sacraments. The individual lay Christian fulfills his function when he bears witness to God by a holy life and discharges his secular duty with a sense of religious vocation. The glory of Lutheranism lies in the spiritual inwardness it has created in its adherents. Its emphasis upon faith, liberty, and brotherly love gave rise to some of the finest expressions of Christian piety, both individual and corporate. Bach, the prince of musicians, was a child of the Lutheran tradition.

The Church has not been regarded by Lutherans as responsible for the secular order. They have consistently maintained that the attempt should not be made to apply the law of love to the realm of politics. Because of sin, the political order does not and cannot operate in accordance with the laws of God's Kingdom. In consequence of this attitude, there has grown up in Lutheranism what must be regarded as an unhappy detachment of the Church from secular society. The latter has been allowed to develop according to its own laws. The Church has not felt itself responsible to dictate to rulers or to influence state policy. It has demanded only that it be left entirely free to preach the Word and to administer the Sacraments, and that all its members shall enjoy freedom to pursue their religious life in tranquillity and peace.

While the accusation is utterly false that to Luther belongs the main responsibility for Adolf Hitler and German Nazism, it is true that the traditional detachment of Lutheranism from public affairs in Germany made it easier for society and the state in that country to pry themselves loose from Christian direction. It is, therefore, an exceedingly important fact in contemporary Protestant history that the great Lutheran Communion, both in Europe and the United States, is beginning to revalue its social responsibility.

2. *Calvinism.* Second in historical order, and first in the order of its influence and the number of its adherents in the Protestant world of today, is Calvinism or, as it is also called, Reformed Christianity.

Reformed Christianity originated in the work of John Calvin, whose passion was to reform existing Christianity so that it might resemble original Christianity. Calvin, a Frenchman, and the only man of his time who was the peer of Erasmus as a Humanist, passed through a profound religious experience, as a result of which, in the words of his follower, Beza, "he renounced all other studies and devoted himself to God." By means of his theological writings, especially *The Institutes of the Christian Religion,* and his activities as a preacher, lecturer, and church organizer in Geneva, where he settled upon his exile from France, Calvin became one of the most revolutionary figures in religious and secular annals. More than any other man in his time, he saved Europe from disaster. While the passion of Luther, the former monk, was the soul and its salvation, the passion of Calvin, the former humanist layman, was truth and a doctrine of God. He was a God-intoxicated man. Feeling himself to be heir to the whole Christian tradition, as expressed in the Bible and the great Fathers of the Church, Calvin became the architect of the most massive and potent system of theology in the history of Protestantism, the Protestant counterpart of the great *Summa* of Thomas Aquinas. Yet, significantly enough, as demonstrating Calvin's sense of continuity with the Chris-

341

tian past, *The Institutes,* his theological masterpiece, is essentially an extended commentary upon the Apostles' Creed. This fact reveals how closely linked Calvin felt himself to be to the historic Christian faith. He became at the same time the architect of an ecclesiastical structure which was destined to exercise a profound influence upon the political history of Europe and the Western world.

Reformed theology, following Calvin, makes several important emphases. Religion does not exist primarily for personal happiness or for public utility; it exists for the worship and service of God. It serves man best when it puts God first. The source of Christian doctrine is Holy Scripture alone, which is "the infallible rule of faith and practice." The criterion by which a doctrinal position must be judged is the influence it exercises upon life, for "truth is in order to goodness." Pure doctrine must express itself in pure living on the part of all who profess it. In the words of that compendium of Calvinistic doctrine, the Westminster Shorter Catechism, "Man's chief end is to glorify God and to enjoy him for ever." The Christian who lives thus, develops in his life an asceticism of a very special character, an asceticism-in-the-world, which leads him to live the life of God in full contact with the secular order. This attitude determined the attitude of Calvinists toward work and public office. Calvin's crest, a flaming heart in an open hand, the oblation of personality in its wholeness to the living God for sacrificial service, constitutes the genius of the Reformed view of life. Its representation in art is Rembrandt's famous picture, "The Syndics."

Reformed Christianity has a high doctrine of the Church and of the Church's responsibility for the secular order. The Church, in Calvin's words, is "the foundation of the world." It is "the holy community which in its life must demonstrate that God has created the world in order that it may be the theater of his glory." In its visible expression the Christian Church is made up of "the whole multitude, dispersed all over the world, who profess to worship one God and Jesus Christ, who are initiated into his faith by baptism, who testify their unity in true doctrine and character by a participation of the sacred supper, who consent to the word of the Lord, and preserve the ministry which Christ has instituted for the purpose of preaching it." [1] The government of the Church is in the hands of a presbytery, which is made up equally of ministers and laymen, ministers who are "teaching elders," and laymen who are "ruling elders." For Calvin, schism is the worst of all evils which can affect the Church. "Whoever departs from the Church," he said, "denies God and Jesus Christ." To the end of his days Calvin longed for the reunion of Christendom. His consistently ecumenical spirit had been reborn, as we shall see later in this study, in a rebirth of Church and ecumenical consciousness in the Protestant world of our time.

The Church, however, does not fulfill its full mission in the world as the instrument of God's glory when it is merely concerned about preaching the Word, administering the Sacraments, producing Christian piety, and carrying on its own institutional life. It has also a mission to the community. Reformed Christianity has profoundly influenced cultural, political, and social life in every country where it has been a dominant influence. In Scotland, John Knox, Calvin's great disciple, established a school alongside every Church. At the time of the American Civil War, the Presbyterian Church led all the Christian Churches in the number of colleges it had founded from the Atlantic to the Pacific. It is also worthy of note that in the American Revolution the only clergyman who signed the Declaration of Independence was John Witherspoon, the Presbyterian President of the College of New Jersey, now Princeton University, and that the first ecclesiastical body to hail the new order was the Presbytery of Hanover in Virginia. It is equally notable as a fact of contemporary history, that Fascism has not appeared in any country in which Reformed Christianity was the dominant expression of religious life. The man whose influence inspired the organization of the Confessional Church in Germany was Karl Barth, the famous Reformed theo-

[1] *Institutes,* IV, 17.

logian who dared Hitler, and sounded the return to Biblical Christianity.

Calvinistic influence in thought is found historically not only in the Presbyterian or Reformed family of churches, but also in the Anglican, the Congregational, and the Baptist churches. The ecclesiastical influence of Calvinism is found in those churches whose polity has been based upon Presbytery, which in the Reformed system takes the place of the hierarchy in Episcopal churches. Reformed churches are widely scattered throughout the world, and constitute together the largest single body of Protestant Christians.

3. *Anglicanism.* The Anglican Church is the Church of England, which since the reign of Henry VIII has been the Established Church of that country. Taking historical form as a separate ecclesiastical entity, following a quarrel between Henry VIII and the Pope, the Anglican Church owes its specific character and spirit not to anything associated with the notorious English monarch or his reign but to great men like Richard Hooker and Jeremy Taylor who, in the reign of Elizabeth, became the creators of Anglicanism as we know it.

The Anglican Church has always aspired to be, as T. S. Eliot has expressed it, "a mean between Papacy and Presbytery." This is true not only in an ecclesiastical sense but also in a doctrinal sense. Anglicanism has had, from the beginning of its separate existence, an intense sense of the Church and of its own continuity with the Church of the Apostles. This sense of the Church, "the Church of Christ which was from the beginning, is, and continues until the end," to quote the words of Richard Hooker in the second book of his *Laws of Ecclesiastical Polity,* has determined the spirit and attitude of Anglicanism throughout its history. Regarding the Church as an extension of the Incarnation, and its own role as that of mediating between the churches of the Reformation, and the great hierarchical churches whose ancient seats were at Rome and Constantinople, the Church of England has followed a *via media.* It has been, as one has put it, "a Catholic Church with prophetic elements." Its genius has not been to revolutionize but to permeate. It has sought to keep within its pale all those who profess loyalty to the Church, however different their emphases may be upon specific issues not relating to the basic Anglican allegiance. While being Calvinistic in its essential doctrine, as this is expressed in the Thirty-Nine Articles, considerations of polity and liturgy rather than considerations of doctrine, have generally speaking, determined Anglican history and decisions. Viewing Anglicanism within the general framework of Protestant doctrine and life, it might be remarked that in its theology, especially in recent times, it has laid great stress upon reason as a necessary supplement to faith. A certain asceticism and an emphasis upon the moral responsibility of the Christian to exercise self-discipline have been marks of Anglican piety.

Some further facts regarding Anglicanism are worthy of note. In full communion with the Church of England, are the Episcopal Church of Scotland and the Protestant Episcopal Church in the United States of America. From time to time, all churches belonging to the Anglican family, meet in conclave at Lambeth, England, at an ecclesiastical gathering presided over by the Archbishop of Canterbury. At this gathering decisions are made for the guidance of the Anglican Church and its affiliated communions. Within Anglicanism are found, as a matter of fact, three main groups of churchmen all of whom are equally devoted to the Church: the Evangelicals, or Low Churchmen, who stress the Gospel and the great principles of the Reformation; the Anglo-Catholics, or High Churchmen, who stress the Catholic element in the Anglican tradition, the importance of Apostolic Succession and the Real Presence in the Eucharist; the Modern Churchmen, doctrinal radicals, whose passion it is to come to terms with secular culture as represented by philosophy and science. In recent years the Church of England, particularly under the leadership of the late lamented Archbishop of Canterbury, William Temple, has given outstanding leadership in the new Ecumenical Movement and in the approach of the Church to social questions. The comprehensive character and mediating genius of Anglicanism appear in the fact that, apart from the Roman Catholic Church, the

Protestant Episcopal Church in the United States was the only Christian communion which remained undivided at the close of the American Civil War.

RADICAL PROTESTANTISM

By Radical Protestantism we mean those Christian groups or schools of religious thought which broke away little by little from the churchly systems of Protestantism described above, or which originated independently of these. Such groups, which have varied greatly in size and importance, have constituted the "step-children of the Reformation." On the one hand, they have been nonconformist in character; on the other hand, by stressing elements in the Christian religion of vital importance for the Body of Christ, they have been not infrequently the very "salt" of Christianity. The influence of the "sect" and the "sect" phenomenon in the history of Protestant Christianity, especially in the United States, has been of a very decisive and transforming character. At the same time it was the spectacle presented by the manifold diversity of Protestant communions, of which there are more than two hundred and fifty in the United States alone, that led the French Catholic Churchman, Bossuet, to write his famous *History of the Variations of Protestantism*. In Radical Protestantism are two main types: the Evangelical, and the Humanist.

The Evangelical type of Radical Protestantism embraces all those Protestant groups, denominations or churches, which maintain a separate existence within the Protestant family through a sincere desire to bear witness to that kind of Christian fellowship or to that form of life or doctrine which, in the judgment of the members, conforms most closely with the Will of God as revealed in Holy Scripture. Their passion has been to grasp and express in both doctrine and life the inmost meaning of Christian discipleship. Under the inspiration of this passion, there have appeared periodically in Protestant history, churches of "gathered" or committed Christians. The "gathered" church is a church whose members are what they are not because of family connections or for conventional reasons, but

346

because of their personal commitment to Jesus Christ and to that for which the fellowship stands. The religion of the "gathered" church has been marked by a certain primitivism in a double sense. It has been elemental religion, that kind of religion, which, in the words of William James, is an "acute fever" and not a "dull habit." It has, at the same time, represented a desire to have daily life conform to the most primitive Christian pattern. In the sphere of morals, the lives of those belonging to the "gathered" church have been marked by a severe, and oftentimes legalistic, rigorism. Their sense of the Church in the classical meaning of that term has been slight. For them the Church is essentially a voluntary association.

Protestant Christians of this type have played a very decisive part in religious and political history since the Reformation. They have been used by God to keep alive certain essential elements of Christian faith and practice. In the political realm, they have played an important part, as did Roger Williams, for example, in leading the state to grant complete religious freedom to all citizens. They have been traditional champions of the rights of man. The British Labor party drew its chief support at first from the ranks of religious Nonconformism.

Most representative and important among the Evangelical expressions of Radical Protestantism have been the Baptists, the Congregationalists, the Methodists, and the Quakers.

The Baptists, who are the successors of the Anabaptists of pre-Reformation times, have stood for the necessity of personal religious commitment as the prerequisite for Christian baptism. They constitute the largest body of Protestant Christians in the United States and have been marked, especially in the South, by great evangelistic fervor.

The Congregationalists owe their separate existence to a polity which makes the individual congregation the ultimate ecclesiastical unit. Congregationalism, traditionally Calvinistic in its theology, exercised a decisive influence on the religious life of New England in colonial days and gave birth to the universities of Harvard and Yale. Today Congregationalists are among the chief supporters of the ecumenical movement, and a considerable number of the leading theological minds in America belong to the Congregational communion. In their polity Baptists are also congregationalists.

Methodism originated under John and Charles Wesley as a movement within Anglicanism to secure that all who called themselves Christians should take their calling seriously and live holy or sanctified lives. Methodists constitute a large and influential group in world Protestantism. More interested in life than in doctrine, Methodists have frequently taken the lead in the initiation of social reform. The largest single ecclesiastical body in Protestantism is the Methodist Church of the United States.

The Quakers, or the Society of Friends, have stood since the days of George Fox, the founder of the Society, for the reality of the inner light in the Christian soul as a source of spiritual insight and a guide to daily living. Members of the Society of Friends both in the Old World and the New have been marked traditionally by a profound human passion and social concern. In time of war they have been pacifists who devoted themselves unstintingly to alleviating suffering.

In the world of today all four of these denominations, which began as "gathered" churches with an intense "sect" consciousness, manifest the same inclusiveness in their membership that marks the Protestant Churches of the classical tradition.

The Humanist type of Radical Protestantism has been supremely concerned with the relation of the Christian and the Church to secular society. One of its major passions has been to vindicate Christianity to "men of taste" and to accommodate it to Reason and the most approved cultural categories. Its representatives have generally been individuals, or groups of individuals, drawn from many churches rather than whole religious bodies in the ecclesiastical sense. Turning from Revelation as the supreme guide of thought, men of this type espoused Reason as the ultimate source of truth. Maintaining that the highest role of religion is to be the soul of culture, they have aimed to fit Christianity into the prevailing cultural pattern. Their ultimate criterion of religious truth has not been the Christian revelation but some discovery of science or some philosophical principle or value. For Protestants of this "modernist" type, the Christian Church has been little more than a sociological institution. It has been to them one of the forces, perchance the highest, "among the various spiritual and cultural forces which are working in the same general direction of the ultimate good." Some would even suggest that the Church is simply "a voluntary association for providing services on Sunday for that section of the community which chooses to take advantage of them."

This highly secularized expression of Radical Protestantism represents the most extreme aberration from the central Christian tradition for which essential Protestantism has stood and continues to stand. Within the Protestant world of today the influence and prestige of this secularized variety of the Protestant spirit are very markedly on the wane. It is important, however, that we take this viewpoint into account in order to obtain a clear conception of the historical range of Protestant opinion. In this way we shall be prepared for a basic study of the eternal core of Protestantism, and of the new and striking developments in the Protestant world which constitute one of the chief religious phenomena of the twentieth century.

DOCTRINAL EMPHASES

From historical description we pass to theological interpretation. It will be our endeavor in this section to express the soul of Protestant Christianity. Amid and beneath all the diverse manifestations of Protestantism in history, we discover certain major emphases which together constitute the inmost core of Protestant faith and life.

The Supreme Authority of the Bible. Protestantism emerged in history with the affirmation that the Bible, the Scriptures of the Old and New Testaments, rather than Tradition or the Church, constitutes the supreme authority in all questions relating to Christian faith and practice. This affirmation was directed against the authority of the Roman Catholic Church, particularly the Papacy, which had vested in itself the authority formerly exercised by the Ecumenical Councils. The Protestant Reformers proclaimed that authoritative knowledge of God and His will is derived from a study of Holy Scripture. The Bible, which in the medieval Church had existed only in a Latin version, was now translated from the original Hebrew and Greek into the several languages of the West. It soon began to be studied not only by churchmen and scholars but also by the common people. The presupposition that underlay the translation of the Scriptures into the vernacular tongues of Europe, and later of the whole world, was and continues to be, that the Holy Spirit, under whose inspiration the writers of the sacred Record had done their work, would lead humble souls to a saving knowledge of God. Tradition, which had come to be regarded as coequal in authority with the Bible as a source of our knowledge of God, and the Church, which had become the proximate rule of faith and the supreme interpreter of Revelation, were now studied and judged in the light of the Bible.

The restoration of the Bible to the supreme place of religious authority which it had occupied in the early Church has had far-reaching implications for Protestant thought and life. One implication touches the meaning of Divine Revelation. The classical Christian affirmation is that God has spoken. The eternal silence has been broken. The inscrutable mystery has been unveiled. There is a word from the Lord. Truth exists. This truth is redemptive truth. It has taken the form of great redemptive deeds wrought by God in behalf of man, and of luminous prophetic words which interpreted those deeds and made clear to man the nature and will of God for his salvation. The record of those deeds and words we have in the Bible. The core of the Bible and the clue to its understanding is the Gospel. The Gospel is the Good News of what God has already done for man in Christ, and is ready to do for any person who believes the record concerning Jesus Christ, the Saviour. They only, however, really understand the Bible and attain a knowledge of God and His redemptive will who come to the study of Holy Scripture not because of intellectual curiosity but through a deep concern to discover authoritative answers to the agonizing questions about God, sin, and destiny.

Biblical truth is moreover personal truth. Being a book about redemption, the Bible is supremely interested in answering the quest of a person who comes to it with the query, "What must I do to be saved?" This question is answered in the form of an encounter between God and the earnest reader in such wise that the centuries are telescoped, and a redemptive encounter takes place again. Not only so: from the hour of the great encounter onward, it is in and through the Bible that the Christian soul holds communion with God. Through the Bible also, the will of God is revealed to the Christian for his behavior in the concrete process of living. The Bible is, therefore, not only the supreme source of our knowledge of God and the supreme theater where God and man meet; it is also the chief medium of our communion with God and the chief guide in the proper conduct of life.

As regards an understanding of Biblical truth, the Bible is to be interpreted in terms of categories which are native to itself. Being a book about redemption, that is to say, about the supernatural disclosure of God to men as a redeeming God, the Bible cannot be understood in terms of any categories and forms of thought which are alien to the basic presupposition that God revealed himself in a redemptive manner in the life of Israel. Basic for a true understanding of the Bible is the recognition, for example, that one of its central categories is that of a "covenant" between God and his people whereby He promises to bless them and they promise to do His Will. Moreover, being a book about redemption, the Bible is authoritative only in its own particular sphere. As a document with a history, it is to be studied and investigated with the most rigorous historical and scientific criteria. Under such scrutiny, a flood of light has been thrown upon the origin of the Biblical records, as also upon the elements that entered into Israel's religion. The important thing about the Bible is, however, that whereas the human, often all too human, elements are abundantly present, God used lowly and unworthy people and religious elements of a plebeian and even exotic character, to communicate himself and his purpose to men. His self-communication moved progressively from the early origins of Israel's history through the great prophets of Israel and Judah, took personal and absolute form in Jesus Christ, and was perfected in the Apostolic era of the Spirit. Revelation as a whole is bound together by the central reality of the Redeemer, so that there is a sense in which one can call the Bible a book about Jesus Christ. It is in the measure in which He becomes known in his saving power that the Bible becomes truly understood. While it is not true that the Bible is the "religion of Protestants," as has sometimes been said, it is true that the Bible produced the Protestant Reformation and has inspired and determined the Protestant expression of the Christian religion.

The centrality given to the Bible in Protestant faith and experience exerted a profound influence upon those forms of cultural development which are Protestant in their inspiration. Popular interest in the Bible gave a great impulse to public education. Literacy was promoted in order that men might learn to read the Scriptures. Where the Bible has been diffused, the common people have become literate, while culture in every sphere has been transfigured. In many instances the Bible itself was the first book to be translated into the language of a people. In other instances, a particular translation of the Bible gave classical expression to the language in which it appeared. The great figures, episodes, and teachings of the Book have entered as a creative force into the main stream of many a literature. It is a striking and symbolical fact that Rembrandt and Bach, two of the greatest masters in the history of art, one in painting, the other in music, were Protestants, and that their greatest creations were directly inspired by the text of Holy Scripture. Both men were profound students of the Bible whose inner meaning they succeeded in interpreting in a way that no other artists have ever done.

The Unmediated Lordship of Jesus Christ. The centrality of Christ in Christian thought and experience, and the unmediated character of relations between him and the souls of men, is a basic Protestant emphasis. Jesus Christ does not submit to control or patronage even by the Church, as the Grand Inquisitor in Dostoevski's famous legend thought he should. He maintains himself in sovereign freedom, using the Church as the agent of his will, but bringing it into judgment when it becomes presumptuous and assumes prerogatives which Christ has never relinquished. A fourfold affirmation makes up the Protestant insight into the meaning and significance of Jesus Christ and his relations with men.

1. *Salvation is obtained through faith in Jesus Christ.* The doctrine of Justification by Faith has been called the formal principle of Protestantism. Its meaning is this: Man is saved, not by ethical striving or achievement, but by the joyous acceptance of God's gift of salvation. Good works do not save men; they are the fruits of men who are saved. God offers to man the complete redemption which was wrought out for him in the life, death, and resurrection of Jesus Christ. To the reality of this redemption, man gives his assent, acquiescing in the fact that he owes salvation not to his own goodness, but to the goodness of Another. By an act of consent or commitment, he gives himself to that Other, the living Christ, with whom he identifies himself in thought and in life. In this view of faith there are, accordingly, two elements: one, the element of assent by which the mind grasps and acquiesces in what God has done for men in Christ; the other, that of consent or commitment, whereby a man identifies himself wholly with Christ in thought and in life. In saving faith, therefore, there is assent to a proposition, and consent to a Person.

Believers in Christ, whoever they may be, enter upon a life of unique privilege and responsibility. They are constituted "priests." As such they have full right or access to God through Christ at all times. It is their corresponding responsibility to live lives of utter dedication to God, in the secular as well as in the religious sphere. The doctrine of the "Universal priesthood of believers" is a basic Protestant affirmation.

2. *Jesus Christ is the sovereign Lord of the Church and of the World.* While affirming that Jesus Christ founded a Church

which is his Body, and that outside this Church there is no salvation, Protestantism affirms that Jesus Christ has not abdicated. He continues to direct affairs in the Church and in the world. As the Lord of the Church, he can bring and does bring the Church into judgment. That being so, a Church that bears the Christian name may so far depart from the mind of Christ in faith and practice, as virtually to become apostate and to be, in the words directed by the Lord of the Church to one of the churches in the Apocalypse, "spewed out" of His mouth. It means also that there may be times when an individual Christian may have to appeal to Jesus Christ against the Church. This is the significance of the famous words of Pascal when he said: "If my letters are condemned in Rome, what I condemn in them is condemned in heaven: to Thy tribunal, Oh Lord Jesus, I appeal." That was the profoundly Protestant affirmation of a great Roman Catholic saint. It was in the spirit of that affirmation that the Protestant Reformers made their appeal to Jesus Christ himself against those who carried on the affairs of the Church in His name.

Jesus Christ should be equally sovereign in the affairs of the state. It is never legitimate for Protestants to make any pact with, or derive special advantages from, a form of government whose principles run counter to the truths of the Christian religion, or which challenges the right of the Church to proclaim God's truth and to live in accordance with His will.

3. A third affirmation is this. *The concrete figure of Jesus Christ as He appears in the Gospels, is the normative standard for human life.* Whenever, as has frequently happened in Roman, Orthodox, and Protestant circles, the way of life and thought which was characteristic of the historical figure of Jesus is not taken seriously, the quality of Christian living immediately declines. The so-called "Back to Jesus" movement, and that of the "Quest of the historical Jesus," which were Protestant in their inspiration, despite all the great limitations attaching to this approach, gave to the Christian Church the concrete living figure of Jesus in a form in which the Church had never possessed Him before. That Figure, divested of the

elements that belonged merely to His own age, sets before each succeeding generation of men a concrete and authoritative standard of human behavior. While it is true that Lives of Christ have been rather autobiographies of their authors than biographies of Jesus, they do enshrine the eternal truth that the most important thing that any man can do is to face the Man and to order his life in accordance with the life of Christ.

4. The fourth affirmation regarding Jesus Christ is: *the Risen Christ is the perennial source of strength for action.* Protestant piety has stressed the reality of communion with the living Christ, not only on the part of great saints but also on the part of simple believers; not only in the sacrament of the Lord's Supper but amid the routine of daily living. "Lo I am with you always, even unto the end of the world" said Christ. These are the words which David Livingstone called the "words of a gentleman." A sense of comradeship with the living Christ, to whom one can go at all times for forgiveness and cleansing, for sympathy and for strength, has been one of the chief marks and sources of inspiration of Protestant Christian personality. Because of the overwhelming fact of Christ as the ever present and living Lord, Protestant Christians have not been aware of any necessity to have recourse to the Virgin Mother or to the saints as special intercessors. Having the living Lord himself, they have felt the need of no other. This Christo-centric character of religious experience amid the routine of daily living and in all the great crises of life has been a characteristic of Protestant Christianity.

The Witnessing Responsibility of the Church. The supreme function of the Christian Church is, in the Protestant view, to bear witness to God. The Church exists to witness to the Gospel, the Good News of human salavation in and through Jesus Christ. Whenever the Church, as the "Body of Christ," thinks and acts as if it were an end in itself, or engages in activities in which the reality of the Gospel does not hold a central position, it fails to fulfill its primary function.

Witness must be borne to the Gospel by word and by life. The centrality of preaching, of proclaiming the Gospel by word, has been one of the chief characteristics of Protestant Christianity. Ideally speaking, the Gospel must be proclaimed with passionate conviction: with conviction because it is true, with passion because it is important and because obedience to it is urgent. It must be proclaimed also with unmistakable clarity in the language of every people. Clarity in the proclamation of the Gospel involves a thorough knowledge of the Bible where such knowledge is obtained; personal experience of the power of the Gospel; an adequate theological system in which the Gospel is central. The form of speech used in proclamation must be such as to convey the significance of the Good News in the most compelling form. The heart of man and the culture of the time must be assiduously studied in order that communication may take place in such a way as to be challenging and luminous.

It is for the Church also to bear witness to the Gospel by life. No witness will be more effective than that of personal piety, of spiritual inwardness, of victorious living, on the part of those who profess the name of Jesus Christ. But witness must be borne no less by a deep human or social passion. If men are to take seriously the presentation of the Good News about God, goodness must validate the presence of truth; good works must prove the reality of faith. However, personal ethical behavior and Christian philanthropy are not enough. The Christian Church must proclaim God's righteousness for all human relationships, and must throw its weight at all times upon the side of righteousness.

Everything which the Church does in bearing witness to the Gospel by word and by life must have as its principal aim that individuals and communities may respond to the call of God. In order to exist truly, the Church, in accordance with the inner meaning of the term "exist," must "set out," "sally forth," along the highways of life, bearing witness before all men, in every circumstance and in every age, to the Good News that God has given a definite and final answer to the agonizing problems of man's life.

356

CONTEMPORARY DEVELOPMENTS

We have now come to the most important part of this study, a consideration of the developments that are taking place in Protestant Christianity in our time. For Protestantism, let it be emphasized, has not yet reached its religious majority, nor discharged its full historical mission. It is still in process of becoming; its heyday is not behind it, but before it. The complete meaning of what happened at the Reformation four hundred years ago has still to be expressed in life and doctrine and ecclesiastical organization. Other things, too, must happen which did not enter into the thought of the Reformers.

That Protestant Christianity is crossing the threshold of a new era in its history is abundantly clear. It is rediscovering its soul. Protestant Churches are becoming increasingly aware of the greatness of their heritage from the past. The glory of the Gospel and its implications for the world have captivated afresh the Protestant imagination. A sense of contemporary mission is deepening. Contact has been established with the Eastern Orthodox Church. The Roman Catholic doctrine of the Church and the bearing of its pretensions upon the future of Christian unity, is being studied afresh, and from a fresh point of view. The expansion of Evangelical Christianity into every represenative area of the world and the coming, in consequence, of a world-wide Evangelical community, has given a new sense of ecumenicity. The global character of contemporary problems, the physical unity of the world and its tragic spiritual disunity, constitute a new challenge to Evangelical action. The connection between human welfare and the religion prevalent in a given country has come up for new study. The devastating effects of religious monopoly and the suppression of religious freedom in large areas of the world, not only in countries where non-Christian religions have prevailed but even in others where the dominant religion has been Christian, have made a profound impression upon the Protestant mind. At the same time, there is much sober reflection upon the fact that the nations which proved victorious in the recent world struggle and which will

357

have to assume a major responsibility for the world of tomorrow, are nations whose religious background has been predominantly Protestant or Orthodox.

Four major developments have been taking place in Protestantism in recent years which will have a far-reaching influence upon the history of Christianity and the future of human civilization. Let us state what these are and pass on to consider each one of them in turn. First: The meaning of the historic Christian faith is being grasped afresh. Second: The reality of the Holy Catholic Church, the *Una Sancta,* and its implications for the Christian community and the family of nations, has caught the Protestant imagination. Third: A reawakened sense of responsibility for the secular order inspires a passion for a new *Corpus Christianum.* Fourth: The formulation of an ecumenical theology, made necessary by the world-wide expansion of Evangelical Christianity and the new problems of culture and civilization, is being initiated by Protestant thinkers.

The Rediscovery of Christian Orthodoxy. After a somber period during which it appeared as if Protestant theology was to succumb completely to a liberalism whose assumptions were derived from Reason rather than from Revelation, a powerful reaction has set in. The way was prepared for a renaissance of orthodoxy by the study of certain thinkers who had been largely passed by. The discussions of Pascal and Kierkegaard on the nature of Truth and of Christian truth in particular; the devastating critique of man and human nature by Dostoevski and Nietzsche disposed men's minds to take seriously the realism of the Bible. God became greater and more transcendent; man became meaner and more problematical. The religious romanticism which had immersed God in nature and divinized man received a shattering blow when in 1918 Karl Barth, a Swiss country pastor, published a commentary on Paul's Letter to the Romans. The number of allusions to Kierkegaard, Dostoevski and Nietzsche, in this epoch-making book show how those thinkers had prepared the soul of Barth to listen with fresh understanding to the powerful voice of Paul as he spoke again to Western religion and culture. Once more the transcendence of God became real in the high places of Protestant theology; the Word of God became potent and authoritative once again; the gulf between God and man, between sin and righteousness, between truth and falsehood, between perdition and salvation, became apparent; while the Bible as the written Word, and Jesus Christ as the personal Word of God, took on new meaning. The tremendous fact was brought home to thinkers that when God speaks, the content of His word is not information to satisfy man's curiosity but a command that summons him to obedience. The inner meaning of religion, as a total response of human personality to God, became clear. The impossibility of understanding the Bible without taking up the adventurous attitude which the Bible demands, also became manifest. Existential theology, that is, theology grounded upon man's total response to God, as against religious romanticism which rooted Christianity in pure feeling, and Protestant scholasticism which reduced it to the mere acceptance of theological formulas and the Biblical letter, had arrived. While so-called Barthianism has few adherents in its original form, and Karl Barth himself refuses to be known as a Barthian, the diffused influence of this German Swiss theologian and of his compatriot Emil Brunner has led to a rebirth of Protestant orthodoxy. That influence may be traced in many thinkers, both Protestant and Roman Catholic, who differ from these two theologians in many respects.

The appearance of a theological commentary on a book of the Bible, as distinguished from a merely critical and historical discussion, was soon followed by a new interest in theology itself. In the Protestant world, theology in general, and systematic theology in particular, had largely fallen into disrepute. Not doctrine but life was the prevailing slogan. The content of theology was determined largely by psychology or sociology, by philosophy or the history of religion. Now the Bible and the Bible alone became the supreme source of theology, as it had been in the Protestant tradition when it first broke upon the world. A new Biblicism was born which, while eager to do the fullest justice to the authenticated results of literary and historical criticism as applied to the Biblical records, was still prepared to affirm with intellectual conviction and passionate faith that the Bible was the Word of God to man. The Record of God's Self-disclosure in redemptive deed and prophetic word, in the person and work of Jesus Christ, in the coming of the Holy Spirit and the creation of the Christian Church, was where God and man supremely met. In the theological construction now undertaken of the doctrine of the person of Christ were blended the Jesus of history and the Christ of Paul, the Word become flesh of the Fourth Gospel and the King of Kings and Lord of Lords of the Apocalypse. The Old Testament soon began to be studied with fresh eyes not as a mere preface to, but as an integral part of, the Christian revelation. Fresh attention was given to the writings of Luther and Calvin and the other great Reformers of the sixteenth century. As a result of this study it was discovered that some of the greatest insights of those great men had been lost or dimmed in the Protestant theology of the succeeding period. When the white light of Revelation was turned upon the study of man and the human scene, it became evident that man was chiefly distinguished from the animals not only by his rationality, but also, and very especially, by his "capacity for self-deception." His characteristic sin was no longer lust, but rebellious pride. His supreme sin, to which he was constantly subject, was to substitute himself or something else for God, his Maker. Thus, in the higher spheres of Protestant theology, a new Christian realism was born. It was also proclaimed once more that the glory of the Christian preacher was to be a "servant of the Word."

In the period between the two wars, and under the double inspiration of the reborn interest in Christian orthodoxy and the growing desire for Christian understanding and unity, two great gatherings were convened. The object of the one was to crystallize Christian truth for the churches which professed it. One of the chief objects of the other was to define the Christian message in relation to the non-Christian religions. The first of these gatherings, called the Conference on Faith and Order, was held at Lausanne, Switzerland, in 1927. The second, an enlarged meeting of the International Missionary Council, assembled for two weeks on the Mount of Olives at Easter time, 1928, to consider the relation of Christianity to the non-Christian religions and the world of our time. Out of the Jerusalem gathering, and under the inspiration of what had taken place at Lausanne the year before, there came forth, in the form of a message, one of the great documents of contemporary Christianity. In the intervening two decades the Jerusalem message has exercised a wide and consolidating influence upon Protestant thought throughout the world. To make clear what is believed in the higher circles of Protestant leadership today, we can do no better than to quote part of this document. The chairman of the commission which drafted the message was the Archbishop of Canterbury, William Temple. The message reads in part: "Our message is Jesus Christ. He is the revelation of what God is and of what man through Him may become. In Him we come face to face with the Ultimate Reality of the universe; He makes known to us God as our Father, perfect and infinite in love and in righteousness; for in Him we find God incarnate, the final yet ever-unfolding, revelation of the God in whom we live and move and have our being.

"We hold that through all that happens, in light and in darkness, God is working, ruling and over-ruling. Jesus Christ, in His life and through His death and resurrection, has disclosed to us the Father, the Supreme Reality, as almighty Love, reconciling the world to Himself by the Cross, suffering with men in their struggle against sin and evil, bearing with them and for them the burden of sin, forgiving them as they, with forgiveness in their own hearts, turn to Him in repentance and faith, and creating humanity anew for an ever-growing, ever-enlarging, everlasting life.

"The vision of God in Christ brings and deepens the sense of sin and guilt. We are not worthy of His love; we have by our own fault opposed His holy will. Yet that same vision which brings the sense of guilt brings also the assurance of pardon, if only we yield ourselves in faith to the spirit of Christ so that His redeeming love may avail to reconcile us to God.

"We re-affirm that God, as Jesus Christ has revealed Him, requires all His children, in all circumstances, at all times, and in all human relationships, to live in love and righteousness for His glory. By the resurrection of Christ and the gift of the Holy Spirit God offers His own power to men that they may be fellow workers with Him, and urges them on to a life of adventure and self-sacrifice in preparation for the coming of His Kingdom in its fullness. . . .

"Christianity is not a Western religion, nor is it yet effectively accepted by the Western world as a whole. Christ belongs to the peoples of Africa and Asia as much as to the European or American. We call all men to equal fellowship in Him. But to come to Him is always self-surrender. We must not come in the pride of national heritage or religious tradition; he who would enter the Kingdom of God must become as a little child, though in that Kingdom are all the treasures of man's aspirations, consecrated and harmonized. Just because Christ is the self-disclosure of the One God, all human aspirations are towards Him, and yet of no human tradition is He merely the continuation. He is the desire of all nations; but He is always more, and other, than they had desired before they learned of Him." [2]

The Affirmation of Evangelical Catholicity. A new sense of the Church and its universality has also been born in recent years within the representative Protestant communions. The Church within the churches becomes more and more the object of thought and devotion. A deeper study of the New Testament, and especially the restoration of the Pauline letters and the other Apostolic writings to their true place within the Christian revelation, has focused upon the Church the attention which in the liberal era of Protestantism had been focused almost exclusively upon the Kingdom of God. The eschatological character of the Kingdom has been grasped afresh. It is recognized that the Christian Church is "the pillar and ground of the truth," that it is "the Body of Christ," God's chosen in-

[2] *The Jerusalem Meeting of the International Missionary Council,* International Missionary Council, New York, 1928, Vol. I, pp. 402, 411.

strument for the doing of His will in history, which must dedicate itself to the coming of His Kingdom among men. This Church came to birth as a fellowship before it became an organization. Its birth was due not to the "consenting wills of men," but to the power of God. Being the creation of the Holy Spirit, the Church is indwelt by the Spirit and must ever strive to maintain the unity of the Spirit.

The last two decades of Protestant history have been marked by increasing devotion upon the part of Protestant church leaders to the cause of Christian unity. They are committed to the proposition that only a united Church can fulfill the will of Christ as expressed in His great High Priestly prayer (St. John 17) and discharge its true mission in the world. Christ Himself is the center of Unity. Allegiance to Him as Divine Saviour and Lord is the bond that binds together the several Church councils that have been formed in recent years, such as, for example, The Federal Council of the Churches of Christ in America, and the World Council of Churches. A wholehearted recognition of Christ's deity is the basis of the new Christian unity that is being sought today in the Protestant world. This does not mean, of course, that the goal proposed is a single ecclesiastical structure made up of all the Protestant churches in any given country, or of a world Church with a single centralized authority. Seriously to entertain such an idea would run counter to the mind of Christ and to the true meaning and structure of the Christian Church, as these are expressed in the New Testament and in the early centuries of Christian history. What is sought is a federated expression of Christianity in which an increasing number of churches would unite organically, while others would manifest a growing unity in their doctrine, life, and practical endeavor, and in their strategy with respect to the secular order.

Thus schism and division are more and more regarded as evils by the great churches that make up the Protestant family. These Churches, however, are not disposed to admit that the historical division of Protestantism into a multiplicity of denominations has been an unmitigated evil. It is freely recognized that Protestant denominational history has many lamentable chapters in its annals. It is equally realized that the Spirit of God has used the witness and work of the great Protestant communions to set forth and to keep alive certain expressions of Christian faith and life that would otherwise have been passed over. The ecclesiastical unity now being sought is one in which each denomination, having studied itself in the light of Holy Scripture, in the light of other Christian denominations and traditions, in the light of its own history and mission, and in the light of contemporary need, shall slough off everything attaching to it which does not belong to the essence of the Christian religion, while it brings the rest, as its particular contribution, into the unity of the Body of Christ. An epochmaking step has been taken in the Protestant world when division is regarded as one of the greatest evils which can afflict the Church of Christ. In the light of Christ and the developing unity which brings the Protestant churches of the world together, schism has a hideous face. And what is the soul of schism but that any one institutional expression of the Church of Christ should presume to be the whole? Those Christians are schismatics in the worst sense who, in spite of the New Testament record and the testimony of history, regard the particular organization to which they belong as *The Church.*

Coincident with a deepened apprehension of the meaning of the Church, and an awakened passion for Christian unity, there has grown up in the Protestant world a new concept of catholicity. The nineteenth century and the first decades of the twentieth witnessed a missionary movement of the Protestant churches unparalleled in all Christian history. As a result of that movement, evangelical missions and national evangelical churches are found today in every representative area of the world. Soldiers, sailors, and airmen recently serving in continental areas and in remote islands of the Pacific ocean found that "The Church Was There." In this way the new vision of the Church, derived from a deepened study of the New Testament, has been paralleled on the plane of contemporary history by an expanded vision of the World Church. The Ecumenical

Church, that is to say, the Church which is coextensive with the inhabited globe, has appeared for the first time in Christian history. Its advent took place just at the time that civilization was entering upon its global era, when in a world that had achieved unprecedented physical unity abysmal spiritual rifts were forming and the earth was about to become devastated by global war. There is no more striking fact in the dramatic annals of the Christian Church than the circumstance that, during the years preceding the outbreak of the Second World War, great ecumenical gatherings were held in Europe and Asia, which were attended by the representatives of all races and of more Christian denominations than had ever come together before in all Christian history. Out of these gatherings there emerged a sense of the living reality of the Church Universal. At Jerusalem, at Oxford, at Edinburgh, at Madras, at Amsterdam, at Utrecht, a new concept of catholicity became real in experience and began to be formulated in thought.

To understand the meaning and grasp the implications of the new concept of catholicity which has emerged in the Protestant world is to take cognizance of the most significant single phenomenon in the contemporary history of Christianity. In a recent article published in the theological quarterly, *Theology Today*,[3] and entitled "The Growing Concept of Catholicity," the Church historian, Dr. Kenneth Latourette of Yale University, compares the traditionally Roman concept of catholicity with the emergent Protestant concept. To that admirable article of the great Church historian some reflections may be added. Evangelical catholicity does not confine the frontiers of the Christian Church to the boundaries of any one Christian institution. Taking seriously the great dictum that comes down to us from the Patristic era, *Ubi Christus ibi Ecclesia,* "Where Christ is, there is the Church," it considers that any Christian group that gives full allegiance to Jesus Christ in its doctrine and bears His marks in the life and witness of its members, gives unmistakable evidence of the fruits of the Holy Spirit, and so belongs to the Holy Catholic Church. Its members may

[3] Vol. ii, No. i (April, 1945), pp. 69–76.

have to clarify their thinking and learn the way of the Lord more perfectly, but if they give evidence of the basic Christian loyalties in faith and practice, Christ's seal is upon them and they belong to His Church. Evangelical catholicity, therefore, embraces all those, whatever their name or sign, who pledge their loyalty to Jesus Christ and manifest the fruits of the Spirit. All such are members of the Holy Catholic Church and are invited to form part of the ecumenical fellowship of Christian believers. They are urged to manifest their unity in Christ, to join in giving more perfect expression in thought and life to the Christian faith and its implications for the human situation, and to develop a common strategy in approaching the world and its problems. The affirmation that underlies Evangelical Catholicity is therefore this: Jesus Christ Himself, by the faith and life which He creates in those who profess to be His disciples, ultimately determines who belong to the Holy Catholic Church.

The coming of the Church Universal in concept and in reality has given birth in Protestant circles to a new science, the science of ecumenics. Ecumenics is the science of the Church Universal, its nature, functions, relations, and strategy. It corresponds in the religious sphere to geopolitics in the secular. Henceforth the Christian Church in its Protestant expression will devote increasing attention to the formulation of an adequate Christian approach to the diverse problems which confront the Christian religion at the present time.

Reawakened Concern for the Secular Order. At the close of the First World War, several movements appeared among the Protestant Churches to bring the message and influence of Christianity to bear upon the life of the world. Two of these were the World Church Movement, which was organized in the United States, and the Life and Work Movement, which was international in character. The latter held a great congress at Stockholm in 1925. Both movements did their work under the influence of the idea that the lights of the coming Kingdom of God were already flushing the contemporary horizon. The churches of that time lacked a sufficiently deep insight into the realities of human nature and of the human situation. What was more, they lacked an adequate grasp of the meaning of the Church and of the great Christian verities. Under the influence of religious romanticism they felt that the transformation of human society could be accomplished if only the Church organized itself adequately for the task.

In the intervening years, the international situation grew worse. Theological insight was deepened; the nature and mission of the Church became clearer. At Oxford in July, 1937, there came together representatives of the Protestant and Eastern Orthodox churches. Members of the clergy and eminent members of the laity were there. At a time when it began to appear that a new world war was inevitable, the members of the Church Universal assembled at Oxford, spent two weeks on issues relating to "Church, Community, and State." Out of that gathering came the slogan that has since resounded around the world: "Let the Church be the Church."

The Oxford Conference, which grasped and formulated the true mission of the Church in the world, faced also, and in a constructive way, the Church's relationship to the whole secular order. The problem of a *Corpus Christianum* became real again. How could human society as a whole be brought under the decisive influence of Christian principles and a Christian way of living?

In the years since this decisive gathering was held, the problems of the secular order have been envisaged with great clarity, in their social, cultural, and political aspects. Protestant leaders proclaim afresh that it is not enough to formulate ethical principles for society, nor yet to regenerate individuals through the preaching of the Gospel. It is necessary, in addition, that Christians should live out in communal form the new meaning of a true Christian life within the diverse spheres that make up Society. In other words, the true meaning of community must be correctly worked out within the representative areas of social life. As regards the cultural sphere it is pointed out that modern culture has become largely rootless. It lacks, besides, a great luminous idea to give life meaning, direction and propulsive

367

power. The great insights of the Christian religion must therefore be given to modern culture. The question is raised afresh in Protestant circles as to the place of religion in public education. God must come again into education; reverence must be taught to youth. The Bible and the great sources of spiritual renewal must be made available for popular study.

In the sphere of politics, and especially in the sphere of international relations, a decisive influence has been exerted in the United States by the commission entitled The Commission to Study the Bases of a Just and Durable Peace. This commission, sponsored by the Federal Council of the Churches of Christ in America, and under the chairmanship of a distinguished Protestant layman, John Foster Dulles, who received a vision of the Church and its possibilities at the Oxford Conference, has been more influential in shaping Christian public opinion in America, and in influencing the international policy of the government, than any single group in recent times that has faced the problems of peace and world order.

Now that the war is over, and the full meaning of the Ecumenical Church becomes more apparent, Protestant Christianity looks forward to bringing the insights and inspiration of Christianity to bear on the secular order with a sense of responsibility unmatched since the great schism divided the Christian Church in the West.

A Demand for an Ecumenical Theology. The new orthodoxy that takes shape in the Protestant mind, the new catholicity that inspires its ecclesiastical outlook, the Christian concern for the human situation in its global aspects that mark the Protestant Churches of today combine to create a longing for an authoritative Ecumenical Council. This was what the Reformers of the sixteenth century desired above anything else, "the next free general Council of Holy Christendom," and of which they were defrauded in their time by the action of the Council of Trent in 1546. An invitation to such a council will undoubtedly be issued in due course "to all whom it may concern." One of the chief tasks of the new Ecumenical Council will be the formulation of an ecumenical theology. Such a theology, grounded upon

Holy Scripture as the supreme source of Christian doctrine, will take cognizance of the light that has fallen upon the Christian revelation under the influence of the Holy Spirit from the first century to the present. It will take account of the global character of human life today, and of the existence and problems of a world-wide Church in a global era. It will formulate Christian truth in relation to the new heresies which have been spawned in our time. The writer may be permitted at this point to reproduce a statement which he recently prepared on this subject and which has appeared elsewhere.[4]

Taking seriously the presence of the Holy Spirit in the Church and realizing that there is no better commentary upon the meaning of both than the history of the Church, ecumenical theology will study the Churches of the great dispersion in the light of the Bible and of Jesus Christ. Now that the Church is coextensive with the inhabited globe, the hour has arrived to survey afresh the whole course of Church history. Let each Church in the three great traditions, Roman, Eastern, and Protestant, be studied for the witness it has borne to Christ in the course of its life, whether in the nurture of saints, the elucidation or defense of truth, or in its contribution to the effective reign of God among men. Let it be surveyed to discover whatever stains of sin, or marks of shame and error, its history may reveal. Such a study will show that no Church in history can claim a monopoly of insight or sainthood, of evangelical zeal or transforming power. Those things which God has taught the Church through the glory and shame of the churches will provide data for an ecumenical theology. A theology of Revelation, which cherishes without idolatry the historic Creeds and Confessions, which studies the life history of the churches in search of insight regarding Christ and the Church, which embraces within its sweep God's dealing with the new Churches in Asia, Africa, and Oceania, can lay the foundation of that theology which is needed by an Ecumenical Church in an ecumenical world.

[4] "The Times Call for Theology," *Theology Today,* Lancaster, Vol. II, No. 1 (April, 1945), pp. 7 and 5.

Let the Churches of the Reformation acknowledge their many sins and shortcomings, admitting freely that the Church can sin and has sinned. In penitence and humility, in faith and in hope, let them prepare for the tasks that await them in the coming time. And about one thing let them be quite clear. The theological statement to which the Church Universal must look forward in the years ahead must be no doctrinal syncretism or theological dilution. It must have at the heart of it no pale, lowest denominator formula. Never must the Church sponsor a blanched, eviscerated, spineless statement of confessional theology. It must give birth in this revolutionary, transition time, to a full blooded, loyally Biblical, unashamedly ecumenical, and strongly vertebrate system of Christian belief.

SELECTED BIBLIOGRAPHY

Protestantism. By William Ralph Inge. London, 1928.

A Compend of Calvin's Institutes, Philadelphia, 1939; *A Compend of Luther's Theology,* Philadelphia, 1943. Edited by Hugh Thomson Kerr, Jr.

The Christian Message in a Non-Christian World. By Hendrik Kraemer. New York, 1938.

History of the Expansion of Christianity. By Kenneth L. Latourette. 7 vols. New York, 1937–1945.

A Preface to Christian Theology. New York, 1941. By John A. Mackay, editor, *Theology Today Quarterly,* Princeton, New Jersey.

Unitive Protestantism. By John Thomas McNeill. New York, 1930.

The Nature and Destiny of Man. By Reinhold Niebuhr. 2 vols. New York, 1941–1943.

Romanism and Evangelical Christianity. By E. J. Paul. London, 1940.

The Vitality of the Christian Faith. Edited by George F. Thomas. New York, 1944.

Protestantism and Progress. By Ernst Troeltsch, translated by W. Montgomery, New York, 1912.

Universal Christian Conference on Life and Work: J. H. Oldham, *The Oxford Conference, Official Report,* Chicago, 1937; W. A. Visser'T Hooft and J. H. Oldham, *The Church and Its Function in Society,* Chicago, 1937.

WHO'S WHO OF AUTHORS

OHN CLARK ARCHER. Hoober Professor of Comparative Reli-
ion, Yale University. Author of *Mystical Elements in Mohammed; A
Jew Approach in Missionary Education; Youth in a Believing World;
aiths Men Live By; The Sikhs; etc. Lecturer at various institutions in
he East and the West. A.B., Hiram College; A.M., B.D., Ph.D., Yale.

EWIS HODOUS, Head of Chinese Department, Emeritus, Kennedy
chool of Missions, Hartford Seminary Foundation. Former President
f Foochow Theological Seminary. Authority on Chinese culture and
eligious thought. Author and translator of works dealing with China.
.B., D.D., Western Reserve; B.D., Hartford Theological Seminary.

). C. HOLTOM. Authority on Shinto. Formerly Professor at Japanese
aptist Seminary; Professor of Theology, Aoyama Gakuin, Tokyo.
Iaskell Lecturer, University of Chicago, 1940. Author of *Political
*hilosophy of Modern Shinto; The Japanese Enthronement Cere-
onies; The National Faith of Japan; The Meaning of Kami; Modern
apan and Shinto Nationalism;* etc. A.B., Ph.D., Chicago.

OSEPH L. HROMÁDKA. Visiting Professor, Princeton Theologi-
al Seminary; formerly Professor of Theology at the University of
rague. A widely known central European thinker and a profound stu-
ent of Russian literature. Author, in Czech, of *Masaryk; Dostoyevski
d Masaryk; Christianity in Thought and Life; The Legacy of Luther;
he Legacy of Calvin;* etc.; in English, *Doom and Resurrection.*
h.B., Vienna; Ph.D., Prague.

DWARD J. JURJI. Associate Professor of Islamics and Compara-
ve Religion, Princeton Theological Seminary. Formerly, Member of
e Institute for Advanced Study; lecturer, Princeton University. Au-
or of *Illumination in Islamic Mysticism;* "Arabic Literature" in
ncyclopedia of Literature. A.B., American University of Beirut;
.A., Ph.D., Princeton; B.D., Princeton Theological Seminary.

)HN A. MACKAY. President of Princeton Theological Seminary;
rofessor of Ecumenics. President of the Board of Foreign Missions,
resbyterian Church, U. S. A. Leading church statesman and inter-
eter of Protestantism. Author of *The Other Spanish Christ; Preface
Christian Theology; That Other America; Heritage and Destiny;*
. Editor of *Theology Today.* M.A., Aberdeen; B.D., Princeton Theo-
gical Seminary; D.Litt., Lima; D.D., Princeton.

ABRAHAM A. NEUMAN. President of the Dropsie College for Hebrew and Cognate Learning, Philadelphia, Pa.; Professor of History. Editor, *Jewish Quarterly Review;* Revising Editor, *Universal Jewish Encyclopedia;* Secretary, American Jewish Historical Society. Author of *The Jews in Spain: Their Social, Political and Cultural Life during the Middle Ages; Cyrus Adler: A Biographical Sketch; Relation of the Hebrew Scriptures to American Institutions.* B.S., M.A., Columbia; H.L.D., Jewish Theological Seminary of America, Hebrew Union College; LL.D., Pennsylvania.

A. K. REISCHAUER. Lecturer on the History of Religions at Union Theological Seminary. Formerly, Educational Missionary to Japan; Professor of History of Religion, Nihon Shingakko; Charles F. Deems Lecturer on Philosophy, New York University. Author of *Studies in Japanese Buddhism; The Task in Japan; Present Day Religion in Japan;* etc. B.A., M.A., Hanover; D.D., New York University.

GERALD G. WALSH, S. J. Editor of *Thought* (Fordham University Quarterly). Formerly, Head of Graduate Department of Italian Studies; Graduate Professor of Medieval History, Fordham. Author of *The Emperor Charles IV; Medieval Humanism; Dante Alighieri, Citizen of Christendom;* contributor to *The Catholic Philosophy of History; Faith for Today;* etc. B.A., London; M.A., Oxford; Ph.D., S.T.D., Gregorian University, Rome.

INDEX

Abd-al-Rahman Rasuli, 321
Abhidhamma-pitaka, 110
Abraham, 226, 309
Abravanel, 239
Absolute, 76–77, the Brahman, 53, 59, 73, philosophic, 72, 74, Truth, 109, Self, 102, Japanese Kami as, 174
Abyssinia, 196
Achiki, 16
Acta Apostolicae Sedis, 315n
Adam, fall of, in Judaism, 246
Adi-Buddha, 129
advaita, 73–74, 76–77
Afghanistan, 194, 214
Africa, north, 115, 196, 214, northwest, 183, Negro, 214, Christianity and, 362, Churches in, 369
agape, 315
Agni, 55–57
Agra, 212
ahimsa, 59, 62
Ahmad Khan, Syed, 214
Akbar, the Mughal, 80, 212
akhlaq, 192
Aki tsu Kami, 173
Akiba, Rabbi, 243
Alexandria, patriarchate of, 288
Ali, the caliph, 197–99
Ali, C. Rahmat, 219
Ali Abd-al-Raziq, 194–195
Aligarh College, 214
All-god, 83
All, the, 74–75
All-India Muslim League, 219
Allah, 196, slave of, 79, of Sufis, 80, doctrine of, 188–191, and Providence, 189
Amaterasu Omikami, 17, 133, 168
Ameer Ali, Syed, 193
America, Jews in, 280
American, nationalism, 177, Catholics, 318, Civil War, 343, 346, Revolution, 343, Declaration of Independence, 343, Christianity, 362
Americas, Moslems in the, 214
Amida Buddhism, *see* Amitabha
amir al-muminin, 196
Amitabha, 108, 126, 135, scriptures, 112
Amsterdam, 365
Analects of Confucius, 2n, 16, 18

Ananda, "beloved disciple" of Buddhism, 95
Anatta, 101–102
Angkor, Wat, 117
Anglican Church, 344–45
Anglicanism, 244–46
Anglo-Catholics, 345
Antioch, patriarchate of, 288
Antonius, metropolitan of Kiev, 298
Apocalypse, 354, 360
Apollo, 160
Apostles, writings of, 310, Creed, 342
Apostolic Succession, 345
Apostolicity, 315
Ara Mikami, 173
Arab, Sea, 47, conquerors, 182, and other races, 184, 210, Isalamization of, 187, people, 214, League, 222
Arabia, 181–182, 211
Arabic, language, 184, 210
Aranyakas, 54
Archbishop of Canterbury, 345, 361
Arhat, 107
Arian, heresy, 325
Aristotelian, concept of habits, 317
Aristotelianism, 235
Arius, 325
Arnold, Matthew, 138
Arthashastra, 52
arya, 60
Arya Samaj, 47, 80
Aryan, 47, 55, 62, non-, 54, invaders, 90
Aryans, 48, 52, 60
Aryo-Dravidians, 58, 67
Aryo-Indian, 47
Ashari, al-, abu-al-Hasan, 205
Asharites, 205
ashramas, 65
Asia, Buddhism in, 92, Western, 115, 182, Christianity and, 362, Churches in, 369, Minor, 46, 284
Asiatic, 46
Asoka, King, 106, 109, 112
Ataturk, *see* Mustafa Kemal Ataturk
Athanasius of Alexandria, 325–6
Atharva Veda, 53–54, 57
Atlantic, seaboard, 182
Atman, 74
Aurangzib, 70, 212
Australia, 322

Avalokitesvara, 129
avatara, 70, 84
avataras, 87, of Shiva, 84, of Rama and Krishna, 85
Ave Maria, 295
Averroës, 208
Averroism, 331
avidya, 75
awqaf, 191
Axis, the, 215
Azhar, al-, 183, 221

Babar, 212
Babawayh, ibn-, 200
Babylon, Jewish academy of, 247
Bach, 352
Badarayana, 73
Baghdad, 211
Balkans, under Islam, 302
Baptists, the, 347
Bar Kokba, 243
Barrett, Timothy, 318
Barth, Karl, 343, 358–59
Barthian, 359
Basilides, 325
Basri, al-, al-Hasan, 204
Baydawi, al-, 200
Benares (Kashi, City of the Kasis), 58, 61, 67, 69–71, 81–82, 97, sermon of, 98
Benedict XV, 320
Bengal, 48, 51, 68, Bay of, 67
Bengali, 83
Berdyaev, N., 298
Bergson, 3
Bethlehem, 295
Beza, 341
Bhagavad-Gita, 85
Bhagavat, 92
Bhagavata, 85
Bhagavata-Purana, 85–86
bhakta, 80–81
bhaktas, 80
bhakti, 72, 78–79, way, 84
bhakti-marga, 77
bhashya, 76
Bible, the, Holy, 80, 350–52, 356, 359, 364, 368–69, anthropomorphism in, 235, Hebrew, 247, Old and New Testament, 291–92, 360
Biblical, tradition, 182, law, 275–81, Christianity, 344, records, 351, 360, belief, 370
Biblicism, 359
bila kayfa, 205
Bodhidharma (Tamo), 125

Bodhi-sattva, 107, Chenrezi, 129
Bohmer Wald, 46
Book of Changes, 2n
Book of God, *see* Koran
Book of History, 2n
Book of Poetry, 2n, 16
Book of Reward and Punishment by the Great Supreme, 37–38
Book of Rites, 2n, 6, 15
Boroboedoer, 117
Bossuet, 346
Brahma, 57, 69, 81
Brahman, 62–63, 65, 77, the Absolute, 53, 57, 73–74, 76, 97, priestly heritage, 87, of Vedanta, 80
Brahmana, 58, theology, 60
Brahmanas, 54, 57–59, 63, 73
Brahmanic, 82, tradition, 83, religion, 91
Brahmans, 50, 58, 61, 63, 66, 70–72, their number, 48
Brahman-Atman, 102
Brazil, 46
Britain, 49
British, 49
Brunner, Emil, 359
Buddha, the, 36, 38–39, 45, 59, 72, 85, 92–95, 97–104, 106, 109, real experience of, 93–94, message of, 96, the Eternal, 105, 108, 120, 127, 132, life of, 110, teachings of, 112, silent on hereafter, 114
Buddhahood, 38
Buddhas, 105, 108
Buddhism, 1–5, 11, 15–16, 19, 41, 72, 90, 143, influence on Taoism, 35, 37, beginnings of, 91, founder of, 92, predominant emphasis in, 93, its stress on solitary life, 95, source on early, 107, older and later, 108, sacred literature of, 110, characteristically Indian, 112, in fifth century India, 113, lost identity in India, 114, its spread in Asia, 115, Dhyana, 125, Tantric, 129, contemporary status of, 138, semi-Christianization of, 140, Japanese, 143, 154, compared with Shinto, 162–63, resolves about compassion, 176
Buddhist, 4, 68, ex-, 17, influence on Taoism, 36, 38, hierarchy, 39, gospel, 59, lands, 93, scriptures, 95, canon, 109, missions, 115, ascendancy in Japan, 157

Buddhists, 16, 38, 45, 66, 87, leading, 96, of Ceylon, Burma, Thailand, and Cambodia, 10
Bukhari, al-, 201
Bulgakov, S., 298–300
Burma, 110, 115, Hinayana Buddhism in, 116, its Buddhists, 118
Busenbaum, Herman, 318
Byzantine, culture, 192
Byzantium, 284, Empire of, 287

Cabala, 239, 276
cabalistic, doctrine, 246
Caesar, 162
Cairo, 211
Calcutta, 83
Calvary, 295
Calvin, John, 341–43
Calvinism, 341–44
Calvinistic, influence, 344–45, 347
Calvinists, 342
Cambodia, 110, 115, Hinayana Buddhism in, 116–117
Canada, 322
Capetown, 183
Cappadocia, 46
Cardinal Hinsley, 321
caritaten, 326
Carpocrates, 325
Casablanca, 183
casta, 60, 64
Catholics, Protestants, and Jews, 322
Caucasian, 284
Celestial Teacher, 32
Celt, culture, 46
Central Asia, 32, 107, 115
Ceremonies of the Engi Era, *see* Engi Shiki
Cerularius, Michael, 289
Ceylon, 110, Buddhism in, 115–116, its Buddhists, 118, Buddhist dominance in, 120
Ceylonese Chronicles, 115
Chalcedon, 328, 332
Chan, 39, 125
Chan-men, 39
Chang, family of Taoist popes, 32
Chang Chueh, 31–32
Chang Ling, 31
Chang Lu, 32
Charnock, Job, 48
Chen Huan-chang, 19
Chen Shen, 8
Chen-yen, school, 127, 132
Chi, 4, 21
Chih, 21

Chiang Kai-shek, his New Life Movement, 20–21, 216
Chih-kai, 126
Chin, 32
Chin Shih Huang Ti, emperor, 31, 35
China, 1, 3, 5, 10, 15–18, 28, 40, 90, 107, 110, 115, Republic of, 19, 41, spirit of old, 20, trend in, 22, ancient, 26, rural, 35, modern, 41, religion in, 42, Mahayana Buddhism in, 121–28, Islam in, 182, Moslem, 214
Chinese, 1, 4–5, 12–14, 16, 19, 37, classics, 17, wisdom, 18, thinking and life, 20, 24, people, 28, pharmacopoeia, 33, ethics, 34, conditions, 38, mystics, 39, society, 41, Mahayana Buddhist canon, 110–111, nationality, 210
Chinese Classics, the, 2n
Chingiz Khan, 212
Chishtiyah, 193
Chou, 1, 2, 8, 27
Christ, *see* Jesus Christ
Christendom, 213, 321, Reunion of, 323, 343, medieval, 334–35, Council of Holy, 368
Christian, 41, 66, religion, 19, world, 50, first centuries, 72, civilization, 301, theology, 324–25, traditions, 337–38, historic faith, 342, and non-Christian religions, 361, life and faith, 364, revelation, 369, belief, 370
Christianity, 19, 41, 84, 90, 115, 182, 362, invaded Europe out of Judea, 161, compared with Shinto, 162–63, as center of Western civilization, 164, and Shinto, 165, revolves about universal love, 176, surpasses Islam numerically, 183, Eastern and Western, 284, Western, 298, paradox of, 307, Reformed, 343, Biblical, 344
Christians, 18, 80, Indian, 44
Chronicle of Ancient Events, *see* Kojiki
Chronicle of Japan, *see* Nihongi
chu, 12
Chuang Tzu (Chuang Chou), 25, 27
Chuang Tzu Book, 25–27, 29
Chu-fu, 1, 11
Chu-Hsi, 2, 4, 21
chung, 7
Church, the, 364–66, 370, Judaism and, 230, Apostolic, 300, is Christ,

311, virtues of, 320, prayer of, 332, Confessional, 343, of England, 344–45, Roman Catholic doctrine of, 357, meaning of, 367
Church of the Resurrection, 196
Chutsze School, 17
Cleomenes, 325
Cohen, M. G., 334
College of Cardinals, 320
Columbia University, 19
Commentary on the Gospel of St. John, 327
Comintern, 216
Commission Study Bases Just Durable Peace, 368
communicatio in sacris, 323
Compendium Theologiae Moralis, 318
Comte, Auguste, 209
Conference on Faith and Order, 360
Confucian, 1, 4, 7–8, 10–11, 15–16, 30, influence on Japan, 17, Church, 19, University, 19, temples, 20, system, 20, virtues, 21, as state religion, 31, pre-, 2
Confucian Temple, 11
Confucianism, 1, 2, 11, 15–16, 41, 122, 143, cult of, 19, revival of, 20, as a religion, 21, eternal order in, 22, ethics of, 22, philosophical, 38, Taoist influence on, 39, Japanese borrowings from, 154, 156, 166, surpasses Islam numerically, 183
Confucianists, 1, 3, 6, 17, 33, 123
Confucius, 1–2, 4–5, 7–8, 10–12, 41, 45, life in French and Latin, 17, ceremony to, 20, metaphysics of, 21, teachings of, 124
Confucius Sinarum Philosophus, 18
Congregationalists, the, 347–48
Constantinople, 285, 287, Church of, 284, patriarchate of, 288, Council of, 326
Contending States, 6, 15
Cordova, 211
Corpus Christianum, 358, 367
Councils, Ecumenical, 328, 330
Cow, Sacred, 57
creatio ex nihilo, 325
Crescas, Hasdai, 238
Crescent, 213
Cross, the, Way of, 307

Daily Express, the, 119
Dalai Lama, 129, 130
Dalton, 22

Damascus, 211
danda, 52
Dante, 37, 332, *Inferno,* 314
Dardanelles, 215
darshanas, 59
dasas, 60
dastur, 88
dasya, 60
Dasyus, 55
David, 45, Psalms of, 224, house of, 243
Day of Atonement, 268–70
Day of Judgment, 180
Dès le début, 320
Delhi, sultanate of, 212
Dengyo Daishi, 132, 135
Deus ex machina, 299
devas, 54
Devi, 70, 82
Deussen, Paul, 74
Dewey, George, 217
Dhamma, *see* Dharma
Dharma, 51, 62–63, 74–75, 85, 105
dharma-shastra, 53
Dharma-stan, 69
Dialogues of Love, 239
Diaspora, 233
Diet of Spires, 338
Divine Husbandman, 9
Djokjakarta, 218
Doctrine of the Mean, 2, 7, Latin translation, 17–18
Dostoyevski, F. M., 298, 353, 358
Dravidian, cult, 62, pre-Vedic maternalism, 81
Dravidianism, 61
Duke of Extended Sagehood, 20
Dulles, John Foster, 368
Durga, 69, 82, 84
Durga-puja, 84
dvijas, 64–65
dyaush, 54
dyaush pitar, 54
dyu, 54

Earth, 8, 24, 30, 32
East, 22
East China, 14
Eastern Church, *see* Orthodox Christianity
Eastern Orthodoxy, *see* Orthodox Christianity
Eastern, world, 39
Ecumenical, the, movement, 284, councils, 292, spirit, 343, gatherings, 365, Church, 368–69

Eden, Garden of, 246
Edinburgh, 365
Egypt, 194, 196, 214, 220, Church of, 284
Egyptian, religious reformation, 183, 192
Eire, 46
élan vitale, 3
Elijah, 243–44
Eliot, T. S., 344
Elizabeth, reign of, 344
Emperor, of Japan, 142, 164
Encyclical, *Corporis Mystici*, 315, *Arcanum*, 318, *Casti Connubii*, 318, *Inscrutabili*, 318, *Divini illius Magistri*, 318, *Rerum Novarum*, 319, *Quadragesimo Anno*, 319, *Immortale Dei*, 319
Engi Shiki, 166
England, 321, 345
English, 51
Episcopal, churches, 344
Erasmus, 341
Esther, scroll, 271
Eternal Word of God, *see* Jesus Christ
Etna, 46
Eucharist, 345
Eucharistic, 295
Europe, 18–19, central, 46, Lutherans in, 341, tongues of, 350
European, Christians, 362
Evangelical Catholicity, 366
Evangelicals, 345

Fa-Hsien, 113
Far East, 152
Farabi, al-, 208
faruq, al-, 196
Federal Council Churches Christ America, 363, 368
feng-shui, 33, 34
Fertile Crescent, 196
Festival of Dedication, 271
Festivals, Jewish institution, 260–67
Festival of New Food, 170
Fifty Years of New Japan, 17n
filioque, 287, 289
Fiqh, 199
Five Classics, 2
Five Relations, 5
Florenski, P., 298–300
Formosa, 165
Four Books, 2
Four Noble Truths, 98, 101
Franklin, Benjamin, 22

Galilee, 307
Galileo, 22
Gandhi, 57, 66, 82
Ganesha, 70
Ganga-ma, 69
Ganges, 58, 67, 82, 112, Valley, 113
Gauri, 82
Gautama (Gotama), *see* Buddha, the
Genchi, Kato, 152, 155, 157
Genesis, book, 247
Geneva, 341
genomenos, 326
gennomenos, 326
German, Nazism, 341
Germanos, metropolitan of Thyatira, 298
Germany, 278, 340, 343
Germanic, culture, 46
Ghazzali, al-, 80, 205–207
Gita-Govinda, 86
Gleanings from Ancient Stories, *see* Kogoshui
Ghaznah, Mahmud of, 212
Gnostics, the, 325
Goa, 48
God, 8, 15, 76–78, 87, 351, 361, 363–64, personal, 21, of all religions, 41, reality of, 72, the Absolute, 74, Moslem, 79, Krishna, 85, will of, 96, of theistic religions, 108, Eternal Buddha as, 120, Absolute Kami as, 174, one true, 175, 362, sovereignty of, 180, 320, Hebrew, 226, Temple of, 227, Jewish vision of, 231, 234, existence of, 235, in Zion, 242, 244, through the Incarnation, 294, the heavenly Lord, 296, Triune, 298, Christ is, 311, Supreme Goodness of, 317, authority is from, 319, doctrine of, 341, worship and service of, 342, knowledge of, 350, in education, 368
God-man, the, *see* Jesus Christ
Gog and Magog, 244
Copala, 86
gopi, 86
Gospel, the, 284, 355–56, 367, the Fourth, 360
Govinda, 86
Gotama Sakyamuni, *see* Buddha, the
Gotama Siddhartha, *see* Buddha, the
Grand Clarté du Moyen Age, La, 334
Great Learning, 2, Latin translation, 17, 18

Great Learning and The Mean-in-action, 2n
Great Supreme, 38
Great Vehicle, *see* Mahayana Buddhism
Greece, 59, 215, Church of, 284
Greek, 45, 52, culture, 46, 332, philosophy, 286
Guide of the Perplexed, 205
Gury, Jean Pierre, 318

Hades, 35, 37–38
Hadi, al-, ibn-Ahmad, 218
Hadrian, Emperor, 243
Haftarah, 272
Halakah, 272
Halley's comet, 10
Hammurabi, Code of, 192
Han, 2, 11, 15, 21, 24, 33–34, 122
Hanbalites, 201
Hanifah, abu-, 201
Hanuccah, 271–72
Hanuman, 87
Hao Tien Shangti, 8
Hardwar, 69
harijans, 48, 61, 65–66, 73
Harnack, von, Adolf, 324–25
Harsha, Emperor, 113
Harvard University, 347
Hasan, al-, 199
Hasidim, 240
Hasidism, 239, 277
Hastings, Warren, 51
Hausa, 210
Heart-cleansing Societies, 19
Heaven, 2–3, 6–10, 15, 22, 24–25, 33, offering to, 19, 21, Tao of, 29, favor of, 30, genii of, 32
Heaven and Earth, 39
Hebraic, prophetic tradition, 185
Hebrew, 69, religion, 332
Hebrews, 45
Heian, 133
Hellenic, civilization, 213, philosophy, 332
Henry VIII, 344
Heraclitus, 208
Hillel, 240
Himalayas, 47, 69
Hinayana Buddhism, 42, 107, 109–110, 113, 115, 120
Hindu, 44, 46–47, 52, 54, 56, 61–63, 67, 69, 79, multitudes, 49, caste, 60, population, 63, social system, 64, history, 68, faith, 70, philosophy, 72, 74, thought, 76, reform-ers, 77, scriptures, 78, 80, theism, 79, family, 88, religion, 89, race, 210
Hinduism, 44–51, 53, 58, 59, 60–67, 69, 72, 76, 81, 88, core of, 48, upper castes of, 64, south Indian, 71, its struggle with Islam, 79, common dogma with Islam, 80, popular, 80, as religion, 89, all-inclusive, 91, renascent, 113, merged with Buddhism, 114
Hindus, 44–45, 47–48, 50, 57, 62, 64–65, 70, 74, 76, 78, 81, 88–89, as a people with a scripture, 80
Hindustan, 47, 67
Hindustani, 210
Hiram of Tyre, 214
Hiroyuki Kato, 175n
History of the Variations of Protestantism, 346
Hitler, Adolph, 341, 344
Ho-O, 133
Hobbes, 332
Hokkekyo, 136
Holland, 218
Hollywood, 49
Holy Land, *see* Palestine
Holy Spirit, the, 291–92, 296, 299, 310, 350, 365, 369, coming of, 323, Life of, 326
Holy Scripture, *see* Bible
homoousios, 325–26
homoiousios, 325–26
Hooker, Richard, 344
Howard, John, 41
Hsi Wang Mu, 32
Hsiao Ching, 18
Hsuang Chuang, 113
Huang Tien Shangti, 8
Hurgronje, Snouck, 218
Husayn, al-, 199, 202

I-Ching, 113
Iberian Peninsula, 182, 211, 217
ihsan, 186
ijtihad, 200
Imamate, dogma of, 198
iman, 186
Immortales, Taoist idea of, 32–33, 36
Imperial Ancestors, 167
Imperial Rescript on Education, 17, 166
India, 42, 44, 46–49, 59, 60, 63, 67, 69, 71, 76, 78, 80, 92, 211, 220, South, 61, Moslems in, 79, genius

of, 88, Buddhism in, 91, northwest, 107, Moslem, 214
Indian, religion, 44, life, 49, communities, 64, villages, 84, view of woman, 95
Indians, thoughtful, 91
Indo-Aryan, 53
Indo-European, 46–47, 54, 210
Indo-Iranian, 47
Indonesia, 214, 218, 220
Indonesian, 210
Indra, 46, 55–57, 86
inkilap, 215
Inouyé, Dr., 17
International Missionary Council, 361
Institutes of the Christian Religion, 341–42
Intorcetta, 17
Iqbal Ali Shah, Sirdar, 219
Iran, *see* Persia
Iranian, culture, 46
Iraq, 194, 214
Isaac, 226
Isaiah, 242
Ise, Mecca of modern Japan, 167
Ishaq, ibn-, 198
Ishwara, 74, 76–77
Islam, 41, 72, 80, 84, 90, 115, 178–222, popular, 48–49, Indian, 79, its coming into India, 114, defined, 182, status of Christians and Jews, 197, its core of religious power, 183–95, its founders and interpreters, 195–210, expansion of, 210–15, its contemporary mission, 215–22, worship in, 186–87, theology of, 188–91, ethics of, 191–95, takes Christianity to task, 194, modern, 194
Islam wa-Usul al-Hukm, al-, 195
isnad, 200
Israel, custodian of religion, 227, its awareness of God, 232, election of, 234, groups within catholic, 240, final triumph of, 241, the suffering people, 245, 279, prophets, 352

Jabala, Syrian Ghassanid king, 196
Jacob, 226
Jagannatha, 67–78
Jagannatha-Krishna-Radha, 68
Jaimini, 73
Jainist, 68
Jains, 44–45, 59
Jamal-al-Din al-Afghani, 193
James, William, 347

Jamna, 58
Japan, 16–17, 19–20, 107, 110, 115, 141–77, Mahayana canon in, 111, Mahayana Buddhism in, 131–38, unique geographical position of, 143, Moslems in, 214
Japanese, nationalism, 141, spirit, 145, ancestor worship, 156–57
Jatakas, 87
Jati, 61
Java, 117, 218
Javanese, 210
Jayadeva, 86
Jerusalem, 196, 361, 365, patriarchate of, 288
Jesuits, 18, 330
Jesus, *see* Jesus Christ
Jesus of Nazareth, *see* Jesus Christ
Jesus Christ, 18, 41, 44, 307–308, 321, 323, 342, 350, 356, 361, 362–63, 369, Incarnation of, 290, 293, 295, nature of, 291, Logos, 294, 296, 329, nativity and Ascension of, 295, Eternal Word of God, 298, God-Manhood of, 299, Incarnate, 302, Body of, 310–11, 364, the Redeemer, 316, Head of the Church, 316–17, Person of, 321, the Shepherd, 323, His Church, 323, Divinity of, 326, Lordship of, 352–53, faith in, 353, sovereignty of, 353, figure of, 354–55, the Risen, 355, resurrection of, 353, Lives of, 355, as Word of God, 359, allegiance to, 365–66
Jewish, people, relation to religion, 224–25, relation to land, 225–26, metaphysics, 233, scholarship, 280, commitment, 346
Jews, 80, 181, their number, 224, Indian, 44
Jimmu Tenno, 155
jinja, 144
jnana, 58, 72, 75
jnana-marga, 77
Jodo, 134
Jodo Shin, 134
Johannine, disclosure, 185
Judaeo-Christian, heritage, 183
Judah, prophets of, 352
Judaism, 115, 182, universal and national aspects, 226, its relation to Christianity and Islam, 226, 228–30, attitude to religions and nations, 227–30, its vision of God, 231–32, under medieval scholasticism, 234–

36, groups within, 24, 280–81, its doctrine of sin, 246, of the here and hereafter, 247–50, Torah as key to, 250–54, institutions of, 254–66, holy days, 267–72, piety, 272–74, Law, 275–81, rabbinic, 275, Reform, 278, 279–81, Conservative, Reform, Orthodox, 280–81
Judas Maccabeus, 271
Julius, Pope, 326
Ju-chia, 1
Jupiter, 9, 54, 160

Kabah, al-, 181
Kabul, 212
Kaifeng, Jews of, 16
kaivala, 73
kalam, 205
Kali, 68, 82–84
Kalighat, 83
kaliyuga, 67, 73, 84
Kalki, 84
Kamakura, 135
Kami, meaning of, 147–52
Kami no Michi, 146
Kang Yu-wei, 19
Karaites, 240
karma, 50, 62, 75
karmic, 50
Kashshaf, al-, 200
Kashi, 58
Kautilya, 45, 52
Kelvin, Lord, 22
Keyserling, Hermann, 213
Khadijah, 181, 197
Khaldun, ibn-, 207–210
Kharijites, 198
Khomyakov, A. S., 284, 298
khulq, 192
Kiangsi, 20, 32
Kierkegaard, 358
Kiev, 284
Kingdom of God, 362, 366, Jewish view, 247–49, 277, mystical, 302, is at hand, 307, is within, 311
kismet, 190
Knox, John, 343
Kobo Daishi, 132–33
Kogoshui, 166
Ko Hung, 25
Kojiki, 156, 166–67
Koran, 50, 80, 178–80, 196, as scripture, 183–86, the uncreated, 185
Koranic, picture of paradise, 191, faith, 215

Korea, 107, 115, 123, 165, Mahayana Buddhism in, 130–31
Korean, 16
kou-tou, 13
Krishna, 68, 72, 82, Vasudeva, 85, Gopala and govinda, 86, the lower, 87, avatara, 68, 84
Kshatriya, 63, 86, 92
Kshatriyas, 64
Kuan Yin, 123
Kuanti, 9, 40
Kufah, al-, 198
Kuoumintang, 216
kurma, 85
Kweiki Kiangsi, 39
kyokai, 143
Kyoto, 132

labbayka, 186
Lakshmi, 84, 86–87
Lamaism, 124, 128–30
Lambeth, 345
Lao Tzu, 25, 41
Last Day, 180
Latin, culture, 46
Latin Church, *see* Roman Catholic Christianity
Latinism, 333
Latourette, Kenneth, 365
Laurentie, 284
Lausanne, 360
Lavoisier, 22
Law, 53, Torah, 80, of Jewish life, 275–81
Laws of Ecclesiastical Polity, 344
Leibnitz, 18
Leo, Pope, the Great, 328
Leo IX, 289
Leo XIII, 318–19
Leontyev, K. N., 303
Lesser Vehicle, *see* Hinayana Buddhism
Lhasa, 129
Li, 3–4, 20–21
Lieh Tzu, 27
Lien, 20–21
Life and Work Movement, 366
Livingstone, David, 355
Logos, *see* Jesus Christ
London, 119
Lotus Scripture, 112, 135
Lugo, de, Juan, 318
Lumbini Park, 92
Lung Hu Shan, 32, 39
Luther, Martin, 340–41

Lutheran, communion, 341
Lutheranism, 339–41

Madariaga, De, Savvador, 211
Madras, 365
Magadha, 113
magatama, 154
Magna Charta, 51
Mahabharata, 49, 54, 72, 86
Maha-Vairo-cana, *see* Vairocana
Mahadeva, 69, 81
Mahadevi, 82
Mahayana, Buddhism, 37, 39, 105, 107, 109, 113, 115, 117, doctrine, 108, canon, 110–111, in China and Japan, 112
mahayogi, 82
Mahdi, 202
Maimonides, 207, his articles of faith, 237–39, 243
Malabar Coast, 212
Malay, Archipelago, 115, Hinayana Buddhism in, 117, language, 210
Malaya, 214, 217
Malayan, 210
Malikite, School, 201
mana, 149, 155
Mamun, al-, caliph, 204
Manar, al-, 183
Manchu, 10–11, 124
Manchuria, 19, 165
Manu, 54, Code of, 61, 72
Manyoshi, 148
Maraghi, al-, al-Shaykh Muhammad, 221
marga, 58
Marxist, ideologies, 215, 218
Maskilim, 240
Mathura (Mattra), 86
matn, 200
matsya, nyaya, 52, avatara, 84
Mauryan, rule, 52
Maximilla, 325
maya, 74–75, 78, 97
Mecca, 178, pilgrimage to, 221
Medina, 181
Mediterranean, 9
Medulla Theologiae Moralis, 318
Megasthenes, 52
Meiji, Emperor, 17
Mencius, 2–4, 7, 10
Mendelssohn, Moses, 238
Messiah, the, 236, Jewish doctrine of, 241–45, promised, 308
Messiahs, fallen, 243

Messianic, hope, 233–34, age, 243, 253, idea, 241–45, dream, 279
Methodism, 348
Mezuzah, 272
Micah, 242
Middle Ages, Jewish philosophers of, 238, Jews in, 276
Middle East, 222
Midrash, 271
Mikadoism, 157
Mindanao, 183, 217
Ming, 14, 25, 124
Mishna, 234, of Sanhedrin, 237
Mission und Ausbreitung des Christentums, Die, 324
Mo Tzu, *see* Moti
Mogul Empire, 212
Mohenjo-daru, 81
Mohsan Fani, 50
Molina, Luis, 330
Mongol, dynasty, 40, 124, race, 210
Monophysitism, 294, 300
Montanists, 325
Montesquieu, 209
Morale de Confucius, La, 18
More, Paul Elmer, 332
Moros, 217
Mosaism, 33
Moscow, 284, 286
Moses, 45, prophetic primacy of, 235–36, five books of, 253
Moses ben Maimon, *see* Maimonides
Moslem, 50–51, 64, 66, interaction with Hinduism, 79, 80, calendar, 197
Moslem Mutual Progress Association, 216
Moslems, 16, 50, 71, 181, Indian, 44, as Koranists, 185, Soviet, 221
Mosque, Judaism and the, 230
Mother Earth, 15
Mount of Olives, 295, 361
Moti (Mo Tzu), 10, 12, 15, 35, influence on Taoism, 32
Motoori, Japanese scholar, 147–49
Mt. Hiei, 132
Mt. Kailasha, 47
Mt. Zion, 46
Muhammad, 41, 44, 180–81, 195–96, first revelation of, 178, new religion of, 182, death of, 183
Muhammad Abduh, 184, 193, 218
Muhammad Ali, of Egypt, 214
Muhammad Ali Jinnah, 219
Muhammad Husayn Haykal, 179
Muhammad Iqbal, 193, 208, 219

Muhammad al-Muntazar, 202
Muhammad Rashid Rida, 183–84
Muhammadiyah, 218
mujtahids, 202
Mumtaz-i-Mahal, 212
munajah, 187
Musar, 239
Musings of a Chinese Mystic, 27
Mustafa Kemal Ataturk, 193, 215
Muslim, 201
Mutazilites, 193, 203–205
mysterium tremendum, 150

Namu Amida Butsu, 134
Namu Myoho Rengekyo, 136
Nanak, 45
Nanchang, 20
Nanking, 14, temple of Confucius at, 22
Napoleon, 220
Naqshbandiyah, 193
nar-singha, 85
Nara, university of, 17, Japan's first capital, 131, sects, 132
Nasatya, 46
Nat, worship of, 117
Nazi, invaders, 221
Nazism, 141, 341
Nazzam, al-, 206
Near East, 182, 220, 302
Netherlands Indies, *see* Indonesia
Negro, race, 210
Neo-Confucianism, 4–5, 39
Neo-Confucianists, 3
Neoplatonism, 235, 330
Nepal, 92, 110
Nepalese, Mahayana canon in, 111
New England, 347
New Testament, 80, 248–49
New Year, Jewish holy day, 267–68
Newton, 22
Nicene, creed, 288
Nichiren, 135–36
Nicholas I, 289
Nietzsche, 358
Nihongi, 148, 166–67
Nipponism, 141
Nirvana, 95, 97, 99, 100–101, 105, 107–108, attainment of, 103
Noah, Laws of his children, 227
Noble Eightfold Path, 99
Nofet Zufim, 239
Nonconformism, 347
norito, 166, 168–69
Nostis errorum, 320

Novissima Sinica, 18
Nyaya of Kanda, 72

Okuma, 17n
Oceania, 369
OM, 57
Omar, the caliph, 195–97
Omito-fu, see Amitabha
Orissa, 67
Orthodox Christianity, 284–85, 337, 357, 367, 369, name of the Church, 285–87, organization, 287–89, nature of Church, 289–93, faith, 293–95, liturgy, 295, sacraments, 295–97, theology and philosophy, 297–302, piety and moral life, 302–306, councils, 328
Ottoman, caliphate, 183, 193, Turkey, 214, Empire, 215
ousia, 325
Oxford, movement, 239, ecumenical gathering at, 365, 367–68

Pacific Ocean, 146, 364
Pai Lien Chiao, 40
Pai Tsung Hsi, 216
Pakistan, 218–20
Palestine, 214, 233, 235, 243, Jewish academy of, 247, restoration of Israel to, 279, 282
Pali, Canon, 106, 110–111, 117, scriptures, 107
panchamas, 48, 63, 65, 80
panchama-harijan, 66
Panchatantra, 72
Panjab, 46–47
panchayats, 52
Panna, *see* Prajna
Papacy, the, 344, modern, 320
Papal, initiative, 321, authority, 326, Jurisdiction and Infallibility, 330, See, 339
parashurama, 85
Pari-Nirvana, defined, 103–104
Parousia, 323
Parsis, 44
Pascal, Blaise, 207, 354, 358
Pashupati, 46
Pasteur, 22
Pater Noël of Prague, 18
Patimokka, 95
Patristic, era, 365
Patrologia Graeca, 327
Peiping, 19
Peking, 19, 41
Pentateuch, 236, laws of, 251–52

Pentecost, 290, 299
Peripatetic, thought, 207
Pershing, John J., 217
Persia, 196, 214
Persian, 47, culture, 192, race, 210
Peter, *see* St. Peter
Pharisees, 234, 248
Philippines, 183, 214
Phis, worship of, 117
Pitakas, 110
Pius IX, 292
Pius XI, 318-19
Pius XII, 321, 332
Plato, 45, 59, 208
Platonic, dualism, 300
Pope, the, 293, 316-17, 344
Portuguese, 48, 60
Potestas magisterii, 292
Prajapati, 56, 67
Prajna, 105
Presbytery, 344, of Hanover, 343
Presbyterian, family, 344
Princess of Azure Clouds, 35
Princeton University, 343
Priscilla, 325
Prophet, the, *see* Muhammad
Protestant Christianity, 286, 301,
    337-38, 367, 369, historical forms,
    338-49, doctrines, 349-356, con-
    temporary developments, 357-70,
    Classical Protestantism, 339-46,
    Radical Protestantism, 346-49, au-
    thority of the Bible, 349-52, Lord-
    ship of Jesus Christ, 352-55, func-
    tion of Church, 355-56, rediscov-
    ery of orthodoxy, 358-62, Evangel-
    ical Catholicity, 362-66, concern
    for secular order, 366-68, Ecumeni-
    cal theology, 368-70, the Human-
    ists, 348-49, thought, 361, world
    of, 364
Protestant Germany, 18
Protestant Reformation, 337-38
Protestantism, *see* Protestant Chris-
    tianity
Psalms, 224
puja, 71
pujari, 71
Purim, Jewish holiday, 271
purva mimamsa, 73
punarjanman, 61
Puranas, 49, 54
Puranic, 68
Puri, 67, 69, 81
Purusha, 56-57

qada, 189
qadar, 189
Qadiriyah, 193
Qandahar, 212
Qasim, ibn-al-, Muhammad, 212
Quakers, the, 348
Questo giorno, 320
Quraysh, 181
Qurayshites, 195-96

Rabbis, the, 275-77
Rabindranath Tagore, 82-83
Radha, 68, 86, *bhagavati,* 87
rakshasas, 87
Ram, Lord, 79
Ram Ram, 70
Rama, 72, 78, 82, 85, 87, cult of, 86
ramachandra, 85
Ramachandra, *avatara,* 84, 86-87
Ramadan, 178
Ramaism, 87
Ramakrishna, 83
Ramanuja, 73, 77-78, 80-81, 87
Ramayana, 49, 54, 78
rathayatra, 68
Ravana, 87
Real, the, 75
Red Revolution, 221
Redeemer, the, *see* Jesus Christ
Reformation, churches of the, 344,
    370
Reformed, Christianity, 343, 344
Reformers, 357
religio, 51
Religion and Life, movement, 321
Rembrandt, 352, the Syndics of, 342
Retribution, 180
Renaissance, of Europe, 182, Italian,
    239
*Revivification of the Sciences of Re-
    ligion,* 206
Rig Veda, 53-54, 56-58, 60
Rig Vedic, 57, 60
rita, 55
Ritter-Orden, 302
Roman, 54, civilization, 332
Roman Catholic Christianity, 286,
    301, 337, 349, 357, 369, defined,
    311-12, numerical strength, 316,
    the Church as Christ's Body, 310-
    11, religious experience, 311-14, the
    institutional Church, 314-17, moral
    theology, 317-23, interpretive the-
    ology and authority, 323-32, his-
    tory of Church, 332-35, Catholic
    faith, 312-14, Sacraments, 312, 317,

323, Sacrifice, Mass, 312, Sacred Heart, 313, Virgin Mary, 313, 355, Holy Places, 313, Councils, 328, the visible community, 332, Orders and Congregations, 335, concept of catholicity, 365

Roman Catholicism, *see* Roman Catholic Christianity

Roman Church, *see* Roman Catholic Christianity

Romans, 71

Roman Catholic, missions in Japan, 164

Rome, 160, 285, 287, 354, Bishops of, 315

Rudra, 82

Ruler Above, 35

Runnymede, 46, 51

Russia, 18, 183, Moslem, 214, expansion in Transcaucasia, 220, Jews in, 277

Russian, philosophers, 284, Revolution, 285, Christianity, 285, 304

Sabbath, the, Jewish institution, 257–60

Sabellius, 325

Sabetti, Luigi, 318

sabhas, 52

Sabians, 80

Sacrificial Official of the Late Teacher, 20

sad-darshana, 72

Sadducees, 234, 248

sadhu, 65

Safed, 235

saisei itchi, 158

Sakyamuni, see Buddha, the

Sakyans, land of, 92

salah, 186

Salahuddin Khuda Bakhsh, 193

Sama Veda, 53–54, 57

saman, 54

Sambuddha, 97

samhita, 60

samhitas, 53

samitis, 52

Samkhya of Kapila, 72

samsara, 97

San Ho-hui, 41

San Tzu Ching, 4

sanatana dharma, 53

Sangha, 95

Sanhedrin, 237

Sankhara, 101

sannyasi, 65, 75

Sanskrit, 47, Buddhist canon in, 110–111

Santze-ching, 18

Saraswati, 84, 87

Sarikat Islam, 218

satya dharma, 53

Saturninus, 325

Saudi Arabia, 192, 194, 214

Saul of Tarsus, *see* St. Paul

Saviour, the, *see* Jesus Christ

Savitar, 57

Scandinavian, countries, 340

Scholastic, theologians, 317

Scholasticism, Thomistic, 330–332

Second Commonwealth, of Israel, 233, 282

Scotland, 343, 345

Second Rome, *see* Constantinople

Self, nature of, 107

Semites, spiritual, 332

Semitic, 50, soil, 182

Sergius of Radonesh, 304

Seville, 211

Shafii, al-, 201

Shah Jahan, Emperor, 212

shakti, 72, 83, Tantric, 84

shammai, 240

Shang, 8, 12

Shanghai, 25

Shangti, 8–9, 15, 21

Shankara, 59, 73, 76–77, 80, 82–83, his formulation of Vedanta, 74–75

Shansi, 19

Shantung, 32

Shen-nung, 9, 15

sheng, 42

Shensi, 32

sheol, 248

Shepherd, the, *see* Jesus Christ

Shiah, 197

Shih Huang Ti, Emperor, 32

Shiite, theology, 198–99

Shingon, 132

Shinran, 134

Shinto, deity, 131, 141, 143, deities, 132, Neo-, 137, organization of, 142, its two kinds, 143, doctrine and sects, 145, National, 146–52, literature of, 155, Pentateuch, 155, Old, 157, 168, characteristics of, 159–77, compared with Christianity and Buddhism, 162, and Christianity, 165, comprehensive sincerity, 176

Shinto Honkyoku, 144

shiva, 82

Shiva, 46, 49, 55, 57–70, 77, 81–83, cult, 84, left-hand *shakti*, 86
Shiva Mahadeva, 46, 74
Shivism, 71–72
Shivite, 68, 70–71, morality, 75, elements, 84
Shoguns, 135
Shotoku-Taishi, 16, 131
shraddha, 76
shruti, 53
shu, 7
Shudra, 65
Shudras, 48, 73
Shun, 15
Shushi, *see* Chu Hsi school
Siam, *see* Thailand
Siddhartha, *see* Buddha, the
Siffin, battle of, 198
Sikh, 66
Sikhs, 44, 64
Simon Peter, *see* St. Peter
Sina, ibn-, 208
Sinai, revelation on, 235
Sinarum Scientia, 17
Sind, Province of, 193
sindhu, 47
Sita, 78
Skambha, 57
skandhas, 98, 101
Slavic, culture, 46
smarta, 70–71
smriti, 53–54
snanayatra, 68
Sobornost, 293
Society of Friends, 348
Soma, 55–57, 86
Sophronius, 196
Sovereign Earth, 9
Söderblom, 150
Solomon, King, 214, wisdom of, 224
Solovyev, V., 298
Son of God, 290
Son of Man, *see* Jesus Christ
Soviet Union, 284–85, Marxism and Orthodoxy, 305
Spain, 211
Spinoza, 234
St. Alphonsus de Liguori, 318
St. Ambrose of Milan, 317
St. Athanasius, 297
St. Augustine, 320, 326
St. Basil, the Great, 297
St. Cyril of Alexander, 297, 327–28
St. Gregory of Nazianz, 297
St. Gregory of Nyssa, 297, 317
St. Ignatius of Antioch, 297

St. John Chrysostom, 297, 317
St. John of Damascus, 297
St. Paul, 285, 311, 315, 358, his interpretation of the Incarnation, 304
St. Peter, 285, 308, 317, 323, 328
St. Thomas Aquinas, 207, 317, 329–32, 341
Stockholm, 366
Stoics, 208
Stone Age, 44
Suarez, Francisco, 318, 330
Sudan, 214
Sufi, 80
Sufis, 80
Sufism, in India, 80, 193
Suhrawardiyah, 193
Sultan Mahmud II, 214
Sujin Tenno, 155
suluk, 192
Sumatra, 218
Summa Theologica, 207, 317, 329–30, 341
Summi Pontificatus, 321
Sun Yat-sen, 6, 14, Three Principles of, 20–21, father of modern China, 22, 216
Sung, 15, 124–25, 135
sunnah, 196, 199
Sunnite-Shiite, difference, 200, 202–203, 221, groupings, 214
Supreme Personal Being, 104
Surya, 70
Sutta-pitaka, 110
Switzerland, 360
Sword of the Spirit, movement, 321
Sydney, Archbishops of, 322
Synagogue, 228, 237, authoritarian, 236, worship in, 254–57, prayer of, 332
Syria, 194, 214, 220, Church of, 284
Syriac, civilization, 214
Syrian, 210
Syro-American, communities, 220
Szechuan, 32

Tabari, al-, 197, 199
Taj Mahal, 212
Talmud, 271
Talmudic, literature, 234, erudition, 277
Talmudists, 240
Tamerlane, 212
Tantras, 54
Tantric, 68, 70, 128, shakti, 84
Ta Tung—World Brotherhood, 16
Tabarsi, 200

Tafsir, 199–200
Tai Ping, 41
Tai Shan, the Great Eastern Mountain, 9, 46, the god, 35
Tai Tsung, 11
Tang, 11, 123
tanzih, 188
Tao, 4, 8, 15, 24–26, 28–31, 39–40, 42, 146, union with the, 27
Tao jen, 36
Taoism, 1, 15–16, 24–26, 29, 31, 34, 37, 41–42, popular, 32, Moti's influence on, 33, Buddhist influence on, 36, philosophical, 38, modern schools, 39–40
Taoist, 15, mystics, 24, 30, philosophy, 26–27, 125, popes, 32, 40
Taoists, 25–26, 28, 32, 34–35, 123
Tao Te Ching, 24–25, 28–29, 31
Tao Tsang, 25
Tartar, 210
Tathagata, *see* Buddha, the
tawil, 200
Te, 25, 40
Temple, William, 345, 361
Temple of Heaven, 9
Temple of Prayer, 9
Tendai, 126, 132, 134–35
Tenri Kyo, 146
tera, 143
Tertullian, 325
Tailand, 110, 115, Hinayana Buddhism in, 116, its Buddhists, 118
Theology Today, 365
theotokos, 327
Third Rome, *see* Moscow
Thirty-Nine Articles, 345
Thor, 143
Three Character Classic, 4
Three Kingdoms, 9
Three Kingdoms, 40
Three Refuges, 97
Ti, 8
Tibet, 107, 110, Mahayana Buddhism in, 128–30
Tibetan, Mahayana canon in, 111
Tibetan Buddhism, *see* Lamaism
Tien Chu, 8
Tien Tai, school, 126, 132
Tien Tao, 21
Tipitaka, 110
Tokugawa, age, 17, Shoguns, 137, Shogunate, 164
Tokyo, 137, allied headquarters in, 141, Imperial University of, 153, 172, 175

Toledo, 211
Torah, the, 236, Jewish conception of, 250–54, core of, 251–53
Toronto, 322
Toynbee, Arnold J., 213
Travel Diary of a Philosopher, 213
Tripitaka, *see* Tipitaka
Tropic of Cancer
Tsankov, S., 298
Tsukiji, Hongwanji, 137
tsung, 5
tu-li, 41
Tulsi Das, 78–79, 87
Tulsi Das Ramayana, 87
Turkey, 193, 214
Turk, 210
Turkish, 210, conquerors, 182
Turkistan, 46, 214

Ubi Christus ibi Ecclesia, 365
Ukrainian, 284
Ultimate Reality, 108, 127
Uma, 82
Una Sancta, 358
United Nations, 215
United States of America, 217, 278, 340, 345, 366, 368, Lutherans in, 341, Episcopal Church in the, 346, Protestant Christians in, 347
Universal Order, 6
Upanishadic, times, 45, 71, theory, 60, 75
Upanishads, 54, 57–59, 73–74, 76, 78
Urdu, 210
Ushas, 55–56
Uthman, the caliph, 198–99
Utrecht, 365
uttara-mimamsa, 73

Vaikuntha, 77
Vairocana, 108, 127, 131, 158
Vaisheshika of Gotama, 72
Vaishya, 64, 66
Valentinus, 325
Valmiki, 54
Valmiki Ramayana, 72, 86
vamana, 85
Vardhaman Mahavira, 45, the Jain, 71–72
varna, 60–61
varna-shankara, 66
varsha, 85
Varuna, 46, 55–57, 67, 86
Varuna-Prajapati, 57
Vasca da Gama, 48
Vatican, 160

Vedanta, 73, 76–77, 80, 127, Shankara's, 74
Vedanta-sutras, 74
Vedantic, tradition, 74, 77, non-duality, 79
Vedas, 54, 56–59, 71, 74, 78, as revelation, 83
Vedic, wisdom, 45, 58, culture, 46, heritage, 47, schools, 53, 73, post-, 54, 60, Hinduism, 56, 67, times, 62, revelation, 72, gods, 76, deity, 82, traditions, 83, religions, 90
Vedic-brahmanic, 72
Vedism, 56
Vergil, 47
via illuminativa, 26
via negativa, 26
via unitiva, 26
vidya, 75
Vienna, 215
vijnana, 75
vinaya-pitaka, 110
Virginia, 343
vishishtadvaita, 73
Vishnu, 55, 57, 68–70, 77, 81, 84, 87, wives of, 87
Vishnuite, 70, tradition, 78, elements, 84, theology, 88
Vishnu-Brahman, 77
Vishnu-Krishna, 49
Vishnuism, 71–72, 84
Vishnuites, 86
Vishveshvara, 69, 82
Vollenhoven, Van, C., 218
Vrindavana, 86
viyoga, 82

Wahhabi, revival, 201, 212–13, 220
Walls and Moats, god of, 35
Wang Yang-ming, School, 17, 124
Wang Ying-lin, 4
waqf, 191
Water, 32
Watt, James, 22
Well of Knowledge, 69
Wesley, Charles, 348
Wesley, John, 348
West, 18, 22, 26, 34, 59, 60, 76, Roman, 288, Christian Church in the, 368
Western, civilization, 17, soil, 46, student, 48, realism, 74, philoso-phies, 215, culture, 278, religion, 362
Westerners, 9
Westminister Shorter Catechism, 342
White Huns, 113
White Lotus, 40
White Russian, 284
Williams, Roger, 347
Wodin, 143
World Church Movement, 366
World Congress of Faiths, 221
World Council of Churches, 363
World War I, 320, 366
World War II, 152, 159, 171, 215, 220, 265, 320
Wu-ti, 8, 123
wu-wei, 29

Yajnavalka, 45
yajur, 54
Yajur Veda, 53–54, 57
Yale University, 347, 365
Yama, 55
Yaman, 194, 214
Yamuna, river, 86
Yang, Y. C., 1
yang, 3, 24, 32, 34
Yellow Turbans, 32
Yen, Governor, 19
Yen Hui, 26
Yi, 20–21
yin, 3, 24, 34
yin-yang, 2–3, 34, 36, philosophers, 24
Yoga of Patanjali, 72
Yu, 15
Yu Huang Shangti (Jade Emperor), 34
Yuan Shih-kai, President, 19

Zamakhshari, al-, 199
Zen, 39, 135
Zeno, 208
Zeus Pater, 54
Zinjani, al-, al-Shaykh, 221
Zion, 241
Ziya Gök Alp, 219
Zohar, the, 235
Zoroaster, 44–45
Zoroastrianism, 115